BIRD

The Making of an American Sports Legend

BIRD

The Making of an American Sports Legend

BY

LEE DANIEL LEVINE

McGRAW-HILL BOOK COMPANY

New York St. Louis San Francisco Auckland Bogotá Hamburg
London Madrid Mexico Milan Montreal New Delhi Panama
Paris São Paulo Singapore Sydney Tokyo Toronto

1 2 3 4 5 6 7 8 9 DOC DOC 8 9 2 1 0 9 8

ISBN 0-07-037477-5

LIBRARY OF CONGRESS CATALOGING-IN-PUBLICATION DATA

Levine, Lee Daniel.
   Bird: the making of an American sports legend.

   1. Bird, Larry, 1956–   . 2. Basketball
players—United States—Biography.   3. Boston
Celtics (Basketball team)   I. Title.
GV884.A2B575   1988   796.32′3′0924 [B]   88-13364
ISBN 0-07-037477-5

Map by Southern Signworks, Paoli
Book design by Eve Kirch

More than just one hero emerges out of this story. Georgia Bird, I believe, is a true unsung hero. Without her incredible strength, the story might have been quite different. To her and all the Indiana basketball fans who have made basketball such a significant way of life across the state, I dedicate this book.

CONTENTS

PREFACE

I first heard about Larry Bird when I was a freshman in high school in LaPorte, Indiana. He was the skinny youngster who had just gone through an impressive growth spurt and emerged at 6'7". He was toiling in relative obscurity down in southern Indiana, but he was starting to draw attention elsewhere. Although he was playing against lesser competition, he had tremendous shooting range and averaged 20 rebounds a game. Plus, he had developed a reputation as a daring passer but still managed to score over 30 points a game. I began following him avidly and read with disappointment the next year that he had dropped out of Indiana University. Later I heard that he had resurfaced at Indiana State.

But no one, including Larry himself, expected that he would explode onto the scene as resoundingly as he did his first year at Indiana State. Averages of 33 points and 13 rebounds a game were nothing short of miraculous for a newcomer. No player had ever before emerged so dramatically out of anonymity to dominate college basketball. Before long, his feats inspired me to keep a file. At 19 (Larry was 21), I believed our fates were tied, not within a specific context, but more within the realm of basketball spirituality, and I even believed that we went through parallel emotions with each win and loss. In truth, the only thing we shared was a Hoosier upbringing, and even then we had been raised at opposite ends of the state.

When I moved to the east coast, I discovered that ignorance of Hoosier Hysteria (the passions that surround high school basketball in Indiana) was far more pervasive among fans and sportswriters than

I had thought. People in the east were trying to understand Larry without any concept of what it was like to grow up in Indiana. The more I heard and read, the more I was convinced that most people weren't fully aware of the roots of Larry's greatness. Not only was there a lack of understanding about the cultural significance of basketball in Indiana but about the unique culture of French Lick and West Baden as well. On top of that, the true difficulty of Larry's childhood had not been known. Of course, it is only logical that such a singular talent should be the product of a rare environment. And just as the roots of greatness are seldom monolithic, an understanding of greatness demands an appreciation of complexity.

Thus, the guiding principle for this book has been to present a Larry Bird that has rarely been glimpsed up to now. I believe that the Larry Bird presented here—a real person—is vastly more engrossing than the mythologized, one-dimensional sports "legend." For the deification of superstar athletes in our society tends to rob them of their humanity. After all, success and failure on and off the court, even if not always flattering, allows a more valid and compelling portrait. Few have overcome the towering adversities that Larry has faced, and I believe a full understanding of these adversities makes his Algeresque story even more remarkable.

1 / A Gift

For a long time a few of Larry Bird's basketball trophies were probably rattling around on the floors of his friends' trucks. He thought. One of his NBA Most Valuable Player trophies was on loan to the Basketball Hall of Fame. Another sat on top of a refrigerator in an apartment in the house where Georgia Bird lives on Abbeydale Road in West Baden, Indiana. West Baden (population 930) sits just adjacent to the larger and better-known city—with which it shares an area known as "the valley"—French Lick (population 2,059). The third consecutive MVP trophy could have been practically anywhere. (All three MVP trophies have now been rounded up by Max Gibson and placed in the MVP Club, a members-only dining room in Larry's new hotel in Terre Haute.)

You see, Larry Bird might be making in the vicinity of $3 million a year (counting endorsements). But that doesn't mean he wouldn't hurry back for the summer—literally, the day the season's over—to the home he built on the property that once belonged to his grandparents, Claude and Helen Bird. Not that Larry's a Mama's boy— far from it. But most of his friends live in the valley anyway—so why not? "I am a hick from French Lick. I lead a simple life. I'm just a small-town kid gone to the city," he said upon arriving in Boston ten years ago.

This is the same Larry Bird who, following his junior year in high school, didn't show up for the basketball team's annual awards dinner—virtually an unpardonable sin in Indiana. The coach at that time, Jim Jones, knew exactly where he must be. So he drove to Larry's favorite basketball court, where he found Larry working on his shooting. Larry reluctantly agreed to attend the dinner after washing his hands and combing his hair. He accepted his award wearing a tee-shirt, jeans, and sneakers.

Not much has changed over the years. Larry is the only recipient of the John Wooden Award (honoring him as 1978–79's best college basketball player) to skip the award ceremony. He had better things to do, namely, fulfilling his student teaching requirements so he could graduate on time from Indiana State. Larry accepted his 1980 NBA Rookie of the Year trophy in absentia (the only recipient to ever do so). Instead he went to Florida, honoring a commitment to give a speech at a banquet sponsored by the Boys' Club of America, an organization he had worked with over a number of summers.

Of course, Larry did show up for the black-tie NBA MVP awards ceremony honoring him as the world's greatest basketball player in 1984. But he arrived an hour late and accepted the trophy in short sleeves—to be precise, a bowling shirt. It seems that Larry had been discovered mowing his lawn in West Baden only a few hours before the banquet and had been persuaded to attend. Oh, and there was also a certain ceremony at the White House with President Reagan following the Celtics' clinching of the 1984 NBA championship. And was the 1984 playoff MVP in attendance? Are you kidding? He "over-slept."

Larry's lack of concern for the formalities that anyone else just automatically accepts is symptomatic of a man who is as unique an individual as he is a player. After all, this self-proclaimed small-town "white boy who can't run or jump, can play this game," as he modestly points out, and is quite possibly the best player of all time. But basketball is a sport that, more than any other, rewards (and almost requires) great leaping ability and great running speed in tandem. And of the twenty-four players in the 1988 NBA All-Star game, twenty-one were black and nearly two-thirds were from predominantly urban areas. So where does this small-town white boy get off? Remember, this is the same guy that Joe B. Hall, former long-time coach at the University of Kentucky, said was too slow to play college basketball! So, this book is about Larry's quirks and turns, "the hum and buzz" of his everyday life in an attempt to make sense of why the conventions lie in shambles at his feet every time he walks onto a basketball court.

A man who couldn't be bothered visiting the President (political reasons had nothing to do with his decision) obviously operates under different imperatives than most of us. Growing up in rural Indiana played no small role in his unique perspective. So did his father's alcoholism and suicide—perhaps a good deal more so. But beyond the environmental factors exists an extremely gifted individual, one born with special talents, and therefore having a different relationship with the world than the rest of us.

It is ironic that the most indisputable truth of Larry's greatness—his "differentness" from the rest of us—should be the exact opposite of what attracts many of us to him in the first place. Like most fans in the NBA, but unlike most of the players (nearly 80 percent are black), Larry is white, and—at least on TV—his physical appearance is, at best, unremarkable. There is none of the incredible muscle definition or muscle mass that some of the other players have. Larry seems to have a body that is, well, more like ours. Why, he doesn't even have good posture. In a game of gazelles he appears to be more of a rhinoceros. He runs flat-footed at a speed that is more comprehensible to most of us. He doesn't seem to lift off into the stratosphere like so many other players. Nor does he seem to defy gravity while he's up there either. He seems to jump, it appears, like a lot of us. After the game he pops open a few beers and hangs out with us, or it seems like it could be us anyway. Why, this guy could be playing on any number of organized softball teams around the country. He'd just be another one of the guys.

Yet, the first thing one notices upon actually meeting Larry Bird is his remarkable size. This is not just another third baseman on the Red Rooster Tavern softball team. This is a man who is a legitimate 6'9". In fact, according to one of his college coaches, he's 6'10" in his stocking feet. For those who forget how tall that is, most of us would look into the middle of his chest. And he isn't weak either. Under the miniaturizing and distorting gaze of the TV camera, he may appear sort of regular. In person, this guy's a rock. That two-hundred-twenty pounds can hold its ground whenever it damn pleases.

Physical size has always been part of what sets Larry apart and, without question, has had a lot to do with his success. If Larry were even 6'6", for example, he'd still be an extremely good player. But the difference between 6'6" and 6'9" is the ability to see over any defensive situation and make the pass; the ability to back up (post-up) a smaller defensive player toward the basket to gain advantage on the inside; the ability to compensate for a lack of foot speed on defense; and last, but not least, the ability to release his shot while rarely having to worry about getting it blocked.

But make no mistake, this man possesses so much determination, so much resolve that he'd be a remarkable player even at 6'6". He'd merely adapt to the greater obstacles in his way. After all, this is the guy who at 16 broke his ankle and would stand, propped up on his crutches, and shoot for hours on end with anyone he could find to chase the ball for him. Later, when he had a walking cast, he'd hobble around working on ball handling as well. "I never saw a kid who played basketball so much. He didn't have a car or much money, so he spent his time at basketball," said Gary Holland, Larry's high school coach his senior year. Of course, not having a car or money doesn't altogether explain what drives a kid to practice at 6:30 in the morning before school (shooting free throws), to work out again immediately after school, and then to start "banging on the windows of the gym" to get back in later in the evening. There were other times when Larry would play after practice until one or two in the morning. Inevitably, he would run out of kids to play with. This was part of the reason Larry developed the solitary ritual he has relied upon to develop and hone his game.

Today Larry follows much the same regimen. He has an assistant trainer rebounding and passing to him two hours before every game—without exception. He will sometimes shoot as many as 2,000 shots in a practice session. No other player follows such an intense schedule, and he makes sure he is always the first Celtic on the court (as opposed to merely in the locker room) for practice. (Some players are known to arrive in the locker room an hour before practice, only to be the last ones on the court for the start of practice.) "I'm the kind of guy who gets here an hour before practice because I want to warm up and practice my shooting before anyone else is out on the court." Not only was Larry usually the first person to arrive for practice; there were times when he never left. Celtics Coach K. C. Jones describes the sometimes-familiar sight of Larry "asleep on the mats in the gym at eight-thirty in the morning. Did he practice all night? Maybe." Larry also makes sure he is the last to leave. A certain mystique has developed concerning the "Bird work ethic." Five years ago, when Tom Nissalke was coaching the Cleveland Cavaliers, he brought the team out onto the court two hours before the game to see Larry and show his players, particularly the younger ones, what it took to be great in the NBA. Even the best player, the soon to be MVP, never stopped working, he explained. When Stan Albeck was coaching the New Jersey Nets, he loved to tell his players about Larry's pregame regimen. For the last game of the 1984–85 season, the Nets were to play the Celtics, and an hour before game time, forward Mike O'Koren noticed that the court was empty. As he ribbed Albeck for his supposed hyperbole, he looked up to see Larry running laps around the concourse of Boston Garden. Larry had come three hours early on this occasion, had already finished his shooting, and was working on his endurance.

Few in the NBA work harder than Larry on improving their game, and few possess his kind of relentless drive and will to be the best. A variety of reasons have been offered to explain why Larry is so driven, but at bottom is one certainty: Larry himself doesn't understand what has always driven him. "When I was younger I played for the fun of it, like any other kid. I just don't know what kept me going and going and going." Yet Larry does recognize that there is something that lies behind his unending quest for improvement and that this something is in the nature of a *gift*. Once he remarked that "strength is not nearly as important as desire. I don't think you can teach anyone desire. I think it's a gift. I don't know why I have it, but I do." Is this desire, this drive, merely a "gift," or is it beyond his and our understanding? There are a number of logical explanations for this drive.

Larry recalls that when he was younger he was consumed with a feeling of fear before every game. Termed by one of Larry's coaches as "huge fear of failure," it continued to inspire Larry to practice longer and harder than other players throughout high school, college, and the pros. Then there is the old Satchel Paige dictum, "Don't look back, because somebody might be gaining on you." Larry is never secure in his sense of being number one and staying that way. He told *Time* magazine in 1985, "Last summer I caught myself shooting around for five hours. I thought, 'What's wrong with me?' It's like I get this guilty feeling that I'm not playing enough, that someone is playing more." Was Larry referring to Michael Jordan or to Dr. J? No. "Some kid in the sixth grade." Yet at other times he expresses the same concern about other NBA players.

But being "at the pinnacle" (as K. C. Jones has described Larry's game) brings about imperatives related only to the game itself. As Larry explains, "You know, Bobby Knight probably had the best quote I've ever seen. He said, 'You don't play against opponents— you play against the game of basketball.' He's right. I don't play against opponents, I play against the game." And now that Larry has set the standard, he feels a great internal compulsion to maintain it. "Once you've got yourself on that plateau, you don't want to get knocked down. You want to stay up there, and you can't do it by loafing around."

Yet others who know him explain his quest for perfection in a different way. "Larry never tries to please anyone but himself, and he isn't hardly ever pleased," says his mother. "The amazing thing is that he is truly never satisfied with his own efforts.... That's his way of making sure he never becomes too complacent," says K. C. Jones. Jones has also commented that in his entire involvement with basketball "I have yet to find anyone who has Larry's determination or plays with more intensity." It was this remarkable drive for perfection which allowed him to overcome the biggest tragedy of his life, his father's suicide, when Larry was just 18.

Georgia Bird believes that her husband's death intensified her son's determination to succeed. Still, it was Larry's toughness prior to the suicide that allowed him to cope with the ordeal to begin with. "If you don't have a strong mind, you won't overcome the adversities, and you just have to keep on pushing and go as hard as you possibly can," Larry says. His father's death was clearly the significant turning point in his life. This is because much of Larry's drive *before* the suicide was related to the nature of his father's interaction with his mother.

Larry's characterization of his drive as being "a gift" is, to an extent, correct. Here was a boy with a solitary, intense, and innate drive, which was fueled throughout his childhood and adolescence by a complex and dysfunctional family situation. "When we find that in the picture presented by a person's character a single instinct that has developed an excessive strength," said Freud, "we look for the explanation in a special disposition.... It [is] probable that an instinct like this of excessive strength was already active in the subject's earliest childhood, and that its supremacy was established by impressions in the child's life."

Those "impressions" fostered an unconscious drive to play all the time and work harder than others. They consisted of a household with an alcoholic father, a mother who had to work all the time while coping with her husband's problem, and older brothers who pushed him to strive and compete. Growing up in Indiana socialized him to channel that drive into basketball. And his family's financial neediness further reduced the number of possible distractions and dictated a kind of survival mentality that made winning in basketball much more important to Larry than to most other kids.

The sublimation that takes place in the children of alcoholics was manifested in Larry in several ways. His father's alcoholism prompted him to find something that would allow him to rely only on himself. The ball and the basket were constants that countered the unpredictability and out-of-control world of the family of an alcoholic. He clung to the ball, rarely letting it leave his side. The anarchy of his home life forced Larry to shrink his world so he could further control it. A solitary game of made or missed baskets therefore became his universe. He either scored or he didn't; there were no excuses. And shrinking his world into a smaller one inside his head enabled Larry to learn how to tune out the outside world. Because of a household that was out of synch, Larry had a need to make things right. Therefore, making baskets and, especially, winning games were ways of making things right, and they were the only things he could control.

However, Larry did have an adult ally. His maternal grandmother helped to moderate the effects of his turbulent family life. At the same time that Larry was toughened by his older brothers and his economic circumstances, his grandmother spoiled him, nurturing him and giving him enough of an ego to want glory later on. These influences were vital to Larry's successful arrival at a conscious drive for success when he turned 14. It was then that Larry started to nail most of his shots, and that gave him a sense of pride. It also made him popular. At the same time, Larry noticed that his brother Mark's popularity was a result of Mark's basketball prowess, and he realized that he wanted people cheering for him too. It would be a kind of affirmation that would make him feel like less of an outsider, a typical feeling for children of alcoholics. And so he began his long journey.

The uniqueness of Larry's journey and his uniqueness as a player are no accident. Yet trying to explain what skills go into making this particular non-black, non-jumping, non-running, non-center quite possibly the greatest player of all time, is no easy task. Not the least of the many inadequate explanations are Larry's own. In one instance he explained his success in these terms: "I have some talent—shooting and thinking. I try to use it to overcome my lack of jumping and speed." Another time he offered, "I would say my vision, my court awareness, and my height are God-given. Everything else I've worked my ass off for." But there have been other tall kids who could shoot well, see the court, and work hard, who not only haven't come close to attaining the success that Larry has, but who couldn't even make the NBA. True, in most cases the before-mentioned attributes would guarantee admission to the NBA, but the greatest player in history? Not even close. So what is it, what is the key element in Larry's success? It's clear that during the season Larry is one of the hardest-working men in all of basketball—though the hard work is more of a symptom than a cause. Behind that hard work is a drive, a tenacity, a will, surely unrivaled in the history of this and maybe all sport. That passion is what fuels not only the hard work, but the competitiveness, the toughness, the will to be the best—" as nearly perfect as you can get," says former basketball great Jerry West. Referred to simply as "desire" by Larry, perhaps this is the "gift."

Larry is the best in the NBA because no other player combines the shooting, the moves and the fakes setting up shots, the rebounding, the passing, the success in the clutch, the game-in and game-out intensity, the leadership, and the appreciation of the dynamics of team play and life. Because Larry seemingly doesn't excel in terms of the three most common barometers of athletic ability—speed, strength, and jumping ability—he tends to be described as a player able to make up for a sparsity of natural talent. But surely there is much more to "natural talent" than these three categories. How many times have strong and fast leapers been defeated in competition by those with an abundance of other skills?

To begin with, Larry is not as deficient in the three basic categories as it is supposed. He doesn't possess good foot speed (especially by NBA standards), but he does have decent quickness. Jay Vincent, of the Denver Nuggets, points out, "People say he's slow, but he has that quick first step." In terms of the all-important first or second step, he is near the top of the league for his size. In terms of jumping ability, again, Larry is deceptive. Bill Russell has commented, "He can get up a lot higher than people think." On a comparative scale, though, he's nowhere near the top of the league. Finally, in terms of strength, Larry is still one of the bigger players at the small forward position. And because much of Larry's power comes from his unusually low center of gravity (for his size), when he is fighting for position under the boards, an opposing player is often forced out of position or out of the lane. This leverage which derives from his hips and rear end is one of the most important measures of strength in basketball.

But even if Larry is underrated in terms of these categories, that hardly explains his dominance in his sport. When writers typically describe Larry, for example, as having "Gifts That God Didn't Give" (the title of a cover story on Larry in the November 9, 1981, *Sports Illustrated*), they wrongly imply that Larry makes up for a lack of athletic talent by sheer hard work. While the work Larry puts in plays a major role in his success, Larry is still one of the better "natural athletes" in the NBA. He excels in a large number of categories (besides strength, speed, and jumping) that go into defining athletic talent. Besides his "desire," he is at the top, or near the top, of the league in terms of competitiveness, toughness, intelligence, memory, instinct, anticipation, and creativity. On the physical side he is again at the top in terms of hand-eye coordination, hand strength and quickness, depth perception, and peripheral vision.

One of the most decisive factors that contributes to the athletic dominance of Larry Bird is his intelligence. The Lakers' Magic Johnson says that "Larry is the smartest in the league." And Michael Jordan has said he is in awe of Larry's ability to think through several possibilities at once. Yet Larry blends this intelligence with an uncanny instinctual feel for the game. "[A lot of the] things I do on the court are just reactions to situations....I don't *think* about some of the things I'm trying to do.... A lot of times, I've passed the basketball and not realized I've passed it until a moment or so later." Jim Jones, Larry's high school coach, remarks that the ability that Larry has to integrate his instincts and his conscious understanding of the game is "like a three-dimensional awareness of the other player." That awareness stems partly from Larry's phenomenal memory. According to Bob Woolf, Larry's agent, "Larry has an incredible memory—it has helped make him the great player he is." Woolf relates one very telling incident. For a segment of the *Today* show, following Larry's first NBA championship in 1981, the producers wanted to show Larry watching a replay of the final game. The videotape was turned on to a random point in the game. Woolf asked Larry if he could figure out what part of the game was being viewed.

"Fourth quarter, 5:40 left," said Larry.

"How can you possibly be that precise?" Woolf asked. There was no commentary on the videotape, and the score had not been shown.

"The song," Bird said.

"The song?" Woolf said.

"That fight song. That's the last time they played it. They played it three times during the game. This is the last time they played it. This is the last time because the crowd is going nuts. Houston came from 17 down, and there's about 5:40 left."

"You mean you were aware of that song?" Woolf asked.

"I was there, wasn't I?" said Bird.

"I was there, too, but I don't remember any song. And I wasn't playing," said Woolf.

Larry laughed and watched the rest of the tape, calling out each play in detail a few seconds before it came up on the tape.

Larry admits to having an unusually acute memory "on a basketball court." Echoing Woolf's recollection, he said, "I can play in a game, and when we watch it later, I can tell you throughout the rerun everything that's going to happen next. If we run the film of the game a week later, I can still tell you what's going to happen. But a year after the game I wouldn't be able to." This pictorial memory pays dividends for Larry, especially in the Boston Garden. "Like, in Boston Garden, I know *exactly* where I'm at. You remember where they put a new piece of tile in. If the defensive player is too far off me, 'cause I know where I am, I can turn and shoot almost without lookin'." And Larry's memory isn't limited to the court. "I can tell him something today, and six years from now, if I tell him something different, he'll say, 'Mr. Woolf, didn't you say this before?' [Larry still calls his agent, neighbor and friend, Mr. Woolf.] It's like a computer, his memory.... He'll play a golf course once and memorize the location of every tree. I can go to a game and swear that Larry never saw me, and days later he'll tell me in which section I was sitting, who I was talking to, what I was wearing."

*   *   *

Larry's uniqueness stems from the prodigious gifts he brings to the court, like his memory, his understanding of the game, his work habits, and all his natural physical skills. It also stems from the priorities he's adhered to in his life. Larry has reacted to the pressures of fame and fortune differently than almost anyone else would. His world remains centered around his friends—almost all of whom he has known for years—and his home in Indiana. His values are still firmly rooted in the soil of southern Indiana. And those roots have dictated that his world is almost as circumscribed as the one in which he was raised. "I've never seen nothin', I've never thought about nothin' other than basketball. It's my life, it's always been, since seventh grade," Larry explained in 1986. Is it any wonder then that this is the same guy who just a few years ago could ask, "Who's Bruce Springsteen?"*

"Larry, he's the you of rock 'n' roll" was the reply.

Laughing, Larry asked, "Where have I been?" He has been listening to the rhythm of another beat, the solitary beat of a basketball against the court. More elemental and familiar than a rock and roll beat, it is the cadence of one man against a game, its history, its perfection. Its final plateau will never be reached, but he has continued to struggle—with his considerable "gift"—to reach a still-higher level.

---

*Recently Larry decided to expand his horizons. Shortly after learning who Bruce Springsteen was, Larry attended one of Springsteen's concerts. He was impressed by how hard Springsteen worked, but not by the loudness of the music.

2 / *Hoosier Hysteria*

In Indiana it has always been a given that Larry Bird's talents were inextricably bound up with the passions for the game that run from Evansville to Fort Wayne and from Toto to Floyds Knobs. All over the state in communities like French Lick, the obsessive devotion to basketball is known as "Hoosier Hysteria." The unique level of intensity and dedication that Larry brings to the game can, to some extent, be traced to the passionate basketball milieu in which he was raised. For example, today, when Larry rubs the soles of his shoes, people assume that it is only one of the unique quirks that belong to the Larry Bird mystique since no other player in the NBA does it. But years before Larry's arrival, schoolboys from all over Indiana would rub their hands on the soles of their shoes for a very practical reason: The grit from the bottom of the shoes provides a better grip on the ball when the player's hands are wet from sweat.

Larry was asked at the beginning of his pro career what he liked to do when he wasn't playing basketball. "Play basketball," was his reply. For those in Boston and elsewhere, such a reply was probably regarded as humorous. For those raised in Indiana, who have watched Larry through the years, it was the only reasonable answer. "We don't play or watch basketball in Indiana. We live it, breathe it, taste it, smell it, sleep it," says Bob Collins, long-time high school basketball expert and sports editor for the *Indianapolis Star*.

For many in Indiana, Larry personifies a proud Hoosier identity. And given Larry's sometimes contentious nature, the humorous story by the late "Hoosier poet," James Whitcomb Riley, about the derivation of the word "Hoosier" is especially apt: "The early settlers... were vicious fighters, and not only gouged and scratched, but frequently bit off noses and ears. This was so ordinary an affair that a settler coming into a barroom on a morning after a fight, and seeing an ear on the floor, would merely push it aside with his foot and carelessly ask: 'Whose ear?'"

The word "Hoosiers" has become better known over the last two years with the popularity of the film of the same name, which has helped bring about a nationwide awareness of the Indiana basketball tradition. That awareness has only now begun to draw the connection between the talents of Larry Bird and the culture in which he was nurtured. The film's popularity derived to a great extent from nostalgia for the heartland and its traditional values that are perceived as purely American. Basketball in Indiana hearkens back to a bygone era, when values were simple, the work ethic pure, the family central, and the community close-knit. In many ways, that bygone era still exists in Indiana, preserved and strengthened with the help of the basketball culture. Larry himself evokes much of the same sentiment as the film, and those antecedents help to define him, as well. "The games draw people in to watch, and they tie the community together...," says Larry. "I have to believe it helps people stay together a little longer, and it starts with basketball."

And one of the film's greatest appeals is its evocation of the American dream—the chance of the little guy, the underdog, in overcoming all odds and succeeding by dint of sheer hard work. Hickory, the tiny school, was able to achieve the impossible—winning the state championship. Like Hickory, Larry was an underdog from a small school who also succeeded against overwhelming odds. Not surprisingly, what Larry loved most about the Indiana high school basketball tournament was that "even though you play for a small school you can win the state tourney. That anything is possible."

The story of *Hoosiers* was actually inspired by a true story, one that Larry and every Indiana schoolboy grew up hearing: the story of Milan (pronounced *my-lan*) High School and its star, Bobby Plump. This tiny school captured the 1954 Indiana State High School Championship and its achievement became known as "the dream," a term which became part of the state's cultural fabric. Milan evokes familiar images, distilling cultural metaphors out of the basketball drama: a gym spilling its light onto a desolate pastoral landscape during a wintry Friday night; a solitary boy shooting baskets at a bent old rim on a weathered barn set amidst endless cornfields; the deserted streets of an empty little town on a Friday night during the game; a caravan of headlights moving down a country road as an entire community travels to the arch-rival's gym for the annual showdown to determine county bragging rights; "downtown coaches" at their daily drugstore strategy sessions discussing the respective benefits of man-to-man and zone defenses. Perhaps no image of the Milan miracle remains more vivid than the one of Bobby Plump releasing the ball fifteen feet from the basket with just 3 seconds to go in the game on March 20, 1954. Here was the shot which epitomized for all time "the dream" and the era of glorious high school basketball in Indiana.

Bobby Plump is from Pierceville (about thirty-five miles northwest of Cincinnati), a tiny town with a total population somewhere between 45 and 50. Yet, it was never difficult to round up ten or twelve players after dinner—not in *Hoosier* country. Outside a barn, Plump and three friends would string light bulbs from a shovel handle under sheets of tin acting as reflectors, which enabled them to play until midnight. When Plump was there by himself, he would work on one move his ninth-grade coach had told him to perfect. He'd cut toward the center of the court on the dribble, full speed. Then, on a dime, he would "stop and pop" the ball from about the free-throw line.

All the boys from Pierceville played for Milan High, three miles down the road. The town of Milan seemed a little scary to Bobby: It was a bit too big. Milan's population was, according to Journalist Herb Leibowitz, 1,150 "on Saturdays when the farmers came to town to window-shop and buy groceries." The Milan High School enrollment was 162; there were 73 boys. Milan had never won a game beyond sectional competition in its entire history.

Naturally, Plump and his friends all went out for basketball. The coach was Marvin Wood, who arrived in Milan by way of French Lick in 1952, just two years removed from his college basketball days at Butler under renowned Coach Tony Hinkle. Under Hinkle, a basic offensive pattern involving two players was learned along with fourteen variations. Wood had learned that a patterned offense could be devastatingly successful, especially in a state where the influence of Branch McCracken's "hurryin' Hoosiers" (of Indiana University) up-tempo, fast-break style had become both an Indiana high school and college tradition. (Needless to say, people in Milan were at first not pleased about Wood's changes.)

In the final game of the 1953 season, Milan was scheduled to play at the gym of its arch rival (Osgood), which was unusually small. Because of the size of the gym and the intensity of some of the players' feelings, Wood was concerned about possible injuries. Though the game was eventually moved to a bigger court site, Wood decided to stay with the unique ball-control strategy the team had worked on called "cat and mouse"—an offense that became the forerunner of all spread-and-delay offenses including, most notably, Dean Smith's famed four corners offense. It centered around Plump, who would stand near the ten-second line (midcourt). His cohorts Ray Craft and Bob Engel would be spread out to each side parallel with the free-throw line. And Gene White and Ron Truitt would be in the corners along the baseline. Plump would hold the ball until a defender came to midcourt. In that event, another player, most often Ray Craft, would come up and meet the ball, with Plump passing to Craft and then everyone else cutting for the basket, looking for the pass. Plump and Craft were free to drive the middle when they saw an opening. Otherwise, the ball was generally passed from corner to corner. If a short-shot opportunity developed as a result of this "spread offense," the players were free to take it. This offense was meant to create numerous scoring opportunities for a team so small that its front line stood only 5'10" and 6'2" at the forward positions and 5'11" at the center position. Milan won the sectional and regional championships* by utilizing the cat-and-mouse strategy, and the team became widely known all over the state as the *tiny* school with the strange, deliberate offense. They went on to win the semi-state championship and advanced to the state finals, where they were beaten in the first game. However, since the players had only known of tourney games on the radio, this experience was to stand the four returning starters in good stead the following season.

The 1954 season had an almost fateful quality as it slowly fulfilled

---

*The first stage of the state tournament, where a team might play as few as two or as many as four games. The next week a regional is played with the winners of each of the two afternoon games meeting in the final that same evening. The following week the semi-state uses the same format as the regional. One week later the state finals take place, which use the same format as the regional and semi-state contests.

everyone's highest expectations. The Milan Indians had finished the season with a 19–2 record, and many experts felt they had a chance to get to the Indianapolis finals again. (A total of 751 teams began the Indiana tournament in 1954, though Milan was not the smallest; Hebron had just 65 pupils—87 fewer than Milan.) At a pep rally just before the sectional, Chris Volz, of the local GM dealership, offered, for the second year in a row, to take the team to the sectionals in a convoy of new Chevys. A convoy of Pontiacs would be provided for the regional, Buicks for the semi-state, and Cadillacs for the state final.

The sectional soon provided little resistance, and the regional proved to be just as easy. The team's good fortune continued at the semi-state. Arriving in Indianapolis the next week in the promised Cadillacs, tiny Milan was once again participating in the state's final four. Opening against Terre Haute–Gerstmeyer, they proved 1954 different from 1953 by winning 60–48.

But the final game would prove a challenge. The first problem was determining who would stay home. With only 900 tickets available and 1,100 townspeople, 200 would have to tend to the ghost town while the rest passionately cheered their team on at Butler Fieldhouse in Indianapolis. The second—and bigger problem—was Muncie Central, considered by many observers the best team the state had seen in a number of years. Central's enrollment of 1,662 students was over ten times that of Milan's. And their front line *averaged* 6'4" to Milan's 5'11". Muncie's size advantage spurred Coach Wood to go with the cat-and-mouse offense the entire game. And in the first half he looked like a genius as Milan pulled out to a 25–17 lead by intermission. But in a disastrous third quarter, Muncie Central briefly took the lead, and the quarter ended in a tie at 26–26. It was in the fourth quarter that the most astonishing strategic move in the history of the Indiana state finals occurred. With Muncie scoring the initial basket of the fourth quarter to go ahead 28–26, Wood told Plump to hold the ball. For the next 4 minutes and 13 seconds (over half the quarter) not a dribble or pass was made. Bobby Plump stood near midcourt, alternately holding the ball against his hip or in front of him, seemingly as perplexed as everyone else. "Some of my teammates were doing calisthenics to keep warm. I just stood there," Plump said. "I remember wondering what the hell we were doing. So I looked over at Marvin Wood on the bench. He was just sitting there with his legs crossed as if he didn't have a care in the world." Actually, Wood was desperately trying to think of something to do. Meanwhile, the fieldhouse and the rest of the state watching on TV or listening on radio was going crazy.

Was Milan conceding the game? Had Wood lost his mind? The state held its collective breath. Then, with 2 minutes to play, Wood signaled for a time-out in order to set up a shot for Plump. But when Plump took the shot, he missed, and Muncie rebounded. Yet the trapping zone press did its job and forced a turnover. Ray Craft then hit a short jumper, tying the game at 28. After a Muncie miss, Plump hit two free throws to give Milan the lead. But Craft missed a chance at a game-clinching lay-up, and Muncie tied the game again at 30. Plump brought the ball downcourt for what would prove to be the last time. With 18 seconds to go, Wood called a time-out.

Wood decided to let the team clear out to one side to enable Plump to go one-on-one against his defender. Wood told Plump to start making his move with about 8 seconds to go. Yet Plump almost didn't get the chance to be a hero. Instead of receiving the ball on the inbounds play, Plump nervously took it out himself. "I passed it to Craft and then he got the ball back to me. It wasn't exactly what Marvin wanted, but we never heard any complaints from him later." With about 5 seconds left, Plump faked left and drove to his right as the defender pulled back to guard against the drive to the hoop. Given an opening, Plump had, nonetheless, figured all along on "stopping and popping" a jump shot—the shot he had perfected in Pierceville four years before. With just a few ticks remaining, Plump let it fly from about 15 feet. The ball's destiny was the bottom of the net. Tiny Milan had not only become the state champion, but that one shot, proclaimed as the "greatest moment in forty-four years of Indiana basketball," guaranteed that Indiana would always hold tournaments without size divisions.

While history had just been made in Indianapolis, the 200 people back in Milan built a bonfire as the postgame celebration began and the team headed back in its Cadillac caravan. No one could have predicted what ensued: crowds lining the streets as they headed out of Indianapolis, planes flying overhead, flags and banners waving in every little town, fire trucks adding on to the caravan in Greensburg and Shelbyville, and cheering crowds in each successive town. Slowly the caravan swelled. There were so many cars that it took thirty-five minutes to drive the eight miles between Batesville and Sunman, and there were still five more miles before Milan. When the last of the Cadillacs reached Milan, 40,000 people were waiting. As the *Osgood Journal* proclaimed a few days later, "Indiana is still the best state in the USA for basketball, and Milan made it a little better Saturday night."

Today, thirty-four years later, Bobby Plump still gets calls in the middle of the night asking him to answer questions or settle bets about his miraculous shot—a shot which is etched into Hoosier consciousness like no other. On the day of the miracle shot, March 20, 1954, an estimated 90 percent of all Indiana families were watching or listening. The next day on the front page of the Sunday *Indianapolis Star,* a picture of a ball, captured just as it was dropping into the net, accompanied the day's bold headline, "Plump!" Not much after that, Bobby Plump received a fan letter addressed simply, "Plump, Indiana." Says Plump, "Hardly a day goes by that I don't meet somebody who asks me if I'm the same Plump from the state tournament."

For years after "the shot heard all over the state" as it came to be known, kids like Larry, on playgrounds, in driveways, and next to barns, hoped to imitate the Bobby Plump miracle. But Bobby Plump had begun with a dream too. His had been inspired by hearing the 1949 state finals on the radio,* in which one Bobby White led his Jasper High School team to victory. This particular triumph had an unusually religious backdrop.

It began in 1937, when first-grader Bobby White took his First Communion and began a twelve-year ritual of daily church attendance. He explained to his mother that the purpose of his life was to be a member of the Jasper High basketball team that would win the state championship his senior year. During his first two years in high school Bobby White was deemed too small to play, but through a fluke he became a starter as a senior.

But by the time the sectional rolled around, there was very little to cheer about in Jasper. The team's overall record was 11–9. No

---

*The state basketball finals were broadcast on TV throughout much of the state beginning in 1951.

team had ever finished a season with such a poor record and then gone on to win the state. However, Sister Joan of nearby St. Joseph's School insisted that Jasper was going to win. Her reasoning? After St. Joseph's school had burned to the ground, St. Joseph's had been allowed to use Jasper's facilities. The state finals were to be held on St. Joseph's Feast Day, March 19, "and God's going to reward Jasper High for letting us use their school."* Following two upsets, Jasper came from behind with White leading the way to win the sectional. For the rest of the week, the other Catholic boys on the team went to Mass with Bobby. After White led two comeback wins in the regional, the three non-Catholics on the team, as well as numerous other citizens, began joining Bobby at Mass. Jasper, the little community of 8,500 whose top priorities had always been religion and basketball, was now beside itself with spiritual frenzy.

The following Saturday in the semi-state, the Jasper Wildcats were down 49–48 against Bloomington with only 1 second to go. But their worst shooter hit at the buzzer for a 50–49 victory. The next morning, the entire town of Jasper attended Mass. One week later, on St. Joseph's Feast Day, Jasper came from behind to edge Auburn 53–48, and White led the scoring. In the final against Madison, Jasper came from behind again for the eighth straight time, to win 62–61. Little Bobby White was Jasper's leading scorer with 20 points. And to this day, in the 75 years of the Indiana tourney, no team has ever won with a record as poor as the Jasper Wildcats. Jasper is only twenty-five miles southwest of French Lick on Highway 56. And, Larry and the rest of the kids in the area grew up with hopes of also repeating the miracle of underdog Bobby White.

On the eve of the 1974 state tournament, twenty years after Bobby Plump and twenty-five years after Bobby White, Larry Bird was just as excited about the pursuit of "the dream," which was now *his* dream. But Larry's dream was not to be. His Springs Valley team lost in the final of the regional. To this day he lists this failure as one of the biggest disappointments of his life. By failing to duplicate Milan's improbable small-school triumph, Larry forfeited his chance for Indiana high school basketball immortality. In the 100-minute

---

*Jasper's large Catholic population was fairly unusual for the region.

video *Hoosier Hysteria,* celebrating Indiana's high school basketball history, Larry rates nary a mention until the closing credits. Plump, who never reached the NBA, received a great deal of exposure. It is ironic that the greatest player from the greatest basketball state is assigned so small a role in the state's high school basketball history.

However, Larry was a late bloomer who didn't really begin to dominate until his senior year. And then he was at a disadvantage because he was at a small school, where he was playing weaker teams and receiving less exposure. Going into his senior year, Larry had not yet won even a sectional title. Consequently, despite producing some of the finest numbers in state history during his senior season, Larry suffered the ignominy of not making first team All-State his senior year. It was only owing to an intensive last-minute publicity campaign that Larry barely made the twelve-man All-Star team that was to play Kentucky after the season. But despite all his disadvantages, people across the state knew about his senior-year exploits. Larry's renown was impressive considering that his rise to stardom was so sudden. He had not built a reputation in the early years of his high school career like most of the other well-known players. But he had learned the game in much the same way.

Kids growing up in Indiana benefit from an elaborate basketball training infrastructure that exists in every county and almost every small town. In French Lick, the program was called Biddy Ball, and like many of the other programs, it provided "stimulation through idolization," because the kids were taught by the high school basketball stars. Jim Jones, who helped develop Biddy Ball, explains that by the time a player has reached the high school level, he is fully versed not only in the fundamentals of the game but imbued with its spiritual ethos as well: "the dream" and his own potential place in the state's basketball history. The precocity of the high school player doesn't stop there: "In a way high school basketball is like the pros in Indiana," says Jerry Sichting from Martinsville (and now with the Portland Trailblazers). "Players get used to playing in front of 5,000 fans when they are young."

Because of this statewide emphasis on school basketball, there is more than a little truth to the adage, "In Indiana you can easily spot the old, dilapidated, one-room, red school house—it is attached to the modern gymnasium." Eighteen of the twenty largest high school gymnasiums in the world are in Indiana. At least thirty-two of the state's high school gyms seat in excess of 5,000 people. And over 150 high school gyms seat at least 3,000 people. New Castle High leads the way with the world's largest high school gymnasium. Built in 1959, it seats 9,325, serving a high school of 1,125 and a town of 19,500. Yet there are smaller schools that represent, in proportion, even greater examples of basketball devotion. In 1951, when Huntingsburg's gym was built, it seated 6,260, almost twice the town's population and twenty times the school population. Clay City, with a total population of 500, built a 3,000-seat high school gym and Carmel, with 1,442 citizens, a 4,500-seat gym.

How could the various city councils justify the cost of such seemingly gratuitous displays of basketball love? Simple: so that the towns with the biggest gyms could host the sectional tournament and maybe even the regional tournament. Any team doing so would obviously have a big advantage in the state tournament. In 1984, Richmond High's brand-new $7 million 8,100-seat gym took Richmond out of the New Castle sectional and into the newly created Richmond sectional. In California, a state with 18 million more people and three times as many high schools as Indiana (in 1984), the attendance at the most popular state tournament ever (1984) averaged less than one-fifth of the Hoosier tournament.

The atmosphere behind Hoosier Hysteria, however, goes far beyond the number of fans who attend the games. It is an atmosphere that permeates every aspect of everyday life. Only religion and the economy rival the influence that basketball has over most of the communities across the state. Even education usually takes a back seat to the importance of a community's high school team. "In the little towns, people sometimes run for the school board on a platform of nothing more than wanting to fire the basketball coach," says a one-time high school coach. "In Indiana, everybody thinks he's a coach because he either played basketball or studied the game. And usually he knows what the hell he's talking about." Many school boards in Indiana have the power to hire and fire only two school employees, the principal and the coach—and not necessarily in that order. It's not unusual for a high school to have four or five and sometimes as many as seven coaches in a ten-year period. "You got to win.... The wife can't even go to the store if you don't win," says Howard Sharpe— the winningest coach in Indiana history with 753 wins in 47 years of coaching. Sharpe recounts the story of one year "when nobody was buried in Indiana for a week. Big snowstorms paralyzed everything. And there were 250 high school basketball games played in the state that week. They just put the people on snowplows and brought 'em to the gyms. This isn't a game in Indiana, it's a religion."

Indeed, the relationship between the church and basketball in Indiana is unmistakable. For Hoosiers, the Sabbath begins on Friday night. Each gymnasium serves to house the communal yearning for basketball salvation. And each gym celebrates its sacred relics, its basketball immortality, in showcases filled with pictures, trophies, and nets cut in triumph, which are dutifully acknowledged by all the faithful upon arriving and leaving.

Despite the almost-mystical quality of Indiana's devotion to its game, there are a number of logical reasons for Hoosier Hysteria. The first has to do with the timing of the basketball season. In 1920, 31 percent of the entire Indiana population lived on farms. In addition, many Hoosiers not living on farms were at least peripherally related to the agriculture industry. Considering that basketball is played exactly between the harvest and the planting season, this then was a time when nearly half of Indiana had much less work to do. The issue of what to do with all this leisure time was further compounded by the large number of tiny hamlets and towns throughout the state. As Hoosier Comedian Herb Shriner explained, "Boy, did we use to have excitement Saturday nights! It was nothing for us to go down to watch a few haircuts."

Many schools barely had enough boys to field a football team, never mind having enough in case somebody was injured. And football equipment was expensive. But it was cheap and easy to nail a hoop up to a barn and play alone or with a few other kids. And unlike other predominantly rural states in the midwest, Indiana was unique in that until recently it did not have professional sports teams to compete with the high schools for fans. Following the community's high school basketball team was for many the sole occupation during the harsh winter months. The social life of an entire community would center on the ball team: the gym became "the nightclub," and everybody went to the club. As Bob Collins explained: "I've been in places where I was having dinner on Friday night, and the owner would shout, 'fifteen minutes and we're closin' up!' and everybody

cleared their plates, settled up and went to the basketball game."
With elaborate bake sales, bands, baton twirling exhibitions, pom-
pon routines, and the most select units of radiant and pristine cheer-
leaders, who could want more?

Yet there were other unique cultural factors that contributed to the
growth of the Hoosier passion. In the forties, fans all over the state
were linked by the *Indianapolis News* basketball column, "Shootin'
'Em and Stoppin' 'Em.'' Columnist Paul Fox's coverage of the sport
by automobile was aided by the relative smallness and flatness of the
state and the high quality of the state's highways. Between 1928 and
1936 Fox and Butler University Coach Tony Hinkle barnstormed
across the state, bringing word from all sixteen regionals. In the forties, towns were entering their third generation of staunch basketball
loyalty. Rivalries and hatreds had been hardened. Today those rivalries are just as intense. In Orange County where Larry grew up, the
hatred induced by the rivalries is just as strong. When Gary Holland
was named head coach during Larry's senior year, there were big
problems because he had grown up in neighboring Paoli. "My father
still owns a store in Paoli," says Holland. "That first year, they shot
his windows through with buckshot. I got calls in the night all winter
long, people from Paoli saying 'Traitor' and hanging up.''

The phenomenon is especially a problem in a community like
Anderson. "They [the teams' opponents] all want you to die, and
they don't care when," says Coach Norm Held of Anderson High.
"It's almost a kind of insanity. You know. Like a cult.'' In Anderson
the rivalry between the city's three high schools is so intense that
"it's like three different cities.'' Anderson, a town of only 65,000 people, had the highest unemployment rate in the nation in 1984 (22.5
percent). Yet in the same year there were 12,000 season ticket holders at an average of $15 per ticket for a total of eleven games. In the
NBA, out of twenty-two cities only Boston, Los Angeles, Portland,
Dallas, and Houston have more season ticket holders.

As Bobby Knight says, "Basketball may have been invented in
Massachusetts, but it was made *for* Indiana.'' Indeed, the state's basketball history goes back to almost the very beginning of the sport
itself in the early 1890s. By 1911 the first official state high school
tournament was held with 12 teams competing. At that point, games
were being staged just about anywhere: at skating rinks; in the driveway of a lumber yard; in halls, garages, and barns.

The barn usually had a wood burning stove to keep everyone warm. On occasion, when a game was very close, the person tending the stove would sometimes forget his duties, allowing a stray ember to burn on the floor. As a result the barn would sometimes catch fire. Hence the term "barn burner" for a close basketball game.

By 1925, the state tournament had 674 participating teams, and Hoosier Hysteria was well on its way. According to the immortal basketball coach John Wooden, himself a member of the 1927 state championship Martinsville High team and later an All-American at Purdue: "For a high school player, winning the Indiana state championship was far more meaningful than winning the NCAA is today or ever has been."

Basketball growth in the Hoosier state hardly slowed down during the depression; the WPA, instead of building roads and bridges as in the other states, built bleachers for gymnasiums.

By the Second World War, Indiana's basketball reputation had spread. "If you went into the military and said you were from Indiana they automatically told you to report to the gym," says Jerry Hoover, Indiana high school basketball coach. Indiana's reputation also spread as a result of the basketball it exported. The coaches of nine Indiana high school championship teams went directly into college coaching in other states. Most notably, Everett Case, former Frankfort coach, brought dozens of Indiana high school players to North Carolina State and built a hardwood tradition in that state which—at least at the collegiate level—almost rivals that of Indiana.

But Indiana's basketball exports started taking a toll on its own college basketball. In 1938, seven of the ten players for the University of Southern California came from Indiana. In 1943 all of Michigan State's starters were Hoosiers. And in 1951 when Vanderbilt played Mississippi, twelve of the twenty players hailed from within a 50-mile radius in southern Indiana, and six of those twelve were from Jasper, population 8,500. Then the next season Bobby White continued the Jasper hardwood tradition. In 1948 when Indiana University finished last in the Big Ten it was Clyde Lovelette, from Terre Haute, who led Kansas to the NCAA championship. That year Coach Branch McCracken vowed to recruit the five best boys from Indiana. With the help of the high school coaches in the state, the best players were steered to Indiana University. Five years later Indiana University won the NCAA with ten small-town Indiana kids.

*   *   *

Considering how important basketball is to Indiana's sociocultural life, it is not surprising that the game has had a dramatic impact beyond the gym and has profoundly affected both the political and educational arenas. The fifties marked a period of change for Indiana politics, education, and basketball—and a positive one for the most part.

Indiana's race relations spurred the first significant change. For, as glorious as Indiana high school basketball has been, its record for racial tolerance has been equally inglorious. The KKK ran the state in the twenties and single-handedly elected the governor of Indiana and the mayor of Indianapolis. In rural counties it was estimated that more than half the men and women were members of the Klan. Close to one-third of *all* males in the state were members. School segregation was actively encouraged or required by either action or law. Then, between 1951 and 1957, all-black Indianapolis Crispus Attucks High reached the semi-state finals six times. They became the first Indianapolis school to win the state championship—an intensely embarrassing fact for people from that city, both because it had taken so long and because it took an all-black team to do it. As a result, says Bob Collins, "the success of Attucks' basketball integrated the high schools of Indianapolis. They had become so dominant that the other schools had to get black basketball players or forget about it." By 1955 a previously all-white school, Indianapolis Shortridge, had four black starters. Before, all blacks, no matter where they lived in the city, had to go to Attucks. Since 1960, there have been only six state champion teams (five were all white) that weren't integrated.

The integration of Indiana's schools changed the way basketball was played in the state. When the black or mostly black teams began to dominate in the midfifties, the small-town, mostly white teams found they were being beaten at the fast-break style of basketball they had emphasized for years. But due to the influence of Tony Hinkle (who had taught Marvin Wood, the Milan coach), a number of coaches in the state had favored a slower, more deliberate style of play. Many small-town teams found this style was the most effective way to match up against the urban schools, which otherwise dominated because of their speed. Throughout the sixties and seventies, more and more small-town teams adopted the deliberate style. When

Bobby Knight came to Indiana in the early seventies with a motion offense that was extremely deliberate, the mold was cast. In the eight years between 1976 and 1984, five teams that were all white, or started white players, won the championship utilizing that kind of offense.

The successful adaptation of small-town teams to the influx of the urban game has been evident. Both the successful assimilation of a more deliberate style of play and the proliferation of integration have doomed the likelihood that big-city schools will ever again dominate the tourney. Integrated teams from small schools have been able to mix both the urban and deliberate styles to their advantage. After Milan in 1954, fourteen of the next seventeen champions were from urban areas or cities with a population of 70,000 or more. Since then, thirteen of the next seventeen have been from towns with populations between 7,000 and 40,000 people. But one thing is certain: most small-town teams will never again play a predominantly fast-breaking style of basketball.

A second profound change occurred in Indiana high school education and basketball: consolidation of school districts. However, its progression was greatly inhibited by the intensity of basketball passions around the state. Generations of entrenched rivalry are not easily overcome. The community where Larry grew up illustrates this problem quite well.

Before consolidation, the rivalry between the West Baden Sprudels and the French Lick Red Devils was fierce. If a West Baden kid went to French Lick or vice versa, there was sure to be a fight. "They fought over that basketball all the time. When I was a kid growin' up, there probably wasn't a ball game when there wasn't a fight afterwards," says Jack Carnes, who runs the kitchen at the French Lick Springs Hotel. And though consolidation inevitably changed the map of Indiana high school education and basketball, the final result was far less sweeping than it would have been without basketball.

Perhaps the most instructive example is the story of Onward. At the beginning of the 1950 school year, Onward High School and Walton High School were ordered to consolidate. A savings of $20,000 for the township and quality education for the students made the merger a prudent move. Onward (population 171) would use its high school for the consolidation's grade school, and Walton (population 835) would use its high school for the consolidation's high school.

When the school year began, all the Walton grade-schoolers reported dutifully to the new Onward grade school. However, with the exception of four traitors to the cause, all Onward High School students refused to report to their new Walton High School. Onward announced it would begin the high school year with the smartest students serving as teachers.

At the same time the citizens of Onward suspected that state authorities and township trustees might attempt to capture the school by storm, so an informal defense and radar system was begun. Men and women were posted outside the school twenty-four hours a day. A small plane monitored the road between the towns by day; at night an air raid siren alerted the town if there were attempts to infiltrate and capture the school by darkness. In the first confrontation, a trustee and fifteen volunteers were met by fifty Onward residents, barring entrance and singing "Onward Christian Soldiers." A week later, the trustee arrived with sixty-seven state troopers, 20 percent of the entire state force. Onward was ready: two rows of trucks encircled the building, the doors were chained, and fifty defiant kids stood guard inside. Though there was some scuffling, the governor ordered a retreat. A new strategy was adopted: a war of attrition rather than confrontation. State aid was stopped; teachers were no longer paid, and accreditation lapsed. Yet the renegade school at Onward continued for another two years, financed mostly by chicken dinners sold to supporters from all over the area. Forty years of fanatical basketball rivalry does not surrender easily.

But with Washington exerting pressure by using federal aid as a bargaining chip for better roads, the Indiana Assembly moved toward consolidation. The pain and frustration for many small communities whose entire identity revolved around the high school basketball team was intense. Losing the school and the ball team for a town like Onward meant becoming a nonentity. The statistics tell the story: In 1938 there were 787 high school entries in the state tournament; in 1985 there were 394. Before the consolidation, 40 percent of Indiana's high schools had 200 or fewer students. Now there are only 32 with less than 200 students (less than 8 percent.) Because of its state championship, Milan has staved off consolidation. But with 305 students, Milan is actually bigger than 90 other schools.

As a result of consolidation, the popularity of football has burgeoned, since school size is no longer a factor in fielding a team.

(Football has even pushed back the once-sacred basketball season's November 1 starting date by three weeks.) Cable TV and its offering of pro and college basketball games every night has also affected the high school game. Consequently, an Indianapolis television station has dropped its high school game of the week. Saddest of all is that many small Indiana communities—once full of the boisterous glories of Friday nights, with all of the main street's rituals before and after the game—are now strangely quiet and vacant on these same Friday nights.

On the plus side, the super-schools have dictated the building of even-better basketball facilities. And as the many little high schools have closed, their remarkable basketball facilities have been bequeathed to the consolidations' junior highs. The junior high school basketball facilities in Indiana are the largest in the world. And, despite consolidation, basketball popularity has largely survived. The state tournament is still the best-attended in the country. And half the state still watches the state final on the last Saturday night in March. For, even in communities that have consolidated, basketball loyalties and rivalries have remained.

Much has changed in Indiana high school basketball, but fortunately, much has stayed the same. Reflecting a large part of the state's personality, the game still rests largely on its traditions, rituals, and history. What once was the result of a unique regional sociology is now forever a determining force in that sociology. To have lived in Indiana is to have rubbed elbows with a passion, a spirit, a state of mind revolving around a game that has reached larger-than-life proportions. People in Indiana view Larry Bird as more than just a sports hero; for he is the greatest player in the greatest sport—and he is their own. As a result, Larry is able to inspire much the same passions as Hoosier Hysteria itself.

Every Hoosier understands intuitively what Psychologist Carl Jung could only guess about when he hypothesized, "It is even conceivable that there are several forms of hysteria which Freud has not yet observed at all." Only a totally jaundiced observer would not relish the thought of the good Doctor Freud at midcourt, ten rows up in the bleachers at sectional time, trying to figure out the phenomenon going on around him.

By the time Larry was 14, he knew exactly what was going on around him at sectional time. That year he saw his brother Mark win a sectional title. It was about then that he understood that he wanted to dedicate his life to basketball. Years of organized play in his childhood had preceded Larry's realization, and the basketball passions of the community had helped to nurture and support his ambitions. There are a number of reasons why Larry continues to live where he was raised—not the least of which is that he and the community of West Baden and French Lick understand the phenomenon of Hoosier Hysteria.

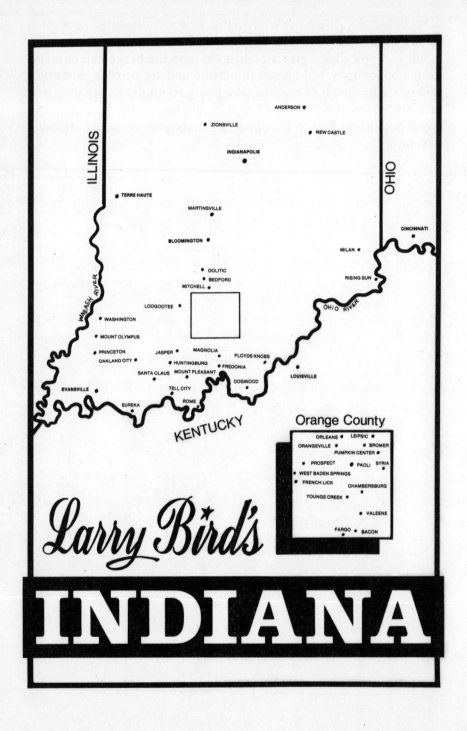

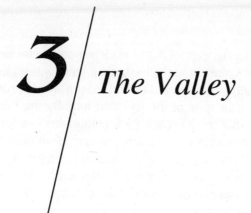

3 / *The Valley*

West Baden and French Lick are the twin communities which, along with tiny Prospect, make up "the valley." All told, the population is about 3,000, of which two-thirds live in French Lick. Though it is only a mile from the eastern end of West Baden to the western edge of French Lick, kids from West Baden rarely venture into French Lick except to attend school. And kids from French Lick seldom feel the need to go into West Baden. Even though the only thing that separates West Baden from French Lick is an imaginary line, everyone is acutely aware of that line. Says one West Baden resident, "[When I was a child], that line, as far as I was concerned, was a brick wall." But today West Baden residents harbor more than the customary resentment because their community is smaller. Thanks to Larry's famous reference to himself as "The hick from French Lick," people still associate Larry with French Lick, even though he currently resides in West Baden and spent his first twelve years there as well. Almost like a microcosm of Indiana high school basketball history, the valley's experience encompasses generations of entrenched rivalry, consolidation, and a fervid passion for the game that involves literally everyone in the community. Like other towns in the midfifties, West Baden and French Lick resisted the pressure to consolidate their schools. The basketball rivalry between the West Baden Sprudels and the French Lick Red Devils was so fierce that, according to Jack Carnes, "Whether you won or lost you had to agitate the other team....I've seen people jump off the balcony [at the old West Baden gym] and onto a player. It was just that violent." Finally, in 1957, with the help of a push from the state and thirteen community leaders, the towns consolidated their schools. The new school was called Springs Valley, and the basketball team was named the Black Hawks. Ironically, that first basketball season would prove to be the valley's greatest, in spite of the fact that initially the West Baden players suspected that their French Lick teammates wouldn't pass them the ball—and vice versa. The team, featuring four starters from West Baden, won 25 straight games and beat three big schools ranked in the state's top ten, though they were defeated in the state finals. Thanks in large measure to that team's success, consolidation has not proved to be a problem since.

Bob McCracken and Marvin Pruett were the stars of that team and both went on to play for the Indiana high school all-star team. Their pictures are displayed in the Springs Valley gym alongside those of Larry and Eddie Bird, Indiana all-stars in 1974 and 1986. And right next to the American flag is, appropriately, the 1958 state finals banner. Still, the most prominent and revered artifact is a near-full-length picture of Larry which looks down magisterially over the gym from the entranceway. As in other Indiana communities, basketball and basketball facilities had taken precedence over education and other school facilities. When the new high school was built, "the first thing that was constructed was a 3,000-seat gym," says a French Lick resident. Actually, the gym is supposed to seat 2,700, but 4,000 were in attendance for Larry's final home game. On average, about 1,600 people attend regularly and another 1,000 listen over WFLQ. That accounts for just about everyone in the valley.

In a sense, the gym and many other aspects of the "new" valley have come to represent a shrine of sorts for Larry. On entering the gym lobby, one is greeted by Larry's 1974 high school all-star jersey and trophy. Just outside is the 15-foot-high basketball-shaped sign marking Larry Bird Boulevard in French Lick. After the renovation of the gym floor, The City Drug Store sold pieces of the floor Larry used to play on for $5.95. Larry's number 33 has been retired, but the number is stitched to each reserve team warm-up jacket.

"When the Converse people wanted to talk to Larry about money, the first thing he wanted to know was: 'Can you get some sneakers for my high school?'" recalled Gary Holland. Indeed, fifty pairs of $40 sneakers were soon delivered to the high school. Now, every year fifty balls and fifty pairs of shoes arrive for the team. "It has really helped out our program more in terms of monetary things than anything," says Holland. Larry Bird symbolizes many things to the valley, but mostly he is a hero. Growing up even poorer than the rest of the valley's residents, Larry now serves as the main source of valley pride. "Larry is a like a God to [the valley]. He came out of the cornfields, and better yet he came out of *their* cornfields," says a former valley resident. His Celtic games are carried locally via satellite, and a "birdwatch" column in the *Springs Valley Herald* chronicles his season's progress. Add the hometown pride and interest in a Larry Bird to an already rabid interest in basketball and it's no wonder that Larry Bird and basketball supply the majority of conversation in the valley. "Well, we've always had a big interest in basketball, but Larry's helped it," says *Springs Valley Herald* Publisher Jim Ballard.

"Who'd have ever thought in French Lick he'd learn the skills he's learned? You'd expect it from someone who grew up playing in New York City, not French Lick," says former Milwaukee Coach Don Nelson. "Somehow he learned to play the game better than anybody." No one can underestimate Larry's remarkable ability for self-instruction, but the valley was an almost-perfect place to grow up and learn to play the game. Indeed, the basketball training comes early in the valley, just as in the rest of the state. The program called Biddy Ball provides youngsters in the fourth, fifth, and sixth grades with their first opportunity to experience organized basketball. Besides Saturday instruction and games, occasionally the Biddy Ball teams come in to play at the halftime of the high school games.

Larry refers to the time when he played Biddy Ball as his "habit-forming days." Jim Jones, who developed the program, and Gary Holland, his assistant, were devoted to teaching a fundamental approach to the game. "I never had the gifted speed, but I always had great coaching, back to when I played Biddy League Ball," Larry says now. "They banged the fundamentals into us. If you made a mistake you did it over until you got it right. They were constantly drilling us on executing back doors, pick and rolls, and using the backboard for a lay-up. No 'fancy Dan' stuff or showboating." Today, Larry is one of the best ball-handling big men in the league, and he is definitely the most effective ambidextrous shooter in the NBA. "When I played Biddy Ball," says Larry, "everybody learned to dribble with his left hand. It was something among the fellows I grew up with to see who could dribble the best with his left hand."

But more than just the Biddy Ball program, the general environment in the county was perfect for a kid like Larry to learn the game and make it the center of his existence. "Just the idea of how important basketball is to people here, in French Lick, helped Larry a whole lot," says Holland. "In general [for] the kids in this county, [basketball is] what they look up to," says Coach Holland. "I grew up in this county [in Paoli], and [basketball] is what we did all the time." Such an environment provides a marvelous chance to receive a lot of individualized instruction. According to Jones, "In a community of that size we try to recruit any kid who can breathe. And you can spend a lot of time with them." Of course, the size of the community meant that the coach was always nearby to provide instruction. "It could be six or seven o'clock and a bunch of us playin' outside, and he'd come by and stop and make pointers. He did it so much that what he said just started coming naturally....He would not listen to a player sayin' 'I can't do it.' He just didn't want to hear it," says Larry.

Understanding then what the valley meant to Larry's basketball development helps to make more plausible his rush to return every summer. Few individuals and their communities value basketball like Larry and the valley. And the sharing of values between Larry and the valley only begins with basketball.

The values of the community have been handed down for a couple of generations, and there is no more instructive example of those time-tested values than the point of view of Larry's grandmother, his primary influence when he was young. Lizzie Kerns still lives in the same house where Larry spent much of his adolescence, two blocks from the school. Larry has offered to build her a new house, but she has adamantly refused. "She likes her little house," says a family member. The only thing Lizzie Kerns has accepted from Larry is a new TV so she can watch her favorite grandson's games. At 82, "she's such a spunky little thing," says a relative, that neighbors down the block can hear her screaming at the refs during the Celtics' games when it's warm enough to have the windows open.

Lizzie did allow Larry to paint the house himself the summer before last. She will accept those gifts facilitating her basketball watching or requiring a little work. And her values have influenced Larry enough so that to this day one of his most cherished activities is working outside with his hands. If he isn't painting Lizzie's house, he's working on the lawn at his home. Along with his preoccupation with his lawn, there goes a rigid work ethic. So when Larry gave his little brother Eddie the Trans Am Larry won for being the playoff MVP in 1984, the gift was contingent on Eddie's maintaining the lawn while Larry was away. Living out on the outskirts of West Baden made it hard for Eddie to get to and from basketball practice without a car. Now Eddie drives a jeep which Larry won in 1986. The same *quid pro quo* exists for the jeep as well. Larry took away the Jeep he had given Eddie when he received a "D" in one of his classes last year. Though Eddie struggles in school partially because of a reading disorder, both the Jeep and the Trans Am were contingent upon Eddie's promise to go to college. And Larry doesn't stop there. In order to adequately monitor Eddie's work, Larry had his mother send him photos of the lawn. "Hell, yes [I had those pictures sent]. Cause it's his job when I'm away." And it is gladly Larry's job when he is back home in the summer.

"I still lead a simple life. I'm still just a small-town kid who is living in a big city for a while," Larry said just a few years ago. And the same holds true today. "[I most enjoy] my privacy, my family, my friends, a little fishing and golfing, a little beer drinking. Those things will keep me happy for the rest of my life," he says. Indeed, hanging out with his lifelong buddies and drinking a little beer is one of Larry's greatest pleasures and provides him a much-needed respite from the pressures of the NBA. "He's pretty much a social drinker; he'll play when he's with friends," says a relative. "He has so much pressure on him during the season that he has to let his hair down once in a while." To that end one of the first extravagances Larry allowed himself when he signed his rookie contract was the equipping of his Ford Bronco with a beer cooler in the console. "He always keeps it filled up, too," says a friend in the valley.

The sharing of values also means that Larry can be accepted for who he is rather than the celebrity he has become. He can lead his life without the difficulty and interruption that he encounters in Boston and elsewhere. In the valley, he gets peace. "I want to go in to eat and get the hell out," Larry says. "Back home, I don't have those problems, and that's why I go back there. People go about it different. They don't follow you around." Not only do the people in the valley understand his needs, but they all go out of their way to protect him. They divulge nothing without his permission—partly out of respect, partly out of distrust of outsiders, and partly out of fear of incurring Larry's well-known wrath. They are even loath to divulge flattering details. "I could tell some stories about some real nice things Larry has done but I wouldn't unless Larry said it was O.K.," says a close family friend. And it is such a familiar refrain that Larry is sometimes accused of hiding behind the valley for fear of the more harsh realities in other places. "I ain't scared of nothin'," he replies defensively. "I think I'm totally fearless. I went off to college by myself. I went off to Boston myself—I mean who wouldn't be scared by that? But I made it."

Larry feels more comfortable and understood in the valley. This is partly because people living outside of the area fail to understand how significant the valley's culture has been for Larry. This is not just in terms of values but in terms of style as well.

While some people tend to think that Larry is dumb because of the way he communicates, that style is the valley's style. Larry makes no apologies. "You'd have to go down to French Lick and that general area to know the grammar," he says. "If you're going to be around people all the time, it's only natural that you pick up their way of talking. It's a very limited small town. You don't need a lot of grammar. Half the time you can communicate with hand signals. I'm not knocking the English teachers or anything. It's just the way the area is. I didn't take school seriously until my junior year in high school. I didn't take it very seriously again until I was halfway through college. My grammar isn't very good, but you know what? I think a lot more people can understand me around here [better] than they can many other people."

It is the springs in the valley that historically have best defined the valley. In 1840 the first hotel was erected in French Lick to take advantage of those miracle waters. Another hotel, a mile away, was built just six years later. The forerunner of the West Baden Hotel, its springs and their adjoining 6,000 acres were what Colonel John Sinclair, entrepreneur, hoped to turn into "The Carlsbad of America," (at the time, Carlsbad had the most popular spa resort in Europe). Sinclair hoped that additional revenue could be generated by the marketing of bottled water from the springs for medicinal purposes. A tremendous promoter, Sinclair began advertising the springs throughout the country as "America's Cure," and he listed fifty ailments (mostly of the nervous system and digestive tract) all curable "through the natural power" of his springs. But it was only when more salts were added, thus producing an effective laxative, that Pluto Water became famous. "If nature won't, Pluto will," said the bottle. Soon Pluto Water was selling over the counter all over the world and even won first prize at the World's Fair in Paris.

The advertising for Sinclair's resort in addition to the smaller (all of 3,500 acres) resort in French Lick, claimed they could "be reached from almost anywhere by railway." In 1900 a special spur was built just to serve the two hotels. Meanwhile, Sinclair had not been content to simply provide miracle waters. Beside making lavish improvements in the hotel, in 1893 he added an opera house, and in 1895 a casino.

The casino proved to be a significant turning point in the fortunes of the valley, since heretofore the area had attracted a wealthy clientele simply for its luxurious accommodations and miracle waters. As the crush of visitors increased, the allure of the casino interested one investor in particular—Democratic Mayor of Indianapolis Tom Taggart. When a fire leveled Sinclair's establishment in 1901, Taggart bought the French Lick Springs Hotel believing he had just acquired a monopoly.

But within four months of the fire, the indefatigable Colonel Sinclair embarked on a grand design for a new hotel to cater to wealthy Americans who had previously traveled to Europe and the Orient in search of both quaint and bizarre surroundings. The West Baden establishment rose from the ashes more dazzling than before.

The valley also gained a national reputation in the first third of the twentieth century as a training center for some of the country's top athletes. Baseball teams like the Cincinnati Reds, Chicago Cubs, St. Louis Cardinals, St. Louis Browns, Pittsburgh Pirates, and Philadelphia Phillies all did their spring training in West Baden. Boxers like John L. Sullivan, Thomas J. Sharkey, and James J. Corbett trained in West Baden before major bouts. Even Joe Louis trained at Sinclair's hotel, though he was required to stay at a "negro" hotel, The Waddy.

The athletes were not the only big names attracted to the sumptuous surroundings. The Astors, Vanderbilts, New York Yankee owner Colonel Jake Ruppert, and Charles Murphy and his Tammany

Hall politicos (including Governor Alfred E. Smith and Mayor La-Guardia) vacationed there regularly. So did Tom Mix, Clara Bow, General Pershing, Howard Hughes, and supposedly Al Capone. There's even a Bird family story that Capone tipped Larry's grandfather $100 for carrying his bags at the French Lick Hotel. When not training, Jack Dempsey would stay in French Lick. Though not a gambler, Irving Berlin would come regularly. He wrote "I'm All Alone" while at Taggart's hotel. Senator Harry Truman would visit and largely because of Taggart's political support, Franklin D. Roosevelt made a significant whistle-stop campaign appearance there in 1931. So it was because of the two major hotels and another twenty smaller hotels that the valley became one of the best-known vacation spots in the country. Frequently anywhere from 120 to 200 private and Pullman cars were parked along the track at a time. The maids and servants for various guests at the hotels would often stay on the train. And chauffeured Rolls Royces, Deusenbergs, Cords, and Auburns would line the street.

Gambling was the primary lure for many of the ultrawealthy visitors. Whether the gambling was technically illegal was never an issue. With 80 percent of the valley's 2,300 residents in the employ of either the West Baden or French Lick Hotels, and with a Democratic power broker owning one hotel and a Republican another, somehow the county authorities were never able to uncover any Indiana gambling law violations. Work for two and sometimes even three generations of most of the valley's families revolved around the hotels and serving the wealthy visitors.

On November 17, 1929, this pattern of life came to an abrupt halt when the great depression hit. For four days, porters worked nonstop around the clock, carrying baggage to the waiting trains and luxury automobiles. Many of the rich and glamorous visitors disappeared, never to return. And West Baden never recovered. For the next ten years, the French Lick Hotel managed to maintain much of its allure, but by the forties, its popularity began to wane. By the end of the decade, a power struggle for control of The Brown (the main casino) and the French Lick Springs Hotel developed, and one week before Derby Day in 1949, Governor Schricker sent the Indiana State Police to enforce Indiana's antigambling law.

The demise of gambling, added to the financial impact of the stock market crash, and the change in people's traveling habits (i.e., planes instead of trains and the resulting emergence of resorts in warmer climates such as Florida's) meant that the glory days of the valley were over.

The valley became much like the rest of the poor little communities spread across the state of Indiana. Yet vestiges of the community's earlier glory days remain. The French Lick Springs Hotel continues as one of the valley's leading employers, but today its popularity derives from its use as a convention center. And an effort is currently under way to renovate the old West Baden Hotel into a resort.

The major employer in the valley today is the Kimball Piano & Organ Company (which arrived in 1975) with approximately 900 workers. Just about everyone works for either Kimball, the hotel, U.S. Gypsum (in nearby Shoals) or the bottling plant (which now produces something called Blue Lustre Carpet Shampoo instead of Pluto Water). Of course, farming is still significant. Yet the poverty of the valley is quite evident, much like that of the other small towns throughout the southern area of the state. For Larry Bird, one of the few ways "out" (of the poverty of the valley), as in the inner city ghetto, was basketball.

The poverty that the valley has endured since the rich and famous abandoned it has not been without its emotional impact. There's a perceptible distrust of outsiders that is even more palpable in the valley than in other towns in the area. Further aggravating the sense of abandonment was the fact that a fair number of the wealthy did continue to visit the French Lick Springs Hotel over the years. Larry, for one, was agonizingly aware of the contrast between his and his town's poverty and the wealth of the outsiders. The great disparity fostered resentment. "When I grew up, it's not that I hated rich people, but I sort of frowned on them. It's just something about being rich irritated me." Today, he resists the temptation of a wealthy lifestyle because he, like many in the valley, has such a fundamental distrust of it.

The human costs of the poverty in the county have been enormous. A Bird relative sighed wearily at the mention of it and summarized that "in Orange County you work hard and you die young." A former resident also points out, "The valley is like a bubble. It is a typical southern Indiana town where all the people live in their own world. They resist change; they want everything to stay the same.

Paoli Square, the hub of Orange County, had the only stoplight in
the county for years. All the businesses were on the hub so when a
strip center was proposed out on North 39, the people fought it. They
liked things the way they were.'' Despite the hardships, most refuse
to move. ''They could work in factories in other places and make
more money, but they don't want to.'' Today there are two stop-
lights in the county (one in Paoli and one in Orleans), and things are
beginning to change.

In French Lick, City Drug is closed, three of the six or seven
downtown stores recently burned down, a new Hook's Drugstore has
opened, and in West Baden there is even a 24-hour market called
Austin's. The people in French Lick aren't too pleased about Maple
Street (the downtown's main street) being cobble-stoned and converted to one-way traffic.

One way in which the valley contrasts sharply with other nearby
communities, however, is in its racial views.

Unlike Orleans in Orange County or nearby Jasper where a black
man risks his neck just by setting foot within city limits, the valley
has by comparison an unusually tolerant attitude in terms of race.
This stems from the significant number of blacks that have been employed by the hotels for the last century. Although the term ''colored''
is still employed by many of the community's older citizens, in this
case it has less of a racist overtone than an anachronistic one. The
attitude is almost paternalistic, as in the common reference to ''our
coloreds.''

It has always been common for whites and blacks to express affection for one another in public and to help each other out in typical
small-town, neighborly fashion. In West Baden especially, black families like the Paytons and the Pointers were held in high regard. Indeed there have been a surprising number of mixed-blood children
who were the result of interracial affairs. There have also been some
interracial marriages. Larry's own first cousin Jerry is half-black. He
grew up mostly with Larry's grandparents and was extremely close
to all the Bird kids, especially Larry. When Larry and his brothers
were quite young, they often played with Jerry and once asked ''How
come Jerry's got a suntan and we don't?'' Larry's mother, Georgia,
relates. ''I just explained that Jerry had been out in the sun more
than they had.'' To this day, Jerry and Larry are still close.

That Larry had exposure to blacks while growing up helped him develop an ability to adapt to all types of people, unlike most small-town Indiana basketball players. Besides, Larry was one of the few in the valley who lived in both West Baden and French Lick while growing up. Despite the communities' rivalry, Larry by necessity developed an ability to transcend any differences. And to this day Larry is a player distinguished by his ability to get along well with players of all types and to effect harmony among them.

The house that Larry has built in West Baden sits on ten to fifteen acres of land amidst rolling hills on the outskirts of town off Abbeydale Road. The Bird estate is bounded on one side by the aqua-blue Shepherd's Bethel Mission Station (an interdenominational parish), which operates out of an old trailer home, and on the other side by the rural landscape that predominates at this distance from town. The most sensational thing about the homestead is not the Bird home, an unremarkable sprawling split-level ranch, but the basketball court beside it: regulation-length blacktop with glass backboards, lights, and bleachers. And that is how it should be; for Larry lives as unostentatiously as possible, independent of his very obvious basketball talent. What other man making $3 million a year would choose to come back to his provincial hometown environment in order to live in an apartment within the house where his mother lives year-round? Yet there's a logic in Larry's annual return to the valley. He, like the valley today, exhibits a simple, almost single-minded focus. And for both, behind that present simplicity hovers an unusual and troublesome past. It is a common bond that provides, for each, a measure of understanding and thus contentment: "Because it's my home, it's the place where I feel most comfortable and where I want to raise a family someday," Larry says. "The people in French Lick want nothing from me, and I want nothing from them. They treat me as just another guy, and that's how I want to be treated, more than anything."

4 / *Joe and Georgia; Larry's Childhood*

Although Joe Bird had been a talented athlete back in the forties, he never had the opportunity to play basketball or other organized sports at the high school level. "I talked to my father about [Larry's] father," says Gary Holland. "I guess his dad was quite an athlete. Some of the older guys said his dad, Joe, if he'd had the opportunity and the drive Larry had, he'd have been just a tremendous athlete." Larry first learned that his father had been a gifted basketball player from a dwarf named Shorty Reeder (owner of what was then known as Shorty's Pool Room). Shorty explained that the elder Bird quit school in the eighth grade to begin making a living, thereby ending what surely would have been a successful basketball career. Joe's family was quite poor. "Orange County is a poor county, and the Birds were among the poorest," says one valley resident. Joe Bird's family was so poor that one West Baden resident remembers her mother taking the good material from dresses that had been worn out and making clothes for the Bird children.

The Birds were looked down upon by many in the community. Unlike Georgia's family, the Kernses, the Birds were not close. There were twelve kids in Joe's immediate family, including twin brothers and a sister who were lost in infancy. "Those [Bird] girls didn't know how to take care of themselves," said one West Baden resident.

Joe's mother was notorious throughout the community for being a difficult person. "Helen Bird was the meanest woman I ever seen in my life," says Georgia. She explains that one day Helen could be nice, but the next day—"Watch out!" Her volatile temperament was a crucial factor in Joe's intense love-hate ambivalence toward his mother.

Not surprisingly Joe himself was the child of an alcoholic. His father, Claude, drank heavily most of his life; although in his last ten years he was "on the wagon." Unlike Helen, Claude was well-liked in town. Joe's impoverished circumstances and his parentage of course figured prominently in shaping the course of his—and later, Larry's—life. Another pivotal experience for Joe was his service in the military.

When Joe turned 18, in 1944, he enlisted in the Navy and saw action in the Pacific. After two years, three ribbons, and a rank of Seaman First Class, Joe was honorably discharged. During those two years Joe had sent much of his pay to his parents, which helped them to build a house just outside of West Baden. Joe returned to his parents' new home after the war and tried a number of jobs, finally settling down at the Travelers' radio parts factory in nearby Orleans, Indiana. He shared in a car pool where he met Georgia Kerns, who had begun working at Travelers' a few months earlier following her graduation from French Lick High. She and Joe became friends, but when Joe left Travelers' for another job they lost contact. The following year—1951—Joe couldn't resist returning to the military; this time he enlisted in the Army. The Korean Conflict broke out during the same year, so Joe went overseas once again. Meanwhile, Georgia Kerns began working at the Lilly Paper Company in French Lick, along with Joe's mother, Helen Bird. Helen gave Joe's address to Georgia, and the two youngsters ended up corresponding for the duration of his duty in Korea.

Joe's first appearance back home following the war was a dramatic one: Joe returned to the valley with both hands bandaged; the injuries were not combat wounds, according to Georgia, but the result of his punching a concrete wall after experiencing a war flashback.

Joe's transition back to civilian life was not a smooth one. He was nervous and occasionally drank too much. Like almost all the boys in Orange County, Joe had gone straight off the farm to a war overseas. The experiences of wartime were terrible enough, but they were especially difficult for the young men from the valley. "All the farm boys who never been off the farm was changed after they came back," says a Bird family friend. "They drank to blot out the memories." The friend added that many of these young men never fully recovered. Larry's fiancée, Dinah Mattingly, remarked to Georgia Bird after spending a few summers in West Baden that "in the valley everybody is either an alcoholic or a teetotaler."

Despite Joe's problems, Georgia pushed for marriage, and within a few months of Joe's return she prevailed. Since Joe was still in the Army, he and Georgia were limited to seeing each other during his leaves from Fort Knox in Kentucky. But even during Joe's abbreviated stays, there were increasing indications of trouble. Joe was displaying many of the symptoms of posttraumatic stress disorder. He suffered from terrible nightmares, and was increasingly nervous and irritable. A family member remembers sitting in a movie theater with Joe when the movie unexpectedly showed bombs dropping and exploding. Joe was so startled that he ducked for cover below the seats. Another time, when a boy from the town who died in the war was honored with a twenty-one-gun salute, Joe "jumped ten feet in the air" in reaction to the sound, says a relative. And Joe's record in the service was affected, too. His prewar record of exemplary behavior contrasted with his continual disciplinary problems following the war. Exploding shells at the Fort Knox training center would cause him to freak out, says Georgia. And he would perform diligently for a while, but immediately following a promotion or just before one, he would get involved in a fight or go AWOL. By getting his rank stripped or his promotion denied, he was able to avoid the added burden of command. On one occasion when he was about to be promoted to sergeant, Joe went AWOL to French Lick. He stayed with a friend, and Georgia was not alerted to his whereabouts until the MPs showed up at her doorstep the following day. Consistent behavior of this sort resulted in Joe's spending much of his remaining time in the service behind bars.

Despite the AWOL incidents and problems, Georgia had persisted in her desire to marry Joe, perhaps because he was so similar to her father. "[Joe and Georgia's father] were a lot alike," says a relative. John Kerns would be warm and charming one moment and cold the next. His inconsistent behavior was exacerbated by a temper that rivaled the well-known temper of Helen Bird, a temper inherited by Joe. Kerns, for most of his life, was a religious teetotaler. But he squandered his income through compulsive gambling. Likewise, Joe went on to squander much, if not all, of his wages on alcohol. Both

John and Joe were not that much different from many in the valley. "This was a gambling town and that's all people knew—gambling and drinking," says a valley resident. John Kerns might have recognized that Joe was much like himself in certain respects, and he was leery of his daughter getting into a marriage as potentially bad as his own. He did feel Georgia was rushing things, but Kerns's resistance to Georgia's wedding plans only made her all the more determined. Georgia was nothing if not "stubborn, strong-headed, and determined," says a relative. It is hardly surprising that Georgia married a man so similar to her father. Many women do. Studies show that at least 60 percent of the daughters of alcoholics marry an alcoholic. And though Kerns was not an alcoholic, his behavior pattern and gambling addiction resulted in the same kind of family constellation.

Georgia's life with Joe would prove to be neither easy nor happy, and her childhood had not been dramatically different. Georgia was named after her paternal grandfather, George Washington Kerns, and her maternal grandfather, George Washington Noble. She was the third of eight children. The oldest kids were worked to the bone; the younger kids had a less difficult time. Her parents' marriage had not been happy. And the marriage became even more unhappy when her 16-year-old brother Rollie died of Rocky Mountain Spotted Fever when Georgia was 17. Kerns had always treated his wife and children severely, and Lizzie Kerns somehow decided that this harshness was related to her son's death. But Lizzie Kerns was a "good Christian woman," says a friend, and she refused to divorce; instead, Lizzie persevered, raising eight kids through the hardest of times, including the depression and the war. Ironically, John Kerns made relatively good money working in construction throughout those years, but most of it was lost to gambling. If the economic hardship weren't enough, John was a stern and relentless taskmaster. Throughout her youth, Georgia worked on the farm doing heavy chores to help the family maintain itself. She even went to live with her aunt Jesse Spoonmore, in French Lick, to help earn a little money baby-sitting while attending high school.

The Kerns family were members of the nondenominational Chrystal Community Church, a congregation made up of mostly Baptists and Methodists. The Kerns family used to walk three or four miles through the woods to church; they eventually wore their own path.

Later they owned a car, but if the dirt roads were too muddy to drive on, they would set out along the old path in the woods. The church was also rigid and strict. Females could not cut their hair, use make-up, or wear pants. One exception that John and Lizzie allowed was the wearing of pants under a skirt when berry picking. Congregants also were not permitted to go to dances or movies or to listen to popular music. At the same time, it was understood that "boys will be boys," so the rules were somewhat relaxed for them. "[Lizzie and John] had been stricter with the girls," says a relative. And at six foot, Georgia was the "odd one out" in the family. Not only was she taller than the rest of her seven siblings, she was also the most withdrawn, sullen, and stubborn of the children. She was the third child in a family of children that got progressively shorter until the last child, Virginia, was only 5'2". (Lizzie was 5'0" and John was 5'10".) However, Georgia took after her mother in that she proved to be a tower of strength in times of adversity.

Georgia and Joe's wedding took place on Sept 20, 1951, the day before Joe's twenty-fifth birthday, on one of Joe's authorized leaves. Georgia was 21. Georgia's older sister Mildred and her fiancé were the attendants. Despite John Kerns's misgivings, he let the newlyweds stay at the family farm until Joe had to report back to Fort Knox. Eventually, Georgia and Mildred rented a house close by, about two miles west of French Lick. Joe would visit when he had a leave. It was on these occasions that Georgia began to learn more of the war's effect upon her husband. Joe would have nightmares about the elderly Korean villagers who were forced to leave their homes by Joe's company. The homes were then burned to prevent Korean forces from hiding in them. These dreams continued even after Joe was discharged from the service and the stockade. Once Joe had settled back into civilian life in the valley, he worked hard during the week, but drank all weekend. In time, his drinking began to stretch on into the rest of the week. At its worst, the drinking culminated in Joe's dismissal after three years from the U.S. Gypsum plant in Shoals. A pattern of job instability persisted until 1962, as Joe worked at the shoe factory in West Baden, hauled wood, and did odd jobs in construction. He worked mostly at the Wilsten Chicken Farms owned by Georgia's brother Amon.

After five years of marriage, on December 7, 1956, the fourth child of Georgia and Joe Bird, named Larry Joe, was born. Mike had been born in 1952, Mark over a year later, and Linda two years after Mark. "All my kids were raised in an environment that was, well, tough," says Georgia. "We just never had much money." Joe and Georgia, both, were proud people and tried hard to keep up appearances. "Georgia was too proud to ask for help from the family. Whenever we went to her house we put milk and food in the refrigerator," says one relative. And though Joe and Georgia often didn't have enough money for food, rent, or heat, they would go into debt just to have a tree and a few gifts for Christmas. "My family has been through the ups and downs and hard times with me.... It's not that we were that poor. We had food, but Mom always had to work," Larry explained in *Sports Illustrated*. "I remember she worked a hundred hours a week and made a hundred dollars, and then went to the store and had to buy $120 worth of food." Larry, however, was always sheltered from the reality of the family's food needs, says a family member. Since he ate at his grandmother's often and was unaware of the food brought in by relatives, "Larry didn't realize how close [the food situation was] to the edge."

Only Georgia's determination kept the family marginally solvent. "Georgia worked so hard," says a friend. "She worked two jobs sometimes, working at practically every restaurant in town." They still endured evictions and the occasional shut off of utilities. During southern Indiana's often severe winters, the family sometimes had no heat or light. But it could've been worse. Georgia sometimes resorted to creative financing to keep the family afloat. "If there was a payment to the bank due, and we needed shoes, she'd get the shoes, and then deal with them guys at the bank," says Larry today, in the same *Sports Illustrated* article. "I don't mean she wouldn't pay the bank, but the children always came first." She also worked at the West Baden shoe factory and at Amon's chicken farm. Then for quite a while she worked at the Medco nursing home. Georgia often came home from working two jobs, exhausted, and then had to do the laundry or clean the house. To make matters worse, she suffered from migraine headaches that along with the fatigue, caused her "to walk around in a daze," says a relative. (Her grandmother Jane Noble and some of Georgia's sisters suffered from migraines as well as Larry's younger brother Jeff.) Between the work, keeping up the house, and the migraines, all she could do at the end of the day was stumble in and "collapse on the bed." Nevertheless, Georgia managed to keep her homes spotless—though they often didn't live in any one house too long. Whenever Joe was fired or quit work, the family would move from their rented home, and so Joe, Georgia, and the kids would go to the Kerns's farm. Then Georgia would walk the two miles to French Lick, where she would work as a waitress. Once Joe had found a new job, the family would move back to West Baden to rent another in a series of decrepit houses.

For the first eight years of the marriage these circumstances were manageable, since the Kerns's farm was always available as a temporary refuge. But in 1960, when Larry was almost 4, Lizzie and John decided to separate. Though Lizzie was not willing to go as far as divorce, they did give up the farm. Since John was in poor health, Lizzie told him that if he needed a place to stay, even after the separation, she would take care of him. Within a year, however, John died, and for the next four years, Lizzie lived with either her mother or with Joe and Georgia. As a result, the family had to make do without the safeguard of the farm. One emergency measure was the purchase of a coal stove to ensure that there would be heat during the winter even if the utilities were turned off. The stove had its drawbacks, however; Linda, especially, complained that kids at school noticed that her clothes smelled like coal. Regardless, Georgia had made up her mind three-and-a-half years into the marriage that she would not rely on her parents again. She started working when she was three-months pregnant with Linda. For the next twenty-five years, she held down at least one job, but usually worked two at the same time, even during her pregnancies. She was working at her brother Amon's chicken farm even when she was eight-months pregnant with Jeff.

In 1965, the burden eased a little when Lizzie moved into a little house across the street from the school and the playground in French Lick. The three boys would stay over with their grandmother as much as they could, which was most of the time. Since Lizzie had no phone, Larry and his brothers spent much of their childhood without the luxury of a phone. Linda, on the other hand, was in the unfortunate position of being the only female child. She received the least attention, and even though she was older than Larry, she was never allowed the privilege of living at Lizzie's like the three oldest boys. Instead it was expected that when Linda was old enough, she would help her mother with the laundry, the housework, and the baby-sitting. And since Linda was nine and eleven years older, respectively, than her brothers Jeff and Eddie, she was expected to be their surrogate mother while Georgia was at work. As a result, from the time Linda was in her teens, there were basically two households: Lizzie's, with the three older boys, and Georgia's, with Linda playing parent to the two youngest boys. Eventually, Georgia and Joe decided to move to French Lick, too, where they went through a few more homes.

In 1969, when Larry was almost 13, the family purchased its first home, on Washington Street in French Lick. But the family's financial burdens didn't end with the purchase of the home. Not only did Georgia still often have to work two jobs, but Mike and Linda sacrificed going to college in order to provide needed financial help. Linda was a talented softball and volleyball player (there was no girls' basketball in the state, then) who had hopes of going to college. However, from the time she was 16, she worked part-time at the Medco nursing home with her mother, and full-time following her high school graduation. Mike also deferred college to work at Kimball's, and Mark worked at Agan's Market during summers to ensure that house payments could be made. Indeed, it was Mike's income which allowed the family to make the down payment in the first place. Joe had received a $200 FHA loan toward the down payment but had blown the money in the bar, and Georgia then had to borrow from her son Mike. "Georgia didn't know what it was to have a home down payment until Mike and Mark helped out financially," says a relative.

Though much of the family's financial burdens derived from Joe's drinking, he was characterized as a wonderful person by all who knew him: "more of a lover than a fighter," "a genuinely nice guy." Larry says that people, today, talk about Joe's generosity: "I always hear he was the kind of guy who would give you the shirt off his back." Joe had a good singing voice, and would often sing to himself or make up funny, nonsensical songs. He also had a great sense of humor. Unfortunately, the drinking often dwarfed his good qualities. "He had a heart as big as the world, but his drinking problem was bigger" was how one relative put it. His finest traits were twisted into destructive ones. He would generously offer to stand rounds of drinks at the Juble Bar and would end up with less or sometimes none of his meager wage to bring home to his family. During a period of time in the marriage when Joe worked during the week in Louisville, he would come home on Friday evening only long enough to deposit his dirty clothes on the floor. He would then head off for the bars for the rest of the weekend only to appear on Sunday night having spent the $500 he had earned the previous week working highway construction. Before he headed off for Louisville again, he would beg Georgia for money so he could eat during the week.

When he was working, he was a hard worker. But he often hurt himself if he had been drinking. Georgia explains that an incident mentioned in *Sports Illustrated* was a by-product of Joe's accident-prone drunkenness. "I remember one time I was thirteen, or fourteen maybe, my father came home with an ankle all black and blue and red," says Larry. In this instance, Joe's ankle was so swollen that he could not remove his boot by himself. "He needed me and my brother just to get his boot off and he was in awful pain, but the next morning we got the boot back on and he went to work.... That really made an impression on me."

Often when Joe drank, the Bird family temper was unleashed, and he would become abusive. Though one relative describes the abuse as being predominantly verbal, another relative says, "He'd slap Georgia around now and then." The reality shows how easily wife abuse can be hidden from others. "I got beat a lot because I was the *enemy*," says Georgia. Asked if she meant the North Koreans, Georgia explained, "I don't know. It was either that, or I was his *mother*. He often had a war flashback.... Larry didn't know much about the beatings. Mike did. The only thing Larry ever saw was when Joe was choking me and pulling his fist back to hit me, and Larry was so scared he started to laugh." Joe broke Georgia's glasses once while she was pregnant with Mark, giving her a black eye and a cut above the eye that required stitches. The following day Joe came out to the farm where Georgia had taken refuge. He was sober and contrite, as always, and begged forgiveness. And Georgia, as always, took him back.

Twice during the fifties, disturbed by Joe's behavior, Georgia had seen a lawyer with the intention of filing for divorce. She had gone at the urging of her father, but at the last moment changed her mind. On the second occasion, in 1959, they separated. Joe, stunned by the turn of events, pled for another chance. Georgia relented. The year that followed was the happiest of the marriage, as Joe stopped drinking. Yet the death of John Kerns, about a year later, in 1961, might have affected Joe more than any other relative. After spending time together at the farm, the two men had recognized certain similarities in temperament, and they worked construction together in the summer and odd jobs in the winter. When the elder man died, Joe "broke down and sobbed," the only time that he allowed his relatives to see him cry.

It wasn't long before Joe started drinking on weekends again. For the most part, however, he was able to confine his drinking to weekends, largely because he had found his niche as a wood finisher at the Kimball factory in Jasper. Joe's eight years there was his longest stint at any one job. And even when his drinking spilled over into the week, the drinking didn't cause a problem on the job. Indeed, Joe had earned a reputation as one of the finest wood finishers at Kimball. "He was real good," says Mike. "Once he was chosen to finish the piano that would be played by someone, I don't remember who, on national television, and we all watched just to see the piano." During the early years at Kimball's, Joe and Georgia managed to build a reasonably stable life together and two more children came along, Jeff in 1964 and Eddie in 1966. Joe became especially attached to Eddie. But gradually, as the decade wore on, the weekend drinking escalated into the familiar binges. And once again Joe's problems began to affect the marriage.

Georgia, of course, wasn't blameless for the marital problems, either. As one family member points out, Georgia was by far the most difficult of the Kerns children; she was stubborn and feisty and often had "trouble with relationships" involving the rest of her family. She would go without speaking to various relatives for long stretches of time. And Georgia didn't always cope with Joe's problem in the most constructive way. She would complain about his drinking until he would storm out of the house and go on another binge. Despite her shortcomings, the family remained supportive of Georgia, sympathizing with the "physical and emotional pain she went through." Georgia was beset with daily anxieties such as the fear that Joe might pass out while water was boiling and the house would burn down. And then there were occasions when Joe chased Georgia around the house with a knife.

Georgia and Joe were dealing with a disease beyond their control. "I always felt sorry for my husband," Georgia says. "Drinking was something he had to do; it wasn't something he *wanted* to do."

Joe wouldn't admit that he had a drinking problem or that he suffered from posttraumatic stress syndrome, but Georgia blames herself for not succeeding in getting him to seek help. Joe's refusal to acknowledge the disease only made matters worse. The one concession Joe was willing to make was to let a mutual friend who was an entertainer and hypnotist put him under. Joe had severe repression about the events of the war, and had very little conscious recall of what had actually transpired. The rationale for the hypnosis attempt was to help discover what events in the war might be at the root of Joe's spiraling problems. Said the friend, "Anytime he gets in trouble, I'll bring him out of it." Once under, Joe revealed a not-uncommon saga for those suffering from posttraumatic stress syndrome: He continually referred to an incident in which a close friend was killed as the two of them entered a bunker. Face to face with the killer of his friend, Joe fired and killed the North Korean soldier. It was a stunning revelation, considering that Joe hadn't previously spoken of the war. In fact, the hypnotist was so surprised that he considered bringing Joe out of the hypnosis in the middle of his reliving the episode. But everyone else argued it would be best to let Joe finish. So Joe continued, dwelling over and over on the dead Korean's eyes, the same eyes he had looked into just before firing. Those eyes, open in death, were the same eyes that had haunted him in visions during the day and in his dreams at night and would continue to haunt him for the rest of his life. Afterward, instead of being better, Joe seemed to get worse.

Only four years separated the four oldest children, but the newest arrival on Pearl Harbor Day in 1956 would be treated as the baby of the family. Larry Joe Bird was born at the Bedford Medical Center in Bedford, "the limestone capital of the world," about thirty-five miles northeast of French Lick. A neighbor, Menta Elliot, helped bring Larry home to Russelville, a part of West Baden where the family was living at the time. Georgia had needed assistance because Larry "was so big I couldn't lift him out of bed." Larry weighed 11 pounds 12 ounces and was 23 inches long. His heritage boasted Irish and Scottish blood, as well as Indian blood on both sides of the family. Though neither Georgia nor Joe was blond like the infant, they had both been blond in their youth. "You just mark my words," Menta Elliot said after holding the infant. "This boy is destined for greatness." The strength that the neighbor had noticed soon became more apparent. Larry was doing push-ups when he was 3 months old. At 7 months he could pull himself up and stand alone. At 9 months he walked alone. At 1 year he had already destroyed two cribs and a playpen, at which time he was placed in a regular bed that he shared with his two older brothers, Mike and Mark.

As a child, Larry was big and husky though he had constant sinus problems. He also suffered the cuts and bruises that active kids often experience. One time he cracked his head open when he fell off his great-grandmother's porch. In his first year of organized football, when he was 9, he broke his clavicle. He never played organized football again, after suffering an injury. Larry sustained his injury while playing quarterback. Anyone who has seen his remarkable floor-length passes can appreciate what a quarterback he would have made. Both Mike and Mark also had promise as football players, but Mike suffered a broken arm, and Mark a broken shoulder. None of the three brothers was willing to jeopardize future basketball seasons with the risk of more broken bones.

But the brothers were not deterred from playing football, or any other kind of ball, on their own. They were also not hesitant about playing rough. "[Mike and Mark] baby-sat for me," says Larry. "Everywhere they went I had to go. Sometimes I would have to pitch for both teams and sometimes I just had to chase balls. They were always pushing me and knocking me, always beating up on me." Of course, Mike and Mark's version of the events was a little different. "Every time we went someplace," Mark complains, "we had to take Larry along. We used to beat him up every day. He was a little smart butt. Even if we just told him he couldn't play, he'd go home and tell Dad we hit him and it'd be all over for us." Larry was demonstrating a certain savvy even then. If his brothers were going to beat up on him anyway, he was at least going to ensure that they let him play.

By the time he started school, "he was just a little bit special to me," says his first-grade teacher, Wanita Beaty. She remembers Larry as much taller and less talkative than the other children, with an unusually strong need for play. "Recess meant more to Larry than anything else. And because he was big, he'd just knock those little ones down as he ran to his desk. Yet he always helped them up and brushed them off," says Beaty. "The kids all loved him. He was the leader." That he attached great importance to recess had much to do with his home environment. Dr. Robert J. Ackerman (co-founder of the National Association for Children of Alcoholics) points out that Larry's use of play as sublimation was quite natural. "[Children of alcoholics] will be characterized by powerful defense mechanisms: among these are...sublimation....Sublimation involves directing feelings of discomfort or anxiety to acceptable activities."

Those feelings of discomfort and anxiety contributed to Larry's moodiness throughout his childhood. Like his mother, Larry was the one child of six who was "different." And like his mother, Larry really cared about cleanliness. When he was young, the family called him "Mr. Clean" because a couple of times a day he would shower and change his clothes. "He always liked clean clothes," his mother remembers. The similarity of many of their personality quirks was uncanny. Both Larry and his mother were intensely private, stubborn, determined, and suspicious. Larry's suspiciousness, in fact, led him to believe that his mother's migraines weren't that bad, explains a relative. He believed that it was just a question of how tough she was. He resented what he saw as her babying herself! Larry's suspicions were aggravated by the resentment he felt over her migraines' depriving him of what little time she had to be his mother. He couldn't help but feel a sense of abandonment, since he saw his mother almost as infrequently as he saw his father. "Larry never wanted me to [work]," says Georgia. "He always cried after me when I went to work and he had to stay home. He was a baby for eight years. We spoiled him until the other boys [younger brothers Jeff and Eddie] came along."

Joe's alcoholism had really deprived Larry of both his mother and his father. "Children need to be able to depend on parents to meet their physical and emotional needs in order to develop trust," says Claudia Black, one of the pioneers in the understanding of children of alcoholics. "In alcoholic environments, parents simply are not consistently available to their children either by being drunk, physically absent, or mentally and emotionally preoccupied with alcohol, or with the alcoholic." Nevertheless, at a young age, Larry demonstrated his unusual ability to adapt to his father's absence, as well as a certain amount of street savvy: He would find out which bar his father had gone to and then go there and ask Joe for money before it was all spent.

And being the child of an alcoholic allowed some moments of normality. Joe and the kids did sometimes go fishing together and he would watch them play ball, but they felt that "they couldn't count on him," says a relative. That lack of predictability was at the core of Larry's discontent as well as his tendency to spend all his free time on the basketball court. On the court, he needed to rely only on himself. Judith Seixas and Geraldine Youcha, leading figures in the literature on children of alcoholics, explain: "When unpredictability results in disappointment after disappointment, it finally gets the children down. As they grow older they may blot out the disturbing incidents, but they never forget the uneasy feeling.... A child who learns early that no one can be counted on learns equally early to depend on himself."

Besides basketball, Larry also occasionally used fantasy as a means to escape. "[Children of alcoholics] managed to survive the chaos of living in a family faced with alcoholism...in their ability to use their imagination," say Seixas and Youcha. Often the fantasy would involve a miracle or magical event, thus providing hope and easing the child's unhappiness. These miracles or acts foster a sense that "something will happen that will change all this" and also serve to lessen anger toward the offending parent. "It takes the blame away at last and puts it on an outside force. 'If something magical can save me, something magical must have put the curse on us.'" Larry's fantasy, which he entertained throughout his childhood, was that he'd find a suitcase by the road. And when he opened it, he would find a million dollars. He'd then take the million dollars to a hole he'd dug under the porch and he'd hide there with the money. "I had that same dream all the time—over and over and over." Larry says today, "I always thought I'd have a lot of money."

For Larry, the impact of Joe's alcoholism was blunted somewhat by the relatively privileged position he enjoyed within the family. It was eight years before another child was born and so Larry was the baby and the one who was most indulged. "We used to send him home crying, and Dad'd come down there and beat me 'n' Mike for beatin' up his baby," says Mark. In addition, that eight-year period was the most stable time of the Bird marriage, and Larry received more attention than he might have otherwise. Still, the greatest palliative to the impact of Joe's drinking was Larry's happy relationship with his grandmother. "Research shows that those children [of alcoholics] who had a good relationship with at least one adult—a relative...tended to function best," say Seixas and Youcha. And Larry spent even more time with Lizzie Kerns, since he often avoided being at home. Lizzie doted on Larry, and he milked the relationship as much as he could, mainly because he just wanted a normal home life. Before 1965, she often baby-sat for the kids either at the farm, at her mother's, or at Joe and Georgia's. In any case, Larry spent more time with Lizzie than he did with his parents.

When Larry reached the age of 8, he was granted the luxury of having a bed at Lizzie's house, and he began to spend more time there than he did at home. Larry mowed the grass, shoveled the snow, took out the trash, and helped Lizzie with her laundry at the laundromat. In return she babied him, cooked for him, and doctored him; she had a home remedy for any illness. It was a good thing that Lizzie was there, for Larry seemed to need a little more attention than the other kids, according to relatives. And Georgia had not been around to fill that need. Says a family member, "Granny always had a special feeling for Larry. They had a unique bond. She could get him to do things that no one else could." Lizzie refused to establish disciplinary guidelines for Larry and his brothers, and she imposed no curfew, which gave the boys even more incentive to stay with her. It was common to see Larry out playing basketball well after 1 A.M. The fact that she lived directly across the street from the school's outdoor courts from 1965 until 1967, and then just two blocks away thereafter, didn't hurt, either.

By the time Mark and Mike were 7 and 8, they were playing basketball constantly. Larry's only desire was to keep up with his brothers. Hence, he received his first basketball the Christmas he turned 4. "My ball was one of those cheap rubber balls. I was so proud of it that I stayed up for hours bouncing it," says Larry. But that same night he left the ball by the wood-burning pot-bellied stove. The next morning, Larry discovered his new basketball had a big knot in it. Georgia and Joe bought him another ball which Larry, with the help of his brothers, promptly wore out. Said Georgia, "My kids were made fun of for the way they dressed. Neighbor boys had basketballs or bikes. My kids had to share a basketball. A friend of Larry's would say, 'if you can outrun me down to the post office, you can ride my bike for ten minutes. Larry used to run his tail-end off."

The Birds' financial circumstances did more for Larry than simply help him appreciate the value of a basketball or the pleasure of briefly riding a bike. Those circumstances helped instill the kind of drive that pushes one kid to run faster than another, regardless of physical ability. This kind of internally generated, externally motivated drive cannot be taught; it is most often born in poverty. Sports are dominated by those from disadvantaged socioeconomic backgrounds. Boxing, basketball, football, baseball, and track assimilate issues of survival; and the competitor who wins in these athletic battles is most likely the hungriest and the most tenacious. Furthermore, since the Birds' financial situation didn't allow for a family car or extra money for recreation, summer camp, and family vacations, there were no distractions to the single-minded pursuit of basketball greatness. That these environmental factors must be in place before any of the other factors contributing to greatness is emphasized by John McPhee, noted biographer and writer for *The New Yorker*. "A great basketball player, almost by definition, is someone who has grown up in a constricted world, not for lack of vision or ambition but for lack of money; his environment has been limited to home, gym, and playground, and it has forced upon him, as a developing player, the discipline of having nothing else to do."

One specific of that environment directly affected the development of Larry's competitive skills. Due to the broken-down condition of the family's many rental homes, any damage done by three unusually competitive and physical boys could not make that great a difference. In the homes that had facing archways, the Bird brothers cut out the bottoms of two coffee cans and nailed one above each archway. With a small rubber ball it was simple to get a good full-court game going. Each boy had the typical Bird temper, and fights resulting in broken lamps, tables, and chairs would often ensue. "Growing up I had fights with my brothers all the time. They'd do something I didn't like, I'd say something; next thing you know we were going at it. But they were still my brothers. I loved 'em. It's [just] the competition."

When his older brothers played pickup games of baseball, Larry was only allowed to pitch; he was not allowed to bat until he was good enough to earn an at bat. But though Larry liked baseball, nothing could be compared to basketball. Regardless of whether Larry had a ball or a bat in his hand, a basketball would be in the other. "[It didn't matter] if he was going to play football or baseball, Larry had to take his basketball along," says Georgia. "I can still hear him coming up the porch bouncing a basketball," says his grandmother. For much of his childhood, Larry clung to the ball he was supposed to share with his brothers. If he couldn't beat them one-on-one, he could at least control the ball. And no matter how many times the family moved or how difficult Joe's alcoholism became, Larry always had the ball to hang on to. "Whatever the kind of control involved, the concern with it is easy to trace to the childhood in the alcoholic household where things may have been literally beyond control," say Seixas and Youcha.

Any excuse to get near the game was enough. Larry remembers going to the school and chasing down the ball so his brother Mark could work on his shooting. But Larry yearned to be involved in the game competitively. The wish, especially, to be good enough to go one-on-one against Mark, instead of being just a ball boy, was another incentive for Larry to excel beyond his years. Being able to compete against older and talented brothers meant that Larry had to be able to take their best shots and then go them one better by playing longer. "Those brothers were so competitive, and they just pounded on the kid. Boy, he'd fight them tooth and nail, and he'd stay around and play after they'd leave," says Jim Jones, who coached Larry in every sport he played from the time he was quite young. "Even at the age of eight I saw him...as someone who played very hard and never backed down." Since Larry didn't have the physical maturity to beat his older brothers, he had to compensate by outthinking them. "I think," says Mike Bird, "he just reached the point where he didn't like to be beat anymore. So he began looking for ways to beat you." That ability to think would prove integral to Larry's eventual success as he developed the cerebral part of his game enough to neutralize any physical disadvantage. "I have a lot of respect for Larry," says Chicago Bulls' Michael Jordan. "Here's a guy who doesn't have the quickness a lot of players in the league have....But Bird has this knowledge of the game to make his ability as good and sometimes even better....He outthinks the defense, which makes it seem like he can jump higher and is quicker. Therefore he has no weaknesses."

From the beginning, Larry showed a willingness to work on his game with a dedication rarely matched by other players of any age. Bit by bit, he improved his game, putting the pieces together in methodical fashion. "When I first started...I just tried to be better every day," says Larry. "I'd go to basics, like trying to go to my left one day, and do nothing but rebound and pass the next." Larry's attempt to develop all facets of his game as well as his understanding of the game was, again, to some degree due to the influence of his brothers. "I think he got some of his court awareness by playing with me and our brother Mike," says Mark. "He'd do a lot of passing. He was always better than the other kids his age." Of course it didn't hurt that Larry was playing against two guys with similarly advanced instincts. "Larry's instinct is just there. I've noticed the instinct in a few of the Bird boys," says Holland. "Even in junior high he would let his man go, and would steal the ball from someone else. He could just anticipate what someone else was going to do. He just picked it up so much faster than anyone else," says Jim Jones.

With the kind of competitive example that Larry's brothers set, his first taste of organized basketball competition would almost necessarily be a letdown. Nonetheless, by the time he was ready to begin fourth grade, Larry's competitive fires were raging in anticipation of Biddy Ball. And, when the time came, his years in Biddy Ball were noteworthy for the wide range of skills he learned, as well as the drive he exhibited. Playing for Agan's Market, Larry played against six or eight teams throughout the summer.

However, Larry continued to be a poor shooter until he was 14. "Mark's the one that got me interested in developing my shooting," says Larry. Yet there is no early evidence of Larry's being determined to become a good shooter, let alone a great player. Larry's drive to constantly play basketball was not something conscious. "I played when I was aching and I was so tired...I don't know why...I just don't know what kept me going and going." Holland recalls that "the drive was just always there, just an unbelievable amount of drive. When one of his buddies would get tired and go home, here comes another one, let's go play some more basketball. [It was] just the love of playing basketball and...being close to other kids that liked to do the same thing."

However, Larry's love of the game went beyond camaraderie because he often played for hours on end by himself. Some of this solitary play was dictated by the small size of the community. There wasn't always a game going when he wanted to play, regardless of the community's passion for basketball.

Yet, another explanation for his solitary practice ritual was that it became the one way in which he could make a chaotic life "right." In so doing he could free himself from the helplessness he felt at home. Practicing by himself provided a sense of control in much the same way that hanging onto the basketball always had. It became his center of focus, a way of shrinking his domain to just a few variables: a ball and a hoop which were subject to his talents and determination. In contrast, Larry's home life was subject to no such limits or boundaries; any attempt at control there was destined to fail. "As is true in so many homes where someone is drinking too much, controls are invisible or nonexistent and children may ask themselves, 'Am I in control? Who is in control? Is anyone in control here?' When no one is in charge, there can be a frightening kind of freedom that is a burden as well as a gift," say Seixas and Youcha.

So basketball became a private kind of universe that Larry could retreat to when the family universe around him was in a state of anarchy. "When I'm out there by myself, what I'm doing is practicing my rhythm. You can play three-on-three for an hour and a half, and you'll take maybe 100 shots. I can go out myself in the same time and take 1,000—maybe more—anywhere I want." Alone on the court, Larry was subject only to his own desires; it was the ultimate control. And it was control on his own terms. "[Attempting to maintain control] was a constant preoccupation for all family members—especially for the alcoholic, who was always attempting to control the drinking and denying that he or she couldn't. The lesson is so well learned by repetition, if no other way, [that] the child continues to strive for control and feels right only when he or she has it," says Seixas and Youcha.

Maintaining concentration is much more difficult in basketball than it is in baseball or football. Basketball is played indoors where the fans in many cases are seated on the playing surface; thus, the proximity of the fans is much greater. And in football and hockey there is a helmet or head gear to be worn. But in basketball, as one writer put it, "It's hard to be strong when you're running around in your underwear in front of 15,000 people who are all calling you a jerk."

Today, Larry's remarkable ability to concentrate is described by many as *total*. And this ability stems from those early days when he was alone with a ball and a hoop. "There can be 15,000 fans jumping up and down and two guys from the other team waving their hands in his face, and all Larry will see is the ball and the basket," says teammate Kevin McHale. Today, Larry's concentration gives him an edge against the competition just as it did on the courts of his youth when he played against his brothers. "When that little picture machine of his goes off, he's in a world of his own," says Bill Fitch, Larry's first coach with the Boston Celtics. "That little voice starts talking to him and he's in his backyard again. He's playing by himself." Similarly, Kevin McHale sees the vestiges of a childhood basketball ritual behind Larry's ability to focus. "The game can be on the line, and for *him* it's just like playing h-o-r-s-e in his driveway back in French Lick." New York Knick Coach Rick Pitino agrees that when he watches him play, "it's almost like the three-point shot is the game of h-o-r-s-e for Larry Bird."

For Larry, as a youngster, the court had become a refuge from the frustrations of the rest of his life. Similarly, basketball provided a private kind of universe even when Larry wasn't on the court. "I'd start out listening to the teacher for about ten minutes—ten minutes, that was it. For the next twenty minutes, my mind would be thinking about one thing: basketball. When I was going to play next. Where I was going to play. How many kids I could get to play with me. How long we could play. It didn't matter what it was: English, math, history—I even *liked* history a little, but it didn't matter. I'd like, go into these trances. [Then] I started worrying about myself. I'd say, 'What's wrong with me, anyhow: Other people don't seem to do this.' I actually thought I should go to a doctor, get checked out. I thought maybe I was like [one of] those kids who go off in their own little worlds; I forget what they're called." But there was a dramatic contrast between Larry's on-court and off-court personalities. Withdrawn and unemotional at home, Larry was explosive on the court. "But a lot of times Larry was overemotional," says Holland. "As he grew up, if he got beat, he would actually cry. Which was good in a sense, because he didn't want to get beat at anything." Yet the touch of a basketball was often enough to put his unhappiness into abeyance. A good game was satisfaction beyond measure and made up for the deprivation in his life. "Right from the start, children who have lived with alcoholism feel their families are different themselves or feel set aside as 'different' by neighbors, friends and relatives," explain Seixas and Youcha. Add to that the fact that the Birds were among the least well off in an already impoverished area, and it is understandable how playing well took on great importance. Larry was not unlike the poor kid in the inner-city ghetto. With little at home, and no car or diversions, basketball became the sum of his existence.

Yet, for all of basketball's therapeutic value, it was less of a cathartic exercise than an imperfect act of sublimation. For Larry demonstrated as hot a temper as his father and brothers. In other words, his tendency to be "overemotional" wasn't always so positive, says Holland. Even as a kid, he often lost his temper when playing Biddy Ball, and he was known to react angrily in seventh and eighth-grade basketball as well. He was notorious for getting into altercations with other players, getting technicals due to overly physical play, screaming at the officials, using profanity, and slamming the ball down on the court or at other players. Not surprisingly, his game was adversely affected by his outbursts. What's more, he was oversensitive to criticism. If he didn't like what was happening during practice or a game, he would storm off the court. All this behavior came to a head when Larry was benched for a couple of eighth-grade games soon after the family moved to French Lick. Obviously the benching didn't register, because not long afterward he missed a practice as a result of a disagreement with the coach. He was then promptly kicked off the team. "That might've been one of the best things that ever happened to him," says Butch Emmons, the eighth-grade coach. For Larry came back the next year with a remarkably changed attitude.

On the eve of Larry's ninth-grade season, Coach Holland echoed the views of Emmons when he told Georgia that "if Larry can learn to control his temper and channel that anger to work for, not against him, he will be one of the best players this state has ever seen." (Today Holland admits he was indulging in a bit of hyperbole. "No one thought he'd be nearly as good as he turned out senior year.") Though he played basketball constantly at this point in his life, Larry had not yet had the conscious realization that he was a good player or that he loved the game. But then around the age of 14, his life changed abruptly when one day he began to make all his shots. It was an epiphany. He began to experience himself in a totally different way. As Psychologist William James pointed out, there are moments when the sudden realization of one's true self becomes the most significant event in a person's life, when one feels "most deeply and intensely active and alive. At such moments there is a voice inside which speaks and says: 'This is the real me!'" Today, Larry vividly remembers that turning point. "I had been playing the game up until then but was not really interested. Then one day—I can remember it exactly—I started making everything. After that, the older guys chose me first.''

Larry was suddenly on the threshold of a new life. He was a freshman that year while his brother Mark was a senior and the leading scorer on the 1971 Springs Valley sectional championship team with a 17-point-per-game scoring average. Mike, at 6'2", had been a top scorer on the previous year's team, which had also won a sectional championship. Mark, at 6'3", was a terrific shooter, and today he claims to have been the best shooter in the family! Mark particularly likes to point out that he is Springs Valley's *fifth* all-time free-throw percentage shooter for a single season, while Larry is nowhere to be found among the top ten. Mark shot 79.2 percent; Larry's best was 75.2 percent. Mark also became the first person in the family to go to college. In fact he was offered a basketball scholarship to Oakland City College, a nearby junior college with a good basketball program. While Mark was starring on the court, Larry was in the stands, gaining an awareness of the wonders of high school glory. "It's funny, I used to go watch my older brother, Mark, play when he was in high school," says Larry. "Everybody was cheering for him. I wanted to be that guy; I wanted the people cheering for me."

As Larry's sense of himself and his desires began to be defined, he started to gain proficiency in more than just shooting. The more his game developed, the more his newfound consciousness developed, too. "By my freshman year, I started to sense that I could do more things out there, and once I realized I could pass the ball, my game completely changed. The first time I dunked was on that court on the old school yard. My life changed then." He was only six feet tall at that point, and only 14 years old. He spent hours practicing dunking. One West Baden resident remembers watching him: "We'd never seen anybody who could dunk like that. Nobody around here could jump like Larry." As well as ordinary slam dunks, Larry worked on "show-time jams" such as throwing the ball off the backboard, catching it, and then dunking behind his head—all in one swoop. He had a whole repertoire of such shots by the time he graduated high school. Basketball was no longer just an internal compulsion: It had become a barometer of self-esteem. Not that Larry's experience was a unique one. Connie Hawkins was also a basketball legend from a deprived environment with an alcoholic father. "Until I got good at basketball," Connie said, "there was nothing about me I liked; there wasn't a thing I could be proud of."

Larry's awareness of the fulfillment which basketball could provide had widened. And accordingly, the game and the dreams it inspired allowed him to endure the unhappiness in the rest of his life. But his dreams were more steeped in reality than anyone would ever know. "I remember in Junior High, we'd sit the kids down and ask them to write down what they'd like to be," says Holland. "Larry said he wanted to be a professional basketball player, and I just sort of laughed." Though Larry was a long way from attaining his dream, he had begun, for the first time, to really excel in competition. He had grown to over 6'0". And basketball began to provide financial rewards for the first time when his father promised him $20 if he made the freshman team. Not only did he make the team, but he received an award for the most free throws made by a freshman that season. Meanwhile his dreams were helping to shape his work habits. "I never wanted to leave the court until I got everything just right. I would practice different kinds of moves for hours on end and worked hard to make my left hand as strong as my right. By then my dream was to become a pro." And Larry went after his dream. But he knew even then that the likelihood of its coming true was minute. "When you're young, you don't think of [playing pro ball]. You dream about it, but you never think you're really going to make it, because there's so many roadblocks in the way."

The realization that basketball was in some way his destiny signaled an important step in Larry's development both as a basketball player and as a person. If his first fourteen years seemed almost fated to produce a player on the edge of stardom, then the next fourteen seemed almost fated to produce a great player. It was not, however, a matter of simple destiny; it was only his sheer will during the next fourteen years that enabled Larry to overcome the "many roadblocks in the way" of fulfilling his dreams.

5 / Springs Valley High, 1971–1974

On the eve of his sophomore year in high school, Larry Bird stood 6′ 1″ and weighed only 131 pounds. He had become a starter on the Springs Valley Black Hawks junior varsity team. Only two games into the season, following a scramble for a rebound, he broke his left ankle. Despite his cast and crutches, Larry continued to participate in any of the team's shooting drills which required no movement. But he could not bring himself to attend games. "Larry is not patient enough to sit down and watch," says Gary Holland. It was that circumstance, as much as any, which intensified his resolve to come back quickly.

Larry's first step in his rehabilitation program was to increase the efficiency of his workouts. He persuaded younger kids in the neighborhood to chase down the ball for him at the playground. Not only did he work on his shooting while propped up on his crutches, but he worked on his dribbling and, especially, his passing. He'd throw the ball against anything stationary or rigid enough to return the ball for his next throw. In fact, the ankle injury helped bring about a change in Larry's playing style that proved to be, arguably, the watershed event in his playing career. Until he was injured, Larry's basketball identity had revolved around his ability to score points. After recovery, he found himself playing an entirely different game. His inability to move had fostered a new emphasis on skills like shooting and passing, which can be practiced while stationary. To Larry, the change seemed magical. "When I came back, I began throwing these fantastic passes like I had never thrown before. I have no idea where it came from, but there it was. I remember being in the locker room after the first day back and guys saying, 'God, Larry, where did you learn to pass like that?' Suddenly, I had a whole new way to play." "It was great because when you pass the ball like that everybody likes you, and it was also great because when you pass the ball well it also makes it easier to shoot. It just gave a whole new dimension to my game."

Since Larry's ankle was still extremely weak and he often had a great deal of pain, Jim Jones and Holland decided to let him come back slowly on the junior varsity team. Holland, who was the J.V. coach, noted that Larry could barely run. "It bothered me to put him out on the floor, because I thought he was hurting." Despite the weakness, Larry badgered his coaches for more playing time. Holland remembers the difficult conditions he and Jones required Larry to satisfy before they would increase his playing time. "We told him we would play him if he could run this one drill we've got—the death valley—in 35 seconds." The "death valley," also known as a "suicide drill," involved running from the baseline to the free-throw line and back, then to the ten-second (midcourt) line and back, then to the opposite free-throw line and back, and then to the opposite baseline and back. According to Jones, "[Larry] practiced very hard, dragged his leg around...and he couldn't do [the drill] and [he'd] get frustrated and almost cry." But eventually, says Holland, he beat the time. "He'd struggle every night just to [meet the time]. Finally, he made it."

Having met his coaches' challenge, Larry began to get more playing time in the J.V. games, even though his physical condition was far from perfect. "I know that after some of the games, if he had to come out because he was exhausted, we'd bring him out and he'd start crying. He'd want to play more," says Holland. Larry played six J.V. games before the season ended. The state tournament loomed fast ahead. "We told him if he could play to a certain level, we'd take him to the state tournament. I didn't tell him that we'd already decided to include him," says Jones.

What Jones never dreamed was that Larry's first varsity appearance—in Valley's first sectional game—would determine the outcome of a tournament game. With about a minute and a half remaining, Larry had the ball and was fouled. He then proceeded to hit the two free throws which won the game. In Larry's mind, at that moment, there had been more than just the challenge of winning the game. "I had to hit the free throws because my brother [Mark] had never missed one in a tournament." Thus, a season that had begun with a broken ankle had ended with the kind of heroic beginning that often anticipates a special career. In the sectionals, he had performed in a way that would have seemed impossible only one month earlier: in two tournament games he totaled 8 points, 8 rebounds, 5 assists, and 2 game-winning free throws.

Coach Jones, who saw Larry more frequently than even his father, Joe, and who had coached Larry in Little League baseball as well as basketball from the time he was 8, became the first in a series of father figures in Larry's life. (Red Anderson, Larry's boss when he worked for the city; ISU coach Bob King; Terre Haute businessmen Lu Meis and Max Gibson; Terre Haute Boys Club leader May Jones; agent Bob Woolf; Celtic Equipment Manager Walter Randall; and Celtic patriarch Red Auerbach are some of the older men who exerted an influence in Larry's life.) But it was Coach Jones, in particular, who was responsible, Georgia believes, for making Larry the great player he is today. "It was Jones who taught him," Georgia says. "He was a great coach." Jones's role as the high priest of Valley basketball was, probably, his greatest contribution. "Jim Jones would say that one man can't win or lose a game, and that got through to a lot of kids in this town," says Mark Bird.

Jones was responsible for more than just helping to develop Larry's basketball philosophy; "Coach Jones had us [the team] down there [at the gym] at 6 A.M. sometimes. He'd let us in the gym whenever school was out. He'd even give us haircuts there. He was a hell of a guy," says Larry. Though Larry showed remarkable initiative for his age, he wasn't yet at the stage (if there ever is one) when getting up at 6 A.M. was a welcome event. "Larry might not have appreciated getting up that early in the morning then," says Jones. "But he is benefiting from those good work habits now."

When Larry's junior season got under way, he had grown to 6' 2½" and weighed 155 pounds. Valley also had installed a new Universal weight system, and Larry had begun to build his strength by lifting weights. While Larry played at every position, he was used mostly at guard to take advantage of his recently developed passing skills—which only enhanced those skills even more. "The big men handled the scoring. I didn't get big until my senior year. I'd pass the ball off a wall, off a fence, didn't make no difference. If the other guys score, you start seeing a gleam in their eyes. Besides, passing is more of an art than scoring. My feeling about passing is that it doesn't matter who's doing the scoring as long as it's us. I just think when a man is open, he should get the ball, whether it's thirty feet out or underneath.''

Larry's primary responsibility was to deliver the ball to senior Steve Land, who was on the verge of becoming the all-team leading scorer at Valley and who had expressed a desire for a college basketball scholarship. Larry explained to his mother that since he himself wasn't planning on going to college, he might as well help make sure Steve got his points and looked good doing it. Larry was true to his word as the season progressed, and Land neared the all-time scoring record. In the fourth quarter of the game against North Knox, Land was within 6 points of the record, but there was little time left on the clock. To make matters worse, Larry was sitting on the bench, and his teammates were having a difficult time getting the ball to Land. Larry told Coach Jones, "Put me back in and we'll get Steve those points." Jones did and Larry did: three passes and Land had the school record. This kind of selfless behavior was typical of Larry's junior season. And he finished the year with dramatically improved statistics over the previous year: He had an average of 9.86 rebounds and 6.18 assists. No other underclassman in the entire state had combined rebounding and assist statistics to match Larry. He had also scored at an even 16 points a game. The team had finished with a 19–2 record, one of the best in the school's history. Unfortunately the season had also ended with an upset loss in the finals of the sectional.

The loss left Larry with a bitter taste in his mouth, and he vowed to work harder on his game over the summer than ever before. He signaled the beginning of his new regimen by skipping the annual team banquet to work on his game. By this time, people in the valley had come to expect that Larry would be a good small-college player like his brother and Steve Land. Land, like Mark, had a scholarship to attend Oakland City College the next year. "Bird was good, but wasn't that great," says Holland. "As far as being a top player that was kind of beyond my belief."

Larry honed his game throughout the summer and worked out with weights as well. At the same time he went through a fantastic growth spurt. "I had been away at college and I hadn't seen him play," says Mark Bird. "Once between his junior and senior years I was workin' with our uncle up in Gary [Indiana], and Larry and a friend came up to see us. Suddenly he was 6'6" and he'd put on some weight." The growth spurt, even for those who saw Larry all the time, was like a revelation. "We hadn't noticed that Larry was growing so fast," says Coach Holland. "Then one day when Larry was standing next to Steve Land [who was 6'5"], someone said, 'My gosh, that Larry Bird sure has grown.'" Larry was constantly seeing how high he could reach. He wanted to be 6'10"—at least." Even more remarkable than the growth spurt itself, however, was that Larry had been able to retain his coordination and ball-handling skills. Larry could still dribble and handle the ball as well as he had when he was only 6'2".

By the beginning of his senior year, Larry's single-minded devotion to the game was greater than ever. "I'd get up in the morning and the first thing on my mind would be playing ball. I'd go right to the gym. After the first period in school, I couldn't wait to get back to the gym again. When school was out, it was no different. And it didn't hurt that at the time we lived right next door to some outdoor courts." Facilitating Larry's devotion were the unorthodox devotions of the basketball program and the community which supported it. "Larry was always [practicing]. We'd make them [the team] practice an hour in the morning, and maybe three to three-and-a-half hours at night," says Holland. Moreover, additional informal practice sessions were the rule rather than the exception. "It was not unusual for people around here to turn on the lights of the gym and play what we called 'get-up' games until midnight," says Holland.

With the beginning of the basketball season, there were also a number of changes. First, Gary Holland had been named head coach to succeed Jones, who had become the athletic director.* Second, Larry would have to learn a new position: center. Larry had played center a little the previous year, yet he had not been required to post-up near the basket. But now that he had grown to 6'6½", it was hardly desirable for Larry to still play mostly on the perimeter. Third, there

---

*"I thought I'd coached long enough. Boy was it a mistake," says Jones, who has since returned to coaching. Since leaving Valley, he has coached at Princeton (Indiana) and is now at Terre Haute North. There have only been forty-one coaches in Indiana history with more wins than Jones; he now has 366.

were new expectations about Larry as a basketball player. He was no longer projected to be merely a good small-college basketball player. According to the athletic director at Valley today, Larry Pritchett: "I hadn't talked to Gary [Holland] during the off-season, but one day he walked up to me in the hall and said, 'We've got an All-Stater.' I said, 'Larry's that good, huh?' And he said, 'Do you realize he's up to 6'6½" now?' and I had to admit I didn't."

Just three games into the season Larry got his first opportunity to prove himself as he went up against 6'7" Curt Gilstrap of Orleans. Gilstrap scored 31 points, while Larry scored 43 and broke the school record set just the year before by Land. However, Valley did manage to lose the game anyway, which left them with a disappointing 1–2 record.

Because of the losses, Larry emerged to take over leadership of the team. His best friend, Beezer Carnes, explains: "I always figured Gary wanted me to be the leader, but after the second or the third game it was clear who our leader was. Larry liked to joke around, but it was always after practice. He'd get his work done first. He could come down on you out there, too. I might be standin' around and Larry'd come over and say, 'You tired? Then why aren't you workin' helpin' us win?'" Though he was one of the quietest members of the team, Larry didn't simply lead by example. He had another unusual ability: "Larry got along with all the kids. He wasn't a loner. Most of his friends were in sports," says Holland. "Larry just seemed like he could adjust to the character of other people."

One week after Larry had assumed the leadership role, its impact was put to the test. The upcoming game against Jasper was being looked at as a true barometer of the team's strength. Jasper (the same school that produced Bobby White) had dominated basketball in the immediate area for the last sixty years. Larry turned 17 the day before, and he responded with 30 points and 18 rebounds as the Black Hawks won going away, 77–63. In fact, with Larry assuming the leadership role, Valley went on to win 20 of its next 21 games. During that streak Larry set the Valley scoring record with 54 points. (Also a Blue Chip Athletic Conference record.) Against Bloomfield, Larry broke both the school and conference single-game rebounding record with a remarkable 38 rebounds.

As Larry's—and the Black Hawks'—sensational season progressed, word began to spread across the state about the mysterious phenomenon who had come out of nowhere, the center playing for the little school down in the southern part of the state. He supposedly handled the ball, passed, and shot like a guard. But he was 6'7", and he led the state in rebounding and was second in scoring. (Peru's Kyle Macy was first.) Many fans were skeptical. They argued that in the previous year when he had been a guard, he was only the number-two scorer on a small-school squad. On top of that, his team hadn't even won the sectional in one of the state's least competitive regions. A 160-pound center couldn't be that good. Coach Holland knew how difficult it was to get recognition throughout the state. But by now he believed that Larry might very well be the best player in the state. However, without any preseason fanfare and no big-school reputation to back him up, Larry could be destined for relative obscurity, no matter how spectacular his performance was.

Therefore Holland enlisted the help of Jerry Birge from *The Jasper Daily Herald,* the biggest newspaper in the area. Birge personally printed numerous fliers with glossies of Larry and sent them to every newspaper and radio station in the state. He contacted Don Bates of the *Indianapolis Star,* who was in charge of selecting the players for the Indiana All-Star team which played the Kentucky All-Stars in an annual series at the end of the season. Selection to the All-Star team was the highest honor a player in the state could receive, outside of being selected "Mr. Basketball," which Larry had virtually no chance of getting. If Bates could be convinced of his talent, Larry would get the deserved recognition from college coaches and fans across the state.

However, despite Birge's efforts, there was little if any effect on Bates, or anyone else, until Bobby Knight stepped into the picture. Bloomington was close enough to French Lick (fifty-five miles) that Knight had heard of Larry before most people. Thus, in the middle of the season, Knight followed his typical modus operandi and slipped quietly into the Springs Valley gym during a game. He ate some popcorn and then left in the middle of the game (or at least tried to do so) as quietly as he had arrived. This typical Bobby Knight recruiting ploy caused a great deal of commotion wherever he went in the state, regardless of his attempts to remain unobtrusive. When Bates heard that Knight was interested in Larry, he decided he had better take a first hand look. He also came away a believer: "[Larry] had great hands, big hands. He scored about 35 points and had about 20 rebounds that night," says Bates.

Knight's interest and Bates's validation of the raves about Larry's play inspired even more interest. College scouts from all over the country began descending upon the valley. Larry did not disappoint them. One weekend he managed to score 97 points: 42 against West Washington and 55 points (a new record)—along with 24 rebounds and 4 assists—the next night against Corydon. One of those assists was a harbinger of things to come. Larry had been on the left side of the court during a fast break, sprinting downcourt toward the left corner when John Carnes (Beezer's cousin) threw a pass toward Larry from the other side of the court. The pass was slightly behind him, but instead of slowing down and waiting to catch the ball, Larry continued his sprint and reached behind his back to redirect the flight of the pass with his left hand. (This type of redirected pass, with a flick or tap of the hand, has been popularized by Larry and is now known as the "touch pass.") The redirected pass, with one bounce, caught Doug "Turkey" Conrad, also perfectly in stride, as he raced down the middle and laid the ball in. The next day, Holland, Beezer, Larry, and a number of others ran the film of the play over and over. "We just sat there laughing. Even Larry had to laugh," says Holland.

The most memorable game of the season was played against undefeated Loogootee, a perennial area power. The star of the team was the coach's son, Bill Butcher. Butcher had announced that his son would play Larry on defense. Valley versus Loogootee was considered the game of the year. If Valley could beat Loogootee, Valley would be regarded as one of the top fifteen teams in the state. No Valley team had been that highly regarded since 1958. Everyone from the valley, plus people from outside of town and Loogootee, were in attendance for the game. In addition, there were no fewer than six college coaches there, including Knight, and coaches from Indiana State, Miami of Ohio, Northern Arizona, and Hanover College. The stands were packed: People were even sitting in the aisles and standing at the edge of the court. Some students had even climbed up on the rails above the stands where they crouched for the entire game. In all, 4,000 fans were crammed into the 2,700-seat gym, the largest crowd in Valley history.

Once the main event began, it was clear that Valley would have a difficult time as Loogootee raced to a 10-point halftime lead. In the second half, Bird's twenty-five foot jumpers from the corner brought the Black Hawks back. Then with 2:55 left in the third quarter there was a jump ball at the top of the Loogootee free-throw circle, and Larry grabbed the tip. Incredibly, Larry then wheeled around and dropped the ball into the Loogootee basket, thus scoring for the Lions. To make matters worse, Larry's mistaken basket proved to be the margin of difference. With 9 seconds left, Loogootee led 64–63, and Springs Valley had the ball. Unfortunately, Beezer tried to call a time-out when Valley had none left. A technical was called, and the Black Hawks ended up losing 65–63. Despite the basket for Loogootee, Larry had impressed the scouts. After the game, Larry consoled Beezer, both of them agonizingly aware of their blunders: "[Larry] didn't criticize me. He just said, 'We'll get them in the regional,'" says Beezer.

Beating Loogootee in the regional became the goal of the team. Valley had finished the season with a 18–3 record, which, like the preceding year, was one of the best records in the history of the school. But the Black Hawks weren't the most disciplined group, and Coach Holland was inexperienced (he was just 27 years old). Valley also had a tendency to stand around and watch Larry as he played. Still, they were clear favorites to win the Paoli sectional. Yet the team from the year before had also been favorites and were upset. So Valley was hardly overconfident its first game against sectional host Paoli, despite having beaten Paoli twice during the year.

The game was close until in a short stretch in the second quarter, Larry scored 8 points and fed Beezer for another basket to break open the game. Valley eventually won, going away 81–60. The next game was the sectional final against Milltown. The team was escorted by an enthusiastic caravan of fans the entire twelve miles up Highway 56 to Paoli. The game began with everyone in the stands up on their feet and screaming—a sectional-final ritual. The Black Hawks ended up controlling the entire game and won 63–46. It was the first sectional championship for Valley since Mark Bird had led his team to victory three years before.

Larry had scored only 16 points to go along with 16 rebounds and 5 assists. He had not taken a single shot in the fourth quarter, content to let his teammates share in the limelight. Beezer, for example, had 20 points. Such unselfishness had been common throughout the season. According to Holland, "You'd see Larry shuttling the ball off to get the other guys their points to make them happy. And then after the game Larry would say, 'I don't want to talk to the press. Have them say something about the other guys.'" On the court, this unselfishness could occasionally cause problems. "A lot of times if you weren't awake you'd get hit in the head [because] he had made such amazing passes," says Holland. "We used to tell them, 'Better have your head up lookin' toward Larry.'" To be sure, occasionally, Larry was too unselfish. "We couldn't get him to shoot enough. He preferred passing off." Nevertheless, on the whole, Larry's unselfishness paid dividends. "Even in high school, he made an average player great."

The regional, the following week, brought Valley one step closer to their goal of avenging their earlier loss to Loogootee. The Black Hawks were to face Jasper, while in the other afternoon game the regional favorite, Loogootee, was to play Bedford. Jasper had been beaten handily by Valley during the regular season; however, they had won the regional the previous two years. If the anticipation of a possible rematch with Loogootee wasn't enough cause for apprehension, the site of the tournament was. The host school, Washington, with an enrollment of 715, had just built a brand-new gymnasium seating 7,200. Larry and his teammates had never played in such large gym. The noise alone was enough to distract the team. However, Valley took a 36–23 lead at the half, and hung on for a 60–58 victory.

The team had come to the brink of achieving their postseason objective, only to find that Loogootee had been upset in the other afternoon game. Valley would, instead, face the Bedford Stonecutters in the regional final. Coach Holland was concerned that the team wouldn't pull it off, and his worries proved well-founded. Throughout the game with Bedford, Valley floundered and struggled, finally attaining a 5-point lead with 2:38 to go. When Larry missed a one-and-one free throw and fouled at the other end, the Stonecutters converted the free throws, which gave them the lead. Beezer then missed four free throws in the last minute, and Bedford won 63–58. Larry had scored only 15 points and missed a free throw in a critical situation. Beezer's free throws were even more important; they could have made the difference. Larry was reminded of all the mornings during the past two seasons when Beezer would stay with Larry at his grandmother's. When Jones would swing by at 6 A.M. to awaken the players so they could work on their free throws, Larry would dutifully get up while Beezer would go back to sleep. After the game, Beezer and Larry went to Shorty's pool hall where "Larry just laid it out to me," says Beezer. "He said, 'Beezer you should have got up and shot them free throws in the mornings.'"

For Larry, who worked on his free throws in the mornings and still missed in an important situation, there was also more work to be done: Larry's free-throw percentage his senior year was 75 percent; in his first year of college it was 84 percent. Still, the bitter loss of the final game could not overshadow his remarkable senior season. Indeed, in the state's basketball history, there has undoubtedly never been a player who improved so drastically within a three-year period. Larry finished second in the state in scoring, with a 30.6-point-per-game average, and first in the state in rebounding, with a 20.64-point-per-game average. He also averaged 4.28 assists per game. Yet when the Associated Press 1974 Indiana All-State team was named, Larry did not make the first or even the second team; he rated only an honorable mention. The area newspapers were more aware of Bird's talents. The *Bloomington Herald-Telephone* named him to their All-Star team and the *Sunday Courier and Press* (Evansville) named Larry as all-area player of the year. Still, Larry could not be faulted for feeling less than confident about his prospects for making the All-Star team (limited to the twelve best seniors in the state). "But my coach told me not to worry," said Bird. "The coaches around the state would have some say in picking the team." Holland was correct; Bates and many other coaches were impressed by what they had seen and heard. In large measure, they believed that if Bobby Knight felt so strongly about Larry, then the kid had to be deserving. Consequently, Larry was named to the twelve-member Indiana All-Star team that would play their Kentucky counterparts in June.

Because basketball dominated Larry's adolescence, it is easy to lose sight of Larry the typical 17-year-old. Of course, in Indiana, Larry's basketball obsession would have alone qualified him as "typical." It should come as no surprise, then, that Larry's high school yearbook makes no mention of a single activity or award outside of basketball. However, Larry was not simply a basketball automaton. He had a social life of sorts, which consisted of things like hanging out at the Shell station in West Baden or playing pool at Shorty's pool hall with friends like Beezer and Kevin Mills. At night sometimes they would go to the drive-in or cruise the strip in Jasper. As one would expect, the main topic of conversation was basketball. During the season, remembers Beezer, he would stay overnight at Larry's grandmother's on the Friday night before a game. In indulging Larry, Lizzie was more than happy to have his friends come over at all hours. Lizzie loved taking care of all of them, especially Beezer. They would wake up around noon on Saturday, the now-imminent game uppermost in Larry's mind. "Larry'd like to talk about who we were gonna play that night. You couldn't keep him from talking about basketball. Then his granny...would fix lunch and we'd go out and ride around."

Larry's physical maturity came relatively late in life: he was still growing at the age of 21. Larry was also a year younger and more reserved than most of his high school classmates. His shyness and dedication to basketball circumscribed Larry's social experiences. Larry's social life did begin to change in his senior year. He became interested enough in girls to acquire a steady girlfriend, a cheerleader named Janet Condra. And Larry began to drink occasionally: Apparently, more than once Lizzie "would find [Larry] out in the front yard drunk. She'd find him out there the next morning passed out in the yard,...[but] she never really disciplined him," says Janet. Once the season ended, Larry had a run-in with Coach Holland. "I went out to his house and talked to him about it," says Holland. "[Larry said] 'Oh, I haven't been drinking any, Coach.' I said, 'Don't lie to me, I know you have.'" But Holland was quick to point out that this was the only problem he ever had with Larry. Beezer did eventually admit that perhaps all their activities weren't entirely innocent. "We did some mischievy [sic] things when we were kids, but I don't know if I should talk about them. We never got in trouble for them, 'cause we never got caught." But Beezer's revelations hardly discredit a perception of Larry's typicalness. If anything, these incidents were emblematic of a small-town Indiana adolescence.

An aspect of Larry's teenaged years which was less typical had to do with his family's financial circumstances. Even for the poverty-stricken valley, Larry's family was unusually poor. Larry not only had to share a bed with his brothers, but he and the family were forced to move practically every year until he was in the seventh grade. Some years the Birds had a car that was a junker, other years they had none. As a driver, Joe was accident-prone. For Larry, the lack of dependable transportation caused assorted inconveniences. He had no allowance, but he occasionally worked for various farmers in the area. "He was a hard-working country boy," one relative says. "The only way he could get spending money was to put up hay in a hay field." Also, people in the community helped Larry out because he was a celebrity. They would lend him their cars, and Mike in particular made sure Larry was able to get to all his games.

Larry was sensitive to his parents' circumstances. "Even in high school he wouldn't ask for a school ring, a jacket, or anything," says Georgia. But the family's social status was a significant source of embarrassment, despite the fact that many people in the area were under some kind of economic hardship. (Incidentally, Orange County is one of the poorest counties in the state.) Because he was a Bird, Larry was somewhat ostracized by the other kids. Georgia explains that when Jim Jones coached Larry's oldest brother, Mike, he was under pressure to play the children of the more-established citizens ahead of Mike. (However, because Mark was one of the best players in the history of the school, there was a lot less pressure to keep him on the bench.) If Larry felt self-conscious about his family's poverty, it was because there was such a contrast between the family's circumstances and the wealth of the tourists coming to the valley. Thus, even though Larry and family lived within blocks of the French Lick Hotel, they never went inside. Says Georgia, "I never set foot inside the hotel until they had a basketball banquet when Larry was a senior in high school." The family's financial situation also occasionally necessitated atypical sacrifices. For instance, unlike many other parents of star players, Georgia would sometimes have to miss Larry's home games because of her extra job.

Despite Joe and Georgia's divorce the summer before Larry's sophomore year, the Bird family maintained a semblance of closeness. Coach Holland explains: "There was kind of a harmony among the Bird family members. The kids respected their parents real well. You'd see them hug their parents. And a lot of times, a young kid, he doesn't want to go up and hug his mom and dad in front of some other people. I think in [Larry's] family, it was only natural to do that." To be sure, despite the inconsistency of Larry and Joe's relationship there was affection and some degree of support. Joe played an active role in determining where Larry chose to go to school, and occasionally attended games. Larry has said, "My father was proud of us, but he wouldn't go see us play. Dad didn't like crowds." One relative disputes this, saying, "Joe went to some [games] in Larry's senior year—if he wasn't going to go out and hit the bar afterward. I also don't remember Joe ever being scared of crowds." Joe also imparted a philosophy which Larry follows even today. "That's where I get a lot of my toughness about playin' with injuries. 'Cause [my father] would always go to work—even with injuries." Yet Larry's respect for his father went beyond mere regard for Joe's toughness. "I just enjoyed being around [my father]. Great man...he was just a tough individual."

No matter how atypical Larry's home environment was, his prowess as a basketball player supplied still more reason for him to stand apart from the experiences of his classmates. Throughout his senior year he was dogged by the machinery of the college basketball recruiting process. For Larry, the end of the high school season only meant more pressure and unwanted attention: He had been contacted by more than 200 schools. Some, most notably, Kentucky, were no longer interested. Joe B. Hall, the Kentucky coach, had seen Larry play a bad game. "[Larry] didn't score very much and he never really got going," says Holland. Hall's complaint was one that Larry would hear again: "He's too slow." (However, Hall and other coaches might have done well to have noted UNLV Coach Jerry Tarkanian's observation, "White guys are never as slow as they look.") Since Larry admired Kentucky's up-tempo game and had always been a fan of the Wildcats, Kentucky's rejection was upsetting. "At first I was disappointed," says Larry, "but then I decided that I didn't want to try and go anywhere that really didn't want me." Larry also politely remarked that Coach Hall was right about him and that he was flattered that Hall had even taken the time to see him. But other schools were more impressed. Some, however, were never seriously considered by Larry. Denny Crum of the University of Louisville, for example, visited French Lick, and when he found Larry less than interested, Crum challenged him to a game of h-o-r-s-e. If Crum won, Larry would visit the Louisville campus. If Crum lost, he wouldn't bother Larry anymore. After five shots Crum was on his way to Louisville—alone. Larry's reaction to all the pressure and attention was to quickly announce that he had narrowed the field to Indiana, Purdue, and Indiana State.

That Larry chose IU (Indiana) as one of his final three choices was no surprise. Bobby Knight was quite appreciative of Larry's talents and had made that appreciation known. He felt that Larry possessed unusually good hands. In fact, he claimed that Larry had the best hands he had seen all year. Knight also liked Larry's jumping ability and believed that Larry had a lot of offensive skills, and yet wasn't above working on the defensive end as well. Ultimately, Larry's willingness to work won Knight over. The results that had come from Larry's work on his jump shot had been impressive. After all, determination can't be taught. Indeed, Knight commented to his star player, Quinn Buckner, "Bird is a special player, one of the best." Knight also felt pretty confident that he could get Larry. Knight himself had seen Larry play twice, plus his assistants had seen another seven or eight games, and "each time we were more impressed. He's a hell of a player," said Knight. (It is interesting to note that according to Jim Jones, if it hadn't been for the loss of another recruit, Knight wouldn't have recruited Larry.)

In addition, Knight had a number of other advantages. The proximity of IU's campus was appealing to a kid who had never traveled outside of Indiana or Kentucky. And the considerable influence that Knight wields in communities throughout the state was even greater in the valley because of that very proximity. For the townspeople, attention from Knight was the most exciting thing that had happened since the 1958 state finals team. Around town, the implicit as well as explicit pressure upon Larry to go to IU was unavoidable. According to Holland, "People just kept putting pressure on Larry to go to school. He showed a lot of interest in [Indiana] State, but he was pushed to IU. All the people wanted him to go to IU." Of course, Larry's own family was no different. "We were all IU fans," says Mark Bird. "My dad was probably the biggest IU fan ever. He'd say to Larry, 'Boy, I seen this red jacket the other day, and I sure would like to buy it and wear it to one of your ball games.'" Maybe the biggest factor of all in Knight's favor was the influence of Coach Jones. "Mr. Jim Jones kept after him," says Georgia. "He said: 'You're the best. You want to go to the best.' And his daddy wanted him to go."

Working against Indiana was Georgia's dislike of what she felt were Knight's dictatorial and heavy-handed methods and Larry's uncertainty about whether he even wanted to go to school. With everyone's expectations and the scholarship offers, Larry actually had little choice in the matter, regardless of how he felt. "He had big pressures on him," says Holland. "The kid was seventeen...and he [had] never thought about college until his senior year. He said 'I'm going to go, because I'm going to get a scholarship.' Before then I don't think Larry thought too much about going to college. He thought, 'Well, I might, but I'll make that decision when the time comes.'" Georgia had always hoped Larry would go to a smaller school like State. But Larry seriously considered skipping college altogether and getting a job. In that event, maybe his mother wouldn't have to work two jobs. Knight, however, was aware of Larry's uncertainty and acted decisively to assuage it.

He sent three of his star players, Steve Green, John Laskowski, and Kent Benson (all three later played in the NBA) to the high school to talk casually with Larry. Of course, it caused a great stir when all the kids' heroes showed up. "They came down, Coach Holland bought a bunch of pizzas, and we just sat around talking for about three hours," says Larry. The chance to sit down with recruiters who were essentially peers appealed to Larry, and he was more at ease. "I was able to ask some questions that I might have been scared to ask the coach, and it also showed me that somebody up there really wanted me. I liked the players, the coaching staff, and it looked like they were going to have a great team next year," says Larry. (Actually, during the next two seasons IU only lost one game, and if not for an injury to Scott May, they probably would have gone undefeated both years.) The severe sinus problems that Larry had always worsened when he was upset, and the night before Knight was scheduled to visit, he was especially nervous. His mother said his sinuses were so painful and his anxiety over Knight's arrival so great that he was crying. "I don't really want to go to IU. But I guess I'd let too many people down if I don't," he told her. Actually, his decision was not his own: With Jim Jones, Joe, and practically all of the valley pushing for IU, his decision was almost a fait accompli. "And not knowing what to do, people said, '[you have] Bobby Knight and a great school here, why don't you attend IU'; so [Larry] tried it," says Holland. On April 24, 1974, at a press conference held at the school, Larry announced for IU. He explained that he liked State and Purdue, but that "I wanted to go to IU, that was always my first choice." If the press conference hadn't been enough, earlier in the week Larry had been named to the Indiana All-Star team, which was scheduled to play a touring Soviet team just three days later. All in all, it proved to be a spectacular week in the life of a 17-year-old.

For Larry, one of the most exciting aspects about making the All-Star team was the exposure he received. While he had the most impressive statistics on the squad, he was one of the least-recognized members of the team because he came from a small school in an unpublicized region of the state. Many, including Coach Kirby Overman from New Albany, believed that Larry was at a disadvantage since he had not played against sufficient competition. "I was scared at first, but after I got going, it was all right," says Larry. "I was ready for 'em." Larry was also competing for playing time with Charlie Mitchell at one of the forward spots. Mitchell, who had played at New Albany for Overman, was consistently outplayed by Larry, according to a number of observers. But Overman naturally favored his own kid. Holland, who watched all the All-Star team's practices, says that Larry's advantage was due, in part, to his ability to adapt and complement different types of personality and style among his teammates. "I think that, overall, [Larry's] game was much better because he was able to play with some of the other kids and the black kids. And that year some of the kids were a little ornery...[yet] they accepted Larry really well." Don Bates, who watched the All-Star practices, says that one reason Larry was more readily accepted by the black players was because of his impressive dunking ability. "He had those big strong hands, and he would throw the ball off the backboard and catch it in one hand and dunk it backwards. The black kids really respected him when they saw that."

Larry bore out Holland's conclusions in the first formal scrimmage. Playing against an AAU team composed of ex-collegians, he led all scorers in the game with 18 points. But in the next game, instead of being rewarded for his performance, Larry had his minutes cut. Against the Soviets, he played only 15 minutes; but he still managed to total 12 points, on 6 of 9 field goals, with 9 rebounds as the Indiana All-Stars won, 92–60. In the All-Star series against Kentucky, the first game was played at Freedom Hall in Louisville. Fans in the valley responded by purchasing 300 tickets at $10 apiece. A caravan was organized centering around a bus displaying signs reading, "The Bird Flies Again," and Patty Nelson's sign, "French Lick's Super Bird." At the game, the French Lick cheering block, outfitted in Black Hawk colors of black and gold, chanted, "Larry, Larry, Larry." The French Lick contingent, along with the other Indiana fans, comprised 8,000 out of the 12,000 in attendance for what was supposed to be Kentucky's home game. Maybe because of the large French Lick group, Overman decided to play Larry a more respectable 25 out of the game's 40 minutes. Larry answered with 12 points, 7 rebounds, and 3 blocked shots as Indiana prevailed, 92–81.

The next week, the second game was played at Indianapolis's Market Square Arena. The game included 200 Kentucky fans among the 16,000 in attendance. Indiana won *again,* 110–91. Indiana had won 34 of the first 53 games in the series. During the Indianapolis game, Larry played for 15 minutes in the first half and scored 6 points while contributing excellent defense. Inexplicably, Larry sat on the bench the entire second half. With "about four or five minutes left," Don Bates alerted Overman that Larry had yet to play in the half. "When I told him that he said 'Oh, shit!' and put his palm to his head. He just forgot," said Bates. Overman then motioned for Larry to go into the game. But there were only a few minutes left and even at 17, Larry was proud enough to believe that he did not deserve to be forgotten. So he made All-Star history by refusing to go back into the game. The humiliation of not being allowed to play for most of the game and then being ordered in to play during "garbage time" at the end of a blowout was the final insult. It was also the third occasion where Larry's basketball ability had recently been questioned. The others were his rejection by Kentucky Coach Hall and his failure to make the AP All-State team.

In retrospect, those episodes, and the anger they precipitated, were crucial to perhaps the most important stage of Larry's career. For, the ensuing development and elevation of Larry's game marked the difference between a very good high school player and a player capable of greatness. It's unlikely that Larry would have ever settled for simply being a very good high school player. However, at least some of Larry's motivation and determination to be a great player was inspired by the questioning of his talent. In the summer of 1974, an already exceptionally motivated player, he stepped up his intensity one more level. Larry had become consumed by his mission to prove himself to the unbelievers.

Today, when Larry is asked what drives him, his first response is, "I don't know exactly." But upon reflection, he hearkens back to that particular summer. "A lot of people there said I couldn't play. So I worked twice as hard as everybody else to prove them wrong. ...I didn't even make All-State my senior year. I came from southern Indiana, we didn't have much press there. I had the numbers, but I guess the voters figured I didn't play anybody. I heard what they said about me. Too slow, can't jump. Country kid, never had the big-city competition. I went to the state All-Star game my senior year, and I got in the last 5 minutes. I wondered if I was really that bad. I look back and realize I was the best player in the state. No one gave me credit for it. But maybe it worked out for the best. It kept me practicing four or five hours a day in the summer, and now it's a habit."

Larry's "habit" proved not only indispensable for the development of his game, but also for his ability to cope with adversity off the court. The coming year would test Larry's emotional resources and strength as he prepared to leave home for the first time. If Larry could prove that he had the strength of character and will to triumph over the kind of adversity awaiting him, then he would emerge from the struggle of the next twelve months stronger, more mature, and more confident than ever before.

Larry's Stats at Springs Valley High School

YEAR	G	MIN	FG	FGA	PCT	FT	FTA	PCT
71–72	2		3	4	.750	2	3	.666
72–73	22		137	279	.491	79	105	.752
73–74	25		395	606	.652	154	205	.751
Total	49		535	889	.612	235	313	.758

YEAR	REB	AVG	A	AVG	ST	BL	PTS	AVG
71–72	8		5	2.50			8	4.0
72–73	217	9.86	136	6.18			353	16.0
73–74	516	20.64	107	4.28			764	30.6
Total	741	15.10	248	5.06			1125	23.0

G = game; MIN = minutes; AVG = average; FG = field goals; FGA = field goals attempted; PCT = percentage; FT = free throws; FTA = free throws attempted; REB = rebounds; A = assists; ST = steals; BL = blocks; PTS = points.

6 / 24 Days with Bobby Knight and the Indiana Hoosiers, 1974

Larry Bird didn't stay at Indiana University—in fact, he didn't last a month.

"Bobby Knight doesn't recruit the boys for what they can do," says Georgia Bird. "He molds them into what he wants. I don't think that would ever have worked with Larry. I think he would have ruined Larry." Today Georgia reflects that "Larry's a leader, and Bobby Knight would've changed him." Georgia's son looks back and sees the hypothetical scenario quite differently, "I love Bobby Knight.* I think he's the best coach in the nation....[Knight] can be a little rough on his players. But if you can put up with that for four years he'll make you a better player....If I knew then what I know now, I wouldn't have left. Coach Knight and me wouldn't have no trouble. He'd have loved my game." It's a moot issue now. Still, it is fascinating to speculate on how different things might have been had Larry stayed at IU. In retrospect, both Larry and his mother base their points of view on valid assumptions. Georgia, more mindful of Larry's vulnerability and immaturity at the time, is aware of Knight's often-insensitive manipulations of his young players. She also acknowledges Larry's stubbornness, which was more of a problem for Larry at 17 than it is now. Larry, with a little hindsight about his resilience, now realizes he could have adapted to a man who knows so much about the game. One can detect a hint of wistfulness as Larry speculates on whether Knight would have improved him as a player.

---

*On a wall in Larry's Brookline house hangs a framed photograph of Knight, Holland, and Larry after Larry signed with IU.

Still, with hindsight, it's obvious that at 17, Larry wasn't ready for college, regardless of which school he attended. According to Georgia, "He was too young to go away to school. I knew it too, the day Bobby Knight came to our house to get me to sign that paper. I just had to bite my tongue [to keep] from telling him, 'Why don't you leave him alone? He doesn't want to go to school.' But nobody was leaving him alone then. That phone was ringing all the time, and guys at the door."

Larry lasted a grand total of twenty-four days at IU. He left before the first practice had even begun. And he gave no warning of his departure to any officials, coaches, or students in Bloomington. When it was discovered that Larry was missing, distraught IU officials called Coach Jim Jones at Valley, who also knew nothing of Larry's decision. Only Georgia, Lizzie, and her brother Amon knew of Larry's plan to leave. Lizzie's attitude about the prospect of Larry leaving IU was, "If you don't like it, don't do it," according to Jones. In fact, Georgia had expected Larry to drop out sooner than he actually did. From the time of Larry's arrival on campus, a number of unhappy phone calls forewarned of his leaving. Larry still argues that he should have stayed at IU and that things would have worked out with Knight. However, Larry also feels that he should have redshirted immediately. "I was seventeen and a half when I got out of high school. And what I should have done was sit out a whole year right then, no matter where I went."

Larry left IU for many reasons entirely unrelated to basketball. He felt completely out of place in a school where the enrollment alone was sixteen times the population of French Lick. "Thirty-three thousand people is not my idea of a school, it's a country," Larry said once. He felt self-conscious about his family's lack of money. Like the tourists who came to the valley, most of the students seemed to have a lot of money. But unlike the valley, where the wealth of the tourists was an exception to the norm, at IU it was Larry who was the exception. His sense of poverty was reinforced daily whenever he opened his closet. His meager wardrobe, compared to that of his middle-class roommate, Jim Wisman, was embarrassing. Though Wisman was the son of a mail carrier from the rural, downstate Illinois town of Quincy, Larry presumed Wisman was wealthy partly because Wisman had a "full wardrobe." Larry, according to Georgia, had "six shirts, three pair of pants, and one pair of dress shoes." And there was more than simple self-consciousness about wealth, or the lack thereof. Larry's financial situation, practically speaking, was also a problem. "I didn't have enough money. I didn't have no clothes. I didn't have nothing. People said I had a free ride, but I didn't have a nickel in my pocket." The irony was that the recruiting process was partly to blame for Larry's problems of adjustment. In fact, it could be argued that at the very heart of recruiting there often exists a fundamental deception. Many kids are told how good they are and how wonderful college life is going to be, but the reality turns out to be quite different. Though, if Larry had been a more important recruit, there might have been the necessary attention, monetary and otherwise, to help assuage his financial and emotional pressures.

One problem was that Larry had never made a firm resolve to make things work in Bloomington. He had so little idea of what to expect that it's surprising no one anticipated the inevitable—that Larry would leave school. "When you're just out of high school, it's very tough to know what you want," says Larry. "It just wasn't what I expected college to be. Plus [I] hadn't been out on my own before. I guess all that got to me....I was just completely out of it there." The college environment was as alien to anything Larry had experienced as it would have been for a kid coming from the inner city. Moreover, at least an inner-city kid wouldn't have been overwhelmed by the number of students. Also exacerbating Larry's sense of maladjustment was the absence of any advice on how to prepare for the huge transition a large university requires of an underprivileged freshman.

When it was first discovered that Larry had dropped out of IU, everyone automatically assumed that Larry had had trouble with Bobby Knight. One valley rumor says that Larry left IU after Knight threw a trash can at him. After all, in Knight's first eight years of coaching, almost 30 percent of his recruits transferred to other schools (12 out of 41). Larry immediately denied that. "People naturally think it was trouble between [Knight] and me, but it wasn't. [The school] was just too big." In fact, Larry told his mother that he never even saw Bobby Knight while he was there. Over the years the denials that Knight had any role in Larry's leaving have been so emphatic and universal, that it has become an accepted bit of mythology that Knight was blameless. However, the truth, it appears, has not been revealed to anyone, including Larry's family. And it begins with the regard Larry then felt for Knight.

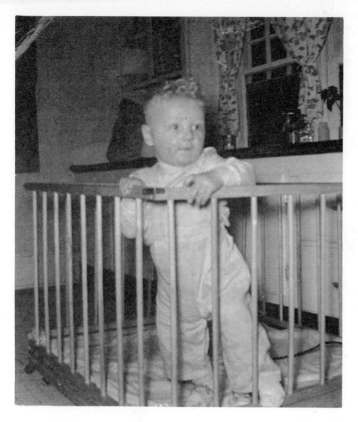

Larry Bird at nine months. (Courtesy L. V. Smith.)

The Bird family home, 1969–1982. (Courtesy Doug Gromer.)

Georgia Kerns Bird.   (Courtesy Georgia Bird.)

Joe Bird.   (Courtesy Georgia Bird.)

Lizzie Kerns.   (Courtesy Georgia Bird.)

At the Kerns's farm. Left to right: Linda, unidentified friend, Mark
(on pony), Larry, Mike.   (Courtesy L. V. Smith.)

Mike Bird. (Courtesy Georgia Bird.)   Mark Bird. (Courtesy Doug Gromer.)

Linda Bird. (Courtesy *Springs Valley*   Eddie Bird. (Courtesy Doug Gromer.)
Herald.)

Jeff Bird. (Courtesy *Sporting News*.)

Dinah Mattingly. (Courtesy George Tiedermann, *Sports Illustrated*.)

Springs Valley High, 1974 sectional champions. Beezer Carnes (35) and Doug "Turkey" Conrad (34) flank Larry. (Courtesy Randy Dieter, *The Evansville Courier*.)

Larry's home on Abbeydale Road, West Baden.
(Courtesy Georgia Bird.)

Larry Bird Boulevard, French Lick.
(Courtesy Kevin Horan Photo Group.)

Larry as a 6′3″, 150-pound high school junior, with his friend, Tony Clark.
(Courtesy Robert Burke, *The Evansville Courier*.)

Perfect form against county rival Paoli
in 1974.   (Courtesy James Qualkinbush.)

Larry's "Globetrotter" form.
(Courtesy James Qualkinbush.)

Janet Condra as a cheerleader for
Springs Valley High, 1974.
(Courtesy James Qualkinbush.)

Larry had been ready to sign with Indiana State. All the kids from the valley went there, and State had begun recruiting him first. However, when Knight suddenly became interested, it was not too late for Larry to change his mind. Larry had been devastated when the most important male influence in his life, Jim Jones, abruptly left coaching following Larry's junior year at Valley. (Jones still maintained some role in Larry's life, although a much more limited one.) So, at that time, Larry was particularly vulnerable to the lure of a strong and older coach. In fact, having the attention of a man as revered as Bobby Knight was almost too good to be true. And Larry never knew that he was a last-resort recruit, anyway.* According to Jim Jones, Larry was still leaning toward attending ISU, until Knight condescendingly told him, "If you're trying to decide between Indiana State and IU, then you don't belong at IU." It was the most effective thing that Knight could have possibly said. "That really made Larry want to go to IU when Knight made that remark," says Jones.

As soon as Larry arrived on campus he was immediately confronted with disillusioning circumstances. The typical Bobby Knight treatment was to let freshmen sink or swim; there would be no support. A player had to be able to cope with the adjustment of college or Knight would assume that the player wasn't up to the task of playing for IU. Larry also had doubts about Knight's personality. Knight's caustic epithets would come raining down upon the players from his perch thirty rows above the court as they went through informal scrimmages before the season started. Besides, Larry had become discouraged at the prospect of learning Knight's system well enough so that he could hope to get even a minimal amount of playing time. "To really shine and look good at IU, you have to get yourself into that system," says Wisman. "Because [the system's] based on motion offense with down picks, if your timing's not there, you're out of synch."

If trying to get the system down wasn't enough, Larry was playing behind four older players (Jim Abernathy, Steve Green, John Laskowsky, and Scott May)—all of whom eventually played in the pros. Not only was Larry's hope for *any* playing time almost nil, but

---

*Knight had lost his first choice, Steve Collier, when Knight signed Illinois prep star Jim Wisman. With Collier's decision to sign with the University of Cincinnati, Knight was left with an extra scholarship and, thus, decided to take a chance on Larry. It was late in the recruiting season, and he had little to lose by doing so.

his hopes of playing even the next year were exceedingly small, since only one of these players was a senior. "He wasn't anywhere near cracking the starting line-up....It might have been two or three years," says Wisman. And even though Larry did show flashes of great talent and potential, especially as a shooter, Wisman says, "there was no way you could have predicted that [Larry] would turn out the way he did." With all those factors, Larry grew increasingly disheartened. "A lot of times [Larry] was fairly unhappy with his performance [in the scrimmages]," so he would shoot alone at one of the dorms after the scrimmages were through. "Larry was much more relaxed when he could just go off and shoot. That's where he was really at home," says Wisman.

Larry was already depressed with the environment on campus. But to have his usual problem solver, basketball, depressing him even more was too much to bear. Making matters worse was his fast-fading hope that Knight would fill the void Jim Jones had left behind. Yet Knight was hardly interested in giving his freshmen any support—especially the recruit who was pretty much an afterthought. Larry's unhappiness with IU and Knight reached its peak when Larry and his fiancée, Janet Condra, were at a restaurant on campus and Knight walked in. Larry's eyes widened, and he was excited but nervous to see his coach, says Janet. Then "Larry spoke to Coach Knight, and [Knight] just totally ignored him, and it just crushed Larry." Janet believes that was the turning point. And Wisman says that he believes Larry would have been too embarrassed to bring up the incident but that it could have happened. "He does things to challenge players—he wants players to develop maturity. The games he plays are all a part of his mental toughness program for freshmen."

The prevailing mythology on Larry's time at IU also emphasizes Larry's confused state at the time and the uncertainty of his future. But actually the evidence points to Larry always having had a clear idea of what he wanted to do. Even before Larry left IU, he was certain about his future. He was going to go where he should have gone in the first place: ISU. Wisman remembers the conversation they had moments before Larry left IU for good.

"I'm going to leave," Larry announced. "I don't want you to say anything to the coaches."

"Where are you going to go—what are you going to do?"

"I'm going to go to ISU."

"Why do you want to go there? You're here to play basketball, right? This is the ultimate place to play basketball. Why not at least stick out the season? You'll lose a year of eligibility anyway."

"I can't stand it here. I'm going back to my old summer job. I was happy doing that. I just got to get out of here."

Bobby Knight recently told another coach, "If I had known how good the kid was going to be, I would have put an arm around his shoulder." Knight has also admitted publicly that his mind-set fourteen years ago differs from his perspective today. "We were right in the midst of having a good basketball team, maybe the best team ever. When Bird left, we hadn't even noticed. It was like 'the hell with him.' I wouldn't chase [Quinn] Buckner. I wouldn't chase [Scott] May. Well, I'll be damned if I'm going to chase *this* kid. That was kind of it. If [it were to] happen today, I would talk to him. I'd tell him what a hell of a mistake he was making, that this [Indiana] was far and away the best place for him....I'm older now. It was a mistake that I didn't do it then." Though Larry claims now that "Knight knew I just didn't know what I wanted to do," it appears more likely that Knight had no idea and that even if he had, he wouldn't have cared anyway.

No matter how wistful Larry is now about not having played for Knight, he hasn't forgotten those awful twenty-four days. So, overall, Larry is ambivalent about whether he should have stayed at IU. On the one hand he claims that if he had known what he knows now he would "have run right back." On the other hand, he also recalls, "I found I wanted a place I could relate to. I didn't like school. Indiana was too big, and I couldn't get adjusted. Sometimes now I wish I had stayed, but sometimes I don't."

Unfortunately, Larry's arrival back home was anything but reassuring for his state of mind. People in the valley reacted to his decision with anger and dismay; they felt betrayed. "People were disappointed. I think a lot of people thought he wouldn't make it after that," says Jim Ballard. That Larry was carrying the burden of an entire community's hopes and expectations would have been unfair to anyone, let alone a shaken 17-year-old. Fair or not, Larry was quite aware of how he'd let everyone down. In truth, many didn't understand the circumstances. Some, like Coach Holland, believed that Larry could have at least persevered for a short time. "Several people, including myself, were mad at him for quitting. We wish he would have stuck it out for one year and tried it....I think we all looked at him and thought, if he doesn't go back to school, it's going to be a big waste of talent." For Larry, the experience was one of the most traumatic he'd ever faced. He felt he needed time to evaluate what he was going to do. Still, it was an almost-impossible task because everyone kept asking him about his plans for the future. Though major colleges had lost interest, junior colleges couldn't wait to get a chance at Larry. "After he came home from Indiana, [the recruiting] started all over again," says Georgia. All the junior college coaches, then. It was awful. Bothering him all the time when he just wanted to work and be left alone."

Larry's solution was to enroll at Northwood Institute, a junior college on the grounds of the old West Baden Springs Hotel. Jones says that one of the reasons Larry went to Northwood was his mistaken belief that he would be able to play immediately and that the school had a really good program. He planned on playing one year for Northwood and then transferring to ISU the next year and playing three years without having to sit out. Larry hoped that his enrollment would remove some of the pressure to make an immediate and more binding decision about his future. He would be able to buy some time and determine whether college was really for him after all. However, Larry was far from being in a position to adequately handle the rigors of even a junior college. He had a difficult time concentrating. Not only was there the pressure of the valley's expectations, but Northwood wasn't at all what Larry had expected either. "He was very unsettled," said Northwood's coach Jack Johnson. "He had trouble attending class and was very undisciplined." Larry left again without warning, as he had at Indiana, and without telling anyone. He just dropped out of sight," says Johnson. "He never told me he was dropping out of school." The core of the problem was that Larry was a 17-year-old kid who was unprepared for college and had never been on his own before. "I guess all that just got to me," Larry says. Plus, when he found out he wouldn't even be able to play ball (for the sake of his future eligibility), there was little incentive to remain at Northwood. So Larry's stay at the junior college lasted a mere two months. When Larry quit Northwood, he further fueled the disappointment of people in the valley and put still more pressure on himself.

The valley had been living vicariously through Larry ever since

he'd started to be a basketball success. When Bobby Knight had recruited Larry, it was almost as if he had been recruiting the community itself. When Larry scored points for Valley it was as if the entire
community supporting the team had scored those points, too. As a
result, many people reacted personally to Larry's decision to leave
school. For these people, when Larry quit Northwood and, especially
IU, he was "quitting on them" as well. In the months following
Larry's leaving IU, some people would even cross the street to avoid
having to talk to him. In their view, Larry had once brought honor
to the community; he had now dishonored the community. Larry had
let himself down and he had let the community down. Never mind
that some of his friends, whose support would have been valuable in
his own time of need, had also let Larry down. Even those who were
simply trying to be helpful aggravated Larry's troubles by persistently
quizzing him about his future plans.

Larry hoped to cope with his crisis in two ways. First, he began
telling everyone that he didn't know what he was going to do—this
despite the fact that he always knew he was going to go back to school
and that he knew it would be ISU. "I got so tired of people telling
me what I should do. But [if not ISU,] I knew I'd go play for some
college," he says. His evasiveness about the future eased the pressure and provided a little distance. More importantly, he also turned
to the one thing that had never let him down, no matter how big the
crisis or how great the anger: basketball. Somehow the necessary
answers, and a clue to the future, would emerge out of the benefi-
cent calm of the basketball court and its routine. As Larry pushed
himself toward a level of excellence all his own, his troubles faded
into the background. That in the end basketball itself would emerge
as the answer was not the point. Basketball had once again, and not
for the last time, provided Larry a refuge from outside problems and
pressures.

Larry unexpectedly found another refuge in plain, old-fashioned
work. After he left Northwood, he worked odd jobs around the valley. Mostly he worked for the French Lick street department with his
buddy Beezer Carnes. "We'd paint benches and pick up trash and
unplug sewers and things like that," says Beezer. "[Larry] was always the kind who wouldn't neglect work if there was work around."
Larry really enjoyed working on the garbage truck, claiming it was
the best job he had ever had. Anxiety about college was, for the time

being, at least, the farthest thing from his mind. "I was with people all the time and very happy down there. My mom kept after me to think about returning to school. She wanted me to play ball and get an education. But at that point I didn't care what anyone said." Larry worked a variety of jobs in addition to the renowned sanitation truck job. He also worked at his uncle's gas station, drove a truck for Hancock Construction (in the town of Mitchell), painted park benches, striped streets, and mowed grass for the city. The kid who had always wanted to work with his hands and pour concrete had gotten his wish. "I'd rather have the ability to fix things and work with my hands than any brainwork in the world," he says. "If I could do anything in the world, it would be to play basketball, but if I couldn't do that, it would be to fix things."

7 / *Joe's Death, 1975*

In the nearly twenty years following his Korean experience, Joe had never attempted to apprehend the meaning of his recurring dreams and memories. His understanding of the experience had been limited, simply, to the realization that drinking had always provided a measure of relief. Such a response to the trauma is common. People suffering from posttraumatic stress disorder have little choice over how they attempt to cope with the vagaries of the disease. Only alcohol had proved capable of helping Joe to forget the dead man's eyes. The hypnosis had made it plain that a recurrent and haunting image of the North Korean's eyes signified the common ground that Joe felt he shared with the other soldier. Both were similarly fearful at the moment of confrontation. Both were thrust into a life-and-death confrontation through no fault of their own. In fact, to a large extent they were all there by sheer accident. Any one or all of them could have met death. And simply by virtue of circumstance, it was Joe's best friend and the young North Korean who had been left dead in the trench and denied the happiness of life and family. Those open eyes served as a constant reminder to Joe that he no more deserved happiness than his friend or the soldier whose life he had taken.

As Joe's sense of helplessness grew, so did the instability of his marriage. Aggravating an already-unstable situation was Joe's increasingly uncontrolled behavior. "[One day] he came up to the house to beat on me, and I was scared for the first time," Georgia remembers. "He acted like he didn't know what he was doing." Once again, the couple separated. But unlike the previous separation, there was to be no reconciliation. Joe and Georgia eventually divorced. A major reason for the divorce was financial. Because of his drinking, Joe couldn't be counted on to provide for the rest of the family. Georgia decided that the only way she could get any money out of him was to divorce him and have the legal system intervene on her behalf. "Nobody will do anything for a woman if she has a man," says Georgia. Despite this situation, Georgia say that "we planned on getting married again after the kids were grown up." And Joe stayed close to the family. Just as Lizzie was willing to take care of her husband after the separation because he was ill, Georgia was willing to have Joe live at the house after the divorce. He slept on a couch downstairs. Georgia allowed this unusual arrangement because Joe's parents' house was far enough out of the way that living at Georgia's was the only way he could pick up a ride to get to work at Kimball in Jasper and therefore continue to make some money for child support.

Another reason why Georgia allowed Joe to sleep at the Washington Street home after their divorce was that the kids, especially Eddie, wanted Joe around.

Not long after, Joe was laid off from Kimball's. The reason, according to Georgia and other family members, was his refusal to give orders, (a reminder of the way he had avoided advancement at Fort Knox). "He was for the men and not the company," says Georgia. Out of work, Joe became increasingly withdrawn and began drinking still more.

Eventually he went back to his old, nonsupervisory job at Kimball's and also moved back into his parents' home. But his attendance at work was sporadic, and his emotional state severely depressed. Living with his parents didn't help. "Helen wouldn't get him up or fix his lunch or help him....It was hell for Joe living with his mother," says Georgia.

After the Christmas break, he never went back to work. And now he was in even worse financial straits than usual. In early December he was given notice to appear in court on January 6 to face charges of nonpayment of child support. He failed to appear as ordered, and the appearance was rescheduled for January 31. On January 20 the county court declared him and Georgia in default of an old loan they hadn't fully repaid. Compounding his woes were several more loans he had obtained by getting someone to forge Georgia's signature.

Around this time, Joe's depression had evolved to the extent that he believed that justice could be served only by his own death. It was a justice represented by a perverse equilibrium, balancing out the death of the North Korean soldier or at least that of his friend. Thoughts of attaining that equilibrium sustained Joe for a while. As Nietzsche has said, "The thought of suicide is a great consolation: by means of it one gets successfully through many a bad night." Nonetheless, for Joe the thought of suicide eventually took on an obsessive power of its own. It became simply a matter of time before the inevitable came about.

He failed to appear in court again, and then, at noon on February 3, 1975, the marshalls arrived at Joe's parents' house to arrest Joe for nonpayment of child support. Joe explained to the officers that there was nothing that could be done. Since he didn't have any money, he'd have to go to jail. The sheriff who knew Joe offered to loan him the money. Joe refused, saying he wasn't going to borrow anymore. He then asked if he could make a phone call to Georgia at the French Lick Medco Center, where she helped cook and serve meals. First Joe called Georgia's house hoping to speak to Eddie, his favorite child. Eddie was at school, and Linda's husband at the time, Ben Campbell, answered the phone. Joe explained that he couldn't take it anymore and that he was going to kill himself. Though Joe had threatened to kill himself before (whenever Georgia had said she was going to leave him), Ben was concerned and tried to keep him on the phone and to reason with him. Joe then told Ben, "Take care of my little girl," and hung up midsentence. Ben called back, but the line was busy. Then, while the officers waited along with Joe's parents in the front room, Joe phoned Georgia. He reached her at the nursing home and announced into the phone, "I want you to hear this." Then he pulled the trigger, killing himself with a shotgun blast to the head. He had made certain, once and for all, that long, overdue "justice" was finally served.

For Georgia, the subsequent weeks and months were intensely difficult; she struggled with the guilt that she should have tried to do more to prevent Joe's death. She says today that she "almost had a nervous breakdown when Joe died." Friends and relatives say that Georgia is still bitter and guilt-ridden over the death. "I think they all blamed me for his death," says Georgia. Mike appears to have been the family member most affected by Joe's death. For his own peculiar reason, Joe had often gone out of his way to give Mark attention while at the same time deliberately shunning Mike. "Mike had a terrible time of it because he felt neglected by his dad," says a relative. When a *Sports Illustrated* story years later implied that Joe's death might have been related to Larry's decision to leave IU, Georgia said, "Sure [Joe] wanted Larry to go to IU, but [his death] was something that built up over many years. It was a tragic death that hurt all of us. Larry doesn't feel guilty. In a case like that, the whole family feels guilty. But life goes on…Larry goes on." Joe hadn't been the only exemplar of toughness in the Bird household. Larry compares his mother's toughness to his father's, "My mother's the same way. She worked her ass off." But more than just setting an example, it was Georgia's outspoken philosophy about work that made an indelible impression on her son. "You can have, and if you don't have to work for it, what do you learn?" says Georgia. "But if you have to sweat and work and maybe not have enough, I think that makes you stronger. I think that makes you appreciate what you got."

Georgia was the embodiment of her theory as she weathered her family's economic circumstances, along with her husband's alcoholism and suicide, and still managed to maintain two jobs. She worked nights throughout the time that Larry was in high school and college. During her stint at Flick's café, she would come to work at two in the morning to bake doughnuts for the next day's breakfast. She routinely traveled the half mile from home on foot. Her example did not go unheeded; Larry learned his lesson well. "My mother had a hard life," he has said. "She worked for everything she got, and that's what I try to do. Every time I play a game I think of my family, I think about things I've done for my mother and my grandmother. It gives me a little inspiration out there." Says Georgia of her son's work ethic, "He is a very poor loser. The thing of it is, if you don't win but give your all, that's no big sin. But if you don't put out your all, that's something else."

Larry and his mother are similar in more respects than just attitude. In looks and in temperament, they are strikingly alike. Not only do they share some similar facial features, but Georgia stands six feet tall (Joe was an inch shorter). Moreover, Georgia, like her son, is also reserved, particularly with strangers. However, both Larry and she possess strong opinions as evidenced by their opposite views of Bobby Knight. And there is no doubt that it's Georgia who has most determined her son's personality. It should come as no surprise, then, that Georgia carries a special feeling for her third son. "All my kids have been good, but to have a superstar, really! Well I usually don't [need to] brag on [Larry]....He always played as though he had to be perfect." That need for perfection may have been born out of the same sense of maternal pride. For, from Georgia's special feeling for Larry, (not to mention the extraordinary doting of Larry's grandmother), there came the needed confidence and the impetus for success. "A man who has been the indisputable favorite of his mother keeps for life the feeling of a conqueror, that confidence of success that often induces real success," says Freud.

Like his mother, Larry had an enormous struggle on his hands in the aftermath of his father's death. "The death crushed [Larry]," says Jim Jones. For a month immediately following the death, Larry waged a fierce battle with his emotions. "Larry got over the death himself," says Jones. In so doing, he allowed few a glimpse of his real sentiments. "[Lizzie and Georgia] knew how deeply affected Larry was, although he didn't show his unhappiness to many people," says Larry's aunt. Throughout his period of unhappiness, which conjoined with his own personal crisis, Larry sought to understand why such a thing had happened. In his own limited kind of therapy, Larry, to an extent, reconciled himself to the death. He came to understand and accept that there were no special insights and no easy answers to be gained. "You don't know what people [who want to commit suicide] are thinking," Larry says. In the period following the death, however, it was Larry's behavior that proved inscrutable. For, Larry withdrew even more, retreating to the basketball court for his solace.

Larry now paints his response in more obvious terms. At face value, it is the response of simple stoicism. But beneath that stoicism operates a much more dramatic kind of pain and denial. Larry now maintains that the death was "not really" devastating or disorienting. "Back then I just lived day to day. And something like [a suicide] is part of life. You go on." In addition, Larry remains philosophical about the universality of both suicide and adversity. It's not so much the nature of the tragedy that counts, he contends, but the strength of those who must cope with it. "If my father was the only one who ever committed suicide, it probably would be something. But he wasn't. [Suicide] happens every day.... Everybody runs into some problems in their lifetime, and it's just how you can adjust to [those problems]." Larry's defensiveness is hinted at in his denial of the extraordinary nature of the event. And his past defensiveness has been even more evident. The responses have ranged from Larry's boycott of the press, following the first public disclosure of the suicide (which appeared in the before-mentioned *Sports Illustrated* article during Larry's junior year at State), to his later refusal to even discuss the matter.

Certainly, the perceptions of others belie the everyday face Larry attempts to present. Such perceptions claim that there is no doubt that the tragedy served to shake up Larry's life. Larry's reflection on that experience explains, to some extent, the process he went through as he reconciled himself to the painful actuality. "At times [the adversity] can tell you to quit and try something else and [you] get frustrated. But if you don't have a strong mind, you won't overcome the adversities, and you just have to keep pushing and go as hard as you possibly can." Other observers agree that, for all of Larry's strength of mind to begin with, the debacle made him stronger. Georgia believes that Larry's commitment and desire to succeed in basketball became even greater in the ensuing months. For his part, Coach Holland says, "I think mentally, [the death] maybe had something to do with Larry straightening himself out...his father meant a lot to him."

Indeed, the suicide had shock value for Larry. For the first time, he sat down and thought about his life: "After doing a lot of thinking and getting my priorities straight, I felt that a college education and some other things are what I wanted in life," says Larry. As important as those conscious decisions were, it was the unconscious decisions, or sublimations, that once again played a vital role in the Larry Bird who emerged from his period of mourning. Armed with a new determination and perspective, stemming from his new priorities, Larry found himself refueled by the familiar subterranean forces intensified by the recent tragedy. Similar to the drive which had fed off his youthful pain, unhappiness, and anger, there had arisen an even more powerful drive. For Larry found psychological refuge on the basketball court, and basketball once again appropriated the unresolved psychological issues in Larry's life.

*   *   *

Larry wasn't ready to commit to college right away. The pain of his aborted college experiences, and of his father's death, was still too fresh. With his mother running interference for him, Larry was able to avoid the pressure of the college recruiters and find some peace of mind. Nevertheless, by February, the first wave of college recruiters began to appear. One of the reasons for their appearance was none too conventional. Coach Holland had gone to school just up the highway in Paoli. One of his classmates had been Eric Dillon, who began publishing one of the more influential scouting report newsletters in the country during the early seventies. Based in Texas, Dillon never had the opportunity to see Larry play until his abbreviated stint in the notorious All-Star game. Dillon, however, was undaunted by Larry's minimal exposure. As Holland explains, "[Dillon is] really a big bullshitter. But he knows his basketball." As a result, when Dillon heard Larry had dropped out of school, "he put in his [newsletter] that 'this kid [in French Lick] could be the number-one player in the nation(!), but right now he's undecided on what he wants to do.'" It was an incredible tout for someone who hadn't even been considered good enough to start on the Indiana All-Star team. The irony was that without this bizarre boost, Larry would have received considerably less attention. After all, when Larry had entered college there had been some question about his ability to handle tougher competition. So, many schools simply wrote him off when he dropped out of IU, figuring that he couldn't compete.

Also contributing to Larry's newfound popularity was his involvement in AAU competition. About the time of Joe's death, Larry became involved with an area AAU team operating out of Mitchell. It was nearing March when Larry led the team to the state championship while being named the outstanding player in the state tournament. Then, on March 7, Larry won MVP honors in the midwest regional which featured six state champion teams from the region. The MVP trophy honored "Larry Byrd." And with the ensuing publicity, a second wave of recruiting began. As it was, Indiana State had maintained an interest ever since their discovery that Larry had left IU. At the same time, State had posted its second straight losing season with a 12–14 record. Attendance had averaged only 4,000 at the school's brand-new 10,220-seat basketball facility, and pressure for a winning season was intensifying. When Bob King was hired as the school's athletic director in 1974, he was told that one of his three priorities was to develop a winning basketball program. Previously, King had been the head basketball coach at New Mexico, where he built a successful program with ten straight winning seasons and four postseason tournament appearances. In 1972, he had been forced to retire due to what was described as "chronic knee problems." But as pressure mounted for bettering State's basketball fortunes, King decided to take over the team. His first move as head coach in the spring of 1975 was to direct his assistant coaches, Bill Hodges and Stan Evans, to recruit Larry Bird.

While King was planning how he might rebuild State's basketball fortunes, people in the valley continued to exert pressure on Larry to go back to college. "The people in town never let Larry forget he had quit, and I didn't like that," says Georgia. "I kept praying that something would happen and he'd go back to school somewhere." Georgia had wanted Larry to go to State rather than IU from the beginning. Still, she was faithful to Larry's wishes in helping to discourage all recruiters, including those from State. "Larry wanted me to tell everybody he wasn't available and I told Coach Hodges just that. But I'm glad [Hodges] didn't give up. The difference was that Indiana State was more persistent than anyone else," says Georgia. From Larry's perspective, it is likely that he had resolved to go back to college, but he was not yet ready to publicly commit to it. Whether he would have gone back to school without the effective persuasion of State's recruiters is another question. But in the final analysis, that Larry Bird had always been the first priority of State's program was an important consideration.

State's continued interest, as evidenced by the persistence of its assistant coaches, was a persuasive factor for Larry. He had been more comfortable with the idea of going to State from the beginning, even in high school. However, because of his immaturity and all the pressure in favor of IU, he had capitulated to the stronger personalities around him. "I found I wanted a place I could relate to. IU was too big for that," Larry says. Yet Larry wasn't above putting up a few roadblocks to interested recruiters before he finally made up his mind. Enlisting the reluctant assistance of his mother and grandmother, Larry succeeded in buying himself some time until State came along. Coach Hodges gives his version of the events that led to

Larry's finally committing to State: "We identified ourselves, and at first he didn't seem to want to talk. But we said we weren't there to pressure him, just to talk and to tell him a few things about the school and the basketball program since Coach King had taken over. He finally consented to let us come over to his grandmother's house and we talked for an hour or so." According to Stan Evans, Larry barely said a word. He spoke to his grandmother a few times but otherwise he just looked down at the floor. Hodges adds, "He didn't agree to come then, but I felt sure that he would. About a week later he said he'd give it a try." With his commitment Larry added a boast that might have seemed a little presumptuous at the time, but now seems remarkable if only for its prescience. "Indiana State might not be very good right now, but it will be when I get there."

Armed with that kind of bravado, Larry moved off to Terre Haute, intent on proving himself to the many skeptics. Despite the outward display of confidence, he had been chastened by the experiences of the past year. He had weathered the worst; he had learned, and this time he was prepared. After all, what surprises could Terre Haute provide after the experiences of the past year? Despite the considerable pain, or maybe because of it, those experiences had been liberating. Larry had survived all the pressures in addition to his own doubts. Everything had been changed, and it had been changed in a way that could hardly have been anticipated. The result was that this time there would be no turning back; the future belonged to Larry.

8 / Bursting onto the Scene: Indiana State, 1975–1977

Larry's move to Terre Haute in June of 1975 helped him, at least consciously, to get over his father's death. Until then, Larry had been even "more moody" than usual. According to Janet Condra, his fiancée at the time, Larry seemed to improve "when he came up to [Terre Haute], maybe because he wasn't in [French Lick]." He didn't talk about the death then or later. "The only time I ever heard him mention his dad was [when] he wished [his dad] could have seen him play ball,...and I doubt that he's talked about [the death] with anyone," says Janet. With his move to Terre Haute, Larry was able to accept the loss of his father and embark on a new life. As Georgia had noted earlier, Larry had become more committed to basketball and had developed a better sense of his priorities. Larry reinforced this perspective with his own comments on his first year in Terre Haute. "I've matured a lot, and I'm ready to play. I know what I want out of basketball now. As a 17-year-old I didn't know."

It was after an unusually difficult practice during the fall that Larry gave an indication of his newfound maturity when he remarked to teammate Rick Williams, with surprising confidence, that no matter how tough the practice is, it's worth it, because "someday this is going to make me a lot of money." In thus defining himself and what he wanted, Larry enhanced his chances of staying in Terre Haute. In addition, Larry had immediately found Terre Haute much more accommodating than Bloomington. Though Terre Haute was twice the size of Bloomington, the campus had one-third as many students. Most were from Indiana and of modest means. The students on the Bloomington campus were more likely to come from out of state and tended to have more money. Then too, Larry's adjustment was furthered by Coach King, who was extremely attentive and fatherly even before school was in session—a marked contrast to the attitude Larry had encountered in Bloomington.

Coach King knew his relationship to Larry would be critical in getting Larry to stay at ISU and was well aware that throughout Larry's life, he had been particularly susceptible to the influence of older men. In Coach King, Larry found exactly the father figure he needed.

The 52-year-old coach was perfect for the role: He was a Mormon and the father of six children, three of them boys between the ages of 22 and 27 (one of whom was also named Larry). With his silvery hair and black-framed glasses, the coach looked closer to 65. Says Rick Shaw, "Larry relied on Coach King a lot." Larry explained the relationship similarly: "[Coach King] helps me off the court as well as on. I've never seen a coach put as much time into the game as Coach King. Whenever I have a problem, I go into his office and talk with him." According to Janet, after Larry and Janet married, the coach even tried to help them with their differences. "Coach King was nice. He tried to straighten things out between Larry and me." The coach also had Larry's unqualified admiration. "Whatever Coach King would want me to do, I'd do it. He taught me how to deal with a lot of situations I was put in. . . . He's the type of guy I would like to be around every day of my life."

Larry's admiration of King was also a natural extension of the fervent loyalty that Larry always felt toward those who helped him. "I think that Larry thought about Coach King that way, because. . . he feels. . . very strongly about people who have been his people, and Bob was one of those people, one of the special people in his life," says Tom Reck, *Terre Haute Tribune-Star* sports editor. The coach inspired a similar devotion among the rest of the players and staff: "He was more than a coach to his players. He was always there, not just with Larry, but with all of them."

According to Assistant Trainer Rick Shaw, Coach King thought about the entire program as a "family." "That phrase [father figure] is probably closest because Coach King was close to his team, but also, the team was close because of Coach King," says Reck.

Beyond the surrogate family structure of team and coach, King created a familial off-campus environment for Larry as well. He arranged for five or six families to "adopt" Larry, to the extent that they "had dinner waiting for me any time I wanted it," says Larry. Also, two of Larry's closest friends from high school, Danny King and Tony Clark, were there to help Larry acclimate to his new surroundings.

Danny King, who had been a year ahead of Larry in high school, had completed his junior college eligibility the previous spring, and not long after Larry committed to State, King decided to use his last two years of basketball eligibility at ISU. King was not only a valuable recruit in his own right, but the ISU coaching staff understood that getting Danny would be crucial in helping to keep Larry in Terre Haute. "Danny King...helped Larry out a lot more than they give him credit for," says Coach Holland. King roomed with Larry that summer, and then for the first few months of the school year before Larry got married. While King was not exactly in a position to show Larry what it took to be a model student—he was something of a ladies' man and enjoyed partying—he did help make Larry more comfortable, especially in a social sense.

Tony Clark and Larry had played basketball together, starting with Biddy Ball in the fourth grade through their senior year in high school. Clark, who had always been one of Larry's best friends, made Larry feel even more at home in Terre Haute. Clark was promised a pre-October 15 basketball tryout, and failing that, a managerial position with the team for the following year, Larry's first season of eligibility. Unlike Danny King, Clark had no hope of materially helping the team—except to the extent that he made its star player feel at home.

Larry, Clark, and King ate together in the dorm, went out together at night, and didn't socialize much with the other players. A teammate remembers Larry as being "extremely shy off the court," but very animated when his French Lick friends were around. Similarly, in practice Larry kept mostly to himself, but had a special rapport with Danny King. They would share private jokes and sarcastic comments. And while competing against one another, they would have their own challenges and put-downs. And they would take every opportunity to beat on each other. As Shaw explains, "Danny was tough. He was a mean son of a gun...just like Larry who was a mean son of a gun. And just like Larry, they were both pretty close-mouthed." And each of them brought their toughness with them on the court to the benefit of the team. "Larry Bird got the ball to the right players. He was the kind of guy who grabbed you by the throat and said, 'Come on. Let's go.' Danny King did that too," says Shaw. They epitomized Coach Hodges' description of the young men he knew from southern Indiana: "hard-nosed and tough."

Young men from southern Indiana like their beer, too. As Larry described himself early in his college career, "I'm a small-town guy who likes to go out with his buddies drinking beer and chewing tobacco." According to Janet, Larry did a lot more drinking at ISU, "every weekend and occasionally during the week." One barroom incident fondly remembered by a teammate was Larry's coming to the aid of a former ISU football player he barely knew. It was typical for Larry to feel a loyalty toward anyone who had ever been part of the athletic program or "family." Mike Deakins, surrounded by four men at the Ballyhoo (one of Larry's favorite watering holes), found Larry coming to his defense (besides loyalty, one shouldn't underestimate the role played by Larry's love of challenges, like two-on-four). Agreeing to settle the issue outside, Larry and Deakins took them all on, and left the four semiconscious in the Ballyhoo parking lot.

Larry wasted little time settling in at Terre Haute. By June, Coach King had arranged for him to get a grass-mowing job at the First National Bank.* A number of players from the upcoming ISU team stayed around that summer. Center DeCarsta Webster, a 6'11" junior college transfer; Danny King from French Lick, the starting point guard; and Rick Williams led daily, informal pickup games. Williams stood 6'8" and weighed 210 pounds. He had been the leading scorer, rebounder, and the MVP for the Sycamores both his sophomore and junior years. For the upcoming season, Williams was receiving All-American consideration.

Though Larry was four years younger, at least 2 inches shorter, and 20 pounds lighter than Williams, they battled evenly throughout the summer according to Assistant Coach Stan Evans and at least one player. Tom Reck argues that Larry outplayed Williams. "He outplayed everybody. You could tell that he was going to be an impact

---

*Mowing the grass is still one of Larry's favorite methods of relaxation. He regularly mows his agent's lawn across the street from his house in Boston.

player at ISU. Former ABA great Mel Daniels, who also watched Larry play that summer, believed that he was already "good enough to play for anyone in the NBA." Coach Evans argues that the memories of both Reck and Daniels have been enhanced by hindsight. Although Larry had been recruited by Bobby Knight, there had been some initial skepticism about him because Larry hadn't stayed at IU. By midsummer, Larry erased a lot of doubts with his performance in Lebanon, Indiana's famous outdoor basketball tournament, which featured several college stars (who eventually played pro). He played for a Terre Haute team called the Hulman Stars and helped them to finish runner-up and won tournament MVP honors. It was clear to the other players that Larry was a potentially dominant player and would be a good college player. Yet, that he would become the best college player in the nation, let alone the best in the pros, was at that point still beyond everyone's wildest dreams.

Once school started, ISU's team worked out together informally until the basketball season opened on October 15. Workouts on Monday and Wednesday consisted of running three miles to the football stadium and then up the stadium stairs. Larry and some of the others would wear weight jackets during this exercise. Then the players would be driven back to the arena, where the more ambitious players, always including Larry, would play. On Tuesday and Thursday, the players would have informal weight training sessions. The first game was played at the end of November. Until then, practices ran about three hours a day. Once a week the starters, the blue team, would play against the white team, the reserves, and any redshirts, which included Larry.

Once the team actually started playing games, Larry's practice role changed. Practices were shorter, usually two hours, and the practice directly before a game would usually consist of a 45-minute run-through of the opposing team's plays. Larry's main role was to imitate their star player. The problem was that Larry always managed to score, whether by design or improvisation. No matter how well the starters played defense, they could not stop Larry. In order to boost the starters' confidence, sometimes the coaches would insert reserve player Don Edmond in Larry's place. When the starters would invariably block Edmond's shot, the coaches would congratulate the starters on their tough defense. Then Larry would go back in and continue to score on the starters every time. As the season progressed, Coach King began to work out an offensive scheme molded around Larry. And as Larry became more comfortable within the offense, his confidence grew. What was most telling, according to Edmond, was that "Larry was always under control. He always knew what to do no matter the situation."

Larry was respected by his teammates because of his hard work. While some team members don't remember Larry playing any longer than anyone else, they do acknowledge that "he played hard.... He wasn't your typical redshirt. Some good players only play hard during the games. But Larry gave a 150 percent in practice," said sports information director, Ed McKee. Tom Reck remembers Larry working after the others had left. "And even then as a redshirt, like he does now, he was probably the last one to leave all the time." Besides his work ethic, Larry's overall play had a great impact on the team's practices; though even Larry wasn't enough to bring the team's weak bench to victory when the blue and white teams scrimmaged. But Larry did stand out. The first vivid memory Assistant Trainer Rick Shaw has of Larry was a moment during one of the first blue-white games. With just a few seconds remaining, Larry picked up a loose ball with his left hand along the other team's baseline. Taking one look at the clock he heaved the basketball the full length of the court, left-handed. On its downward arc, the ball appeared to pass through the arms of gangly senior forward Janis Ludeks on its way into the basket. Stunned, the entire team ended up on the floor convulsed with laughter.

Larry was as true to his roots on the practice floor as he was on the bar floor. Just as he'd done at the Ballyhoo, Larry was quick to demonstrate unconditional loyalty to those he considered on his side. When Mike Route, a big player from the starting blue team, went after a much smaller player from the white team, Larry leveled Route with a flurry of punches. It was the last time a player from the blue team went after someone from the white. It wasn't the first time that Larry had earned the respect of his teammates. Larry had previously demonstrated his toughness in a practice-ending drill in which a ball would be rolled out on the floor and two players lined up opposite each other to go for it. The player who gained control of the ball would try to score. If he did, he could leave. The losing player would have to get back in line and do the drill over. Anything went in this drill: forearms, elbows, tackles, and punches. The more tenacious and aggressive the player, the more successful he was. Larry consistently dominated the drill.

Larry was well into his redshirt year before he began to feel comfortable in Terre Haute. "You have to find a place you can relate to. I had to be relaxed. If you don't like some place, make up your mind quick. It took me three to six months to realize I was happy with my decision." Looking back at this year of sitting out an entire season, Larry states that it was at times one of the most difficult things he had ever done. Even though Larry told the press on one occasion, "It wasn't all that bad sitting out the year without actually playing in the games," in truth, it was more painful than he let on. "That was really hard for him. He's not a watcher. The coach had to make him come to the games," says Mark Bird. Assistant Coach Evans qualifies Mark's claim and explains that Larry was encouraged to attend games, but in either case, watching could not have been an easy experience for Larry. The following season on the eve of his first game for ISU, Larry emphasized, "Man, I'm glad it's over, though. Last year I spent all season looking ahead and now it's here."

At the beginning of his sophomore season, Larry claimed to the press that he had improved a lot because "I worked on things a lot of players don't get to work on. I went through practice as if they were my games." However, players from the team say the only perceptible difference in his game between the beginning and the end of his redshirt season was his increasing confidence within Coach King's offensive system. When practice began for his sophomore season, Larry himself admitted, "I don't feel I improved half as much as I wanted, but I sat out two years waiting for this opportunity and I'm not going to blow it." When he finally began to play, it would be with a drive and a passion that had rarely been seen within the confines of the college game.

On November 8, 1975, Larry married Janet Condra. He moved out of the dorm room that he had shared for two months with Danny King and moved into married student housing with his new bride.

Janet and Larry had had a stormy romance. They had been dating for two years and had originally become engaged following high school graduation. At that time, Janet's family had paid her way to allow her to attend IU along with Larry. When Larry dropped out,

Janet felt she should finish the term for her parents' sake. They still continued to see each other on weekends and occasionally during the week. Janet had just turned 18 and Larry was 17. Both youngsters were insecure about themselves and each other. Furthermore, Larry's moodiness, uncertainty, and low self-esteem, especially after leaving IU, put an additional strain on the relationship. That Janet's life had been as circumscribed as Larry's only reinforced the obvious: The two immature adolescents were stumbling, trying to make their way through an adult relationship. The fact that she "worshipped the ground he walked on" didn't help balance the relationship either.

Larry broke off the engagement in November. The liaison had been one burdened by the couple's inability to communicate. Janet was just as shy and introverted as Larry. That Larry tended to express his feelings through actions rather than words only aggravated Janet's insecurities. Even though Janet was crushed by the broken engagement, she accepted it. "I said fine. I was really upset, so Mom and Dad drove me back to IU." But eventually Larry had a change of heart, and they got back together. An example of the couple's difficulty in communicating is the way they dealt with as important a matter as their rapprochement. "He was [at IU] that week; he drove all the way up there. Then we ended up making up. That was his way of coming up and telling me that [breaking the engagement] was not really what he wanted to do. For a lot of our relationship, I just guessed things."

Janet was homesick, and she "guessed" that Larry wanted her to be with him in French Lick, so once the term ended she left IU. Yet, despite their renewed plans to be married, the relationship continued to lack any real intimacy. Larry rarely confided in Janet. And, though he didn't necessarily confide in anyone else, he was more likely to express himself to his friends. "I'd always have to find out [how he felt] from somebody else." Larry's difficulty in expressing himself was compounded by his intense pride. The end result was that in their four-and-a-half years together, he was able to apologize to her only on one occasion. Since Janet had her own difficulties communicating, the relationship continued on a rocky course.

However, a year after the broken engagement, Janet and Larry were married. It was a marriage that seemed doomed from the start. The morning of the wedding Larry remarked to a relative that "he felt like taking off and disappearing.'' But Larry fought his instincts and stayed at the church. Janet settled in, and Coach King helped her get a job as a teller at the First National Bank. That fall, Janet claims she helped Larry with his homework and term papers, and bought his food. Yet, it was a winter of discontent. Larry would often go out with his friends and Janet would be left alone in a new city where she didn't know very many people. ''He didn't want to take me out. But if I wanted to go out with the girls, he hid his car keys from me one time so I wouldn't get to go out. But he didn't want to come out and say, 'Don't go out.' We were both really young.'' Unfortunately, when they did go out, it didn't help matters. ''He was always putting me down....It was like he was ashamed of me. But there was a lot of insecurity, and it really affected me later on.'' With time, Janet grew even more unhappy. Larry's ambivalence and frequent moodiness only served to further baffle his young wife. ''He's not a very open person, but I got a lot of conflict from Larry. We were really in a kind of odd relationship.''

By late summer, Janet was beside herself. In a desperate attempt to spur a change in the relationship, Janet filed for divorce. ''I got to the point where I'd gone bananas. And I thought, here I am, just turned 20, what am I going to do? I didn't really intend to go through with [the divorce], not really. But I followed up on it, maybe that was to scare him, wake him up or something. So I just filed.'' Even though Janet claims neither she nor Larry wanted the divorce, they had become entangled in something beyond their control. ''We were both stubborn, and I didn't want to back down, and he couldn't either. Several times I was going to drop [the divorce suit], and I didn't, and it was like [playing] chicken—who could hold out the longest.'' The day of the divorce proceeding, they were still living together. And neither desired to go through with the action. ''Right in the middle of the divorce, I just wanted to stop. It just seemed like it was finally too late.'' On October 31, 1976, they divorced.

Janet moved out only one week short of a year after the wedding. But their relationship was hardly over. Though Janet had moved into her own apartment on the other side of town, she continued to stay in married student housing with Larry much of the time. Larry and Janet even started thinking about remarriage. However, Larry's brother Mark, and a friend, Jeff Willoughby, moved into the apartment with Larry, and if Larry and Janet were unable to control their own destinies, at least Mark would try. "Mark was always telling Larry, 'Do this, don't do this.' I think Mark was a lot of the reason why we didn't get remarried. We were going to get married again, and I knew Mark was saying no, because Tony [Clark] used to tell me." The ultimate evidence of the lack of control Larry and Janet exerted over their lives was manifested a month after the divorce: Janet became pregnant. Though Larry never discussed the topic, some of Larry's family and friends mistakenly believed that Janet had duped Larry into thinking she was still on the pill after their divorce. Janet explains that she had not been on the pill since the first few months of the marriage because of medical reasons and that of course Larry was fully aware of this. The pregnancy occurred on, or within a day of, Larry's first college game, which in many ways symbolized Larry's first real chance at freedom and control over his life. Soon it began to seem that the only time Larry ever had complete freedom in his life was when he was on the basketball court.

As the season progressed, Larry's basketball success and sense of worth grew. He became nicer to Janet, which is not to say that his sense of frustration and helplessness over Janet's pregnancy didn't sometimes overwhelm him. On the court, he was experiencing the rapture of total commitment, freedom, and near-perfect execution. Away from the court, he was experiencing the same old sense of being a slave to the external circumstances of his life. Two incidents highlight Larry's tormented ambivalence as well as his unconscious longing to end the only romantic relationship he had ever known. As his self-esteem grew, he no longer felt as dependent upon the relationship with Janet as he once did. But Janet's pregnancy only served to intensify Larry's guilt over wanting to leave, as well as his resentment at being "sabotaged" from doing so.

One night about two months into the pregnancy Janet became very ill after taking some medicine. In fact, she'd been ailing all week. This time she woke Larry and asked him to take her to the hospital emergency room. Larry refused. "He said I was [being] a big baby," Janet says. "So Tony [Clark] had to take me to the emergency room, and then they [admitted] me." As it turned out, Janet's condition wasn't serious and the pregnancy continued unharmed. But for Larry and Janet, the incident was the beginning of the end. Yet Larry could not bring himself to face the inevitable fact that he wanted to end the relationship, even when it had become apparent to everyone around him. "Larry didn't come to see me until the day I got out of the hospital. I guess that my mom had really chewed him out, and she told him that he was going to come in and tell me that he didn't want to see me anymore. But he came [into the hospital room] like everything was fine. After that...I didn't stay over all the time, maybe two nights a week. Then it just kind of tapered off until he started the [new school] year." Obviously, things were coming to a close, but it had taken the arrival of fellow student Dinah Mattingly before Larry could completely make the break. Dinah, who like other students spent a lot of time at the popular Ballyhoo, knew and dated several players on the team. One evening at the Ballyhoo, Janet's sister heard Dinah say that she was interested in Larry. Others affirm that Dinah had announced her interest in Larry before. The interest was obviously mutual for by spring, Larry and Dinah had become a couple. (Dinah and Larry have been together ever since; they announced their engagement in the summer of 1987.) But the entrance of Dinah upon the Birds' domestic scene created a great deal of hard feelings. According to Janet, "It got pretty bitter in the end." About six months into her pregnancy, Janet confronted Larry about Dinah as he returned home from the bar with Tony Clark. An argument ensued, and Larry hit Janet in the shoulder and shoved her, which caused her to fall. Janet was not really hurt, but Larry went into his room, and didn't emerge until some time the next day. Says Janet, "I just picked myself up in embarrassment and I'm thinking, God, I can't believe he did that." However, Larry had never before, and has probably never since struck out in such a fashion.

The summer before Larry's first year of eligibility, the Sycamores were coming off their first winning season in three years with a 13–12 record. And Shaw, for one, believed that the presence of Larry in practice probably had made the difference. The new school year brought Harry Morgan, a standout junior college transfer, who was designated to handle one of the forward spots on the team along with Larry. The other three designated starters, DeCarsta Webster, Danny King, and Jimmy Smith, had started most if not all of the time the previous season. Morgan and Larry worked together in the summer, first at the First National and then at the Terre Haute Boys' Club, where a lot of ISU players played when Hulman Arena was closed for the summer.

One day, when Larry and Morgan were playing at the Boys' Club, Larry suddenly had trouble catching his breath. He was taken to the hospital, where it was discovered that he had suffered a collapsed lung. Larry was unable to play for about two months. Still, the lay-off didn't affect the impact that numerous observers, and especially Coach King, expected him to have in the coming season: "Larry is a great college prospect. He does everything well and although he hasn't played a minute of college basketball yet, we know he's the complete player." Evans notes today that King was particularly anxious to hype State's program due to past attendance problems. And Larry was the best candidate for that hype because he was an unknown and a better player than anyone had expected. King said, "Larry is as fine a player as I've ever coached and that takes in a few [including ABA great Mel Daniels]. I think he's going to be super." Evans adds that no one connected with the program at the time believed King's statement, not even King himself.

Expectations for ISU's 1976–77 season were not high. Seasoned observers believed that a .500 season was unlikely. A player with only two years of organized basketball experience, who was not even considered to be one of the state's top high school seniors, doesn't single-handedly turn around a team's fortunes. Yet that is exactly what happened.

On November 15, Larry made his unofficial debut, in an exhibition game against the Brazilian National Team. Of the mere 5,000 fans in attendance, more than a few had come simply to see if the kid could play. With 31 points, 15 rebounds, and 8 assists, and a 96–76 win, Larry convinced both the curious and the dubious. His official debut came on November 27, and this time Larry scored 31 points with 18 rebounds and 10 assists, in an 81–60 victory against Chicago State. Indeed, when the smoke had cleared, ISU had won its first four games (not counting the exhibition), and Larry had averaged a remarkable 27.5 points and 16.7 rebounds per game. He had shot 52 percent from the field. Larry had also been named the MVP of the third annual Hall of Fame Classic held at Hulman Arena, along with Danny King, and Bob Heaton of the University of Denver (the latter would transfer to ISU at the end of the season), who made the all-tourney team. The fifth game of the year came on the road against nationally ranked Purdue, and though ISU was defeated 82–68, Larry convinced the last of the remaining skeptics with 27 points, 18 rebounds, and 6 assists. Three games later, ISU's record stood at 7–1. Even Coach King, with all of his high expectations, was impressed. The 7–1 record was no fluke; Larry was excelling at a variety of aspects of the game. "Larry's really fluid," said King. "And he's quicker than he appears. He can handle the ball and pass it better than most of the guards in the country. ISU physiologist Dr. Robert McDavid, who tested Larry's agility, supported his claim. "When a person is 6'9", he's usually not average, not even in the 50th percentile. [Larry] is in the 90th percentile."

King explained how Larry's athletic talents enhanced the offense designed to revolve around him. "Larry just likes to play. He's a kid that is a reaction type of player, so we give him a lot of freedom; we just let him play his game. We're not a pattern ball club. Anybody who runs a passing game will have to have a few general rules, but you need to let the players use their natural abilities. That's the strategy of our offense. And Larry is ambidextrous...so that helps him create even more situations for himself." Similarly, in a veiled reference to Bobby Knight and Indiana, Assistant Coach Hodges spoke about how much the ISU offense had helped Larry's game. "I think had Larry gone someplace else—to a more disciplined team—he might have become more inhibited. We've given him a free rein here to move anywhere he wants without the ball. We set the offense to go where he goes, and I think that's helped him develop into the all-around player he is." Ironically, ISU's system did not allow nearly as much freedom as King and Hodges implied. In fact, the offense, based on Johnny Wooden's offensive patterns at UCLA, was quite structured. But, since coming to Terre Haute, Larry had improved his game. Coach King, he said, had helped him defensively and to become a better all-around player. "I shoot better outside now, have more power moves inside, and I can tell where the ball's coming off on a miss. I can jump better, and I'm quicker now." It also didn't hurt that he had grown about three inches and gained around twenty-five pounds.

ISU had just become a member of the Missouri Valley Conference (though they would have to wait until next season to compete for the conference championship) so everyone was excited about their first MVC opponent, West Texas State. By now, Larry had begun to attract considerable regional interest, and the postgame questions often came around to the NBA. "If [playing in the NBA] happens, great," he would reply, "but first I'm looking forward to playing in the Valley [MVC]." In the meantime, press curiosity continued to grow about the kid who had come out of nowhere, the one who looked so uncomfortable talking to the media. Explained Ed McKee, ISU sports information director, "Off court, Larry is real shy. But once he's on the court, it's a whole new world—*his* world." Increasingly, fans went to ISU's games just to witness Larry's world on the court, including the 100 fans from French Lick who would travel the seventy miles to Terre Haute for every home game. When Larry had gone home to the valley for Christmas he had been treated even better than when he had been the valley's high school star; quite a contrast to his treatment only two years before when he'd dropped out of Northwood. The valley, forever living through Larry, was feeling good about itself again.

The turning point of the season in terms of Larry's popularity came on December 28 against Drake. The weather had been terrible all week, and many people had free time because of the holidays. Unexpectedly, a huge walk-up crowd appeared, forcing a delay in the start of the game. They were treated to an exciting 79–73 double-overtime win that dispelled the impression left by King's predecessor, Gordon Stauffer, that ISU basketball was a boring and slowdown affair. Larry's play also inspired what was to become a new generation of ISU basketball fans.

Fan interest was further heightened by Butler star John Dunn. He challenged Larry and made a few inflammatory comments to the Indianapolis press. Even though the temperature was 25 below and a blizzard was raging outside, 7,838 fans cheered inside as ISU beat Butler 90–67. Savoring the challenge, Larry totaled 42 points, 11 rebounds, and 7 assists. It was the start of an amazing hot streak, in which over the course of 10 straight games, Larry averaged 40 points per game. And just two games after the Butler game, Larry broke the ISU single-game scoring record with 47 points against Missouri–St. Louis. With that victory the cagers boosted their record to an impressive 15–1. One victory later, with a streak of 12 wins, ISU entered the national spotlight for the first time, gaining the 19th ranking in the UPI poll.

Unfortunately, in their next game on the road, against Illinois

State, the winning streak came to an end, despite Larry's 40 points and 16 rebounds. The game was the first in a series of highly volatile and wildly contested games between these two teams throughout the Bird era.

Larry's aunt describes the atmosphere at the game: "A few of the Redbirds' fans, sitting next to the sparse Indiana State rooters, aimed a vulgar, nonverbal sign at the visitors, while also shouting obscenities. As Larry began racking up his score,...he was greeted with chants of 'Birdshit' every time he got hold of the ball. At one point, Larry was fouled and landed on the sidelines, lying on his back. A Redbird 'fan' yelled right into Larry's face." But ISU would get its chance for revenge soon enough. The two teams would play again in a mere six days, this time in Hulman Arena. So, with the largest home crowd in ISU history on hand (10,102), the Sycamores paid back Illinois State, winning by 16 points as Larry again scored 40 points.

Four victories later, ISU hosted its final home game of the season, beating Loyola of Chicago, 83–72, in a game which produced the earliest sellout in ISU history. Although Larry scored 45 points, the most telling part of his performance was a series of plays when he didn't score. Johnny Nelson, a 5'7" senior, had become a crowd favorite in spite of, or maybe because of, the fact that he rarely played. In the last moments of the game Larry passed up an easy lay-up that would have allowed him to tie his school scoring record with 47 points. Instead, Larry kicked the ball outside to Nelson, so he could score in his last home game. Nelson missed, but Larry got the rebound and again passed up a shot in order to get the ball back to Nelson. When Nelson missed again, Larry somehow managed to get another offensive rebound, refused to put the ball back up, and delivered the ball to Nelson once again. By now Nelson was laughing so hard that he couldn't even shoot. Larry's behavior was typical of the selflessness that so endeared him to his teammates.

ISU's next-to-last game was a rematch with Butler and the brash John Dunn. This time, Dunn was not so provocative with the press. It didn't matter. Larry was even more dominant than he had been the first game, tying his single-game scoring record of 47 points. After a methodical win over Valparaiso, the team finished the season with a school record, 25 wins and 2 losses. Even though there was some criticism of the weak schedule, the Sycamores were still ranked 16th in the nation in the final season poll. As a result, they were invited to play in the National Invitational Tournament, held annually at Madison Square Garden in New York. It was the first time ISU had ever received a postseason bid to a major college tourney. But in order to get to New York, the team would have to win a first-round game against the University of Houston at Hofheinz Pavilion in Houston. In the Pavilion's seven-year existence, the Cougars had lost fewer than ten games. Houston was led by first team All-American guard Otis Birdsong, captain of the United States Pan American basketball team the previous year. Of course, the game was being labeled a showdown between Birdsong and Bird.

For Sycamore fans, it was unfortunate that there were eight other players on the court, because, although Larry won the battle, ISU lost the war. He had a brilliant game, outscoring Birdsong by 14 points with 44, and leading both teams with 14 rebounds. Still, the Cougars prevailed, 83–82. There would be no New York trip. Larry had missed only 9 out of 28 shots. However, one of the misses was a shot at the buzzer from the baseline which had just rimmed out, and many observers thought he had been fouled. When asked to comment on the alleged foul, Larry shrugged and said, "I thought I was fouled too, but I can't blame the official for not calling a foul like that in front of those fans down in Houston." While Larry managed to hide his disappointment fairly well, one Sycamore fan couldn't mask hers: "I missed only two home games this year," said Georgia. "I was hoping to go to New York. I've never been to New York. I haven't been any place."

Upon their arrival back at Terre Haute's airport, Hulman Field, Larry and his teammates were greeted by more fans than had been at several home games one year earlier. After a long ovation, Larry responded, "We don't want no applause, we want money." From the crowd came the reply, "You'll get yours in two years!" It was an ironic statement, because in a matter of days, there was speculation that Larry would "go hardship" and turn pro at the end of the year. The rumor appeared to be based solely on the Bird family's financial status in tandem with Larry's spectacular season. But anyone who knew Larry realized that Larry was determined to stay in Terre Haute. His mother's comments basically reflected Larry's feelings on the matter. "Money isn't everything. We've not had any real problems, and he has two years to go. I would like for him to stay. That is what I hope. He's real satisfied with school.'' Moreover, Larry had just begun to feel comfortable in Terre Haute; he was hardly ready to begin considering living in a big NBA city. He was also not ready to abandon the fan support that he'd just gotten a chance to enjoy. "It's really a great feeling knowing you have people behind you," he said following the season. Indeed, he couldn't wait for the next college season. "We'll be a better team next year and I know I'll be playing more basketball this summer. I had a collapsed lung last year and missed about two months....I need to strengthen my legs, I know that.''

The thought of Larry working harder over the summer to improve his game must have been a frightening one for future ISU opponents. Overall, Larry had achieved one of the most extraordinary first seasons in college basketball history. And according to Mel Daniels, a former ABA star with the Indiana Pacers, Larry was already playing at a professional level. "We brought a bunch of players from [the Pacers]; we brought Freddie Lewis, Roger Brown, and Bob Netolicky to Terre Haute to scrimmage against the Bird. Larry dominated them as a sophomore.'' Coach Evans remembers that not only were the three Pacers at the end of their careers, but they came in out of season and out of shape.

However, Larry's postseason recognition was pretty impressive considering the grumbling by the press and other coaches about the team's weak schedule and the fact that no one had even heard of Larry four months before the selection of the All-America teams. He was rewarded with third-team All-America recognition from the UPI, honorable mention from the AP, second team from the U.S. Basketball Writers Association, special mention from the *Sporting News,* and first team from *Sportfolio*. In addition, Larry finished tenth in the voting for the Adolph Rupp Award, the AP college player of the year. As the journalists' voting indicated, Larry was well received by the press. And Larry's relations with the press had been pretty good all season. Even so, Larry was still extremely guarded. The seeds of his basic discontent with press attention were already present. And he worried that the media's singling him out would affect the other players: "I felt embarrassed about them always doing stories on me instead of the team. The team deserved the publicity.''

A similar note of humility slipped into Larry's comments about Harry Morgan, though in this case, it was also part and parcel of a shrewd understanding about what makes a team work well together.

For, on several occasions, Larry had remarked to the press, "There is one guy [Harry Morgan] on the team, who is better than me." While Harry was good (he had been second leading scorer with a 16.8 average), the claim was ridiculous. Yet Harry believed, or wanted to believe, that what Larry was saying was true. And Larry at some level, understood Harry's need. Says Rick Shaw: "Larry was smart enough to try to bring out the best in each one of his teammates." For his part, Harry greatly respected Larry's talent: "They talked about all this Kent Benson [who played with the Indiana All-Stars one year before Larry] stuff. I couldn't wait for Larry to start playing with us last year. I knew Larry could show [Benson] up.... He's got such a great all-around game. He makes things happen. If he sees you open, he'll get you the ball. I've learned a lot from Larry as far as scoring is concerned. I've watched him a lot. He takes his time and just puts it in the hole."

Overall, it was becoming increasingly evident that Larry was an extraordinary talent. "I knew he had the ability to turn a program around all by himself...that he was special," said Coach King. The key to Larry's greatness, he claimed, was in Larry's hands. "He's naturally left-handed even though he shoots with his right.... He can throw an outlet pass the length of the floor left-handed, and he eats and writes left-handed." Larry's appraisal of the program's newfound success was, as usual, more modest. "Building a sports program means getting the right people in the right places at the right time. I just lucked into it." Perhaps more accurately, ISU "just lucked into it," which isn't to say that Larry didn't have his own share of luck. For one thing, Larry had been lucky to avoid injury. Since he was the kind of player who would dive after every loose ball, his coaches and teammates held their collective breath every time he hurled himself into the stands. However, during the season, Larry suffered nothing worse than a bad knee bruise.

In June, twenty of the top undergraduate players in the country were selected to try out for the World University Games to be held in Sofia, Bulgaria. The tryouts and the initial practices were to be held in July at the University of Louisville, since Denny Crum was coaching the team. Then the team was to travel to Italy for a two-week tournament, to Yugoslavia for another, and then to Bulgaria for the World Games. In all, the team would be together, and on the road, for eight weeks, six of them in Europe. When Larry received his invitation, he was flattered, but when he heard about the amount of traveling, he began to have second thoughts. Coach King understood that without a push Larry was unlikely to go. He pushed.

Upon arriving in Louisville, Larry was quickly named as a starter —the youngest of the starting five. Georgia was excited: "I never imagined one of my sons would be going to Europe." Needless to say, neither had Larry. But by the middle of July the team had arrived in Rome.

Playing against the national teams of various European countries, the Americans were frequently pitted against much older players. Nevertheless, they prevailed in 13 of the 17 contests played in Italy and Yugoslavia. In one four-game tournament, Larry was named the MVP. In Sofia, after beating the Soviets early in the competition, the Americans played them again for the gold medal, winning again as Larry scored 14 points. In all, the US had won 8 out of 8 games. Larry was named the team's MVP.

If few of the games ended very dramatically, that was fine; the Americans had had quite enough drama in their game against the Cubans. At the beginning of the second half, a fight broke out. Larry wasn't sure just what precipitated the brawl: "Things happened so fast. It lasted about ten or twelve minutes. I was swinging. I really didn't know what I was doing." Mostly Larry was trying to protect himself because "chairs were flying, bottles were being thrown. They had us outnumbered....They won [the fight]." But the Cubans "fell apart after that." And the US won the game.

Larry's European experience was tainted by a combination of dysentery and home sickness. He lost about twenty pounds, down from 225. A postcard Larry sent his mother (which was reprinted in a book by his aunt) sums up his attitude:

> Dear Mom:
>
> Just a note to tell you that I'm never leaving the U.S. again. This place is a dump. We are playing on an outside court. But that's the way it is. I'm a Hell of a long way from home, and we are six hours ahead of you in time. Got to go.
>
> Larry
>
> I want to come home.

Larry was also unimpressed with the European women, the major caveat being their unshaven legs and underarms. Upon arriving back in Terre Haute, Larry was greeted by news reporters and TV people, who asked him what the biggest thrill of his European trip had been. "Landing in Terre Haute," Larry replied. Yet the trip had not been a total disaster, at least in basketball terms: "Over there I tried working on my rebounding, and I tried to play more defense because I knew I could use it and I knew I wouldn't shoot as much as I would on my own team."

In Larry's first two years in Terre Haute, he had gone through as remarkable a series of events as could be imagined. When his odyssey began, he was a shell-shocked adolescent who had never been away from home before. When it ended, he was a nationally known basketball star arriving home from six weeks in Europe. If not for a concerned and fatherly coach, it's possible he might have bolted school for a third time. He had grown, both emotionally and physically. In a three-month period, he had confronted the dissolution of a marriage and the fathering of a child. What's more, he had become an overnight basketball sensation, in a painstaking journey in which he consolidated the trust and respect of his teammates by his toughness, hard work, and loyalty. A naive unknown had metamorphosed into the most dominant college player in the country.

9 "A Phenomenon": Indiana State, 1977–1978

At the beginning of his junior year, to his shock and dismay, Larry found that he had become something of a national celebrity. His heretofore sheltered and comfortable world had been opened up and subjected to intense scrutiny from the media and the fans almost overnight, his cherished and zealously guarded privacy put under siege. As a nonprofessional but scholarship athlete, some of the new intrusions were warranted, others were not. These added pressures would prove difficult for him, both on and off the court. Larry had to grapple with the burdens of expectation, injury, losing, the press, and the temptation to cash in by going pro. "All of a sudden the world seemed to surround me in my junior year in college, and I really wasn't prepared for it. Being on top of the world is probably a phenomenon I'll never understand," Larry said.

Larry was ill-prepared for the revolution in his status. After all, it had only been a year since he had traveled on an airplane for the first time. Now, one year later, Larry had been chosen to grace the cover of the prestigious college basketball issue of *Sports Illustrated*, a de facto confirmation of his position as the premier college basketball player in the land. The *SI* cover was also a revelation of sorts. Since the ISU team had never before appeared on national TV, many fans outside of Indiana (automatically) had assumed that Larry was black.

The cover photo itself almost hadn't happened. Larry had flown to Chicago for the photo session only at the urging of Coach King. Cheerleader Sharon Senefeld, who posed in the foreground of the cover shot explains: "He couldn't understand why he should be there." Larry's puzzlement at all the sudden interest in him reflected more than a lack of understanding; it evidenced an authentic humility and shyness. "He's a very humble person, he has no star syndrome," says Hodges. "The national exposure doesn't mean a whole lot to me," he said just after doing the cover. "I didn't really want to be on the cover, but the coach told me I should, so I did."

The *Sports Illustrated* photo session wasn't the only photo feature that required King to persuade Larry. The 1977–78 *Playboy* All-American team was another situation that necessitated travel, this time to Lake Geneva, Wisconsin. "One of his friends said he wore his Caterpillar cap* right up until the time they went into the Playboy Club and had it on again as soon as they walked out," says King. But at least one member of the Bird family was excited about the photo opportunity. "*Playboy* was the best," says Georgia Bird. "It was the first [*Playboy*] I ever had in my whole life or even looked at."

Georgia entertained quite a different perspective from her son on more than just the *Playboy* publicity. Remarking that her son had no concept of how famous he was, Georgia believed that "[the realization] will hit hard one of these days. It may hit him so hard it will knock him down." But not long after the season began, he appeared to have a better grasp on his notoriety. "You know, you've got to put up with the good and the bad. The good of it is that people look up to you. But the bad of it is they're always wanting to be around you, and sometimes it's bothersome. I like to be alone. I'm from a small town where you have a lot of privacy. But as far as changin' my attitude toward things, the publicity, and all that,...I do what I want to do and if someone doesn't like it...well, that's the way I do it."

Such a vow of independence was not unusual, and the commitment to hold his ground was something Larry managed to do rather easily. At the same time, he harbored some sensitivity about the way his attitudes were perceived. Larry's defensiveness was rooted in the realization that to some people, particularly those outside Indiana, he came off as a hayseed. Even Coach King had to admit that "he's an odd kid. He drives an old clunker [he paid $100 for it] and doesn't care about clothes or material things. He'd sidestep all the publicity he could." And he avoided outsiders as much as he could. "At Indiana State I know everyone," he said. How much Larry appre-

---

*Caterpillar, a midwestern-based industrial machinery company, sells "Cat" caps that have come to be a personal trademark for many young men and farmers across Indiana.

ciated the intimacy and privacy afforded at ISU is clear in his comparison of ISU and IU in an interview: "At a place like [IU], you feel you're on the go all the time, but if you're in a smaller school, you can get off to yourself and have some quiet....Classrooms are smaller at Indiana State, and you get more individual attention."

Larry's independence from more conventional motivations and interests was amply demonstrated in his third photo session. In mid-October, once again persuaded by Coach King, Larry traveled to New York for another photo session with *Sports Illustrated*. He landed at the airport, took a taxi to the hotel, ate dinner, watched TV, slept, ate breakfast, walked to the studio, did the session, went back to the hotel, spurned an opportunity to see the Yankees and Royals in a playoff game, and left. "Larry didn't much like New York," said Sports Information Director (SID), Ed McKee. "He thought it was awful that they charged $6 for a hamburger and a Coke. I remember at the time he said, 'I could never play there.'"

From Larry's view, the publicity was simply a necessary evil. "This publicity is all for the school, not me. They knew I didn't want to do it. But I ain't the one who has the final say-so." Once the season started and the team's ranking began to climb, so too did the intensity of the fans. Since the beginning of the season, Larry had appeared on the covers of *Sporting News* and *Basketball Weekly*, in addition to *Sports Illustrated*. By the end of December, with the team still undefeated, fan exuberance reached a crescendo. As the massive winter snows fell on Terre Haute, blanketing the entire city, the hysteria was so great that basketball seemed to be the only operative institution. This was in keeping with a time-honored Terre Haute tradition. The harsh midwest winter often brought subzero temperatures and so much snow that the city's snowplows were rendered ineffective. Terre Haute's former mayor, Lee Larrison, had become renowned for his reply to complaints about the city's lack of efficient snow removal: "God brought the snow, and God will take it away." And throughout that winter of early 1978, even as the snowplows were idle, thousands of fans managed to arrive hours before the beginning of the games that still managed to sell out.

Fan frenzy in Terre Haute went way beyond mere sell-outs in blizzards. For example, the student uniform included the obligatory "I'm a Bird Watcher" tee-shirt, to which Larry strongly objected. "They should have the whole team on [those shirts]," he said. When the record "Indiana has a New State Bird" was released, Larry's reaction was the same. In addition, autograph requests, in person or through the mail, from both kids and adults became commonplace, a situation with which Larry was considerably less than enamored.

Midway through the season, Coach King assigned Rick Shaw to help shield Larry from the fans, the autograph seekers, and sometimes the media that would congregate outside the locker room. "It was my responsibility after I was done with [Bob] Behnke [the head trainer] to get everything shipshape and then get Larry out of [the locker room]....[My job was] to physically push people out of the way like I was a ramming board. And I'd get him to the bus, and throw his stuff on for him, so all he had to do was get on the bus....I was the little fat guy in front of Larry pushing and shoving all the kids out of the way, and Larry's just hanging onto my collar and we're just going out through there—it reminded me of those Elvis Presley movies that you see where you got all those guys flying down a runway."

The sheer number of autograph requests through the mail began to resemble those directed to a rock star as well. Shaw was also assigned the task of learning to copy Larry's signature and handling the requests himself. Shaw believes that Larry probably had the time but that King thought Larry had enough daily distractions as it was. "I autographed the basketballs, the pictures, the 'horrible hankies.' I also autographed ten pairs of bikini underwear, and a garter or two. I signed about a thousand autographs in all," says Shaw.

The crush didn't let up when Larry went home for Christmas break either. Georgia explains that "there were all sorts of calls and letters. People would send basketballs and things that they wanted to have Larry sign. Or they would just want him to send an autograph. [Larry] thinks it's silly." For Georgia, however, the attention was more enjoyable. "Oh, he'd do it, of course. He's not one to say no to those kids. But they'd come from states away, and he'd just wonder, 'Mother, what do they want with my autograph?' He signed 'em and I mailed 'em. It's kind of flattering, I guess. I got a kick out of it. It got expensive, though, for postage."

From Larry's point of view, his mother sometimes seemed to relish her role with the press a little too much. "He tells me to keep my mouth shut. He was all mad at me...about something I said to a reporter from a Chicago paper. I don't know exactly what it was that made him so mad. He wouldn't tell me. That's the way Larry is, though. He won't say much. He just tells you just what he wants you to know and that's all. He wishes the rest of us would do the same way."

The Sycamore schedule for the 1977–78 season was tougher than the often-criticized schedule the previous year had been. In the new season, 24 of the 26 games would be played against Division I opponents. The year before, only 21 of State's 28 opponents had been Division I teams. However, Larry was confident: "I think we can play with any team in the nation right now." Many agreed. State returned almost all its players from the top-twenty team of the previous season. The starting lineup would be essentially the same. The only changes involved junior college transfer Leroy Staley, who would replace the now-graduated Danny King at one of the guard positions, and 7'0" transfer center Richard Johnson, who would come off the bench. For the upcoming season, the Sycamores would be eligible for their first MVC postseason tournament and were picked to win the conference title and, thus, qualify for their first NCAA bid. Most notably, it was the first time that an Indiana college team other than the big three—Indiana, Purdue, and Notre Dame—would begin the season nationally ranked.

The season unofficially opened with a 79–74 exhibition game victory against a touring Czechoslovakian team. In the game Larry, almost predictably, put up big numbers once again, with 19 points and 17 rebounds. Following a perfunctory victory against the first of the season's two Division II opponents in the opener, State immediately prepared for the challenge of the year, a home game against perennial Big Ten power, Purdue. Purdue had soundly beaten State on its home court the year before and boasted future pro stars Joe Barry Carroll and Jerry Sichting. Going into the November 28 game at Hulman Arena, Purdue was the early season favorite in the Big Ten, so anticipation was great, inasmuch as the game would prove a test of the true strength of the ISU team. That the *Sports Illustrated* issue featuring Larry came out that very day only heightened the interest in the contest. Yet not even the most ardent Sycamore fan could have expected ISU's victory to be such a rout, 91–73. After totaling 26 points, 17 rebounds, and 8 assists, Larry was unsurprised by the lopsided margin: "We expected to beat them by that much." The win over Purdue legitimized State's claims as one of the premier teams in the country. In their succeeding games the team only reinforced that view.

On the heels of the Purdue game, State beat St. Louis 84–61 behind Larry's 31 points, 19 rebounds, and 8 assists. Then one game later, in a 93–77 victory at Central Michigan, Larry made one of the crazy shots his teammates often had seen him make in practice.* Falling out-of-bounds to save a rebound, Larry collected the ball behind the backboard and flipped it back over the backboard into the basket. According to teammate Brad Miley: "It went over or under the backboard or... somehow. And it hit nothing but net." Larry hit nothing but net more than once in the game as he scored 45 points and managed 14 rebounds.

It had been a tough opening-five games for Larry, as he had been bothered throughout by both a sore hip and a bad ankle. But as usual he refused to take any medication, even aspirin. According to Shaw: "All you could do was ice [the ankle] down, do some manual resistance exercise, and tape it up, and he was going to play. And he would hobble on it, and [Bob] Behnke would keep him out until he was able to play. And that was worse than if you had shot him in the head with a gun. I mean he wanted to play on one leg." Larry had the good sense to know that in his position as a possible pro draftee at the end of the season injuries were not to be made public if possible. His relationship with Behnke and Shaw helped ensure confidentiality.

Larry had to deal with injury yet again in the early-season game against Tulsa. He chased an errant pass across the sideline and dived to keep it inbounds. He rubbed his right arm, but continued to play as if nothing had happened. But his scoring was affected as he totaled only 16 points to go along with his 15 rebounds.

Larry's injuries and their probable effect on his confidence resulted in a mild shooting slump lasting the first five games of the season. He broke out of the slump with the Central Michigan game. But five months later, Larry was still burning from the criticism of

---

*He would even practice these shots very seriously since he was in the habit of betting money on his ability to hit them. Shaw tells the story of Larry betting the maintenance man that he could hit 10 out of 10 over the guide wire from behind the basket. And as the team watched in amazement, Larry collected on his bet.

the press. Asked in an interview what he hated the most, Larry answered, "When you're shooting bad and people talk about you in the newspaper." His response to a question about his supposed shooting slump: "I'm never in a shooting slump. You practice all your life to make shots, and the ball either goes in or it doesn't. When the going gets rough, I'll make them. And I'll get away from the publicity if I need to." However, getting away from the publicity wasn't easy, especially after State won the eight games following the Central Michigan game. With those wins, the Sycamores pushed their season record to 13–0 and earned the number-four ranking in the country.

To be ranked among the top-four teams in the country was almost unimaginable to many State fans. One result was the frenzy of expectation among the fans, which was further fueled by some of Larry's remarks: "We're coasting a little bit right now," he said, "but I honestly don't think we'll get beat." Larry's comments were quite reasonable in light of the way the team had been winning. None of their games had been close; the average margin of victory for all thirteen games had been a whopping 20 points. Larry himself was playing brilliantly; his statistics were similar to the season before. That his scoring and rebounding were down slightly, while his assists were up, was quite logical. As he had anticipated at the end of the prior season: "I think I can have just as good a year [in my junior year], although our schedule is going to be tougher. And my role could be different. [My sophomore year] I figured I had to score more so the team could do well. [My junior year] we may have several guys who can score." Harry Morgan was averaging 20 points a game, and Leroy Staley had also contributed offensively. Speaking of Morgan, Larry was typically effusive. "Harry Morgan is a great player and could score a lot if we needed him to." By playing up Morgan's talents, Larry hoped to deflect even a little press attention away from himself. "But I don't know why you want to talk to me," he'd say. "I think Harry is a better player than I am."

But the better the team played, the more Larry and the team found themselves the subjects of intense press attention on the one hand and great expectations from the fans on the other. Yet, after climbing to the fourth ranking in the country, the Sycamores faced pressure of a different sort. They would play six of their next seven games on the road. In the first game the team suffered the initial blemish on its record, falling to Southern Illinois 79–76, despite Larry's 38 points and 9 rebounds.

Two nights later, at dreaded Illinois State, a remarkable free-for-all erupted. Of the many fights Larry was involved in during his college career, Shaw believes that this one was the worst: "Oh my God, it was a brutal fight. First of all, we got screwed by the refs a couple of times. Larry stole the ball and went down and dunked it, but they had blown the whistle. And I don't remember what exactly started it, but all of a sudden, fists are flying... Larry got quite a few punches in... people are coming out of the stands, onto the edge of the court; they're trying to get in, but the cops are holding them back, and it was wild." Despite all the tumult, Larry did manage 37 points and 17 rebounds, but, to add insult to injury, the team lost its second straight, 81–76. A tough overtime loss to Wichita State and what would be the only home loss in 55 games during Larry's career (against a tough Creighton team) followed.

When the dust had settled, the Sycamores had lost 5 straight games. There were no obvious reasons for the losing streak. It's difficult to win 5 of 6 on the road, to begin with. Then there had been a bad flu bug that had plagued Larry and almost the entire team during the road trip. Valuable reserve Richard Johnson had been sidelined with a serious foot fracture. But still it was odd that such a previously dominant team would fall victim to such an abrupt turnaround. What's more, even when he was fighting the flu, Larry had been his usual brilliant self during the losing streak; but the other players had gone cold from the field. State averaged almost 14 points less than it had previously, despite Larry's increased output.

Following a victory at West Texas State, the team traveled to New Mexico State. In a rowdy game that went down to the wire, State was nipped, 83–82. At one point, Larry fell into the stands after going for a loose ball, and he was grabbed—apparently—by two New Mexico fans sitting next to each other. Larry came up swinging and decked both. Rick Shaw recalls: "You don't know about people like that, do you? They're crazy. They could have done anything to him." No doubt some of the frustration over the team's last six games played some role in this altercation, as it did in the closing of the ISU locker room to the press after the game. When the press loudly complained at the door, a member of State's entourage merely shrugged and said, "Sometimes he talks to the press and sometimes he doesn't." On that sour note, the team went on to lose 2 of its next 4 contests. And although State went on to win the remaining three games, they finished the season with a disappointing record of 19 wins and 7 losses.

State would have a chance to redeem itself in its first-ever MVC postseason tournament. Seeded second, they quickly disposed of their first two opponents. For their third game they would be matched against New Mexico State, a team they had lost to on the road and beaten at home. Just as the game at New Mexico had been close, this one was even closer as the Sycamores squeezed out an 80–78 double-overtime win. Larry led with 40 points and 11 rebounds. The victory assured ISU of facing the number-one seed, Creighton, in the finals. Creighton had won both games during the season. Their strategy in both games had been to slow the tempo. In the final they would do it again. That game would go down to the wire. In fact, it was the son of the Creighton coach, no less, who hit a seventeen-foot jump shot with 2 seconds to play to give Creighton the win, 54–52. Larry had done everything humanly possible; he had scored 29 of the team's 52 points and also grabbed 10 rebounds and handed out 6 assists.

Still, the most remarkable aspect of Larry's performance was that he had played at all. Just 45 minutes before game time, he was receiving treatments for his back at an Omaha hospital. Though it was announced that Larry had hurt his back in practice, he had actually injured himself at the hotel horsing around with his teammates. One of them had leaped onto his back. The resulting lower-back pain became so great that Larry could barely walk, let alone run or play. Bob Behnke took him to the Creighton team physician, who declared that Larry would not even be able to move unless he took some painkillers. It was quite a dilemma for Larry. "Boy, was Larry upset, because he didn't want [the painkiller]," says Shaw. "But he did take it. That's the only time I ever heard him doing anything or taking anything like that. He's so dead-set against drugs."

The team was disappointed at not winning the conference championship, but they were invited to the NIT (National Invitational Tournament) again. Their first opponent would be old rival Illinois State. As always the game was nip and tuck. State emerged victorious, 73–71. Larry's contribution to ISU's first major college postseason victory ever, was 27 points, 10 rebounds, and 7 assists. The team's next opponent would be east-coast power Rutgers—featuring one of

Larry's teammates from the World University Games, James Bailey. And Rutgers played a box-and-one defense (one man guards Larry man-to-man while the rest of the team plays a zone defense) to attempt to stymie Larry. Usually State would react by simply sending Larry inside and allowing him to muscle in his points. Rutgers' defense, however, was the best the team had faced.

Larry did get 20 shots, but just barely; he managed to shoot 50 percent and to lead all players with 23 points and 11 rebounds. However, it wasn't enough to prevent a 57–56 Rutgers victory.* What was interesting about the contest was how similar the ending of the game had been to the season-ending NIT game in Houston the year before. In the waning seconds, Larry was hammered, but no foul was called. Just as in Houston, the referees appeared to be intimidated by the partisan crowd. The difference between the two games was in the way King and Larry reacted at the end. King stormed onto the floor and nearly tackled the referee, as Larry screamed in disbelief, barely managing to keep from clobbering the official. A few moments later both King and Larry collected themselves and headed toward the locker rooms.

Then ensued one of those incidents that speaks volumes about sport and its capacity for inspiring mania among its fans. Larry and Bailey had congratulated each other on their way off the court, but then a Rutgers fan, enraged over Larry's taking issue with the call, leaped out of the stands onto Larry's back, where he began to pull Larry's hair and pound on his back. Larry threw his assailant off and then proceeded to knock him senseless. Shaw recalls, "Larry just decked the guy with both fists. He was so pissed off that we lost. I was about three steps in front of that. I mean I got hit with blood. I mean it splattered. This guy's nose looked like a Heinz Ketchup bottle. It just exploded.... I've seen Larry rearrange some dentures before, but this guy was just laying out there." It was, if nothing else, an appropriate way to end a season that was both bizarre and frustrating. But Larry was not about to bow out on such a note.

Larry had been extremely disappointed in the second half of the season. After the 13–0 start, the team had slumped to 10–9 the rest of the way. The statistics told the story. The team had averaged more

---

*Though Bailey scored only 13 points, his basket, with 17 seconds to go, put Rutgers in the lead.

than 10 points less per game over the last 19 games than in the first
13. Even when a team is playing good defense, they are going to give
up more points if their offense is less productive. Perhaps the most
acute problem was the team's extreme scoring imbalance. After Larry
and Harry Morgan, not one player was remotely close to double figures. And when in the second half of the season both Morgan's and
Leroy Staley's figures began to fall off, the team was doomed, especially because they were playing at a slower tempo. Larry averaged 30 points, Morgan 18.6, and Staley, the third-highest scorer,
only 6.3.

Larry's statistics had remained almost identical through the two
halves of the season, no mean feat considering the inconsistency
around him. For the season, Larry had averaged 11.5 rebounds and
almost 4 assists along with his 30 points per game. He was the second leading scorer and the eighth leading rebounder in the country.
Plus, shooting 53 percent from the field, especially in light of the double teaming and box-and-ones he often faced, was quite an achievement. Most amazing of all was that in 2 years and 60 games, Larry
had not once failed to score in double figures. And in those 60 games
he had led the team in scoring 54 times and always led the team in
either rebounding or scoring. For that statistical excellence, Larry
was rewarded with first-team All-American status from the AP, UPI,
U.S. Basketball Writers, the *Sporting News* and *Basketball Weekly*.
In addition, he received National Association of Basketball Coaches
and Citizen's Saving Hall of Fame All-American honors. But, although he was generally regarded as the nation's top player in college basketball, Larry was edged out for the Adolph Rupp Award
(AP player of the year); similarly, he was only third for the UPI Player
of the Year award because the usual sentiment was that the award
should be given to a senior if at all possible. (Butch Lee of Marquette
won.)

The State team had definitely played over their heads much of
the season, and one of the major reasons was Larry's presence on
both the practice and the playing floors. One of Larry's biggest contributions was the example he set. Larry consistently played 45 to 60
minutes after practice, believing that the most effective practice comes
after fatigue has set in. In the same way, Larry's refusal to be deterred by injury also inspired his teammates. And no matter how well
Larry played, his performance never affected his ego. As Hoover

Agan* of Larry's old neighborhood points out, "Nice thing about it all, [Larry] don't blow about it." Larry preferred to compliment his teammates.

Yet, while Larry was generous with praise, he was also shrewd. Whether hyperbole or not, his laudatory comments were appreciated by the other players. Such public gratitude goes a long way toward building the kind of goodwill essential for a good basketball team. After all, it was the thrust of Larry's comments, not the literal detail that mattered. The sincerity of Larry's affection stands behind his public expression. "When somebody wants to do a story on me, I want them to do it on the team. Without them I would be nobody." And because Larry's support of his teammates was unconditional, it was returned in kind.

The roots of Larry's sentiment about his teammates were embedded in his southern Indiana upbringing. Tom Reck, born in Dubois, just a few miles from French Lick, understood the importance of "family and friends," in addition to a strongly felt "loyalty" and "sense of duty." "A lot of people make little of [such an emphasis on family and friends], but that's Indiana," says Reck. Indeed, Larry went so far as to take a familial view of the team wherein King, the father figure, was granted "loyalty" and respect. That respect was very important to Larry. One example of this is cited by Rick Shaw: "I heard that we were recruiting a white kid, a transfer.... The kid sat down with Coach King and Larry, and the kid pulls out a cigarette and starts smoking. And Larry said, 'Any guy like that who has so little respect, we can't use on the team.' So that's it."

Larry's attempts to create a harmonious atmosphere extended to keeping his teammates loose. In locker rooms, the rule of thumb is usually this: the more sophomoric the prank, the more effective it is. And Larry, early on, acquired a reputation as the team's humorist and prankster. Not only did he induce the entire team to start chewing tobacco, but also to use his favorite chew, Levi Garrett. There was no end to the jokes and pranks that ensued once Larry had gotten everyone to carry around a paper cup with a paper towel wedged in the bottom, serving as a spitoon. When the team was flying to an away game, the air was heavy with tobacco juice. Even Bill Hodges

---

*Hoover Agan owned the grocery store where Larry and his brothers practiced their jump shots with potatoes when they were younger; they also bagged groceries for Agan.

chewed. Those Larry cared for the most were the most likely targets. Coach King says, "I had this habit of developing a nervous cough just as we would go into the final briefing in the dressing room prior to the tipoff. Larry would always have something planned for that. One time I came in hacking,...and there is the whole team coughing and hacking, with you know who conducting."

Throughout the season Larry had had various problems with the press. The pressures in his first year had been less because then he had been an unknown and Coach King had done a good job of shielding him. Larry would have gladly accepted the mild irritations and inconveniences of his first year could he have foreseen the environment in January of his junior year. Larry believed that in his first year he had more than accommodated the press, but the net result was that his teammates had been ignored and the press had taken up all his time. "But we got seven guys who play. They deserve to be talked to, too." Larry decided to no longer do interviews; though at Coach King's request he subsequently moderated that position. On the occasions when Larry did, finally, grant interviews, he made a point of depersonalizing them: "Coach King says [interviews] are part of the game. So, I say, 'I'm not representing myself, I'm representing my teammates and State.'"

To begin to understand the nature of Larry's unique complaint requires some perspective on his background. "[He's] small-town Indiana. He does like his privacy, he doesn't like it invaded," said Hodges. "But he's not antisocial in any way except with people he hasn't gotten to trust. That was a trait of mine; I had to get over a mistrust of people I didn't know. That's not uncommon in southern Indiana." It is a basic mistrust rooted in a region scarred by its severe poverty. In Larry's case, that mistrust is further intensified by the social temperament of his hometown, the uneasy wariness toward outsiders by an abandoned tourist mecca.

Moreover, the valley's limited population closes off opportunity for exposure to a variety of experiences available in larger communities. Says Coach Holland, "There are three small towns in the county, and none of them have more than 2,000 people." And reporters were no doubt influenced by Larry's southern Indiana argot, a regional dialect that seemed inarticulate to many. As a result, Larry was self-conscious about the way he expressed himself. "He does not talk like an Oxford don, that's sure," says ISU President Richard Landini. "And every now and then there are some very gross indiscretions in the agreement of his subjects and verbs." One of Larry's responses to a question on TV is a prime example. "The team wuz real tarred [tired] at the aind [end] of the game. But we wuzn't goin' to quit. We didn't want no overtime."

Further complicating Larry's communication problem was a basic reticence. As a child, Larry had always been painfully shy. Speaking in class was something he dreaded. It was doubly difficult for him to communicate with the press or strangers. "He's just not very comfortable talking to people. The way he handles it is to avoid it," says Coach King. King is, however, careful to avoid labeling Larry as shy. "He is shy, then he isn't shy. That's not quite right. He isn't shy. He's a little reserved until he attains a relationship with you. He has to know you before he trusts you. But then he's outgoing and fun to be around." Of course, that doesn't mean that Larry's friends have difficulty getting him to shut up. As Janet had indicated earlier, he's pretty closemouthed even with his friends. "Larry only tells you exactly what he wants you to know," says Georgia.

But Larry had come a long way toward overcoming his shyness. Each year in Terre Haute brought him greater confidence and self-esteem. According to Ruth Myles (secretary for the Sports Information Office), instead of looking down or averting his eyes when he talked to people he didn't know well, he would now look straight at them. Larry became more adept in his responses to the media. Said King at one point, "I think he expresses himself very well now.... He is developing confidence in meeting people."

Despite Larry's added confidence, he grew increasingly estranged from the press as their demands on his time became greater: "Every day there was five or six guys who wanted to do a story. It got to botherin' my teammates. It wasn't that they were mad 'cause I was gettin' all the pub, just that we'd come in, and they couldn't even get to their lockers. We'd be out havin' a beer and there'd be five guys waitin' to talk to me. You can't have no fun in college like that, so I said, 'If you wanna talk, talk to these guys.'" What might have been the greatest irritant of all was the increasingly personal nature of the questions. In Larry's first season, the questions had been mostly limited to basketball. In his junior year, the press became more interested in Larry as a feature, a personality.

For Larry, their questions were a violation. "You gotta be careful what you say around sportswriters because a lot of them want to find out what goes on inside you, the private you.... Hell, that's mine, you know."

Compounding Larry's initial irritation was a continuing problem of misquotation or "twisting my words." It was especially problematic on the road. "You say just one thing, and they're gonna pick it up and throw it right in the paper so it'll make you look bad, or the team mad. At home you can control that a little bit." While Larry's sensitivity to the abuses of the press on the road had some justification, ISU supporters had developed an extraordinary sensitivity to anything written that was less than glowing about their favorite son.

From their vantage point the most egregious incident involved *Sports Illustrated,* which had done a feature primarily on Larry, but also on the team. The passage that provoked everyone said, "The Indiana State coaches even seem disinclined to give Bird instruction, much less raise their voices to him. If Bird is receptive to anyone, it is King. 'Whatever Coach King wants me to do, I'll do it,' he says. About the only thing King seems to want his star to do is play exactly the way Bird wants to play." King, Hodges, and others were outraged at the implication that King allowed Larry to do whatever he wanted. But what is most fascinating about the exchange is how little basic disagreement exists between the conflicting points of view. The writer, Larry Keith, had pointed out that Larry would do anything King asked him to do. Keith's further point was merely that King was disinclined to give Larry instruction. Keith's comments were in line with those of other observers who had pointed out that Larry had pretty much free rein in terms of the offense and that the offense was molded around him. Given Larry's success with that role there was not a lot of occasion for Larry to require instruction, especially since much of that success was due to his ability to improvise. And it is true that due to Larry's close relationship to King, Larry was probably more responsive to him than to other coaches. Overall, what the *Sports Illustrated* controversy pointed up was the state-of-siege mentality, the "us against them" attitude that would ultimately erupt into outright warfare by Larry's senior year.

*   *   *

Larry's worries regarding the press increasingly began to center on his future—specifically, when he would go pro at the end of the year. Larry had entered college four years earlier, and despite dropping out of school and beginning as a freshman a year later, Larry was still eligible for the pro draft. In other words, he would not even have to apply for hardship in order to be drafted. Accordingly, the NBA teams with early first-round draft picks began inquiring whether Larry might forego his senior year of college eligibility. Larry didn't have to commit one way or another. He was going to be drafted, regardless.

The important distinction was that in order for a weaker team to select him, it would be necessary for Larry to declare hardship. Weaker teams could not afford to pass up immediate help to draft a player who wouldn't play for a year. The stronger teams, on the other hand, could wait. If Larry did commit, it was virtually certain he would be the first to be selected. If he didn't, he was likely to be picked seventh or eighth, and the team that drafted him would have one year (until 5 days before the next draft) to sign him. Otherwise, he would be subject again to the next draft. The Indiana Pacers had the first draft pick. They and a host of other teams, who were willing to trade players or picks or both for that spot, expressly wanted Larry. The Pacers played in Indianapolis, only seventy miles from Terre Haute. Not only did many of Larry's fans want him to play ball locally, but so did Larry's mother. Here was a golden opportunity for Larry to exert some control over his future, for the likelihood of his having a second opportunity to sign up with the local team was almost nonexistent. All his worries about adapting to a far away major city would be eliminated. On top of all these considerations came appeals to Larry's Hoosier loyalties. "Larry feels like he could do for the Pacers what he did for Indiana State," said Georgia. "He would probably mean 3,000 more fans a game for them." But at the same time there were also concerns about the Pacers' financial status. They had just received a $1.5-million line of credit in order to make it through the 1980 season. "I don't want to have to worry about my paycheck," said Larry.

The 1977–78 season was not very old when the speculation began. King immediately stated that Larry would not give up his last season. Yet Larry, in one of his first public comments, said, "I don't know what I'm gonna do." His indecision served to open the flood gates of press scrutiny, and it didn't take long for Larry's already rocky relationship with the press to worsen. After having refused to answer personal questions about himself and his family, Larry found himself besieged with questions about his future. He responded by opting to discuss only the present. "Basketball has been my whole life. I imagine it will be my future, too, unless I get hurt. But I treat the future like the past. I don't want to talk about the future or the past. I'd rather talk about the present—the now."

From the beginning of his sophomore year on, Larry had seemed inclined to stay at State and earn his diploma. What was surprising was one of his stated reasons for staying—the role that injury had begun to play in his decision making. "During the course of a season my body takes a beating from drawing charges and pushing around other players. I don't know how much more of that I want to take. I don't know if I want to keep doing that year after year. When I was a kid I used to dream about being a professional player. But now it doesn't seem like that big a deal. I would like to concentrate on getting my degree and taking it from there."

Larry's growing appreciation of the threat of injury also tempted him to consider the pros early. In the pros, for example, there would be less need for one player to play with nagging injuries—or so he believed. At the same time Larry appeared to acknowledge another advantage of the pro game: "I like the idea of playing basketball every night, but I don't know about the rest of it [the travel, the big cities, the news media, etc.]."

Both King and Georgia were confident that Larry would stay in school, but his occasional comments about the pros put them on the defensive. Georgia was quite clear that she wanted Larry to finish at State: "Oh, Lord, let him stay in college. I hope that's what he does. Larry's happy and contented in what he's doing now." King also understood what an adjustment Terre Haute had been for Larry. If it took at least six months and some extraordinary measures to help Larry accommodate to a city of 60,000, what chance did he have of making it in a major city? Said King: "This is a quiet, shy kid who feels comfortable in only two places, French Lick and Terre Haute. ...He likes to be with his friends, and they're kids just like him. He'd die in the big city."

Overall, then, the decision appeared to be a "nondecision," except for one factor: money. In March, a group of sportswriters asked, "What pro team would you like to play for?" Larry said, "I'm best-suited for the team that has the money." It was estimated that Larry would be offered a contract well in excess of $250,000 per year. Many people who had known Larry for years thought he should go for the money. One was Hoover Agan: "He may sign for the big money. I would, wouldn't you?" It was understood that if most people would take the money, that didn't mean that Larry would.

Georgia immediately discounted the money factor. "He's very happy and loves what he's doing, and what does money mean if you're not happy? We've never had anything. And I don't think Larry even realizes how much money that is. Besides, the money will always be there." Conventional wisdom also didn't take into account Larry's unique relation to money. Says King, "He doesn't care for material things, they don't have to do with his way of life, so he doesn't need the pros yet to be happy. A lot of things in the rich life aren't so super." However, Larry was in fact quite alert to the dilemma the money presented. But his point of view was similar to his mother's: "Sure [my family] never did have much money, but we have always been able to get by. If my mother needed the money real bad, then I'd go professional. But we are doing all right without the money."

Additionally, Larry wondered if the prospect of money might taint his enjoyment of the game: "Just as soon as you start seeing the money aspect of it you forget about it as a game. It's a job, and although I don't feel that way right now, I can't say I won't in the future. If I get to that point, I've got to have good money." Larry had come a long way from his high school days of living day to day. He had begun to seriously consider his future. "Right now I'm not really worrying about professional basketball. I've got a college career to finish up, and after I get through with [that], we'll start talking about professionals. But you can never tell, I might get hurt or something and never get a chance to play." When someone in Terre Haute asked him what he'd do if he couldn't play in the NBA, Larry humorously quipped, "Oh, I would try selling Avon."

It was clear to Larry that a diploma would not only be important if he didn't play in the pros, but it would also be important if he did. For when his career was over, he would still have his diploma. A degree would pay dividends in the end. Georgia had come to a similar conclusion, "Getting that diploma means more to him than money." But the press, to both Larry's and King's irritation, continued to harp on the "pro" question. A perfect example is the transcript from Larry's press interview with the writers covering the MVC for their postseason tournament in early March. "(*Q*) How many times have you been asked if you are going to sign with the pros this season? (*LB*) Every time I turn around. (*Q*) One more time then, are you going to turn pro? (*LB*) I've said time and again that I'm not interested now. (*Q*) Who is helping you make that decision? (*LB*) Nobody. I make my own decisions."

Not only did Larry make his own decisions, but he was largely unswayed by anyone else. And he was willing to stand by the consequences of his decisions. King: "He thinks things through pretty good, and when he makes a decision, that's the way it's going to be....He's never said anything else but that he would return to school next fall."

Nothing solidified Larry's decision more than the unsuccessful way the season ended. Larry was determined to make his senior year better than his junior one. Larry also desperately wanted to prove that he was a better basketball player and that the junior season had been a fluke. And improving his game was going to be necessary if he was going to play in the NBA anyway.

Larry also had very personal reasons for staying in school. According to Bill Hodges, whose background is very similar: "First, he wants to get his degree. No one in his family's ever done that and I can relate to that. I was the first from my family to get a degree, and once you get started on that, it becomes an obsession. Second, he wants his family to be proud of him. I think when he went back to French Lick from Indiana, he lost some of that. Not amongst his family, but amongst friends. I think he's stubborn to where he's saying to them, 'I'll prove I'm not the kind of person who's going to pull up stakes and run.'"

Once the season was finished, the pro draft loomed directly ahead. At the same time, in Boston, strange maneuverings were going on which were to have a decisive effect on Larry's future. Boston Celtic General Manager Red Auerbach had fixed his eyes on Larry Bird. How to get him became his overriding preoccupation.

During Larry's junior year, Auerbach had sent then Assistant Coach K. C. Jones to scout the potential hardship case. One play was all Jones needed to see to be convinced about Larry's talents. "Larry is being double- and triple-teamed every time he gets the ball," K. C. remembers. "He gets away on a fast break, but there are two guys hanging on him as he goes down the court. Larry fires the ball off the backboard at an angle, simultaneously zigging away from the two defenders. They think he's just thrown up a crazy shot. Larry goes right to where he knows the ball would come off the board, and in the air he takes the pass he's just made to himself and dunks the ball. I had never seen anybody have the presence of mind and the self-confidence and the ability to put something like that together."

Considered to be the greatest coach in the history of the NBA, Auerbach had proved to be a brilliant general manager as well. He had been involved with all thirteen of the Celtics' World Championships, either as a coach or as a general manager. But the Celtics had fallen upon hard times under new owner and meddler, John Y. Brown. With their thirteenth world championship in 1976, the Celtics became the winningest professional sports franchise in history. In 1977, with the loss of forwards Paul Silas and Don Nelson, vital cogs in the championship team, the team fell to 44–38 and was beaten in the conference semifinals. In 1978, the team's fortunes continued to decline. The team finished with a 32–50 record, which was only the second losing record in the 27 years of the Celtics franchise. The fans were miserable, but in the middle of that season Auerbach was able to pull off a miracle of a trade that seemed anything but that at the time. It would prove to be only the first step in a complex strategy.

First, Auerbach pleased many of the Celtic fans by trading Charlie Scott (notorious for his hypochondria and selfish play), for Los Angeles Laker "problem" Kermit Washington,* a consistently hardworking player. The Scott-for-Washington trade would have been fair enough. But Auerbach also received veteran defensive ace Don Chaney in the deal. Auerbach also managed to finesse LA's firstround draft choice, too, which was the number six pick. Then, following the end of the season, Auerbach immediately signed 7'3" free agent, Kevin Kunnert. Kunnert was a good enough player to provide solid help at both the forward and center positions. Auerbach

---

*Washington had been mistakenly maligned as a "problem" because he punched Rudy Tomjanovich during an altercation which resulted in numerous facial operations for Tomjanovich.

felt that signing Kunnert would allow the Celtics to hang in while they were waiting for Larry to finish his college career.

Meanwhile, the Indiana Pacers continued to maintain that they planned on using their first pick to get Larry. At the same time, they insisted that they needed immediate help and could not wait a year. As Red Auerbach commented about the first three teams with draft picks: "Portland, Kansas City, and Indiana all would have taken Larry in preference to a Mychal Thompson or Rick Robey if they could have signed him." It was also true that none of the first five teams could afford to wait on Larry.

Portland, the NBA champion in 1977, which had the third and seventh picks, was determined to take Larry with its latter pick and wait. Nonetheless, they were also interested in immediate front court help at the forward spot as well as the center position. Besides Larry, they coveted Mychal Thompson of Minnesota. The Pacers were interested in Rick Robey if they couldn't have Larry. When it became clear that Larry was going to remain in school, there was little point in the Pacers hanging onto their first pick if they could get Robey and a starting guard in exchange for swapping their first pick for Portland's third pick. And Portland was willing to trade because they wanted to prevent Kansas City from choosing Thompson. The Pacers' compensation was in the form of star guard Johnny Davis; Portland was more than happy to give up Davis to acquire the first pick while also preserving the seventh pick. However, Portland had originally thought that Boston could not afford to wait for Larry. But when Auerbach acquired Kunnert, they began to worry. To ensure getting Larry, they offered Auerbach a player merely to move up from the seventh to the sixth pick. Auerbach refused. Portland had been right to worry, but now it was too late. Wily Red Auerbach had pulled off the coup of the decade.

On June 8, 1978, the Celtics surprised most uninformed observers by taking Larry with the sixth pick of the first round.

On the morning of June 9, 1978, Larry had gone fishing. He had left a "fill-in" statement with Ed McKee, the Sports Information Director at ISU. "I'm pleased to have been selected by the————. I will be happy to discuss a possible contract upon my graduation next year." Auerbach also made a statement. "I talked to Bob King before the draft and told him that if we drafted Larry, I would not try to persuade him to play. I drafted him for the future. I'm making absolutely no effort to sign him now. Next spring I hope to sign him."

Auerbach's excitement to the contrary, there were some in Boston who criticized the pick, saying that Auerbach had virtually conceded the next season.

Auerbach candidly admits that he didn't know Larry would be great, though that is not the common assumption: "Back in 1977 we started hearing rumors about this kid out at Indiana State. No one ever said he was great...but the word was that he was good, very good. So I watched him on TV a couple of times, and then, during his junior season, I went to see him in person.... Like [Bill] Russell, Larry Bird showed me what I wanted to see the first time I laid eyes on him. Here was a kid who could shoot and who knew how to handle the ball.... He was drafted solely on the premise that he was a damned good ball player who could put some points on the board and move the ball around. That's all I was expecting, just as I was only expecting Russell to get us the ball."

However, before Larry became a Celtic, he almost became a San Diego Clipper in what was undoubtedly one of the most bizarre trades in the history of professional sports. John Y. Brown and his silent partner, Harry Manguerian, owned the Buffalo Braves. Brown was willing to do anything to get out of Buffalo and had settled on moving the Braves franchise to San Diego. The Celtic owners were Irv Levin and his partner, Harold Lipton. Levin, originally from California, was anxious to get out of Boston. Levin met Brown, and proposed incredibly, that they swap their respective franchises. Levin would go to San Diego with the Braves (to be renamed the Clippers) and Brown would come to Boston to take over the Celtics. In addition, Auerbach's recently acquired players, Kermit Washington, Kevin Kunnert, and the Celtics' second first-round draft choice, Freeman Williams, would be traded to San Diego for Nate Archibald, Billy Knight, and Marvin Barnes. It was the first time that a player transaction had been made without Auerbach's consent since his arrival in Boston in 1950. The one newly acquired player the Clippers wanted, and didn't get, was Larry Bird.

Larry had had no feeling one way or the other about being drafted by Boston. Over the summer he had concentrated on getting ready for his senior season. He was also again invited to represent the United States in international competition, but he didn't accept until he found out that the games were going to be played in the United States. The team was to play in a round-robin tournament in Lexington, Kentucky, with national teams from the Soviet Union, Cuba, and Yugoslavia. Ironically, the coach who had selected Larry for the team was Joe B. Hall, who declined Larry's services as a potential recruit four years earlier. The selection of Larry, in itself, could be construed as an admission of sorts that Hall had been wrong about Larry—though Hall could hardly have gotten away without inviting the best collegiate in the country. But as it turned out, Larry hardly played. Four out of the twelve players were from Kentucky, and they received the most playing time. In fact, in the final game, Larry received a total of 13 minutes playing time. (Another reserve on the team who didn't receive much playing time either was a freshman from Michigan State—named Earvin Johnson.) The US defeated Cuba in their first game since the broken-bottle incident, 109–64. The US then went on to beat both Yugoslavia and the Soviet Union to win the tournament.

Larry himself went on to win another tournament that summer, and he got some good playing time. He and his two older brothers played on the Terre Haute 500 Platolene-Carpet Center team, which won the Indiana Class A slow-pitch softball championship. The team, with Larry's considerable help, also set a tournament record for home runs. Larry was very much at home in his small-town, southern Indiana environment. He hung out with the boys, drank some beer, hit some home runs, and tenaciously clung to his desire for an ordinary, normal life. But regardless of how much his values remained the same, his life no longer was. Larry Bird had become a public figure.

10 / *The Final Four:*
Indiana State,
1978–1979

As summer turned into fall, Larry's final season began to look ill-fated. In July, Coach King had suffered a heart attack from which at first he seemed to have recovered. However, by September it was apparent that he was still not well. Then, during the first week in October, King suffered a brain aneurism that would require surgery. As a result, he was left with about a week before the start of practice to decide what to do about his future and who, if necessary, would be his successor. There shouldn't have been any decision to make: King was supposed to have stepped down at the beginning of the previous season and let Assistant Coach Stan Evans take over. But King had enjoyed his tenure and the limelight as Larry Bird's coach too much. After all, when he had hired Evans, how could he have anticipated that a recruit of last resort would turn out to be the best college player in the country?

Evans had agreed to come to ISU three years earlier, only with the understanding that he would become head coach in two years, at which time King would go back to the AD (athletic director) job, exclusively. When King initially approached Evans, he was about to fire the then ISU Coach Gordon Stauffer and take over the basketball program himself. The problem was that he had moved up to the AD position in the first place because hardening of the arteries had robbed him of much of his effectiveness as a bench coach. Unlike most coaches, who want to move from coaching to administrative positions as they get older, King wanted to do the opposite. Some witnesses suggest that this counterintuitive desire may have had something to do with his hardening of the arteries problem. In any case, an assistant with head coaching experience, who had talent for making quick and effective decisions, would enable King to resume coaching again. Evans was just the man King was looking for. Yet, Evans was content as head coach of one of the strongest junior college programs in the country, Miami Dade Community College, and was hardly interested in going from head coach to assistant coach, at a program with athletes no better than he was presently coaching. King knew that Evans desired a major college head coaching position and had been cultivating relationships to that end with coaches such as Bobby Knight and Dean Smith. King also knew that the time frame for such a promotion was often at least five years. King played his trump card. He offered Evans the head job at ISU in a mere two years if Evans would take the assistant position immediately. In two years, King explained, he would be ready for the AD position exclusively. Evans considered the offer for a long time, and finally decided to accept it.

But as the two years passed, King appeared to have no interest in stepping down. Evans's only solace was that King's physical deterioration made it likely he would have to step down anyway. However, Evans had other worries. The second assistant coach he himself had hired was bent on bypassing him for the head job. This was ironic since Evans, careful not to take any chances in this regard, had hired a coach he felt safe with: Bill Hodges, a former insurance salesman, who had been assistant coach at Tennessee Tech.

Faced with major surgery, King had to make a decision. Ever the optimist, King believed he would come back from the surgery as good as new. Therefore, it made sense to appoint an interim coach only. He knew Evans would not stand for an interim position. Even if he would, King knew it would be near-impossible to reclaim the head coaching position later on because of Evans's personality and ability. Hodges, on the other hand, inexperienced and, by all accounts, not very talented, would doubtless happily step aside upon King's return. King made his decision known to both Hodges and Evans on October 11, four days before practice was scheduled to begin. That day, without a formal announcement, Evans once and for all severed his connection with basketball coaching.

Once the decision to hire Hodges had been made, a new assistant coach to replace Evans was needed as quickly as possible. In July, King had brought in Mel Daniels, his former star player from New

Mexico, who had gone on to pro fame with the Indiana Pacers as a third assistant. It was logical that Daniels should step into Evans's old position.

The players had a sense that something was going on, but they knew nothing for sure until the first practice on October 15. At that time, equipment was passed out, and Hodges and Daniels explained the situation. Just two days earlier, King had undergone brain surgery to remove the blood clot in his brain, which necessitated the removal of some brain tissue. It was not certain that he would survive. The players were stunned. They had hardly expected such a dramatic reorganization, let alone the revelation that their beloved coach was fighting for his life. Larry, in particular, was greatly affected. Yet the adversity served to strengthen the bonds of the team, and they quickly came together as one: "[Coach King's illness] had an impact not only on me, but on the whole team," said Larry. "We've dedicated the season to him, and we're going to do the best we can."

The single greatest dividend from King's illness was that essentially it allowed Larry to coach the team. Evans's staunchest supporters as well as Evans himself admit that he would not have finished the season with as good a record as the cagers eventually compiled. "I would have ended up coaching the team too much," says Evans. Hodges had never served as a head coach at any level, but he did have the good sense to let Larry coach the team on the floor. According to Craig McKee (assistant to SID Ed McKee), Hodges had the "courage to let Larry do what he wanted to do." Indeed, Hodges himself, at one point during the season, maintained that his primary contribution as coach was "not messing up Larry Bird." But few took seriously the idea that Larry was literally coaching the team. Insiders, however, admit that Hodges wasn't even close to being able to coach a major college team. It was really Larry's show. Rick Shaw details the unusual amount of discretion and influence Larry was allowed in coaching decisions. "Sometimes, Hodges would want to switch from man-to-man to zone, and Larry would say, 'No, we got to where we are doing what we're doing; let's keep going with it.' And it worked. There were times in the huddle when Hodges would say, 'Okay, we're going to do this,' and Larry would say, 'No, let's stick with what we're doing.' Then Hodges would stop [and say] 'Okay, okay.'" Whether the success of his coaching style was attributable to his prescience or to his lack of skills is probably best explained by Hodges' subsequent record.

The year after Larry left, the team's record fell to 16–11—despite preseason predictions of at least a Top-Twenty year. In the following two seasons, which were to be Hodges' last, the team could only manage identical 9–18 records, the two worst since 1937. But, nonetheless, Hodges' approach did work as long as Larry was there. And despite King's infirmity,* Hodges still relied on King a lot, according to Rick Shaw. That Hodges instituted no changes also smoothed the transition the team had to make. As Larry explains, it was in reality much like dealing with the same coach. "Coach Hodges yells a little bit more, but...the only thing he changed was the outlook of games—he was a little bit easier on us as far as after games [is concerned] and let us do what we thought was right. Coach King was more of a guy that we did it completely his way. Coaches are different. I played well under both coaches and I respect both coaches."

Nevertheless, minor adjustments were made. With Larry running the show from the floor, the offense necessarily opened up a little more, which ultimately served to further enhance Larry's skills. Another key difference involved the use of personnel. King had wanted to pair Leroy Staley, his returning starter, at the two-guard spot with dynamic transfer, Carl Nicks, at the point. Staley had shown great promise in the beginning of the previous season, but had tailed off badly. King had hoped to develop him into a power guard. However, Hodges believed that Carl might be best utilized at the two-guard position. As the point guard, the responsibilities of taking care of the ball and running the offense might stifle his shooting and ability to score. Furthermore, Staley was really a forward in skill, if not size, at 6'4½" and 193 pounds. Thus, it was decided he might be best utilized coming off the bench as the third forward. The most inspired decision was to start sophomore Steve Reed at point guard. Reed was especially adept at getting the ball downcourt quickly and making good decisions when distributing it. Beyond that, his greatest strength was probably his ability to pressure the opposing team's ball handler. So, a lineup featuring a starting backcourt of Reed and Nicks with Staley coming off the bench at forward was put into place.

---

*King returned from the hospital in October. He was able to do some work in an administrative capacity, but it took months before his memory, which had been affected by the surgery, began to come back.

*   *   *

As if losing Coach King so close to the start of the season wasn't enough, Larry also had to deal with a series of bad encounters with the press. It had begun with an article subtly insinuating that Larry was money-hungry. Then, in Larry's first effort to put his best foot forward with regard to the press, he got burned badly. It was at the annual preseason MVC press conference in early November held in Des Moines; Larry was the featured player in attendance. Since there were, according to Tom Reck, fifty or sixty reporters who wanted to speak to Larry, it was determined that instead of speaking to individual reporters, he would field questions from all of them at once.

One of the reporters asked how Bill Hodges' new role as head coach had changed his duties, remembers Tom Reck. "Larry just made some general comments about what Bill's duties were before, and one of them was that 'Bill [Hodges] was the one who would check with the professors if there was any work that the players had to do while they made road trips.'" At the time Reck's newspaper was one of two Terre Haute newspapers which eventually merged. Both papers were stretched to the limit with only two full-time sports people for each. So they both used college kids to help out. In this case, the *Tribune* had sent a college kid whose version of Larry's answer to the Hodges question came out something to the effect that Bill "got us out of classes."

Hodges was furious when the story came out, and Larry was embarrassed for Hodges and also because it appeared that Hodges had tried to curry favor in the classroom. But it didn't take long for Larry to be at least as angry as his coach, when a professor chastised him in class for the reported comment. Larry was livid. His aunt claims he actually packed his bags and left ISU after the incident.

Reck remembers walking into practice in the following week to get some information on the upcoming preseason game against the Soviet Union. Reck was prepared for the worst: "That's when Bill told me...'You're going to be upset with what I have to tell you.' He said Larry's not going to be available to the press this year. He proceeded to tell me why. One thing he did elaborate, it's not only to avoid being misquoted;...it would be better for the rest of the team." Hodges eventually made a public statement. "Larry will not be talking to anyone from the printed media. He has been misquoted repeatedly. I'm sure there's no malice on the writers' parts, but it's a lot of little things." Hodges encouraged the report that it was Larry's decision to not talk to the press. However, people close to the situation, including Reck and Shaw, believe differently: "I think it was mostly Hodges' decision, and Hodges said he'd take the heat for it," says Shaw. Craig McKee explains that the boycott probably came about because Larry was unhappy, and Hodges wanted to assuage Larry's feelings as well as refocus press opinion to himself as the coach using the boycott as the solution. Others affirm that not only Hodges but King as well was interested in maintaining the coach's role as the center of press attention: "It was definitely an ego thing," says Evans. "Of course there was some ego involved," says Craig McKee.

Hodges later had several different explanations for the boycott: All of them place the decision squarely on Larry's shoulders. Indeed, Hodges portrays himself as obligated to go along with Larry: "Whether it was right or wrong, I have to honor his feelings. I don't know that he's completely wrong."

Larry, like Hodges, defended the action: "It was getting to the point where they wanted to spend two hours a day after practice. I don't have that kind of time. I'm in college. Why should I waste my time? I'm not getting paid for it."

Larry did make two minor exceptions to his boycott. He agreed to talk to TV and radio people on occasion, "because they can't change my words." And he talked to the only writer he trusted, Tom Reck. According to Shaw, "SID Ed McKee got to the point where he would call me and say, 'Can you get Larry to do this, and we got Channel 6 coming from Indianapolis to do an interview, would you talk to [the reporter] before he talks to Larry.' So I'd talk to the guy, and I'd say, 'Look just tell him you don't want to ask him anything about his personal life, and you'll be very brief.' ... And Ed wouldn't even come, his assistant Craig McKee would."

Ed McKee didn't attend because he had become the lightning rod for both Larry's and the media's anger. "It was Ed's job to promote him, and Larry really didn't want that, he just wanted to play basketball," says Shaw. But since most media people wouldn't take no for an answer, McKee spent hours every day explaining to media people that they shouldn't waste their time traveling to Terre Haute. "I know [the boycott] made Ed McKee's job very difficult, and Ed got a lot of raps about it," says Reck. "[Larry] still really doesn't trust me," said McKee. "He's afraid I'm going to give away some

Larry can dunk, although he rarely does as a pro. (Courtesy James Qualkinbush.)

A 77 percent free-throw shooter, senior year in high school. (Courtesy James Qualkinbush.)

Receiving an award from Coach Holland. (Courtesy James Qualkinbush.)

April 24, 1974, Larry signs a letter of intent for Indiana University. (Courtesy James Qualkinbush.)

1974: Holland, Larry, and the legendary Bobby Knight—and what might have been. (Courtesy James Qualkinbush.)

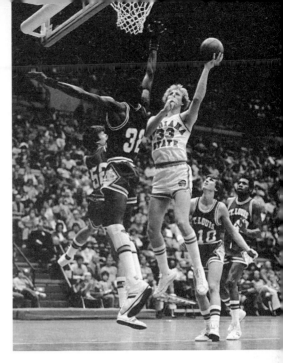

Early days at Indiana State—Larry is still a secret: Note the empty seats.   (Courtesy I.S.U.)

Larry's ambidexterity against St. Louis. (Courtesy I.S.U.)

Finding the open man (senior year), Leroy Staley, underneath.   (Courtesy I.S.U.)

Mid-air improvising against Tulsa. Eric Curry
(32) to the right of Larry.   (Courtesy I.S.U.)

Celebrating a big win over
Illinois State.   (Courtesy, Rich
Clarkson, *Sports Illustrated*.)

Larry and Magic collide in Larry's final college game.   (Courtesy UPI/Bettmann.)

The 1979 National Association of Basketball Coaches Player of the Year: Larry receives Eastman award from Kodak's Hunter Law. (Courtesy UPI/Bettmann.)

UPI's Player of the Year: Larry receives the Naismith trophy. Bill Hodges on the right. (Courtesy UPI/Bettmann.)

First visit to Boston Garden. Bob Woolf on the left, Red Auerbach in the rear between Woolf and Larry. (Courtesy UPI/Bettmann.)

Larry signs his first contract with the Boston Celtics. Auerbach on left, Coach Bill Fitch on right. (Courtesy UPI/Bettmann.)

Larry signs his second Celtic contract. Auerbach on left, Coach K. C. Jones on right. (Courtesy UPI/Bettmann.)

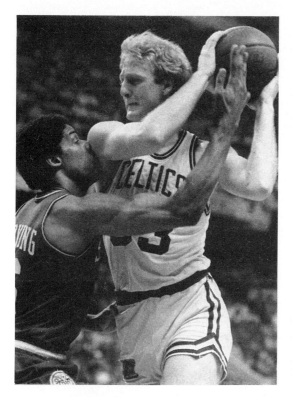

Big-game intensity: the seventh and deciding game of Celtics–Sixers 1981 playoff. Larry's shoulder is in Julius Erving's face. (Courtesy UPI/ Bettmann.)

On the way to the dressing room after 1981 series win over Philadelphia. (Courtesy UPI/Bettmann.)

Larry smokes Red Auerbach's cigar after Celtics win 1981 World
Championship.   (Courtesy UPI/Bettmann.)

In Boston, Larry dedicates his first NBA World Championship (1981) to
French Lick.   (Courtesy UPI/Bettmann.)

deep, dark secrets.'' Larry didn't realize all the abuse McKee had to take while running interference for Larry. Larry merely viewed McKee as another adversary.

Several people in the program expressed concern about Larry's relations with the press. After all, part of the college experience is to learn to deal with those who are different, even if it is initially a difficult experience. Unfortunately, Larry was being unnecessarily handicapped in terms of his future dealings in the pros when press scrutiny would be more constant and unregulated by the coaches. The NBA locker rooms are always open, and reporters travel with the teams. And neither coaches nor teammates would be available to protect him. ''I still run into people who are anti-Larry Bird,'' says Reck. ''I just don't think it is something that should be held against him.'' Not all journalists shared Reck's point of view. Some, like David Israel, then of the *Chicago Tribune,* had been expressly critical of Larry, Hodges, and the entire ISU program from the beginning.

As was usually the case with Israel, some of his criticism hit the mark and some was completely off-base. In one column on Larry's boycott, the intense sarcasm ultimately overwhelmed the few good points he did raise. His first point was telling, despite its contemptuous tone: ''One of the best-known facts about this college basketball season is that Larry Bird, a pretty good player from some place called Indiana State, does not speak to reporters. This is excused because Bird is just a shy, white farm boy from the small town of French Lick, Indiana. You have to wonder if this same unsociable conduct would be excused if Bird were a shy, black city kid from the housing projects of, say, Chicago. But I guess Larry Bird doesn't owe anything to his race, not even if basketball is giving him a chance to escape riding on the back of a garbage truck and make a few dollars.'' Israel went on to draw blood about Larry's being white and his obligation to talk to the press because of that: ''Has anyone tried to impress upon you how much the NBA is going to try to capitalize on your skin color? Do you realize that many members of the NBA's ruling class think their television ratings and attendance are down because there are too few white stars? Do you know that you are going to be asked about being the Great White Hope.... How come if you don't want to talk about it, you're willing to trade on it and take all that money, money that would not be so plentiful if you were Larry Bird, black forward from the ghetto?''

*   *   *

As the team prepared for an exhibition game against the Soviets, the outlook for the coming season was almost as bleak as it had been on the eve of Larry's first season. While they had the probable national player of the year, the rest of the team members were unknown, inexperienced, and therefore considered weak. That a new coach with no previous head coaching experience had been so abruptly appointed made matters all the worse. The Sycamores were predicted to finish somewhere in the middle of the pack in the conference, third in one poll and fourth in another.

The starters would be Brad Miley up front along with Larry, with Reed and Nicks at guard. Miley had started a few games the previous season, but had proved to be a woeful shooter. At 6'8", however, he was quick and was the best defensive player on the team. Completing the front line was another transfer, Alex Gilbert. An aggressive rebounder, Gilbert possessed a 40-inch vertical leap and was strictly an inside scorer. Therefore, despite being only 6'7", he was listed as the center. The other transfer on the team, Bob Heaton, was 6'5". Now eligible, Heaton had been penciled in as the sixth man, ready to fill in at forward or guard.

On Sunday, November 19, ISU served notice of what their season might bring, beating the Soviet national team which had already beaten Indiana and Notre Dame (the preseason favorite to win the NCAA) by a score of 87 to 79. Maybe because of the dire preseason forecast, there were only 7,000 fans to witness Larry's fouling out in the second half. That ISU had been able to win without Larry for the last stretch showed that the team was likely to be far better than expected. ISU opened their regular season against Division II school Wisconsin-Lawrence, and won easily, 99–56.

Then ISU played Purdue at Purdue and won for a second time in a row, 63–53. One thing was certain: fourth place teams from the Missouri Valley Conference don't go into Purdue's Mackey Arena and win by 10 points. However, some perspective was restored in the next game, which was at Evansville, as the team barely hung on for a 74–70 win. Arch-rival Illinois State visited Terre Haute next, and here too ISU barely hung on to win, 78–76. The team hardly looked like the "world-beaters" that had defeated the Soviets and Purdue. One problem was that starters Brad Miley and Steve Reed, while not counted on to score heavily, had contributed only 3 points combined against Evansville and 4 points against Illinois State. Against Purdue they had scored over one-fifth of the team's points.

But over the next five games, three of which were played on the road, the team won by an average of 27 points. One of those wins, against Cleveland State at the Mad Hatter Tournament at Stetson University in Florida, featured a side of Larry that was not always under control: his mean streak. This was part of what made him competitive and aggressive enough to often intimidate lesser players. But here Larry had become enraged at one of Cleveland State's coaches. "At halftime Bird tried to knock down our locker room door," says Cleveland State's SID. "He was trying to get at Larry Shyatt, one of our assistant coaches. I guess [Shyatt] was on him from the sidelines. A security guard and someone from Indiana State had to pull him away." Even when he wasn't chasing assistant coaches, Larry was "surly and mean" while he was at the tournament, said the SID.

In the team's next game, against Morris Harvey, Larry broke Jerry Newsome's 11-year-old ISU career scoring record of 2,147 points. Given a standing ovation, Larry was awarded the record-breaking ball. He considered giving the ball to his mother, who was in the stands, but at the last moment gave it to Newsome, who was standing on the sidelines. In Larry's words, after the game, "the whole town of French Lick" had come to see him break the record. Over the last seven games Larry had averaged more than 36 points along with 15 rebounds a game.

Now, with a 9–0 record, ISU was ready to begin playing its conference schedule. The cagers responded with four dazzling wins—by an average margin of over 20 points a game. Larry was having his finest season: against West Texas State, he responded with 32 points and a career high 20 rebounds; against Bradley, he scored his second triple-double of the season with 27 points, 18 rebounds, and 10 assists. At this juncture, the team had compiled a 13–0 record and was the only one ranked in the Top Twenty to still have an undefeated record.

Despite ISU's 13–0 record, there were many skeptics. After all, ISU had been 13–0 at this point the year before, too—only to go downhill. And the remaining schedule was composed of teams like the University of Wisconsin–Lawrence, East Carolina, and Morris Harvey. But there were significant differences between the two seasons. The

Sycamores were not facing a long road trip, there were no illnesses, and, more importantly, the chemistry as well as the overall talent level were much improved from the year before. Larry's point production and shooting percentage were slightly up, but basically on a par with the season before. He was shooting 53 percent and averaging about 32 points per game. The major change was that there were five other players on the present team who accounted for 400 more points than the third through eighth players the previous year.

Much of the team's improved chemistry stemmed from Larry's assuming more of a leadership role. Larry was especially more willing to assert himself because the last year's team chemistry had been so adversely affected by the personal concerns and problems of Harry Morgan, Richard Johnson, and Jimmy Smith. Morgan had been playing for the pro scouts and had become quite selfish; Johnson had numerous discipline problems and eventually left school altogether; and Smith was not one of Coach King's chosen few and, therefore, became disgruntled. And with Larry taking the lead to ensure that the team stayed more closely knit, many potential problems were avoided. Team morale was also helped by Hodges' more relaxed approach to discipline.

Confident that this season would be different from the last, the Sycamores took on New Mexico State but, like the fourteenth game of their previous year, the team played poorly. Despite playing at home, ISU was trailing at halftime, when an all-too-familiar sight appeared in the locker room: the president of the university. Richard Landini was probably as big a fan as any university president in the country. What other president would pace the sidelines every home football game? He would often appear in the Sycamore locker room during a game, ready to boost morale. His appearance with ISU trailing New Mexico State was the last thing Larry needed that day, and in line with his newfound leadership role, Larry let Landini know what his feelings were: "Get the fuck out of here." Landini left without a word. Hodges was obviously in a difficult position and remained silent. "But you know, how as a coach do you approach that? You can't say 'Can you come back later?'" says Shaw.

Regaining their concentration without the help of Landini, the cagers came back to defeat New Mexico State, 73–69. Though the next two league games were on the road, the team won handily, and then easily won its next two home games to boost their record to

18–0. And ISU found itself the only undefeated major college basketball team left in the country. It was possible that ISU would be officially ranked number one. At this point, every major magazine and newspaper was more desperate than ever to talk with Larry. It was the ultimate in frustration for Ed McKee: For ten years he had worked diligently with little success merely to get the Indianapolis papers to cover ISU ball games. Now everybody wanted to speak with him—about a player who didn't want to speak to anyone. Besides *Time, Newsweek, Life,* and all the sports periodicals, *The New York Times* and the *New York Post* were calling. Even the National Solid Waste Association called; they wanted information on Larry's days as a sanitation worker.

When the rankings came out, ISU was still ranked second; despite a loss, Notre Dame continued to be ranked first. There were still plenty of skeptics about ISU, led by NBC Commentator Billy Packer, who maintained that ISU did not deserve to be ranked number one, considering its weak schedule. The ranking was symptomatic of the lack of respect and recognition which the school had received, especially among the sport's more traditional elites. Those elites, mostly veteran coaches like Packer and those voting for the UPI, regarded ISU as an unproven upstart. ISU would have to win the conference and then beat good teams in the NCAA tournament in order to silence the critics. But the team had to concentrate on their next game, anyway. And it would be a tough one, at Las Cruces against MVC title contender New Mexico State, whom the Sycamores had only defeated by 4 points in their earlier meeting at Hulman Arena. By the close of the first half, in front of 14,000 fans, ISU validated its high ranking by shooting 60 percent and jumping to a 51–39 lead. The Aggies crept back into the game in the second half, however. With less than a minute left, New Mexico State had a 2-point lead despite Larry's 37 points, 17 rebounds, and 9 assists. Then Larry committed his fifth foul. The crowd was ecstatic, and it looked as if the nation's longest winning streak was in big trouble. With just 3 seconds left, the Aggies' Gregg Webb stepped to the line to add to the 83–81 lead. He missed the front end of the one-and-one, though, and Brad Miley controlled the rebound, immediately outletting the ball to Bob Heaton. Heaton, out on the wing on the left side of the floor near the ten-second line as the clock ticked down to 1 second, let it fly from 55 feet. The ball hit the backboard as the buzzer sounded and fell through to tie the game. The Aggie fans had started celebrating and were already running onto the court when the shot fell in. They and the Aggie team went into shock. The ISU team was jubilant, and, in the huddle, vowed to pull it out in overtime without Larry. And ISU held on at 91–89, as seldom-used reserve Rick Nemchek scored two crucial baskets. It was the most dramatic and perhaps the most satisfying victory of Larry's career. Everyone had contributed, and ISU had won as a team and not because their star had won the game by himself. Over the course of the season the team had come together like no previous team in Larry's career. Eight players were capable of making vital contributions at any given moment of the game. And considering that this occurred despite a wide disparity of talent was a tribute to Larry's selfless influence. To celebrate, big booster Max Gibson, who often flew to games in his own plane, treated the team to a postgame meal. Though technically a violation of NCAA rules, there is probably not a program in the land that doesn't occasionally violate the rules regarding meals. And often there are only a few restaurants still open after the games. "[After the game] we go back to the motel. It's like midnight, it's real late, we get our meal money, $2.50 or whatever the hell it was, and Max says, 'Hey, we're going out to eat.' We load everybody in the damn trucks and vans and everything. We go out, and we have the biggest damn Mexican food meal. Oh, it was fantastic. Got back at about two in the morning, the next morning we toured Juarez. It was a fantastic trip," says a member of the team.

It was on that trip to Mexico that Larry contracted a virus that was still troubling him at the completion of the road trip at Tulsa. Despite the virus, Larry managed his career high in rebounds with 22 to go along with 22 points, helping the team to a 66–56 victory. But Larry was too sick to celebrate with the 3,500 fans who greeted the cagers upon their arrival home at Hulman Arena where the team's 20–0 record and number-two ranking were celebrated, along with the official announcement that Bill Hodges was now head coach (instead of interim) and that Bob King was returning to take over as athletic director.

Immediately upon arriving home from their road trip, the team was faced with controversy when the widely anticipated *Sports Illustrated* feature on them came out. Writer Dan Newman had spent time with the team earlier in the season, but because he had been denied access to Larry, there was worry that the article would be critical. Those worries proved to be well-founded. The article, "Flying to the Top," was less about the team than it was about Larry—despite Newman's having promised, according to Coach Hodges, that the focus would be on the team. The only quoted player in the article was Carl Nicks, who felt his portrayal was slanted to imply that he was jealous of Larry. "Like most of his teammates, Nicks likes and admires Bird, but he is also bored by questions from reporters about Bird's personal life. "I don't understand why they don't want to talk about me," says Nicks. "I can play." Nicks was, to put it mildly, upset. "Carl Nicks is the most giving person anywhere," said Hodges. "I thought Carl was going to cry when he read that article. It almost totally destroyed him. He said to me, 'Oh, Coach, I can't believe he made it sound like that.'"

And maybe because of the denial of access, Newman, with the help of Larry Keith, decided to publish background material on Larry that Keith had accumulated for an *SI* article the year before. In that article, Larry Keith had taken great pains to be discreet after Georgia Bird had divulged a lot of personal information. He had only mentioned the failed marriage. Newman, however, described the marriage in greater detail, in addition to bringing up Joe's suicide. It was the first time these matters had ever been mentioned publicly, and Larry was particularly upset. He wasn't the only one. His younger brother Eddie,* who had been especially close to his father, was devastated. When Eddie read the article he "broke down and cried."

The article also discussed the subtle and not-so-subtle control that Larry exerted over the team. "Bob King...who allowed Bird to have his way in just about everything, endorsed Bird's silence. Hodges...has continued to indulge Bird to the extent that both he and many Indiana State players seem afraid of Bird."

The following Monday, February 5, Hodges used a press luncheon

---

*Eddie is, presently, a 6'6" forward on the Indiana State basketball team. He was named Freshman of the Year in the Missouri Valley Conference after averaging nearly 20 points per game in the latter part of the season. Georgia believes that Eddie, 21, isn't quite as talented as his brother, especially since he has yet to commit himself to working as hard as Larry. But Eddie and his older brother Jeff came from a much less financially deprived environment than the four older siblings. Both kids were "spoiled and never had to work like the four older kids," says a relative.

to respond to the accusations in the article: "I think both stories [including the Larry Keith story from the year before] were very derogatory.... I think [the *Sports Illustrated* writers] look for controversy. If they can't find it, they fabricate it."

Did Newman, in fact, "fabricate" as Hodges suggested? If Newman didn't fabricate, did he present a misleading picture of the team and its relation to Larry? Did Newman break assurances he made to Hodges regarding his writing about the team instead of Larry? Did Newman have a general moral obligation, or at least a specific one toward Eddie, not to mention Joe's death? There were only a few quotes in the article, and none of the participants, including Nicks, denied saying what was attributed to them. So the outward facts of the article weren't in dispute. Regarding Newman's assurances to Hodges about emphasizing the team instead of Larry, Newman disputes Hodges' claim. But writing about Larry and the team could not be separated into categories of relative emphasis. To many basketball pundits, Larry *was* the team.

While it was unfortunate that Eddie was pained by the article, his brother was after all a public figure. Newman had the right to print relevant information as long as it was true. So, when finally distilled, the article yields very little substance for objection other than that its tone does not deify Larry, the coaches, or the team, as other sports features had done.

What can be debated is the perception that King "allowed Bird to have his way in just about everything." King, like Hodges, had often deferred to Larry's judgment. Newman's comment is hardly controversial at face value. The implication that Larry would take advantage of his position at the expense of the team is. But it is a stretch of the imagination to derive even that implication from the context of the article. Less clear is the dispute whether Hodges and many of the players "seem afraid of Bird." The statement appears overstated, but it is not unreasonable to believe that Newman could have come to such a conclusion in the highly unusual and cryptic environment that had come to envelop the team.

King argues that Larry was treated the same as the rest of the team, except regarding the press. But the significance of granting Larry this special accommodation shouldn't be minimized. In the history of college sports it was an unprecedented one.

Moreover, the environment for the press was even more repressive than it would appear on the surface. In one instance, when a Chicago *Tribune* reporter walked into the locker room accompanied by a Terre Haute man known to the team, the mood abruptly changed. The reporter was immediately asked to wait outside, where he encountered student assistant Danny King. "I'm doing a story on Larry Bird," the writer said, "and I wonder if you have a few minutes to talk about him." King answered, "I don't talk about him unless I have his permission. That's the way we work." Larry was clearly the man on the team that everyone listened to, including Coach Hodges. If Larry didn't want anyone talking about him to the press, then nobody was going to do so. Similarly, when Larry wanted something done, corrected, or simply maintained on the court, everyone listened. It wasn't that everyone was afraid of him, but the players respected his role in the team's success enough that they were going to respond to his wishes at all times. Hodges felt the same way.

Larry was not about to let the lingering effects of a virus or the controversy surrounding the *SI* article deter him from his central task on the basketball court. Thus, only three days after the Tulsa game and one day after the news conference, Larry led the cagers to a rout of Drake. Larry recorded his third triple-double of the season, with 33 points, 10 rebounds, and 10 assists. With only five conference games remaining, ISU next faced conference doormat, Bradley, in Peoria. Bradley Coach Dick Versace, desperate for any edge, reasoned that if Larry's game accounted for well over half of his team's points, then shutting him down at the sacrifice of a defender for the rest of the team made sense. After all, what did he have to lose? His team had lost by 19 in their first meeting with ISU. So Bradley played a triangle-and-two of some sort (two men play Larry and the other three play a zone), with a permanent defensive sandwich on Larry. Larry was fronted by one player and defended by another at all times. Larry's response was to not force any shots and to set up as many shots as possible. Although ISU had a comfortable lead at halftime, Hodges was furious. He felt that the defense was illegal and, on top of that, that Larry was likely to lose his position as the number one scorer in the nation. But Larry prevailed on Hodges not to make any changes in an effort to get him the ball. The Sycamores won anyway, 91–72, with Larry totaling only 4 points and 11 rebounds.

If ISU fans were bemoaning Larry's loss of the national scoring lead, they didn't have to suffer long. The next AP poll finally acknowledged that ISU should be ranked number one in the country, given previously top-ranked Notre Dame's three losses. It was quite a triumph for such a small school. Terre Haute was jubilant. Larry and the team were the main topics of conversation everywhere. And in Terre Haute itself a fierce civic pride had taken hold. The city's self-esteem increased with each new victory. And in the courthouse, restaurants, bars, and, of course, barber shops, Larry Bird and the Sycamores were the main topic of conversation.

ISU's rapid climb to fame was not merely local or regional, however. It had finally, almost reluctantly, become national. The team had only just been featured on HBO two games earlier against Tulsa—their first national exposure. And the ISU juggernaut was not going to stop with HBO. NBC shifted its schedule to arrange for the final home game of Larry's college career to be televised nationally. NBC also switched announcers, pulling Billy Packer because of the uncomplimentary remarks he had made about the team. Thus, Al McGuire, who had been sympathetic to the team's fortunes, and Jim Simpson were to cover the telecast.

The team won its three games following the Bradley victory, including a squeaker at Southern Illinois. That particular game was notable for what happened off the court. For, well after the game was over, Shaw prepared to run interference for Larry through the fans waiting outside the locker room door. However, Larry decided just as they emerged that he wanted to sign autographs. And, for the rest of the season, he mostly continued to sign autographs after the game.

Larry was never a prima donna. His resistance to things like autographs and interviews was based in humility, not arrogance, and in the ever-present desire for his privacy. But Larry often went out of his way to fulfill those responsibilities which did not cry out for Larry Bird the celebrity. On his own initiative he had penned a thank-you note to Creighton Coach Tom Apke for Creighton's effort in helping him with his injured back the year before. He also made sure to pay a fine that Shaw had incurred while driving Larry's car on the way to pick up shoes at the airport. "He knew I was out doing something for him, so he paid it. But that's the kind of person he was." And when Larry accidentally knocked down a 9-year-old boy while running to the locker room, he picked him up and carried him into the locker room to meet his teammates and get autographs. And Larry saw to it that the boy received a basketball as well.

ISU went into the final game of its regular season with a 25–0 record. On Thursday night, fans started lining up for tickets to the Saturday afternoon game. But a typical late-February snowstorm blew in on the eve of the game, and by the morning of the game, temperatures were subzero with blizzard conditions. With the sudden accumulation, snow had piled up on the roof of the arena and begun melting, causing leaks to drip all over the floor. But paid work crews labored on the roof removing the snow, and volunteers helped spread a tarp over the floor until game time. The airport and all the roads were closed, yet most of the fans arrived hours before game time, each with a "terrible hanky" (the Sycamore blue handkerchiefs that ISU fans waved when excited). The program for the game was entitled, "A Collector's Edition: Larry Bird's Home Finale." Neither the TV audience nor the Hulman Arena crowd were disappointed as ISU won, going away 109–84.

Even more impressive than the lopsided victory was Larry's performance. At one point, early in the second half while standing 25 feet away from the basket in the left corner, Larry made a remarkable ball fake, as if to pass. The defender, Eric Kuhn, scurried toward the basket in search of the ball while Larry calmly popped the jumper from the corner. Then, with 2:30 remaining, Hodges prepared to substitute for Larry, but Mel Daniels noticed that he had 45 points, only 3 points away from his own scoring record. Though Larry passed up a couple of good shots to get the ball to the substitutes, it didn't take him long to go out in style by breaking his own single-game scoring record with 49 points and adding 19 rebounds and 5 assists. After the game, no one left, for, following Larry's NBC interview, the senior team members were to be honored for their careers at ISU. First, Rick Shaw, the manager–assistant trainer, was recognized, then the three senior members of the team: reserve Tom Crowder, Leroy Staley, and then Larry. Leroy and Larry, upon being introduced, ran over to embrace the recovered, but still frail, Bob King, standing at courtside during the celebration (King attended all of the team's home games). The ceremony finally ended with the Hulman Arena crowd singing, the "Amen" chorus, which had come to be the team's victory song.

ISU had yet to win the Missouri Valley Conference title. Their undefeated season had merely earned them the number-one seed and home-court advantage in the MVC postseason tournament. Thus, just two days after the emotional home-court finale, the team took the home court again, hosting West Texas State in a first-round game. The Sycamores had beaten the Buffaloes by 21 and 25 points during the season, but they gained the lead for the first time only near the end of the first half. Larry finished with 29 points and 14 rebounds, helping ISU to a 94–84 victory. Next was a semifinal tournament game against Southern Illinois, a much tougher opponent. The final outcome was fairly close, 75–70. Now only the championship final stood between ISU and the preseason goal that many skeptics had scoffed at: qualifying for the NCAA tournament.

To get there, ISU would have to get past the same New Mexico State team they had miraculously beaten one month earlier. Making things tougher for ISU was the Aggies' decision during the game to slow the ball down. But that worry paled in comparison to an incident just seconds after the start of the second half when Larry took a swipe at the ball, which was being held by an opponent, and was seen to cringe in pain. When he grabbed the rebound, he called for a time-out. Leaving the court for the locker room with Bob Behnke, Larry didn't return for six minutes, finally reentering the game with a thick foam pad on his thumb. Though obviously in pain, he immediately proceeded to steal the ball and score on the other end, thus helping the Sycamores close out a 69–59 victory.

Afterward, there was speculation that the injury might be serious enough to prevent Larry from playing in the NCAAs. But Larry wasn't about to let a little thumb injury affect the postgame celebration as he led an effort to throw all visitors to the locker room into the shower. That one of them was U.S. Senator Birch Bayh hardly mattered to either Larry or, as it turned out, the senator. Says Shaw, "Champagne was everywhere. . . . Of course, then the senator comes out, and you got to get him a sweat suit to wear home."

Once the fun was over, Behnke and Larry went off to get the thumb x-rayed. The results could have been worse, but they were not good. The thumb had been fractured in three places right at the tip so that every time it was touched, Larry experienced a great deal of pain. One doctor argued that Larry shouldn't play, because the thumb would swell up like a balloon. Larry asked Behnke if playing would make the thumb any worse. Behnke said no. So Larry was determined to play. Still, there were restrictions. NCAA rules did not allow metal or certain kinds of plastic as protection. According to Shaw: "I think [the thumb] hurt like hell. It was like a T fracture, and there's very limited things you can do with something like that, because of the rules that govern basketball. It can't be hard, you can't do this, you can't put a stick on it. You can't put plastic on it. God, it was just real limited." However, Behnke did come up with a solution. "Behnke made a plastic thing for him. And of course, everybody wants to tell Behnke what to do. He gets a call from Dick Gregory [the comedian-activist]. Everybody in the United States has a cure for his thumb....[Behnke is] an 'I'm-doing-it-my-way' type person and is usually right," says Shaw.

Meanwhile, both the UPI and the AP proclaimed ISU the number-one team in the country in their final regular-season poll. However, many voted for ISU in the poll not because they believed the Sycamores were the best team, but because the next-highest-ranked team had at least three defeats. However, ISU lacked the respect and recognition of the sport's more traditional elite. Moreover, the sudden elevation of Hodges to head coach had only aggravated the "legitimacy" factor. Hodges was hardly a member of the coaches' club. As a consequence, in the Coach of the Year voting, there were votes for "Bob Hodges," "Tom Hodges," "the coach who replaced Bob King," and, most tellingly, "Bird's coach." Even though Shaw had said earlier that Hodges hadn't made a coaching mistake all year, many people connected with the program believed that Larry deserved Coach of the Year.

Meanwhile, Larry flew to Atlanta to accept the Naismith Trophy, basketball's equivalent to football's Heisman Trophy for best player of the year. Appearing in shirtsleeves, Larry was to be interviewed by the TV and radio people, but did not object to being interviewed by the print media as long as his remarks were being televised. The Larry Bird who emerged from the interview was an unexpectedly poised, confident, and blunt young man, with a good sense of humor. Upon accepting the trophy, Larry said, "You couldn't have picked a finer guy for this award." Asked if he was aware of how important he had been in ISU's rise to fame, Larry replied, "Well, when I came there, they were drawing [only] 2,000 a game. Now every game is a sellout." It was a stellar performance for someone who usually appeared both shy and humble in public.

Larry's newly acquired poise derived from the confidence that fueled him on the court, the kind of attitude that had prompted Coach King to say, "Larry's confident. I've never been around a more confident player." Yet Larry had never exhibited that confidence to strangers off the court before. It was representative of how far he had come in his four years at ISU, especially this last year. In the press accounts that appeared the next day, Larry had earned glowing reviews.

One week after Atlanta, ISU was seeded first in the midwest regional and slated to play Virginia Tech. With the NCAAs under way, an unusual plea was made by Wayne Duke, the commissioner of the Big Ten, who was also chairman of the NCAA basketball committee. He begged Hodges to relent on Larry's press boycott since the regular season was over. Hodges was favorable to the suggestion, so when Larry agreed, it was settled; Larry would appear before groups of writers during the tournament. Meanwhile, as only the team knew, Larry was unable to rebound in practice during the week because of his injured thumb.

Before the game Larry refused to go along with any adjustments in the team's plays because of his condition, even though everyone was nervous about the thumb—including Larry. One fear was that an overzealous player from the rival team would try to take Larry out. "All he has to do is touch it, and he's gonna be in great pain," said Brad Miley. "I just hope someone doesn't go pounding on his hand just to get him out of the game." And once the game began, it seemed there was reason for concern among the 3,000 Sycamore loyalists who had traveled to Lawrence, Kansas. Larry didn't grab a rebound for the first 7 minutes, and with the first half almost halfway over, ISU was trailing, 18–14.

But as the game progressed, Larry and the rest of the team slowly found their rhythm. Larry shot a little less than usual, but still managed 22 points, 13 rebounds, and 7 assists. Moreover, the game was no contest, with ISU winning 86–69. In the game's closing minutes, TV viewers were granted an unexpected perspective on the injury. Larry was sitting on the bench, with Behnke stripping foam padding away from his thumb, as the TV camera panned in to witness Larry wincing in pain and mouthing a very obvious "Fuck." Afterward,

Behnke said, "Most guys would have been sitting and watching after an injury like that. But not Larry. He didn't give sitting a second thought. He is the toughest athlete I've seen in eighteen years in this business."

A few days after arriving back home, Larry, Hodges, Landini, and ISU booster Lu Meis flew to Chicago to accept the AP player and coach of the year trophies, respectively. Larry had won the AP award by a landslide. He adopted a more humble tone in accepting the AP's Adolph Rupp Award, obviously having prepared his remarks rather than ad-libbing as he had in Atlanta. "I want to thank the AP for picking me. I know there are a lot of players out there that are great, and I'm happy to be the one picked. It means a lot to me and my family. If it were not for my teammates, I would not be here. I want to thank them for everything they've done for me." However, Larry did make one characteristic departure before he began answering questions. "Is David Israel here? [He was not.] Too bad. I always did want to see what a real live prick looked like." (Israel, the Chicago *Tribune* columnist, as evidenced by his remarks quoted earlier, had often been very critical of Larry and the team.) While this hadn't been the classiest way to open an acceptance speech, Larry proceeded to surprise the writers in Chicago just as he had in Atlanta. For someone previously thought to be so naive and shy, he was now displaying an unusual degree of self-assurance, if not tact, in dealing with public interview sessions.

Preparations for the Sycamores' next game, against Oklahoma, were under way. The game was close for the first 13 minutes but ended in a blowout, with ISU winning 93–72. Larry's thumb had not been much of a problem as evidenced by his fine showing: 29 points, 15 rebounds, and 5 assists. But fatigue, more than anything, was beginning to wear Larry down. As he explained to his mother after the game, all he wanted to do was come back home to French Lick so he could sleep and avoid having to talk to any more people.

ISU was now beginning to convert some of the skeptics, but their first real test loomed on the horizon. In just two days after the win against Oklahoma, they were to be paired against fifth-ranked Arkansas, which was coming into the midwest regional final with a 15-game winning streak. Going into the game, Razorback Coach Eddie Sutton announced that his team would attempt to shut down Larry's passing game. But Larry adapted to this strategy and shot the ball more.

The lead seesawed back and forth. With 6 minutes remaining, Sutton stumbled into a great coaching move when he decided to front Larry to prevent him from getting the ball. And then when Larry did get the ball one of the frontcourt people would rotate to a position between Larry and the basket, resulting in an effective double team.

The new defense did prevent Larry from taking over the game. Arkansas forged to a 71–69 lead with a minute and a half left. But Larry hit 2 free throws to tie. With 18 seconds left, ISU had the ball and called for a time-out to set up their last play. The play was designed for Larry to shoot, with options for him to pass if he was double-teamed. Larry quickly passed to Steve Reed, cutting down the lane with 7 seconds left. As Reed drove to the basket, forward Scott Hastings jumped out to contest his drive. Reed spotted Bob Heaton to his left near the basket. The surprised Heaton bobbled the pass and, with 2 seconds on the clock, shot-putted the ball, left-handed, at the basket. The awkward shot rolled around the rim and dropped in as the buzzer sounded, giving the Sycamores a 73–71 victory.

The ISU partisans broke into the "Amen" chorus for the third time in the tournament, but this time the chorus seemed far more appropriate. It was a remarkable victory, if only for the fact that Arkansas shot 64 percent from the floor, 85 percent from the line, outrebounded ISU 25 to 20, committed just 10 turnovers, and still lost. ISU's 56 percent shooting wasn't too shoddy, either. And Larry led the way with 31 points and 10 of State's 20 rebounds. With the game over, the ISU fans had surged onto the floor and bedlam reigned as NBC's Bryant Gumble attempted to finesse an interview with Larry amidst the celebration. While Larry was still on the floor, a fan, probably only trying to shake Larry's hand, grabbed Larry's thumb. The pain was so great that Larry reacted by knocking the fan out. "I don't think he knew what he was doing," said Larry. "I dropped him to his knees with a punch to the mouth. It was just a reaction."

The win over Arkansas assured the team of a spot in the Final Four to be played in Salt Lake City, Utah. The Sycamores would take their 26–0 record against DePaul.

Meanwhile, circumstances weren't going to get less exhausting for Larry, tired as he was from the long season combined with the side trips to Atlanta and Chicago. Larry was scheduled to receive the Eastman Trophy in New York during the week before the Final Four. And he would have to submit to interviews again. Hodges had told him at the end of the regular season, "When you receive an award, you talk." The award, sponsored by Eastman Kodak, was the result of a vote for best player of the year by the National Association of Basketball Coaches. After saying, "I want to thank everybody. I am happy to get it," Larry submitted to over an hour of questions. Will Grimsley described the session as often "personal queries—mundane and provocative." Yet what was most impressive about Larry's performance was his giving the lie to the myths about him that the press had encouraged during the boycott. "[The reporters] were not dealing with a sullen, snarling, resentful ogre at all. What they got was just a big, overgrown kid from the little town of French Lick," says Grimsley.

On Thursday, March 22, as the team prepared to leave Terre Haute for Salt Lake City they had a surprise in store. Upon boarding the bus at Hulman Center that was to take them to the plane, the players were informed that they would be part of a motorcade through downtown first. Initially reluctant, the players became enthusiastic about the detour when they realized the tremendous enthusiasm of all of Terre Haute. Once airborne, the team and about 90 other fans and supporters were treated to Larry's famed scatological humor routine via the plane's intercom. Of course, everyone on the team was wearing his omnipresent cowboy hat and boots and chewing his Levi Garrett.* That the players joined in these off-the-court rituals was testimony to the intense fellowship and camaraderie that had developed within the team.

Indeed, much of the team's success could be traced to the support the players gave one another. That and the selflessness that had developed on the team could be traced to Larry's example. As Larry explained after the season, "We didn't worry about who was scoring the points, or who did this or that. We had a very unselfish basketball club. We had guys who wanted to win and guys that could handle everything emotionally. We were very loose as a team. It was enjoyable to play with the guys." Each player had been able to achieve the submerging of individual ego that is usually necessary for superlative team performance. "People really jump to help Larry. And maybe it wasn't so much Larry, it was anybody on that team,"

---

*Assistant Coach Mel Daniels had started a trend for all the team members to wear big cowboy hats and big boots.

says Shaw. "We all stuck together. We'd have done anything to help each other."

Still, the most important factor in the team's success was Larry's role as leader, or as coach, on the floor. In previous years he had been content to lead by example. But in his senior year Larry was well-aware of the responsibilities of his leadership role on the team. He took it upon himself to make sure that all the team members were in bed early the night before a game. And he always tried to promote the idea of the team as a group: "If we were out eating and somebody did something wrong, I'd say, 'Hey, this is a group and this is going to reflect on all of us.'" And of course, much of Larry's leadership was still by example on the playing floor.

"[Larry] gets along great with teammates, and a lot of that is because of the way he plays," said Hodges. "He passes the ball. If you are open, he gets it to you." Teammate Reed added that Larry's example was contagious. "Just being around a player of Larry Bird's calibre, you pick up a lot of things. He's such a super player and such a fantastic passer. I think some of his passing has rubbed off on me a little." In the final sense, much of the goodwill and harmony engendered on the team came from Larry's effort to give everyone support. "Larry's a great player, and another thing, he respects his teammates. He says, 'Hey, great job.' and I think this gets him respect," says Hodges. To put it quite simply, as Bob Heaton did, "Everyone gets along with Larry."

Larry had also played a major role in literally bringing and keeping the team together. He was instrumental in getting Carl Nicks on the team as well as in keeping Bob Heaton there. Said Nicks about Larry: "He brings out the best in all of us. I would like to play with him forever."

In the Final Four, after Michigan State obliterated Pennsylvania 101–67 in the first semifinal, ISU took the floor to face DePaul and their 65-year-old coach, Ray Meyer. The second game was drastically different from the first, with the two teams tied fifteen times as neither was able to take a commanding lead in the opening half. DePaul had shot 60 percent from the field but was still losing 45–42, because ISU was shooting 75 percent, a percentage directly attributable to one of the finest semifinal shooting performances of all time:

Larry simply could not miss, hitting 11 of 12 shots for the half, although his thumb appeared to be bothering him.

When Larry hit a sixteen-footer with 7:30 remaining, ISU led by only 69–65. And Larry was to take only one more shot the rest of the game. With 5 minutes left, DePaul took the lead. But with 50 seconds left, Heaton put ISU into the lead, 75–74. With 4 seconds left, Aguirre launched a desperation fadeaway. Staley garnered the rebound and was fouled. DePaul's desperation pass with one tick on the clock went for naught, and ISU emerged with a 76–74 semifinal victory.

It had been an impressive performance for Larry. He had tied Charlie Scott's semifinal record for most field goals with 16 and, more remarkably, accomplished it with just 19 shots. Not only did Larry score 35 points but he also recorded 16 rebounds and 9 assists. But Larry committed 11 turnovers and shot just once in the last 7½ minutes, leading many observers to wonder how much his thumb was bothering him. Larry discussed the thumb after the game: "Some days I can play with it, sometimes I can't. Today I couldn't use it." Larry added with a touch of bravado, "I felt sorry for the other team, I was shooting well and begging for the ball. Some days you have it, some days you don't." Larry would have all of two days to rest his thumb and make sure that he "had it" when Michigan State and Indiana State met for the national championship.

Sunday was a designated day for interviews, and Larry was scheduled to speak before some 300 press people at a brunch honoring him as the player of the year. Such an event was the last thing Larry was going to give up his much-needed sleep for. Hodges appeared in Larry's place and promised that Larry would appear in a few hours. Near noon, Craig McKee drove Larry over to the Salt Lake City Hilton, where the news conference was to be held. He remembers that Larry was quiet and seemed a little nervous. Once there, Larry assumed a more self-assured persona, though he had arrived wearing a white tee-shirt, warm-up jacket, Levis, and sneakers. His responses were not the typical cliché-ridden, say-nothing answers to which the reporters had grown so accustomed. They got terse answers to stupid questions and thoughtful answers to better ones: "(*Q*) What do you remember about [Magic] Johnson when you played with him in an All-Star game? (*LB*) He wouldn't pass me the ball. (*Q*) How is your thumb? (*LB*) Broke. (*Q*) (Laughter) You seem to have a great feeling for passing. (*LB*) My feeling about passing is that it don't matter who's doing the scoring as long as it's us. I just think when a man is open, he should get the ball whether it's 30 feet out on the wing or underneath. We had guys last year who didn't care about passing. They thought scoring was important.... We didn't expect to be here. (*Q*) You didn't expect to be here? (*LB*) (Smiling) Did you expect us to be here?''

On Monday, March 29, it was evident that the upcoming game featuring Larry Bird and Magic Johnson would be the most popular college game ever televised. The game, for many, had become more of a "Bird versus Magic" contest than an Indiana State versus Michigan State battle. Earvin "Magic" Johnson had transcended position just as Larry had. At 6'8" he was the best point guard in the nation. Considering that most point guards were a half-foot smaller just made his achievement that much more impressive. Magic had also amazed fans and experts alike with his ability to determine games without scoring. He wasn't the leading scorer on the Michigan State team, but there was no doubt he determined the game's outcome. And though he was only a sophomore, he was the leader of probably the best team in college basketball. His maturity was further evidenced by the speculation that he would declare hardship after the tournament and then be selected as the top player in the NBA draft. Some observers believed Johnson was a better player than Larry, and many more believed he possessed greater potential for the pro game than his counterpart at Indiana State. So the matchup of the two players took on an added significance. Larry and Magic were not only considered two of the finer players to be matched up in a championship game in some time, but each possessed a certain aura of greatness. Magic had an effervescent personality and a style of game to match. And no point guard had ever been so big or rebounded so well, since the legendary Oscar Robertson, who had been at least 3 inches shorter. As for Larry, he was one of the best shooting big men to play college basketball since Jerry Lucas and Rick Barry, but he had a more effective game than they did. He was a better rebounder than Barry and a better passer than Lucas. On top of all those skills, Larry had a very marketable quality: He was white. And the game was desperate for white superstars; there had not been one since Bill Walton left UCLA in 1974. Since then there had been a growing sense among many fans, most of whom were white, that a white player was incapable of being the best in the game. When Larry had been unanimously chosen as the best college player in the nation, it alleviated a sense of inferiority that many white fans felt. The professional game had experienced a vast drop in popularity and the college game had stagnated. But with the Bird-Magic matchup, TV ratings would be the highest ever. To this day a greater percentage of viewers watched Larry's and Magic's NCAA final game than any other televised basketball game. Thirty-eight percent of the TV sets that were on at the time (24.1% of all homes with a TV set) were tuned in. And though there were a number of reasons for the appeal of the matchup, the racial factor should not be underrated. Many experts were estimating that Larry's presence in the NBA could mean as much as 5,000 added attendance per game. When Larry received the Adolph Rupp Trophy in Chicago he was peppered by questions about being "the great white hope." Indeed, even Al McGuire, with an unmatched reputation for racial sensitivity, told it like it was when he too admitted that Larry was the great white hope.

Thus, even though the pundits were predicting a potential mismatch in Michigan State's favor because of MSU's superior talent, the two superstars' marquee value overrode the question of which team was stronger. There was some doubt about the outcome. After all, ISU was 33–0, and Larry was such an unusual player that many believed he could will his team, inferior or not, to win.

Michigan State, however, had been truly dominant in the tournament. They had manhandled Notre Dame in a powerful exhibition of basketball strength. And what they did to Pennsylvania was embarrassing. Larry was right to the point when he said before the game, "All I know is, we better come to play 'cuz we'll get blown out if we don't." Not only did MSU have Magic, but also two other likely first-round draft picks and pros, Greg Kelser and Jay Vincent. Moreover, insiders knew that Larry and his teammates had never seen anything like Coach Judd Heathcoate's 2-3 matchup zone. Though a zone, it matched up with one man on Larry at all times, no matter what zone of coverage he was in. Unlike the box-and-one, the man on Larry varied depending on his position on the floor. Plus, another defender would switch to guard Larry just enough to be more than a single team but less than a double team. The defense retained the best parts of the zone and the man-to-man with double teaming. Yet the defense did not appear to have the weaknesses of either. While in recent years, coaches have developed a variety of techniques to handle this defense, in 1979 it was new, and no one had yet figured out how to defuse it. MSU had the further advantage of having been able to practice the defense against Magic, whose game was similar to Larry's. If the defense could prevent Larry from shooting, it could, at the same time, prevent him from passing as well.

In the Sycamore locker room Monday evening before the game, an unusual situation occurred. Shaw recalls the incident by prefacing his remarks with the comment that Larry had the greatest desire to win he had ever seen. "Behnke taped [Larry's] ankles for the final game. And Larry looked at whoever was sitting on my table—I think it was Heaton—and [Larry] said, 'I hope you got it tonight 'cuz I just don't feel it. I don't think I have it tonight.' And I looked at him and I said, 'You better have it tonight. This is what we waited for, all that time, when Billy Packer said, "Ah, you guys don't belong here," and Al McGuire is taking up for us.' And son of a gun, I don't know what happened."

The fact that one week earlier Larry had been complaining that he wished he could just be back in French Lick to sleep and not be bothered provides a clue. And since then Larry had flown to New York and Salt Lake City to fulfill press responsibilities. On top of that, he had played another grueling game with a thumb that was still not up to par. His aunt claimed he was having breathing problems because of the altitude and the dryness of the climate. No wonder Larry hadn't been able to get out of bed Sunday morning. All the traveling above and beyond the team's 33 games was finally starting to take a toll, as was the burden of carrying a not-terribly talented team. Larry had been required to go to the well once too often, and on his last trip he had come up dry. As Larry had said after his hot shooting against DePaul, "Some days you have it, some days you don't." That night, he didn't have it.

Within five minutes of the opening tip, MSU took the lead and never lost it. They went into the intermission with a 37–28 lead. MSU had shot 52 percent to ISU's 38 percent from the field, which was due mostly to Larry's inability to hit from outside. He had been frustrated by the matchup zone and shot poorly throughout the half, hitting on only 4 of 11 shots. The team had hoped to make the necessary adjustments to the matchup zone during the intermission, but Hodges was unable to come up with an offensive scheme to counteract the zone. Of course, without Larry on top of his game, the chances of beating a team as powerful as MSU appeared remote, anyway. Yet it was not an insurmountable lead. If the cagers could control the first couple of minutes, they could make up the four field goals that separated them.

The few hopes that remained were dashed quickly after the beginning of the second half. MSU role player Terry Donnelly hit four straight jumpers to widen the deficit to sixteen at 44–28. MSU closed out the game decisively, 75–64. The game's results could be summed up in Larry's statistics; he shot only 7 of 21 from the field, and could add a mere 2 assists (all in the first half) to his point total. Judd's matchup had done its job. And Magic had finished with 24 points, 7 rebounds, and 5 assists in being named the Most Valuable Player of the tournament.

For Larry, the NCAA's fifth leading all-time scorer, it was an ignominious way to end a glorious career, let alone a near-perfect season. The TV camera slowly panned while Larry, crying, buried his head in a towel at the game's conclusion. He had been so frustrated by the combination of his own ineffectiveness and the success of the zone that during the game he had continually screamed, "Give me the ball," at his teammates.

Larry did not appear after the game as scheduled to talk to the press. Coach Hodges explained, "You have to realize that when you play as hard and as intensely as Larry has, and you lose, you have to have emotion." For Larry, it wasn't just the end of a game; it was the end of a career. But Larry's inability to appear after the defeat left a sour taste in the mouths of even his most ardent defenders. As Will Grimsley wrote, "It is Bird's right as a free man in a free society to take the press or leave it.... Less understandable was his failure to tighten his jaw and show up for the postgame press conference—a slight that reflected on his team, his college, and himself. He had proved more accessible after the Sycamores' first victory. His teammates showed, as did the stout-hearted kids of DePaul and Penn, whose hurt and disappointment certainly were as deep."

Instead of appearing, Larry had had Ed McKee pass out a mimeographed statement: "Michigan State is an excellent team. They played very tough defense and had a real good zone. Unfortunately, the ball wouldn't drop for us, and we missed too many free throws. I hate to lose, just like all the other guys on the team, but I guess we did all right. We won 33 games. We gave it the best we had; we just didn't hit the shots tonight.'' There were few who would claim that Larry was arrogant or spoiled, but not having to appear for the press was a special privilege that had not been granted to any other player. The pullout made him look like a sore loser, who couldn't take the heat of a big loss. That the team so willingly accommodated Larry in his whims made it seem all the worse.

Though he was not willing to excuse Larry's actions, Grimsley understood why such an incident had occurred. "This majestic giant of a man, although a campus idol, shows no trace of being spoiled. Misunderstood? Yes. Arrogant? No. The kink in his rugged armor is naïveté.''

The "losing" team arrived home to 5,000 cheering fans at the airport. Not only that, the team's plane had been escorted through the skies by four Indiana Air National Guard F100s, which saluted the players as they debarked. On each jet was written, "ISU is Still No. 1.'' At the airport the players boarded buses for a tribute to be held at Hulman Arena, but were greeted by thousands lining the route of the motorcade. At Hulman, some 15,000 fans stood for three minutes applauding and shouting, "We're number one.'' Larry served as M.C. and roasted Coach Hodges, several teammates, and himself. Throughout he displayed the wit and humor which his teammates had long appreciated but which the fans had not been privy to. In summing up, Larry said: "I'd like to present this so-called second-place trophy to the community of Terre Haute, and anybody else who thought we'd be here.''

Larry's senior season was a fitting conclusion to quite possibly the greatest collegiate success story of all time. For, when it was over, only Pete Maravich, Freeman Williams, Oscar Robertson, and Elvin Hayes had scored more points. But only one of those five had been recruited while working on a sanitation truck, a two-time college failure with only two years of organized basketball experience. And the high point of such an unprecedented rise to stardom was Larry's senior season. Larry had finished as the second leading scorer in the country, with a 28.6 point average; he had been national runner-up all three years. He was also fourth in the nation in rebounding with a 14.9 average. And his average of 5.5 assists per game was by far the highest of his career. He had maintained his shooting from the field at 53 percent, for all three seasons. And his senior year produced a healthy improvement in free-throw percentage at 83 percent.

In a tribute to his senior season, as well as his college career, Larry had swept every significant player of the year award, including the Adolph Rupp (AP), the Naismith (UPI), the Eastman, the Wooden, and the USBWA trophies. If that weren't enough, the *Sporting News, Basketball Times, Basketball Weekly,* and every significant basketball publication tabbed him as Player of the Year. In his college career, Larry broke at least 16 ISU records, setting career marks in scoring, rebounding, assists, and, probably, steals. Besides averaging over 30 points a game, he had averaged 13.2 rebounds and 4.5 assists. In 94 games he had maintained a 53.5 field-goal percentage and an 83.3 free-throw percentage. Furthermore, he was the first Sycamore to score 900 points in a season, and he did it all three years. Overall, in 94 career games, he had failed to score in double figures only once and had failed to score at least 20 points only seven times. As a model of consistency his career could not be questioned. He scored at least 30 points in 49 of the games and 40 points another 15 times. But most important of all, in those 94 games, Larry led the Sycamores to a 81–13 record, including a 50–1 mark at home.

He had created his own era. And with that era he had changed an entire community forever. "Look up there at those white flags," says a fan today, pointing to an NIT banner, two NCAA banners, and an NCAA runner-up banner. "There wasn't any before *he* came, and there haven't been any more since *he* left." The atmosphere during the Bird era did not grow overnight. The attitude of the typical Sycamore fan had become cynical over the years. However, the Bird era not only changed student consciousness in a way the Vietnam War never had at ISU, but revolutionized the entire city's consciousness too. About halfway through Larry's first season, in 1976, attendance had more than doubled to an average of 6,200. For the start of Larry's second year, in 1977, season ticket sales had increased to 5,300. And once the season was under way, nearly every game was a sellout (maximum capacity, 10,220). And this was so even at the games played during hazardous weather conditions. By Larry's senior year, in 1978, ISU basketball—or Larry Bird Ball—had become the winter's top activity.

During the Bird era, the university experienced a revolution in its image of itself. "I can knock on a hundred doors, which I have," said Landini, "and give 95 speeches to service clubs throughout the state of Indiana, and go to 115 alumni meetings,...but he can do more, you see, in a single three-game road trip in calling attention to the institution." Student enrollment increased 5 percent in Larry's senior year, the largest jump among all of Indiana's public universities. Graduates of ISU in the Bird era were known to put on their résumés that they had attended "Larry Bird University."

In 1984, when the Celtics won the world championship, Larry, on TV, dedicated the championship to Terre Haute. (He had dedicated the first championship in 1981 to French Lick.) Larry had always felt badly that he had not been able to bring the 1979 NCAA championship back to Terre Haute. He believed he had let the community down. Yet the city's passion for Larry had remained strong. And when he dedicated the 1984 championship to Terre Haute, the city's Bird craze became obsessive again. Since then, Terre Haute has not been able to reach its Larry Bird threshold. Larry responded to the city's support by holding his first annual Larry Bird Golf Classic, with the proceeds going to the Terre Haute Boys' Club, where he used to work summers. There have now been five golf classics which have probably raised in the vicinity of $150,000. Larry's desire to give something back to the community that so strongly supported him comes from a genuine gratitude toward a place that made him feel comfortable in a not-always-comfortable period of his life. Many of the values that Larry still believes in derive from the valley. Those same values flourish in Terre Haute. If only for that, Terre Haute deserves credit for contributing to Larry's ultimate success.

Larry's final collegiate season could hardly have been more dramatic. But it was only a kind of apprenticeship for the next twelve months of attention, publicity, and change that Larry would soon be experiencing as he prepared to make the transition into the pros. But the end of his collegiate basketball career didn't mean that his academic responsibilities were finished.

At the beginning of June, two weeks after finishing his student teaching, Larry became the first member of his family to receive a college diploma, with a degree in physical education. (His brother Mark played out his eligibility at Oakland City College where he was "a good small college player," according to Jim Jones. Mark thought he had enough credits to graduate, but then found out at the last minute he did not. He was so discouraged that he did not finish.)

When he had first arrived on campus, Larry's attitude toward education was one of indifference. He, like most of his French Lick friends, had never planned on going to college anyway. He thought, "What am I going to use this diploma for? I'm just going to go back to French Lick and get a job," says Coach Evans. Indeed, Larry had been so lax about his studies in high school that he was threatened with ineligibility in his senior year if he didn't get his grades up. That he did so only reflected his desire to play. Janet claims that she helped Larry get his grades up. "Larry would have never played in his senior year of high school if it hadn't been for me," says Janet. When Larry arrived at ISU, Coach King was concerned that Larry's attitude would prove to be a problem: "But he didn't have the trouble we thought he might have. And he blended in as a student very well right away." Nonetheless, Larry confided in Georgia that he was uncomfortable with his lack of preparation for college. "I didn't know a noun from a pronoun. I was ashamed." Georgia says that Mark helped Larry write his papers when Mark was in Terre Haute. And before that, Larry relied heavily on Janet for help with his homework and papers because "he just didn't know what to do or where to begin," says Janet. Eventually, with the help of tutors and because of his increasing awareness of the value of education, he was able to acquire the skills to better handle his academic demands.

But Janet and others remember that Larry was very diligent about going to class—at least, until his senior year. Janet says that she heard that he often missed his classes then, but others claim that Larry continued to be conscientious. Probably both versions are correct, since Larry was on the road much more frequently during his senior year. Other classmates confirm that Larry was not one to miss class. Says Baseball Coach and P.E. Instructor Bob Warn: "He never missed a class, was always on time, and always worked as hard as he does on the basketball floor."

Despite Larry's less-than-sterling grades, others testify that it was a point of honor for Larry to make it on the same terms as the rest of the students. Coach Evans admits that Larry could have gotten away with a lot. He didn't choose to do so. And it should also be considered that for all of Larry's evolving interest in school, his potential for a high grade-point average was mitigated by his status, not his intelligence. The time consumed in traveling to basketball games alone was a major impediment to his studies. And even with the efforts to shelter Larry from the press and fans, his free time was still more restricted than that of the other players.

Larry's primary problem in school stemmed from his worries that others would perceive him as dumb. According to Larry's mother, "Larry never thought he could make it in school. He wanted to play basketball, but he feared the schoolwork." King disputed Georgia's account, saying, "No, I don't think he's afraid of anything. He just didn't feel comfortable in certain situations."

Larry was quite candid about his academic abilities. "Basketball is my whole life, and it will always be my whole life. I'm a lot smarter on the court than I am in life. I get schoolwork done, but I ain't no genius in school. In the classroom, my mind is always on basketball." After his graduation he spoke of the attitude he'd had to overcome. "I never thought I'd graduate. Not because of basketball, but because I didn't think I was smart enough." But by the end of his junior year, Larry had become interested in getting his diploma as an end in itself: "In education, like they say, whether it's used or not, it's always a great thing to have."

Given his background, that Larry graduated was quite an accomplishment. (Eighty percent of the players in the NBA never receive a degree.) Characteristically, Larry downplayed the achievement when he got his diploma. "It proved one thing—if I can get a college education, there's hope for everyone else. When I got out of high school, I didn't have great grades, just enough to get by. So a lot of people laughed at the idea of me going to college. But my mother used to tell me, 'Son, you're going to be the first one from either side of the family to earn your degree.' It was always on my mind: get an education."

And before Larry's college education could be finished, he would begin to undergo a financial education, with agent and contract negotiations in full force within weeks of his final college game. Moreover, in his personal life, Larry was still reeling from the aftershocks of decisions that had been made years before. Even more dramatic was the impending adjustment to big city life that would have to be made. It had taken Larry almost three years to fully adjust to Terre

Haute and even then it had been a fragile accommodation. Some people wondered whether he could even last a month in a large urban locale. But Larry's ability to adjust to change had grown markedly since he had moved to Terre Haute just four years earlier. He was no longer the insecure teenager uncertain of what the future might hold, and unaware of the full extent of his talents.

Larry's Stats at Indiana State

YEAR	G	MIN	AVG	FG	FGA	PCT	FT	FTA	PCT
75–76	Did Not Play—Transfer Student								
76–77	28	1033	36.9	375	689	.544	168	200	.840
77–78	32			403	769	.524	153	193	.793
78–79	34			376	707	.532	221	266	.831
Total	94			1154	2165	.533	542	659	.822

YEAR	REB	AVG	A	AVG	ST	BL	PTS	AVG
75–76	Did Not Play—Transfer Student							
76–77	373	13.3	123	4.4			918	32.8
77–78	369	11.5	125	3.9			959	30.0
78–79	505	14.9	187	5.5	85	27	973	28.6
Total	1247	13.3	435	4.6			2850	30.3

G = game; MIN = minutes; AVG = average; FG = field goals; FGA = field goals attempted; PCT = percentage; FT = free throws; FTA = free throws attempted; REB = rebounds; A = assists; ST = steals; BL = blocks; PTS = points.

11 / *The Committee, the Contract, and a New World, 1979*

Just two weeks after losing the national championship Larry became the first person in the history of the prestigious John Wooden Award to decline to attend the acceptance ceremony. Larry claimed his student teaching requirements prevented his appearing in Los Angeles for the honor. But Larry didn't like these affairs to begin with, and his tolerance had been diminished even further by the sheer number of banquets he had attended in the last month alone. With his diploma in the offing, Larry had to draw the line somewhere. Plus, despite initial misgivings, he had fulfilled yet another commitment, playing in an all-star game only days before. Two days after the loss to Michigan State for the championship, Larry flew back to Las Vegas to participate in the Pizza Hut All-Star Classic. He had received more votes from pizza buyers than any player ever before, over 2 million. At first, Larry had declined to play. This all-star game was essentially an opportunity for college players to showcase their skills for the pro scouts on the eve of the pro draft. Thus, the game had little to offer Larry. But the owners of the Terre Haute Pizza Hut, Chuck Culp and Gary Fears, told Larry that local kids would be disappointed with Larry's decision. So, Larry changed his mind. More than just the local franchise and kids profited from Larry's change of heart as Max Gibson flew Larry's girlfriend, Dinah, and his little brother Eddie out to see the game. Larry rewarded his guests and the voters' confidence by earning MVP honors to help the East beat the West.

On Wednesday, April 4, three days after Larry's return from Las

Vegas, Bob Woolf was announced as Larry's "sports attorney."*
"[Larry] is a throwback to the old-time athlete who played sports
because he loved to. Meeting him has been like a breath of fresh air
for me," said Woolf. He had been chosen to represent Larry by a
group of Terre Haute businessmen otherwise known as "the committee." The committee had been put together by Terre Haute department store president Lu Meis. Meis, along with the late Max
Jones of the Terre Haute Boys' Club and Max Gibson, who was not
on the committee, were older men whom Larry had come to trust
and rely upon during his college career.

Meis, whose family had been a fixture in the community for over
a century, had taken over the family business and greatly expanded
it to include stores throughout Indiana, Illinois, and Kentucky. Larry
admired the hard work and vision that helped determine Meis's success. So in his senior year, he asked Meis for guidance on his future
pro career. The first task on that agenda was screening agents. Meis
devised a unique and extraordinarily effective plan which insulated
Larry from the burdens of selecting an agent and at the same time
ensured that he would be able to choose the agent best-suited for his
needs. What Meis evolved was the idea of "the committee"—having a group of four Terre Haute businessmen guide Larry through
much more than just the intricate maze of agent selection. They would
also advise on contract negotiations, financial decisions, and other
assorted responsibilities suddenly appearing on the horizon as Larry
prepared to make the transition from sheltered college star to professional athlete.

The members of the committee constituted a fairly representative microcosm of the Terre Haute business community. The four,
whose offices were within a couple of blocks of one another on
Wabash Avenue, were, besides Meis, John W. Royce, president of
Merchant's Bank and Trust, one of the two largest banks in Terre
Haute; Paul Dennehie, Meis's vice president for advertising and sales
promotion; and Ed Jukes, a vice president at Merchant's. The four
men were friends, and had worked with one another on various
projects over the years. They may have represented a certain homo-
geneity of interest, but at least they weren't wanting for religious di-

---

*Woolf eschews the term "agent." "I'm a sports attorney. I'm a lawyer, and my sole
business now is representing athletes."

versity. "We've got a Jew, a Catholic, and a Presbyterian on the committee. We've covered all the bases."*

The committee understood Larry's values and his desire not to be bothered by labyrinthine financial concerns. He just wanted to play ball. And as far as material needs went, Larry's desires were very simple. As a committee member put it, "All [Larry] wanted was a garage full of six-packs and some way that a six-pack could automatically be replaced each time he took one out. We're doing all this for him. He doesn't really want much." Still, the committee set out to secure for Larry as much as the market could bear and then to protect and invest Larry's income. The committee's first challenge was to stave off the wave of agents ready to besiege Larry during his final season and to act as a buffer between them and Larry.

By February the committee had already been approached by some thirty-five agents; the committee itself had approached nine. At least two members of the ISU basketball staff were backing their own choices for agent. One of those agents had already tried to ingratiate himself with Larry a year and a half before. Sensing that Larry was a rising star, the agent managed to get himself appointed as a basketball referee for the World University Games, as well as for a number of the tournaments in Italy and Yugoslavia beforehand. There he attempted to befriend Larry, but Larry would have nothing to do with him. Larry also understood there might be a possible conflict of interest for the NBA Players' Association legal counsel Larry Fleisher (who nevertheless continues to represent a number of NBA players). Thus, Fleisher was never seriously considered. Another agent came into the process late and tried to intimidate Meis. Asserting he knew relatives of Meis, the well-known agent at first claimed to have a lucrative contract from 7-Up in hand, and only if Larry signed with him in the next two days would the contract be Larry's. When Meis said, "Absolutely not," the agent pelted him with obscenities. Later, the agent called back, contrite, explaining that he should still be considered because, he told Meis, "If Larry likes a prick like you, he's going to love me." Still other notable agents arrived too late in the process to be considered.

Finally, after the committee had completed many hours of inter-

---

*The decision was made that Bob King would be, more or less, an honorary member, providing input from a coach's perspective.

views, two finalists were selected: Reuvan Katz and Bob Woolf. Katz, the famed Cincinnati attorney for Pete Rose, Johnny Bench, and Tony Perez, had the advantage of being well known to the committee. Moreover, he was considered both shrewd and scrupulously honest. Katz had earlier negotiated Pete Rose's then record-setting $800,000 per year contract. Katz also had an edge with the committee because he charged a standard hourly fee. Katz was a little reluctant to handle Larry by himself, however, because he had never had a basketball client. So, he asked another associate with some basketball connections to join him in representing Larry. But when the committee interviewed the associate, they were immediately put off by his boasting that whenever one of his clients was in a slump, he immediately consulted with the client in an effort to help break the slump. With that, the interview came to a swift close, and Katz was subsequently informed that his associate was unacceptable.

While his chances had been greatly enhanced by the above episode, Woolf first had to overcome some doubts on the part of the committee. Although Woolf claimed to be the first attorney to have ever negotiated a contract between player and management (he advised Earl Wilson of the Detroit Tigers), his influence as a sports attorney, or agent, had greatly diminished over the years. Woolf also boasted that he had represented more than 300 athletes over the years, including Boston stars John Havlicek and Carl Yastrzemski. But in truth, though both Havlicek and Yastrzemski remained close to Woolf, both had negotiated their last contracts on their own. In fact, Havlicek had called the committee on behalf of another aspirant, Larry Fleisher. Woolf was also elusive about his fee. He refused to charge by the hour, arguing that such an arrangement placed a premium on stringing out negotiations. He nonetheless refused to quote a percentage, claiming he liked to set his fee on a case-by-case basis.

The committee felt that Woolf was unduly evasive, and they did not want to settle on him until they had some assurances about his fee. Woolf was well-aware that there were interested agents willing to settle for a lesser fee, and he did not want to tip his hand. Still, he was favored by the committee though Katz came back and agreed to handle Larry by himself. To Woolf's advantage was his representation of baseball player Thurman Munson and basketball players like Otis Birdsong and Calvin Murphy. And the committee had been impressed by Woolf's intellectual credentials. His autobiography, *Be-*

hind Closed Doors, was the first-ever by an attorney representing athletes, and he had also published in scholarly legal journals. Furthermore, Woolf had a considerable reputation for honesty and integrity. (Rivals claimed that Woolf had an edge because he had an in with local Terre Haute lawyer Joseph Anderson, who later did some legal work for Larry. However, a committee member explained that Anderson had absolutely no input on the committee; thus the attorneys' relationship was irrelevant.) And most important of all was the fact that Woolf lived in Boston. Woolf pretty much clinched his selection with a handshake agreement which proposed that in a year he would submit a fee based on the final negotiated contract. If that fee was not acceptable to the committee, he would tear it up. In agreeing to Woolf's terms the committee conceded that Woolf was a tough negotiator, if only for his refusal to acquiesce in disclosing a specific fee.

Larry did not have a large role in the committee's deliberations, by choice, but he did have final say and veto power as in the cases of Fleisher and the agent cum referee. And the committee was willing to commit only after a three-hour dinner with Larry determined that Woolf and he got along well. They got along so well in fact that Larry had no hesitation in joking with Woolf. When Woolf later asked Larry why he had chosen him over Katz, Larry wryly replied, "Well, Mr. Woolf, that other guy was just too smart for me, so I chose you."

It was fortunate that Larry and Woolf got along so well. For the committee knew how important it was to gain Larry's trust and affection. It was hoped that Woolf could develop a close relationship, or at least some kind of bond, with Larry. Such a bond would go a long way toward reducing the chances of Larry bolting Boston because of difficulties in adjusting to a big city. These were not idle worries. Larry fueled them when he informed a Terre Haute reporter during his senior year that he wanted to play for the Indiana Pacers, not the Celtics. The committee was also mindful of how tenuous Larry's staying in Terre Haute had been. Similarly, they were well-aware of the importance of King's efforts to provide a kind of surrogate family for Larry. Thus, the committee believed that Woolf's role in keeping Larry in Boston might be even more important than the contract he eventually negotiated.

Woolf and the committee were not the only ones worried that Larry might bolt Boston. This was a particular concern of the Celtics as well. And Larry wasn't about to give assurances that it wouldn't happen. One NBA general manager pointed out that much of the problem could be attributed to Indiana State's overprotection of Larry. "He's a country boy. He was terrified in Bloomington; how's he going to relate to a big-city situation? He's been shielded from the press; how's he going to relate to that? It's foolish. They haven't prepared him. There's no question he has a major transition ahead of him." Nevertheless, the same GM explained, the Celtics really had no choice except to go after him. "Nobody will run away from Larry because [of fears that he will flee]. The Celtics will wade in with both barrels. They can't afford not to. They have to have him." There were, of course, the same concerns in the Celtics' front office. "Sure, there are worries with every untried kid," said Red Auerbach's assistant, Jeff Cohen. "Hell, he could come out, stay two months, hate the big city, and go home. But what we hope to get back is the family situation we had here [before 1977]. If we can get back to that, we can make him feel at home. I think he'll relate well to David [Cowens], too. Even though David was more sophisticated when he came out of school, he was self-protective. He'll know what Larry's going through. We feel we can handle him."

Of course, that was assuming that Larry and Woolf could come to terms with Boston. Although Woolf was experienced in dealing with Red Auerbach, the fact that Woolf and Auerbach didn't like each other wasn't going to help the situation. And the fact that they held a grudging respect for each other didn't help either. One reason that Woolf dreaded negotiating with Auerbach was that for Auerbach, negotiation wasn't just business, it was personal. "Negotiating with Red is so hard because he starts off with a figure which he thinks is fair and then he's hurt if you dare think otherwise," says Woolf. "And worse for me, I always believe that he's completely sincere." Asked how he thought Auerbach would react to the announcement of Woolf as Larry's agent, Woolf said, "I don't imagine he'll be too happy about it." Furthermore, Woolf made it clear that he had no vested interest in Larry's going to Boston. "We're going to try to obtain the best-possible contract for Larry, no matter what team it's with," said Woolf. Larry did, however, publicly acknowledge that Boston had earned its opportunity to sign him and that it was, therefore, likely he would end up there. "The way it looks now, I'll be playing with Boston. They've been real nice to me. They stayed away and everything's been fine." However, there were indications that Larry didn't particularly want to play in Boston, according to Coach Hodges. "But if they have money to provide security, he might do it. He'd live with it. He's going to have to make adjustments anyplace. He knows there's no Terre Haute in the NBA." Larry had told a reporter during the season that he wanted to play with the Pacers, but Larry later said, "I knew I wanted to play for the Celtics. But I was lyin' like hell [about wanting to play for the Pacers] because I was scared to death to come [to Boston]. I had never been out of Indiana in my life except to play basketball and come right back home."

Ironically, Larry had decided that where he really wanted to play was New York. Only a year-and-a-half earlier, Larry had exclaimed about the high price of a hamburger and a Coke, and said he could never play there. But Larry's new rationale for playing in New York represented quite a dramatic change in perspective. "I would like to play in New York because that's where everything is at. The media is there, TV, there's more people. I belong in New York....I can handle any situation." While Larry's change of heart did reflect how much he had developed and matured in the last year-and-a-half of college, it is still hard to believe he could have uttered such a statement. But Larry had always been capable of great rhetorical flourishes. One such flourish was a more facetious comment he made, at about the same time, to Coach Hodges. When Hodges pointed out that Larry would probably make more money in a year than he would make in a lifetime, Larry commented, "That's what I'm aiming to do."

Woolf's initial plan was to show Larry around Boston. If Larry thought he could be comfortable and live there, then Woolf would proceed with the negotiations. Thus, two days after the announcement of Woolf's appointment, Larry set off for Boston. On Friday evening, April 6, 1979, Larry made his first appearance at the Boston Garden for the Celtics' game against the Denver Nuggets. He arrived at halftime in the company of Woolf, Auerbach, and new sole owner Harry Manguerian. Despite a typically small crowd, Larry received a standing ovation. Later, at the press conference, Larry complained, "Actually, I was kind of disappointed. Rick Robey [a Celtic Larry had known for a couple of years] told me they'd stand and cheer me and wouldn't stop. They stopped after one minute." Larry, perhaps with a change of heart, or just out of diplomacy, went on to say that Boston was his first choice to play pro ball, if only because they had drafted him. "I have to love them for that. Now we have to see what happens." Larry ended up staying in Boston for three nights. Even today, Woolf will pull out the bill for that stay and marvel at its stark simplicity. "Three nights. Nothing but room and tax. Not a room service charge. Not a phone call." As Rick Shaw once said, "Larry doesn't do room service."

Just two days later, in the Celtics' locker room after a game against the New Jersey Nets, Woolf and Auerbach renewed their on-again off-again feud, ending with Woolf storming out of the locker room yelling, "Auerbach is trying to intimidate me." Woolf's and Auerbach's histrionics were only the start. Almost immediately word leaked out in the press that Woolf was after a six-year $6-million contract. *Newsweek* and *Time* printed that Woolf demanded a four-year $4-million contract. That Auerbach and the Celtics were only offering $400,000 per year indicates the gulf separating the two parties. Auerbach was furious that both figures, especially Woolf's supposed demands, had been made public, and he blamed Woolf. Woolf denied Auerbach's allegations. The demand that Woolf did put on the table was a multiyear, $1.2 million-per-year deal which he had said was developed by the committee. Woolf used his supposed responsibility to the committee as a negotiating tactic. During negotiations, he would say, "The committee wants it" or "The committee won't let me." In reality he merely kept the committee members updated. In defense of that dollar amount, committee member Paul Dennehie said, "Look at it this way. If Dan Roundfield is worth $500,000 to the Hawks, then what is Larry worth to the Celtics? They need him."

The only thing the first three weeks of negotiations produced was a Celtic withdrawal from the bargaining table. Auerbach's response to reporters was that "I gave them my best shot, and they said, 'No way.' I may just sit back and wait for the draft. If I blow it, I blow it....I could eat [the contract]. If I do, he'll never get the contract I'm offering. I guarantee that. No one will pay him if he doesn't play." Of course Auerbach's comments were largely bluster. The street-tough Jewish negotiator was trying to intimidate Woolf, the Jewish intellectual. "[Auerbach] broke off the negotiations," said Woolf. "I've negotiated some 1,800 contracts in my career, and I've never had anyone do that before. Frankly, I was surprised. Maybe it's an effort to put us on the defensive.'' Woolf added that Auerbach ''treats everyone like he used to treat a referee when he was coaching. ...He's more of a dictator than a negotiator.'' Woolf's comments to the contrary, Auerbach was a great negotiator, but this time he was over a barrel, and he knew it. He wasn't about to let Larry get away to another team. He was just establishing his position and trying to bring the price down. He was also not about to be upstaged by a committee of upstart midwest businessmen.

Yet someone like Lu Meis was hardly a provincial. Meis had dealt with Red Auerbach types before. Still, the committee members knew it was in Larry's and the negotiation's best interests for them not to come off too savvy. ''We're all small-town men who've never been involved in something like this,'' says Meis. ''We're not big-time slickers. We're probably in over our heads.'' But Meis wasn't quite so self-effacing when Auerbach called and tried to bully him over the phone. Auerbach claimed that the committee was guilty of inducing and allowing tampering by other NBA teams over the past year. ''I've been to more than nine county fairs, you can't intimidate me,'' Meis replied. Later Meis tempered his comments about Auerbach to say, ''Red Auerbach is my idol in pro basketball, [but] he has to give and take some, too. He just can't make one offer and sit there with it.'' Because of the negotiating impasse, however, charges about the possible tampering were hurled at the committee by the Boston papers as well as the Celtics. And Woolf was the target of a great deal of abuse around Boston for what was perceived as his role in the bargaining breakdown.

On April 27, Woolf flew in to Terre Haute for the weekend, ostensibly to attend two banquets honoring Larry and an ISU baseball doubleheader with Larry at first base. But more importantly, Woolf wanted not only to discuss the status of negotiations with Larry and the committee but to take the offensive in a more hospitable environment by holding a press conference in Terre Haute. In Boston, Woolf had received hate mail, abusive phone calls, and obscene gestures whenever he ventured out onto the street. ''The Hundred Days War'' was how the negotiations had come to be known in the Boston papers. And the negotiations received almost daily coverage even when nothing occurred. The question of whether Larry Bird would be signed had become the burning issue in all of New

England. Fans were pinning their hopes on the belief that Larry would be able to single-handedly restore the past greatness to the now woeful team.

So on April 28, Woolf announced to the Indiana press that the next move in the contract stalemate was up to the Celtics. They had yet to move beyond their original $400,000-per-year offer made at the beginning of negotiations over three weeks before. "If the Celtics wish to remain with their first and only offer, then as much as we would like to be with Boston, we will choose to go elsewhere or enter the 1979 draft in June," said Woolf. Woolf played to the sympathies of his audience by emphasizing the Celtics' tactics as a violation of Larry's privacy. "Larry Bird is a very private person, and he considers his contract negotiations to be a private matter. He further considers the Celtics' public announcements of real or fictitious figures to be an invasion of his privacy." For Larry's part, he merely said with no hint of exaggeration, "I suspected last year something would go wrong in my contract talks. That's one reason I decided to stay in college."

The month of May was not only a difficult time for the contract negotiations, but for Larry, also. He broke his index finger playing the outfield in a pickup softball game with his two brothers. "Mike hit a shot that knuckled like nothing I ever seen, and that sucker hit my finger and I dropped it. So I picked it up and threw to second base, only the ball tailed up and away and clear over the second baseman, and Mike went all the way to third base laughing like anything. I had to laugh too, because I didn't know why the ball did that until I looked down at my hand and saw my finger broken at about a 90-degree angle." Following two separate operations in Indianapolis, the finger was still bent at a 45-degree angle and so stiff that Larry could only bend it halfway to his palm (to this day, Larry can't touch the finger to his palm.). Since the index finger is critical to proper release on the ball in shooting, Larry was concerned about how the injury would affect his shooting. Later in Larry's career, a writer asked Larry what kind of shooter he might have been in the pros if his finger had been straight. "That's what Red was telling me when I was trying to sign," said Larry.

In the meantime, Larry closed in on the completion of his student teaching requirements and spent a great deal of time with his old high school coach, Jim Jones, then living in Princeton, Indiana. The two did a lot of fishing and some mushroom hunting as Larry tried to ignore the continuing stalemate saga on the east coast. However, Larry gave a hint of his frustration at the time when he discussed the impasse. For, just as Larry would remember even insignificant acts of friendship for years afterward, he was prepared to carry a grudge indefinitely if he felt someone was trying to cheat him. "I don't know what I'm worth, but I want to feel that I've gotten what I honestly deserve. I don't want to feel that some one tried to cheat me.... The way things are being prolonged really does a job on me." After Larry finished his student teaching responsibilities at West Vigo High around the middle of May, he then stayed on with the baseball team as J.V. coach and assistant for the varsity. "I was a little apprehensive when he was assigned to us," said West Vigo head coach, Dick Ballenger. "You know, a superstar and all. But he's done a whale of a job... everything we asked him to do and more." Larry was only too happy to add to his list of coaching duties one of his favorite relaxations: lawn mowing—only this time on a big scale. "Twice he's gone out and mowed the field. That takes about three hours," said Coach Ballenger. "School was out three weeks ago, but he's missed only one or two practices and games. That was when he went in for surgery on that broken [finger]."

Regardless of whether Woolf held press conferences, maintained silence, or went back to the bargaining table, nothing seemed able to break the contract impasse that existed through the month of May. The Celtics, on the other hand, attempted to break through the impasse by alleging that the committee was illegitimate or, at least, improper. The Celtics' charge that the committee was inappropriately acting as an agent, regardless of Woolf's "official" status, was intensely debated by the Boston papers. If the committee was, in fact, acting as Larry's agent, they were almost certainly violating NCAA rules. And like Villanova eight years before, there was the chance that ISU would have to surrender its NCAA runner-up trophy. In 1971, Villanova had given up its runner-up trophy in the NCAA basketball tournament because its star player, Howard Porter, had made an agreement with an agent before the tournament began, thus violating NCAA rules. As a result, Villanova also forfeited revenues of several hundred thousand dollars from the tournament. (Similarly, in 1987, Alabama was forced by the NCAA to give up its tourney revenue and forfeit games because player Derrick McKey had signed with an agent prior to the NCAA tournament.) In response to the charge, committee member Paul Dennehie asserted, "We were very careful to observe all the regulations."

The dispute regarding the committee's status as an agent came about because the Celtics learned that the original contract offer which Woolf had presented was derived from months of research done by the committee. Even worse, charged the Celtics, that research had included improper contact with other NBA teams and agents. In other words, the committee had actively pursued both direct and indirect information about what other teams would be willing to pay Larry. Part of the problem was that the committee had set out to study the various features of numerous top NBA contracts. And they sought to gain information on Larry's potential market value at the same time they interviewed prospective agents. The result, however, was that some of those agents went to teams on the pretext of discussing one of their clients on that team but then broached their opportunity to represent Larry. How much would the team be willing to pay Larry? they asked. While the committee reaped an abundance of information, the Celtics felt they were being manipulated into offering an artificially inflated contract. Worse, they perceived it as an effort designed to prevent them from coming to terms with Larry while allowing him to find the best contract with a more desirable team in a city better-suited to Larry's needs. Moreover, in the first week of June, the atmosphere surrounding the contract negotiations was so incendiary that the normally staid *Boston Globe* raised questions about Bob King, an honorary member of the committee, having allowed Don Nelson, the coach of the Milwaukee Bucks, to stay at his home during the middle of the season. Since Larry's draft rights belonged to Boston, the *Globe* thought it improper that a rival team's coach should be allowed such proximity to Larry and his "representatives." However, the subject was never raised again and was obviously a borderline issue at best.

It was understandable that Auerbach was sensitive to such unusual and possibly unethical practices. But from the committee's view it was a highly creative approach toward acquiring as much information as possible. And it was in Larry's best interests to have this information at Woolf's disposal when he came to the bargaining table.

Meis explains: "I'd have to say that by the time we were done with everything, we probably knew more about the NBA than any one agent ever has. We knew as exactly as possible what the top players made; we knew exactly what the top-ten rookies of each of the last three years made, what kind of money different teams might be likely to offer Larry, and what teams to avoid." The result was probably the greatest resource of contract data ever put together prior to negotiations. And from that data was distilled a hybrid contract offer. In answering the charge about the committee's input into negotiations, a committee member admitted, "We talk to Bob from time to time and there is some input, but [Woolf] is the one doing the bargaining. In any case, the final decision will be up to Larry. There is no way we can be unhappy with anything that Larry agrees to, because if Larry is happy, we'll be happy."

Despite all the acrimony, Larry and the committee continued to insist that Larry would be most happy playing in Boston. Yet the committee wasn't about to relinquish its ample bargaining leverage to insist that Larry only play pro ball in Boston. "If it starts looking like [Larry won't be signed by Boston]," said Meis, "then its going to be like a big bluff in a poker game. Who's going to have the guts to stick it out? Larry will lose some money, sure, but the Celtics will lose more. They'd be left with nothing. Signing for $100,000 less or whatever with another team won't mean that much to Larry. He's going to be signing for a lot with somebody." And given Larry's unique attitude, the Celtics were well-aware that Larry's playing in Boston was hardly a sure thing. In fact, Larry was even considering sitting out the entire season. "He could always sit out and play in the Olympics," said committee member Ed Jukes. "Don't laugh; he's independent that way." Jukes added, "Larry's as tough as nails. If he doesn't like what he is offered, he might stay here and teach. He likes the student teaching he's doing now over in his high school. Everybody laughs when I say that; I don't." Nevertheless, the committee's comments about the likelihood of Larry sitting out were, for the most part, a negotiating tactic. No one really believed Larry would do it.

The committee had done its work so thoroughly that they were certain of what they wanted. The $1.2-million demand was simply an opening gambit. Woolf and the committee had determined that Larry's worth to the Celtics was in the $600,000-to-$800,000 range. And though it was still the first week of May, Meis believed owner Harry Manguerian would find it necessary to enter the negotiations in the next month "because he knows the franchise needs help now." Indeed, the committee was hardly ready to panic. "We're not worried about what's going to happen," said a committee member. "We even have a pool going of how much he's going to sign for. I like the chances of one guy on the committee. He has Larry going for $600,000 a year. Those figures and the anticipation of Harry Manguerian's intervention proved prophetic. Just as the committee had predicted, in the first week of June, Manguerian decided to move the negotiations along. Within a week a tentative agreement on a five-year $600,000-per-year contract had been reached. Larry was to fly in to Logan Airport on Wednesday, June 6, where he would be greeted by Woolf and his wife.

Larry knew he would be deluged by the media throughout his brief stay in Boston. He therefore extracted a promise from Woolf that there would be no reporters waiting at the airport. One reporter managed to make an appearance anyway. Woolf beseeched him, "I'll introduce you if you promise not to tell him you're a reporter." Of course the first thing Larry did once he got off the plane was to say to Woolf, "Are there any fucking reporters here?" And Woolf quickly assured him that there were none. Thus, after entering the baggage area, Mrs. Woolf queried the reporter loud enough for Larry to hear, "So, how's the hardware business?" The next day, only because Woolf reminded him, Larry called Georgia to tell her that he would be signing the contract on Friday, June 8, and that he hoped he would be back in Terre Haute to help West Vigo High in its first-ever baseball semi-state scheduled on Saturday. There were some who believed that Larry chose June 8 as the signing date so it would not interfere with West Vigo's tournament game. The next day, while staying at Woolf's house, Larry awakened around 6:00 A.M. to jog. However, the soon-to-be-richest-rookie in sports history got lost and had to flag down a motorist to help him find his way back. "Some guy picked me up and I told him I was lost. He said, 'That's a helluva way to begin here.' Somehow I finally got back to Mr. Woolf's house. I guess I'm still a hick from French Lick." The next day the newspapers all printed accounts of the incident. Larry's remark became famous, and throughout that summer and the rest of the year, there were many quite derisive articles about Larry and his small-town background. Many people in the valley were offended, and Larry was deeply hurt.

For the press conference, thirty-one TV and radio stations, plus over fifty reporters crammed into a private club room, above the Boston Garden, called The Boards and Blades. Larry's guaranteed contract was worth $3.5 million for six years, making Larry then the highest paid rookie in the history of any sport. David Thompson's $500,000-a-year contract in 1975, until then, had been the largest rookie agreement. Seven years later, Auerbach said, "I knew Larry was going to cost us some money, and I was prepared to pay a reasonable price, but the point I kept hammering home was that no forward ever *made* a franchise in our league. And historically, I was correct. The only guys who ever had the ability to turn around an entire franchise were centers: Mikan, Russell, Chamberlin, Reed, Jabbar, Walton, Malone. All of your other players, no matter how great they were, were contributors. Look at Dr. J.—as great as he is, he didn't win it all until Malone joined him. No forward could do it by himself, because forwards are at the mercy of the guards; the guards control the ball. That's why no forward ever *made* a franchise—until Larry Bird made ours. He was the first exception, and he may go down in history as the only exception."

Given these extraordinary circumstances, Auerbach, in introducing Larry, felt it necessary to obviate the historic amount of the contract. "He came here for a lot less than he could get someplace else." This, despite Auerbach's claims that no one would pay more than the $400,000 contract he had offered. Larry subtly sparred with Auerbach, a moment later, when he responded to a question about how it felt "to be wealthy at the ripe old age of twenty-two." "Don't tell Mr. Auerbach, but I'd have played for nothing. Seriously, I come from a small town, and my family never had money. I guess right now I'm thinking about the family and about being able to give my mother the kind of security I've always wanted for her." And through the rest of the press conference, Larry handled other reporters' questions with aplomb. Asked "about the pressure" of "being counted on as the Celtics' savior," Larry replied, "That is not in my contract." Unfortunately, Larry proved a little too glib in another public appearance. Before heading home, Larry had agreed to talk to some teenagers in Providence and admitted he was nervous because he was talking "to a bunch of kids." As a consequence, Larry made a statement that was attributed to him in many an article over the next five years. "I only plan to play pro ball five years," he said, explaining that he would then like to coach at the junior high level. In face of the public reaction and disappointment, Larry immediately disavowed the statement. But, in fact, the comment was in line with another he had made not too long before. "I'd like to play pro ball for a couple years, but I'm not going to stay if there's no interest from the fans or if the team is doing bad and we don't get along. That's important. And I'd never stay and embarrass myself in basketball because I've gotten too much out of it."

Larry's contract for $3.5 million would not prove to be his sole means of support. Numerous endorsement opportunities soon became available, including the 7-Up contract that one agent had claimed to have in his pocket. Larry also signed a $200,000 contract with Spaulding, entitling them to put his name on basketballs, and a $125,000 contract with Converse to wear their shoes for three years. Since then, Larry has signed a second contract with Converse for $100,000 per year, and today he receives in the vicinity of $500,000 per year to wear their shoes. The initial Converse deal was most interesting for what it didn't reveal. That is, during Larry's college career, State didn't have a standard shoe contract. Part of the reason was that shoe contracts were less common in the late seventies than they are now, but more significantly, State's program was considered too small for a contract. Hodges considered himself close to the Converse representative in the area, former Indiana high school great Billy Shephard. So, for the most part, the team wore Converse shoes that Shephard supplied. But players could wear shoes other than Converse, if they wanted. Often players would wear the brand they had worn in high school. Moreover, Shephard didn't do a particularly good job of supplying the team. Deliveries were often late, and the needed sizes weren't always readily available.

During Larry's senior season, he decided to wear Adidas, after having worn Converse his first two seasons. Rick Shaw was in charge of buying Adidas with neutral stripes and painting the stripes baby blue, because that color wasn't available then. However, near the end of the season, Larry started switching brands at random. "Then [Larry] started to play mind games and he drove me absolutely nuts," says Shaw. At one point, Larry decided to wear Pony. Then he agreed to wear Converse for the MVC postseason tournament. Next, Larry decided he wanted to wear Nike at the NCAA tournament in Cincinnati. By the time the team arrived in Salt Lake City for the Final Four, there was a real power struggle about which brand Larry and the rest of the team would wear. Adidas came in first, giving Shaw (who was in charge of dispensing the shoes) all sorts of complimentary shoes and bags. The representative, George Trumble, even announced that Adidas had come out with a radical new shoe. At the time, it looked like "a moon shoe," according to Shaw. The shoe was spongy overall, with an extremely spongy tongue and holes across the top of the toe. There were blue stripes, and Trumble announced excitedly that Adidas thought about naming the shoe, "The Sycamore" when it came out commercially. (Incidentally, the shoe came out the following year and revolutionized the standard look of the basketball shoe. When it was released, however, it was called The Top Ten.)

In the meantime, Billy Shephard heard about the Adidas attempt and immediately went to the players' rooms and gave them all shoes. At that juncture, Shaw was under the impression that Larry was going to wear Adidas, because "they were more comfortable." At the last hour, however, Al Harden, the Converse representative for all the midwest, arrived. Harden had a son Roger, who like Shephard, was the best high school player in Indiana during his senior year. (Dave, Shephard's brother, had also been named Mr. Basketball, and Roger's brother Rob had been a runner-up for the award.) Harden had also been the head coach at the University of Denver until the program had been disbanded. His star player had been Bob Heaton, Larry's housemate and roommate on the road. Heaton mentions a pre-Final Four get-together with Larry and Harden in which it was understood that Larry's wearing Converse shoes in the Final Four would be helpful for the contract offer he would receive from Converse after he turned pro. The Adidas may have been more comfortable, but Larry was not just a "hick from French Lick"; he wore Converse in the Final Four.

The Larry Bird who was emerging at the time of the contract signing was beginning to break out of his cocoon. Of course, the shock of the big city would prove jarring, and Larry's overall naïveté was still predominant. Larry had, however, gained a certain savvy and bravado off the court. At the same time, Larry had come to acknowledge that even as difficult a city as New York—expensive hamburgers and all—could be advantageous to his career. If all those circumstances weren't enough to symbolize the revolution under way in Larry Bird's life, understand that this 22-year-old kid had just become a millionaire. A new era loomed ahead.

12 / Rookie of the Year: The Boston Celtics, 1979–1980

On the eve of Larry's entrance into the NBA, professional basketball was emerging out of a seven-year period which had produced dramatic changes throughout the league and which also had significantly altered the once-optimistic forecasts for the game that had been described in the early seventies as "the sport of the seventies." Rooted mostly in the late sixties, the changes had not manifested themselves, at least to the average spectator, until the midseventies. By then, the league had embarked on a decline as rapid as had been its rise to popularity in the late sixties and early seventies. Much of the onus for both the rise and the decline rested with TV. In the mid- to late sixties, TV provided a medium for large numbers of new fans to develop loyalties and follow the game. In turn, as TV blossomed, commercial products became an important part of the game's burgeoning popularity. Suddenly, with endorsement money and huge TV contracts, the sport had become a major commercial instrument. As a result, there soon came unbridled expansion and the addition of another league. In 1965, before TV had seriously championed the game, there were nine teams in the NBA. Two years later, there was a rival league, the ABA, with twelve teams to go along with the NBA's twelve teams. By 1976, on the eve of the ABA's merger with the NBA, the NBA had eighteen teams and the ABA had eight teams. In 1979, there were twenty-two teams in the NBA.

With expansion, TV, commercialism, and new fans, the NBA found itself in the grip of economic forces over which it had little control. As the league became big business, the very integrity of the game quickly began to erode. Super-agents and a powerful players' union emerged. Huge TV contracts helped some teams flourish, but more often than not had merely propped up weak franchises. And the rival league had prompted elaborate bidding wars for many players. The players' union had managed to win free agency through the courts by 1976; and in 1980 they had been able to halt compensation to the free agent's former team. With all-out bidding between the leagues and powerful agents handling the negotiations, long-term, no-cut guaranteed contracts became the norm. Moreover, the numbers in those contracts were staggering. Between 1967 and 1973 salaries in the NBA increased 700 percent. In the late sixties, a superstar might earn $75,000 a year, but ten years later, a superstar often earned upward of $600,000.

One result of the salary revolution was a breakdown of the traditional loyalty and camaraderie among players, their coaches, and their teams. For the salary battles had produced a great deal of turnover and instability as trades, releases, and free-agent signings became the rule rather than the exception. Players increasingly performed according to the ascending dictates of the dollar, rather than those of team loyalty. New superstars appeared to be more concerned about their statistics than about whether their team won the game. In the sixties it had been shocking if a superstar was traded even once. In the seventies, a year-end trade of the team's superstar was often expected.

Furthermore, expansion brought expansion drafts which accelerated personnel turnover since players were plucked from the existing teams to help stock the expansion clubs. Traditional rivalries, which had historically been so important both to the league and the fans, began to erode as expansion drafts also depleted the depth that had kept traditional powerhouse teams strong. Similarly, rivalries and team loyalties ceased to play an important role in players' careers with the infusion of expansion teams which, of course, lacked any history. The new and greater demands of travel didn't help the game either. That is, as the league expanded, so too did the schedule, frequency, and distance of travel. In self-defense, players wisely chose to pace themselves more, saving their greatest efforts for the all-important playoffs. Thus, by the end of the seventies, economics, rather than the pleasure of the game or loyalty to the team, dominated players' motivations. Not surprisingly, a profusion of lackluster performances was the result.

Unfortunately, these changes in the game happened to coincide with the proliferation of the black player throughout the league. The consequence was that the league's almost completely white gate and mostly white television viewing audience often thought the lethargy on court was racial in origin. Simultaneously, all of the most popular white superstars of the previous decade (the sixties) either retired or saw their games significantly decline with age. They, in turn, were replaced by a new core of black superstars who completely dominated the game. It eventually became axiomatic that whites could not compete with blacks on the basketball court. Indeed, the league was well over 70 percent black at the time of Larry's arrival. And the retirement of great white players like Jerry West and John Havlicek, along with the decline of careers for players like Rick Barry and Bill Walton, * contributed significantly to the NBA's popularity problem.

Besides these superstars, perennial all-star players just a notch below superstar status had left the league in the seventies. Billy Cunningham, the Van Arsdale brothers, Dave Debusschere, Gail Goodrich, Jerry Lucas, and two popular players from championship teams, Don Nelson, and Bill Bradley—had all retired by 1977, leaving the league with a dearth of any white talent, let alone superstars.

Another important factor in the NBA's decline was the decline of the great New York Knick teams of the early seventies. For the Knicks' plunging fortunes closely paralleled the league's fortunes. The great teams of the early seventies featured white players like Debusschere, Bradley, and Lucas, who played disciplined, team-oriented basketball. They were then the focus of the national media, and pro basketball was being hailed as the sport of the seventies. In addition, the Knicks' vaunted rivalries were vigorously promoted by national television. It didn't hurt that those rivals were the Celtics, featuring Havlicek, Cowens, and Nelson, as well as the Lakers, with West and Goodrich. But when the Knicks started to falter, an already-weakened league became even more vulnerable. TV, so crucial to the sport's rise in popularity in the early seventies, deemphasized and televised fewer games. And it was no coincidence that the Knicks and the Celtics, the two most popular TV teams by far, had also begun to crumble.

---

*Walton, in 1974, had been the last in the superstar class to enter the league, and his injuries had cut his career short.

With the traditional rivalries nonexistent and the New York Knicks so weak, the non-TV media based in New York also began to lose interest in the NBA. Even more devastating for the league was a sea change in the NBA's balance of power with the rise to basketball success of the little-known western teams. Between 1974 and 1979, the Golden State Warriors, Portland Trailblazers, Washington Bullets, and Seattle Supersonics, respectively, won four of the five NBA championships. The only nationally recognized west-coast team was the Lakers. So to have three west-coast teams other than the Lakers win the championship was devastating. Worse, two of the teams, Portland and Seattle, were expansion clubs with only the most local interest. Thus, the formerly concentrated media focus on teams like the Knicks, Celtics, Lakers, Sixers, and Baltimore Bullets became increasingly diluted as four other teams with no national following swept to titles.

Even more problematic was the racial composition of these new championship teams. The Celtics' championship teams through most of the sixties had seven or eight black players on the twelve-man roster. But by 1969, as the league ushered in its most popular period, there was more racial balance on its top teams. Both the Knicks and the Celtics featured six whites and six blacks from 1969 through 1973. But in 1974, ten out of the twelve players with Golden State were black. And the rest of the championship teams in the decade had at least seven black players. At the same time, the Knicks, once the model of racial balance, had become increasingly black; the team had lost all of its popular players and had begun to lose games quite often. By 1975, the team had not only fallen below .500, but Debusschere, Lucas, and popular captain, Willis Reed, had retired. By 1979, after the team's record had fallen to 31–51 in the previous year, the team had no white players. The coach, Reed, was also black. The problems attendant on a white gate supporting a mostly losing black team was epitomized by an ugly nickname for the team that had once been so popular among New York sports fans. For, in the late sixties and early seventies, die-hard Knick fans had insisted on referring to the team by its original name, the Knickerbockers. It was an affectionate tip of the hat to the traditional, white type of game that the team played. But in the late seventies, the original name was being invoked in quite a different context. As the fans stayed away in droves, the Knicks became to be known as the Niggerbockers.

Analogous to the Knicks' decline was that of the Celtics', which was precipitated by the changes in the league's financial hierarchy. Red Auerbach had been slow to see the forces that threatened his almost-placid dynasty of the last twenty years. But tradition was the first victim of the new financial structure in the NBA. And between the end of 1976 and April of 1978 when John Y. Brown acquired the team, Auerbach lost players like Paul Silas, Don Chaney, and Paul Westphal, largely because of his financial inflexibility. Unfortunately for the Celtics, by the time Auerbach had finally realized that the big salaries were a permanent fixture, the team had a new owner, John Y. Brown. Auerbach was to find his power strapped by the very kind of parvenu owner that had proliferated throughout the league, helping to accelerate its decline. Brown had no loyalties, no interest in basketball, no sense of what it meant to be a Celtic. He, like most, if not all, of the new owners was only in the game to gratify his ego and maintain some sort of perpetual adolescence.

Brown's meddling crippled the Celtics. After winning the NBA title in 1976, the Celtics were defeated in a tough seven-game Eastern Conference semifinal against Philadelphia. The team then suffered through an injury-riddled and dissension-fraught season in 1978, when they slumped to 32–50. As Auerbach sought to rebuild the team, every move he made was counteracted by a Brown move about which Auerbach was never consulted. Auerbach's first step had been to gain some discipline and racial harmony on the team by firing Coach Tommy Heinsohn, who was white, and replacing him with Satch Sanders, who was black. Auerbach thought that Sanders might be able to communicate more successfully with black players like Sidney Wicks, Curtis Rowe, and Charlie Scott. When Sanders arrived, the team had won only 11 of its first 34 games. Sanders was able to coax only minimal improvement from the team, as they won only 21 of the remaining 48 games.

But the worst event to come out of the dreadful season was the retirement of John Havlicek, fueled both by the internal dissension on the team as well as a foot problem. Havlicek might have tolerated the dissension and foot problems had Auerbach been willing to compensate him more generously. Havlicek was the last connection to the distinct and dominant Celtic eras. His career had spanned eight championships and the three eras beginning with the Russell-Cousy era in 1962, continuing with the Russell era throughout the middle ·

and late sixties, and ending with the Cowens-Havlicek era in 1976. So his leaving was especially portentous. As Phil Jackson, who had participated in so many titanic New York Knick–Boston Celtic battles over the last decade, said, "My God, it's gone; the [Celtic] magic is gone."

Auerbach moved quickly to restore the Celtic magic as best he could. Following the season, he dumped Sidney Wicks, who had been a cancer on the team morale. Auerbach had also moved during the season to rid himself of Charlie Scott and his personal problems by trading him for a first-rounder (the pick that was eventually used to get Larry) plus former Celtics Don Chaney and Kermit Washington. However, owner Brown had intervened in short order, dealing away Washington as part of the notorious franchise-swap cum Archibald-Barnes-Knight deal. All in all, there were a remarkable seventeen new players on the roster during the course of the season.

The 1978–79 season started even more disastrously; so center Dave Cowens became player-coach, succeeding Sanders, fourteen games into the season. The team's record was 2–12 at the time and was 27–41 the rest of the way, marking a slight improvement, though it was still the worst in Celtic history. Auerbach again moved to alleviate the internal strife and help build for the future. Former Celtic great JoJo White, who had become bitter and injury-prone in the twilight of his career, was traded to Golden State for a first-round draft choice on January 30, 1979. It was also obvious that the Archibald-Barnes-Knight acquisition was a complete fiasco. Barnes played in only thirty-eight games before getting waived out of the league. Knight was to be traded, and only Archibald remained.

Meanwhile, the Pacers had let it be known that they were interested in dealing Rick Robey, the Kentucky player they had drafted when they learned that Larry was going to stay in college. Robey had become the symbol of strong-willed Coach Bobby Leonard's unhappiness with the team. His availability also had much to do with the severe financial problems the Pacers were experiencing. So Indiana unloaded Robey and his hefty rookie contract for the Celtics' Billy Knight. Auerbach was jubilant at the acquisition. But as long as Brown was involved with the decision making, there were bound to be more short-term disasters. Brown's actions were the subject of much ridicule around the league. Two of Brown's trades almost succeeded in driving Auerbach himself away forever—a remarkable feat, given that the names Boston Celtics and Red Auerbach have always been virtually synonymous. But the Celtics between 1977 and 1979 weren't the Celtics of old. Brown's Bob McAdoo deal was the coup de grace. McAdoo had been the epitome of the high-scoring superstar, interested only in his own stats, who proliferated in the league in the mid- to late seventies. McAdoo had won league scoring titles with Buffalo and then had been traded to the Knicks, where he continued to amass lots of points with little concern for who won the game. New York was only too happy to get rid of him.

The inside word was that Phyllis George, former Miss America cum fried chicken magnate's wife cum failed TV personality cum first lady of Kentucky, had been the force behind Brown's decision to trade for McAdoo. While Auerbach had often held to the principle of not giving up a first-round draft choice in a trade, that rule had been violated in the McAdoo case when Brown surrendered the *three* first-round draft picks that Auerbach had marshaled for the upcoming draft. This time it took seven months, just before the 1979–80 season, for Auerbach to compensate for Brown's foolishness. Auerbach was able to induce Dick Vitale, the GM and head coach of the Pistons, into signing McAdoo and then was able to con Vitale into giving up two first-round draft choices as free-agent compensation. Still, the McAdoo deal had been more than Auerbach could bear, and he gave Brown an ultimatum that either he would sell his share of the team to limited-partner Manguerian within two weeks or Auerbach would accept a standing offer from Sonny Werblin of the Knicks. Fortunately, Brown acquiesced.

The Celtics' problems weren't limited simply to personnel turnover. The internal dissension was exacerbated even further by racial divisiveness. There were seven blacks and five whites on the team, all the whites in one camp and all the blacks in another camp, except for the fiercely independent Don Chaney, who established his own camp. "Boston is the most racial city in the country. And when we began losing, people suddenly became aware of a player's color," said Celtic Vice President Jeff Cohen. Auerbach, knowing that he must somehow put a winning product onto the court, also felt obligated to at least attempt to put a few more whites onto the team to mollify the fans. "My job is to get a ball club out there the town will like," said Auerbach. So, of the fifteen players in the next training camp, *eight* were white. And by the time Larry had arrived in Boston, season ticket sales had reached a record 6,000 before a game had even been played.

    That Boston had been unhappy with a losing basketball team which was also predominantly black was an understatement. The team had been playing before crowds so sparse that the Garden had often been two-thirds empty during the past two seasons. But the Celtics had not sold out the Garden even when they won eight consecutive championships with black superstar Bill Russell. And after the local favorite Bob Cousy retired, it was near-impossible to sell out, though the team was just as successful. The same team that consistently filled houses throughout the rest of the league could not fill its own. Indeed, throughout the late sixties, while the Celtics were winning one championship after another, the all-white Boston Bruins hockey team, which had yet to win a Stanley Cup in almost thirty years, enjoyed the greater popularity. Part of the Celtics' problem was that Auerbach was as progressive as the city was racist. Auerbach had been instrumental in breaking all of the color barriers in the league. Just after being hired in 1950, Auerbach and Walter Brown, the team owner, drafted Chuck Cooper, the first black to play in the NBA. In 1963, Auerbach had the first all-black starting five in the league, with Sanders, Russell, Sam and K. C. Jones, and Willie Naulls. Then in 1966, Auerbach hired the first black head coach because Russell "was simply the best man for the job."

    Bill Russell had had a difficult time dealing with Boston, and it was no wonder. Here was the most dominant basketball player in the game, and he wasn't even close to being the most popular player on the team. That honor was reserved for the team's white point guard, Bob Cousy. The situation was both absurd and frustrating for Russell. Auerbach did what he could to boost Russell, but to little avail. "[The Boston press] would write: 'The Boston Celtics streaked to another victory yesterday, 112–94, thanks to a sterling performance by Bob Cousy, who scored 22 points.'..." Says Auerbach, "They'd go on and on, and never mention the fact that it was Russell's 12 blocked shots or 10 fourth-period rebounds that dominated the game. ...Who knows what might have happened if the city had embraced Russell in the same manner it had embraced Cousy from the beginning?"

The racial issue, of course, wasn't limited to Boston. Indeed, it had become one of the more worrisome problems in the league. Larry's arrival was regarded as a godsend by the NBA owners, who were doing an increasingly poor job of selling a black game to a white gate. White fans had been demoralized by the dawning realization that whites were clearly inferior to blacks in their ability to play basketball. That realization in and of itself had a devastating effect on the gate. It had been five years since a dominant white player had appeared on the scene. Many felt that a "dominant white ball player" was an oxymoron; the species had become extinct. That view had become so total that there was a remarkable amount of doubt whether Larry would be able to dominate a game in the NBA. Even an unabashed fan and expert like Al McGuire expected Larry to post merely adequate numbers, such as 14 points and 7 rebounds per game, as a pro.

The doubt about Larry's abilities was pronounced among fans, too. And the perception about whites being inferior was at least as common among black fans as white. One writer caught the essence of the black fan's reaction to Larry during a college game in his senior year: "Two blacks were watching the game. 'Man, he ain't white, is he?' one of them asked. After Bird made a fantastic shot, one of them said, 'Say, that's white magic.'"

In this light, Larry's national popularity in college, despite his intransigence with the press, becomes more intelligible. Had Larry been black, it is hard to believe that his hostility to the most basic obligations toward the press would have been tolerated.

Beginning with Larry's acceptance of the Adolph Rupp Trophy in Chicago, he was peppered with questions about how it felt to be regarded as "the great white hope," and represent the "difference between 7,500 and 12,000 in attendance" across the league. Larry bristled at the question, remarking that "it implies racism."* And

---

*Jim Wisman, Larry's roommate during his brief stay at IU, felt that Larry got along better with black players than with white players because in most cases their backgrounds were similar. Larry had always identified his own basketball success with that of black players. It was a success based less on physical differences than on cultural and socioeconomic ones. In Larry's worldview, individual distinctions were always tied to desire, striving, and, in this case, "hunger." "I don't think of myself as any kind of great white hope.... On the whole blacks are the best basketball players in the world. I think it's because they're hungrier. They crave success. A lot of white kids are too spoiled. They get cars and other luxuries."

once the season was under way, Larry commented directly that "great white hope" was "just a label somebody puts on you. You hear it night in and night out. When you're on the court, you don't care who you're playing against—black, white, Mexican, or whatever. You just go out there for one reason—to win a basketball game. If a white guy is guarding you, you don't try any harder than if a black guy is guarding you."

Regardless of Larry's views about the label, it was very much in everyone's mind. As Pat Williams, general manager and vice president of the Philadelphia 76ers, explains, "There are very few outstanding white players in the league. They're very rare, and that makes Bird an asset." "I don't think we're racists," said an NBA executive. "But Bird is going to make more money because he is an unusual commodity in our business." Yet it was not a foregone conclusion that Larry would be a success in the NBA. One article stated that Larry "is not particularly quick, is only so-so on defense and is a bit too reluctant to dribble under pressure." One writer who had seen Larry play three times said: "He's slow afoot and deficient in individual defense.... He could be an excellent goalie on a zone defense but may develop a sore neck watching faster forwards speed past him." Jerry West, the former Laker great and general manager who had scouted Larry, felt he would be a good pro, but probably not a great one: "Boy is he slow.... It's a shame he couldn't be as quick as the other guys out there." Similar sentiments were expressed by one NBA coach, who went so far as to say that Larry "will join the slowest players' club." Even Coach Hodges admitted that "he has some weaknesses. He doesn't have blinding quickness, and he isn't an extremely good runner." Dr. Jack Ramsey looks back on the general consensus around the league: "I don't know anybody who accurately predicted the kind of player he'd be." Of all the appraisers, however, Mel Daniels had the best perspective. Daniels, a star in his own right, had coached Larry in his senior year, in addition to going one-on-one with Larry after practice. "To me, Larry will be on the same par as the Doctor [Erving] in a year. And the Doctor, to me, is a fantastic player." But Larry did not expect to be more than a good NBA player. Similar to his experiences before his first season at ISU, Larry had no idea that he would be able to dominate games at the new level of competition. Larry himself predicted, "I pass good, so I'll probably pass a lot. I doubt that I'll be a big scorer in the pros." (He was to average 21.2 points and 10.9 rebounds per game in his rookie season.)

In early July, Larry had another operation on his finger and then prepared to go to Boston. The first order of business for Bob Woolf was to help Larry get settled. After touring a number of affluent areas, Larry informed Woolf he didn't want to live in any of them. "Who would I talk to?" Instead, he decided he liked the relatively modest three-bedroom split-level home across the street from Woolf in suburban Newton. The house was also only two minutes from the Celtics' training camp. That the home was not for sale didn't deter Larry. He simply offered enough money to persuade the owners to sell. The Celtics were "shocked" over Larry's decision to move next-door to Woolf, and according to a friend, even made an attempt to separate Woolf and Larry. Unfortunately, the Celtics ended up working at cross-purposes with Woolf, who had exactly the same aims as they did: that Larry be happy in Boston. Of course, the Celtics had their own grand design for this. They had acquired Rick Robey and drafted Jeff Judkins with an eye toward more than just increasing attendance. Robey and Judkins were two of Larry's closest friends in college basketball outside of Terre Haute. That the Celtics, with Robey and Judkins, had added to the number of whites on the team didn't hurt, either.

The most important role that Robey and Judkins played had been in the initial recruiting of Larry. On February 12, 1979, Robey, Judkins, and Player-Coach Cowens quietly slipped into Terre Haute to watch Larry play and, as Cowens said, "answer any questions [Larry] might have on our city, organization, players, or my coaching philosophy." Following the game, Larry escorted the trio on a tour of Terre Haute bars during which Cowens felt the three Celtics made an effective case for Boston. Back in Boston, Cowens said he had found Larry to be quite different from his press: "He's a good guy, a guy with a sense of humor. He's not that sullen, unstable hick we've been reading about in the papers."

Larry's attitude about interacting with others seemed to be gradually changing. "I'm not really shy, but it depends on what situation I'm in," said Larry. "I'm just accustomed to a small environment. When I was young, I was never around more than five or ten people at once." Jim Jones said, "Larry doesn't open up to many people. He simply wants to be known as Larry Bird, the basketball player."

Larry's newfound public confidence proved helpful, at least, in terms of commercials. For, no sooner had Larry quietly bought his Ford Bronco pickup than Ford called to say that they had heard he was a customer and that they would like him to do a commercial. Similarly, 7-Up immediately developed a spot featuring Larry and filmed it before the beginning of rookie camp in mid-August. Larry's greater ease in public translated into a desire to do the commercials. "I can sell something, I know that. [Basketball] isn't the only thing I know how to do."

The attention that Larry commanded was not limited to Boston. French Lick was not immune. People would stop in front of his mother's house on Washington Street and ask for autographs. Huge amounts of mail poured in, much of it requests for money.

Larry's elation over his financial wherewithal was not unequivocal. Larry's aunt reports that shortly after signing his contract, Larry said, "I wish Dad was here. I would take care of him and give him anything he wanted." It was one of the few occasions Larry ever mentioned Joe's death. Moreover, Larry was circumspect about handouts to his family. He realized that they could do more harm than good. "It would be easy for me to give my brothers $10,000 apiece, but it would hurt them more than it would help them. But if one of their wives gets sick, I will send them her paycheck for that week."*

However, Larry had no qualms about supporting his mother. "I want to take care of my mom. She deserves it." After signing with Ford, Larry wanted to get Georgia a new car. Her only request was for a pickup truck with the stick shift on the steering column (three-on-a-tree), which Ford agreed to customize for her. But although he wanted to take care of his mother, Larry wasn't altogether happy when she stopped working due to assorted physical problems relating to her hip, legs, and heart. "Larry thinks I should work," says Georgia. "He thinks everyone should work." Aside from her physical ailments, Georgia was embarrassed because people were teasing her for mopping floors now that her son had become a millionaire.

---

*Apparently, Larry subsequently relented on his initial stricture; he did, in fact, give money to family members. Today Larry claims that some members of the family have taken advantage of his generosity.

A sadly ironic aspect of the situation was that now that Georgia could finally afford to take some time out from work to spend with Larry, he was off in Boston playing with the Celtics and fulfilling the time-consuming commitments of a public figure. She now feels great sadness that having to work so hard kept her from getting to know her son better, and she cries softly when she reflects that "they took Larry away from me before I could be with him."

Nonetheless, Larry himself couldn't have found a more ideal situation outside of Indiana. The Celtics provided the close friends, and the committee had provided the father figure. Referring to Woolf and his wife, Larry said, "I feel like a son to them." Once in Boston, Woolf came to be the most significant person in Larry's life. In those first few months, not to mention years, Larry rarely made a decision without consulting Woolf.

Larry's adjustment to the big city was going reasonably well. Larry's oldest brother, Mike, and Larry's girlfriend, Dinah Mattingly, helped smooth the adjustment. Following his second divorce, Mike had moved to Boston to be with Larry. Through the rest of the summer and the first few months of fall, Larry rarely left Newton other than to go to practice. His experience in Boston was limited to occasional and unfortunate forays into the area traffic. Other than getting used to the city, the most significant adjustments Larry would make involved money and his dealings with the press.

Fortunately, Larry's frugality dictated a lifestyle not all that different from the valley. "The way I live, I'd be happy making ten or twelve thousand a year." The only deviance from that lifestyle was his purchase of the house, the Ford Bronco black pickup truck, and a gravestone for his father. He decided to let Woolf's office handle the decorating and furnishing of his home. But his frugality made the process a slow one, since Larry liked to buy only one room of furniture at a time.

The adjustment to Boston had gone better than Larry's initial adjustment to the Boston press.

The ridicule he had endured in the press during his first summer in Boston rekindled his skepticism about the tactics and motives of the press. "They're probing into my personal life, which has nothing to do with basketball. I'll talk to reporters after games, but I will not waste any time doing it. It's going to be a rough enough year for me anyway to get adjusted to all the travel and everything.''

There was no doubt that the issue of Larry's need for privacy versus the rights of the media would be more sorely tried in the pros than it had been in college. However, it didn't have to be as imposing a task as might be assumed. Dave Cowens, who by all accounts had a similar need for privacy, had established some basic guidelines over the years, protecting his privacy while fulfilling his responsibilities. ''The fans here are pretty knowledgeable and know [Larry] can't carry the whole weight. The writers tend to support the Celtics. All Larry has to do is put his best foot forward and play like a bastard.''

As the Celtics' rookie camp at Camp Milbrook prepared to open in the middle of August, there were two new veterans along with the rookies. Auerbach had obtained M. L. Carr, a free-agent swing man from Detroit, and hired Bill Fitch, the first (and only) coach in Cleveland Cavalier history. Carr had led the NBA in steals the year before, and would undoubtedly play the celebrated sixth-man role. In Cleveland, Fitch had turned an expansion franchise, once one of the laughingstocks of the league, into a contender. Auerbach had never gone outside the Celtic family to hire a coach before, but he was ecstatic to find Fitch suddenly available. Fitch was known both as a tough disciplinarian and a meticulous preparer. Auerbach felt Fitch was exactly what the teams in the previous two seasons had been lacking.

But the 2,000 fans that packed into the cramped gym in Marshfield all week were not there to get a glimpse of either Carr or Fitch. They were there to get a glimpse of the savior, whether it was in his contract or not, and he did not disappoint. Still, it was not an easy camp for Larry. First, his finger had not yet healed from surgery. And, in addition, he was completely unprepared for the conditioning demands of Fitch. Despite all that, Larry was eager to compete and earn his money. Carr, for one, tested Larry right away. ''I started banging him around a few times. I popped him with a forearm across the chest. The next time up the court, he stood there and popped me. He meant it, too.''

''It takes a while to get to know him, but I think Larry helps to create a harmonious atmosphere,'' explained Mel Daniels, Larry's former assistant coach at ISU, when asked how difficult it would be for Larry to adjust to the pros. To be sure, before the week was out, Larry's attitude had started to spread to the other players. Like Larry, players started working together instead of against each other, as well as hustling around the court and diving for loose balls. Norman Frank, the owner of Camp Milbrook, could only marvel: "In ten years I've never seen anyone throw himself around like that. Most of these guys are too worried about their careers to risk. Now he's got Robey and Carr diving, too." And by the end of the week, Larry was also a part of the environment off the court too. Celtic Vice President Jeff Cohen said: "Some of the guys had a party after rookie camp. It was just a little breakup party, and it was just at a bar. It was the kind of place where you could see a million dollars flying out the window. But when I got there, there was [Larry] and Cowens....They were just sitting around like everybody else. They fit in." At the same time, Larry wasn't above getting a little homesick, calling home every day. He wasn't interested in talking about basketball, said Georgia, he simply wanted to know what was going on in the valley.

One reason why Larry wasn't interested in discussing basketball when he called home was that he had been unhappy with his playing during the camp. His injured finger was bothersome, and he looked to pass instead of shoot most of the time. But Auerbach was ecstatic. What impressed him had little to do with a bum finger. "To Larry, winning is the most important thing, whether he has to pass, shoot, or rebound to do it. He has that kind of personality....This kid is in that class [with Cowens and Havlicek] at this point in time. He's in the Celtic mold as we know it." From Larry's perspective, the game was fun. And one of the keys to having fun was winning. "I've never played on a losing team in my life. I don't worry about anything except showing up to the games and practice on time. Basketball is fun for me. I don't consider it being work." Still, Auerbach and the Celtics hadn't even begun to see the real Larry, for his true abilities only came to the fore in an actual game, where improvisational talents and the ability to make rapid decisions were critical. As Stan Evans had observed in college, Larry was a different player when the game began.

When the Celtics began their two-week-long training camp in the middle of September, Larry was also flu-ridden and nowhere near peak physical condition. So it's hardly surprising that Larry wasn't the most impressive player in the training camp. The player who really wowed the observers was Cedric Maxwell, a third-year man out of North Carolina–Charlotte. Despite Larry's infirmities, Maxwell himself was impressed. "This white boy can play," said Maxwell. And M. L. Carr found it hard to believe that Larry was a rookie: "Rookies just don't come in the way he did: making creative passes, joking confidently, and then going out and backing up his words with his play."

In earning the respect of his older teammates, Larry diffused the potential jealousy that a great white hope publicity wave generates. Larry's modesty was appreciated by his teammates. Before the exhibition season started, Larry said, "Very few people can turn a team around by themselves, and I'm not one of them." Larry was also appreciated because of his ability to "joke confidently," which in sports parlance means being able to pull sophomoric pranks with the best of them. The most adolescent male behavior is rewarded, and Larry was as adept at this as he had been in college, with his one-liners, phone impersonations, and chewing tobacco stunts. In training camp, however, his repertoire was considerably more simple— after all, he was still getting to know his new teammates. Larry tended to rely on the old standby of finishing a shower and encouraging a waiting teammate like Carr or Robey to take his shower. "M. L.! Come on in here, the water's ready for you," Larry had announced, in front of a couple of writers. Of course, when Carr arrived the water was ice cold. Carr's payback was a little more creative. In anticipation of their exhibition game in New York the following evening, Carr confided to those present, "I'll jump out of a taxi and leave him in all by himself."

In August, Diane K. Shah, a west-coast writer, was allowed a glimpse into this side of Larry. Shah's article in the inaugural issue of *Inside Sports* hit the newsstands about a month later, and Larry was the big selling point of the issue. As is evident from her account, Shah had been allowed to follow Larry and Woolf around as part of a day-long interview. She had been granted this extraordinary access only as an effort by Woolf and Larry to establish a new era of better relations with the press. But Woolf and Larry claim that the interview was granted only on condition that nothing be written concerning Larry's past. Yet in the article Shah not only brought up Georgia and Joe's divorce, but Joe's suicide, and a pending paternity suit against Larry.

However, the editor of the publication claimed he had heard of no such promise by Shah and that she had done background research in Terre Haute and French Lick long before the interview. Despite Larry's anger at having been taken advantage of another time, there was a small sign of a new maturity in his final comment: "I'd rather that happen to me again than for me to be in the papers using drugs, or something."

The paternity suit Shah had allegedly promised not to mention went to court within a matter of days after *Inside Sports* hit the newsstand. It had been over two years since Larry's ex-wife, Janet, had initiated the paternity suit–child support case. Georgia and others mistakenly believe that the delay in the hearing of the paternity suit was due to Janet's desire to take advantage of Larry's ever-increasing wealth. However, many of the delays came at the request of Larry's lawyers, and Janet could always have obtained an adjustment had the suit been settled earlier. Furthermore, she had originally decided to file suit at the urging of her parents, when she was eight months pregnant, and she had been certain for over a month that her relationship with Larry was finally over. It was the summer of 1977, and Larry was trying out for the World University Games. With Larry gone, and a baby due in a month, Janet started to worry that she wouldn't have enough money to support the child. At that time Larry had no money, and it was evident that Larry was not entirely convinced that the child was his. The lawyer Janet saw initially told her she would be lucky to receive $10,000. Janet's parents urged her to see another lawyer, feeling that any settlement should last until the child was 21. A new lawyer, George Tofaute, also thought a $10,000 settlement was absurd. "The attorney said Larry would pay me $10,000 lump sum if I would be really lucky. And I was going to sign, but my Mom and Dad just had a fit.... They said, 'You really think over 18 years $10,000 is not very much.' So I took the papers to my attorney George Tofaute. He looked them over and...said, 'Don't you dare sign that.'"

Janet was making only $100 a week before taxes working at the First National Bank in Terre Haute. "All I wanted was Larry to pay the baby-sitter. That's it. If he'd pay $40 a week, that's all I asked for. And he refused. He said the baby wasn't his. So we had to go through these blood tests. I had Corrie, she was a little baby, and I had to take her to the clinic and have all these blood tests drawn on her. It took three weeks. So he was saying that [the father was] this other guy that I had dated after Larry and I were divorced, and it came out that no, he couldn't be, and the chances of that are just like one in a million for it to say no positively no. And that's what happened. And it said that this other guy couldn't have possibly been her father. And he still didn't want to help me." Larry, of course, was in an even worse financial position than Janet. His scholarship covered room and board, but he had no other income except from a summer job (which he mostly had to forego because of Europe). For Larry, $40 a week was prohibitive. After all, it was Janet who supported Larry when they were married, though as she says, "I was trying to get along, not cause any trouble. But then he refused to even pay the baby-sitter." Ed Jukes, a member of the committee and still a trusted advisor on financial matters, explains some of Larry's motivations (or his attorneys' motivations) in denying paternity. "First, $40 a week child support, relatively speaking, was a huge amount of money. Often four kids will only produce $25 a week support," says Jukes. There was no way Larry could pay that money. Also, some people might have said, "If you can show that she has a legal basis to go after your money now, then she can go after your money later, when you have much more," he explains. Janet says she ultimately scaled back her request to $25. But the stubbornness of both parties, not to mention the hard feelings that had developed, militated against a mutually satisfactory agreement.

Larry is still bitter twelve years later. In a *Sports Illustrated* article he discussed his feelings: "Getting married was the worst mistake I ever made. Everything that ever happened to me, I've learned from it. But I'm still scarred by that. That scarred me for life. That and being broke are the two things that influenced me most. Still." The depth of Larry's ill-feeling is revealed by a recurring dream. "The bad dream. I still have it sometimes. My wife is trying to get me to come back to her, but Dinah is there too. And I keep saying to Dinah, 'I don't want to go with her. I don't want to go.'" Ironically, Janet says she has almost exactly the same dream herself—a dream in which she finds herself struggling with Dinah over Larry.

Corrie Bird was born on August 14, 1977, while Larry was still in Europe. (Janet had to pay $75 for Corrie's use of the Bird name. She has not used the name herself since the divorce.) About a week after Corrie's birth, Larry arrived back in Terre Haute. But relations with Janet were so strained that Larry only saw his daughter for the first time by accident. Janet had gone to see Larry's best friend, Tony Clark, and his wife to show them the baby. It had been a spur of the moment decision, and Larry wasn't at Tony's at the time. But shortly thereafter, Larry drove by and noticed Janet's car parked outside and stormed in. "He was screaming and hollering because I was there, and Tony was *his* friend, even though I've known Tony since I was in first grade....And he put on this big front. I'm sure a lot of it was for Tony's benefit." The relationship between Larry and Janet had deteriorated so badly that Larry would not even acknowledge his child at first. Finally, on the way out the door, and probably because Debbie Clark was holding Corrie, Larry succumbed to some kind of paternal sentiment. "He went over and picked [Corrie] up and kissed her and then he left. Stormed out. He had me in tears. I was so embarrassed."

Though Larry would not see Corrie for another year, Georgia accepted Corrie as her granddaughter. Janet would regularly bring her daughter to French Lick from Terre Haute to visit Georgia as well as her own parents. In fact, Georgia had appeared to accept the inevitability of Janet's needing some financial help from Larry. "I told her I was going to [file]. There was nothing else I could do. Larry wouldn't help me." But as motions began to be filed and requests for interrogatory statements were made, Georgia began to withdraw from Janet, and Janet eventually stopped taking Corrie to see her. Georgia continued to shun her granddaughter once the court case had been consummated. The basic reason behind the resistance of Georgia and many of Larry's friends to the paternity suit was the belief that there were affairs which had led to the dissolution of the marriage and which could have produced the child. Georgia says that she first began to doubt that Corrie was her granddaughter approximately six months after Corrie's birth, when Linda told her that Janet had an affair with a man who had blond hair and blue eyes. Larry never discussed this possibility with his mother—indeed he never talked about Corrie with her at all. Janet responded to the charges by saying that the man had black hair and brown eyes. The paternity test corroborated her claim that Larry was the father.

Despite her doubts about the child's parentage, Georgia did have some infrequent contacts with Corrie. When she was five, Corrie in-advertently reinforced her doubts when she told Georgia, "You're not my grandmother." Janet says Corrie said this because she considered Janet's parents her "grandparents" and didn't realize you could have two sets of them. Today, Georgia doesn't see Corrie, though Larry's brother Mark will often take Corrie and spend time with her.

Janet currently lives just outside of Terre Haute with her third husband. "Larry's mother caused a lot of problems for us," says Janet. And the similarity in the way both Larry and Georgia responded to Corrie was no coincidence. "[Georgia] is actually like Larry. She's a real proud person. And that may be where Larry gets some of that. She would never admit to her emotions, but she was bitter," says Janet.

The second time Larry saw his daughter was on Corrie's first birth-day when Larry arrived with $100 as a gift. An ISU staff member "had given Larry $100 to give to me for this birthday, thinking this would soften me up over this paternity thing. [At the time] I didn't know where he got it, but I found out later."

When Larry brought the money, he gave Janet the impression that another reconciliation was possible. "He really got my hopes up. And he goes, 'Well, what do I have to do?' And the only thing I could come up with was, don't see Dinah. And then he goes, 'Well, I don't know if I can do that or not.'...I was still in love with Larry....But he did come and see Corrie. I got Corrie up and he held her and everything....When he drinks, either he's real angry or he's real sweet, but you never know, and he was in one of those real sweet moods, so I knew he still cared, just from the way he was still act-ing. But then I never saw him again until Corrie was five."

Actually, Janet did see Larry a little over a year later, though it was from the other side of the courtroom, and they didn't speak. On October 3, 1979, the case finally made it to court. It had been sched-uled for that date because the Celtics were playing an exhibition game that evening in Hulman Arena. Janet was working as a secretary for the Terre Haute Police Department. Supporting Corrie by herself, Janet was still earning only a little more than she had before. She was also taking computer programming courses three nights per week at Ivy Tech, a trade school. The case had now become a battle of wills, and Larry wasn't about to listen to anyone else's advice about the case. "[Larry's lawyers, Phil Adler and Joseph Anderson,] tell me they just really did not agree with what Larry did," says Janet. "Well, everybody knows how Larry is. He's not going to do anything. Larry wouldn't tell [his lawyers] nothing either. He's very private."

Despite Larry's intransigence, Corrie was awarded a large trust fund as the court judged Larry to be the father and primary provider. On the eve of the verdict, Janet summed up the situation by explaining that "Larry is a very nice person, but sometimes he just forgets about other people. He sort of forgot about us." Larry was not to see his daughter again until she was five. Six years later, Larry would look back and say, "Nothin' that ever happened was [Corrie's] fault."

As the Celtics prepared to open the regular season, there were considerable doubts about their ability to turn around the dismal 29–53 record of the previous season. The team that had become the patsy of the league would need a remarkable year from Larry if it was to become a contender again.

A sellout crowd in the Garden gave Larry a standing ovation before the Celtics' opening-night game against the Houston Rockets. After the reception, Larry's performance was pretty much anticlimactic as he played only 28 minutes because of foul trouble. Thus, he could manage only 14 points, though he did get 10 rebounds and 5 assists in helping the Celtics to a 114–106 victory. Larry's relatively meager offensive production in the opener was a harbinger of things to come as he struggled with his shooting through the first ten games. He had been playing with his middle finger taped to his still-stiff index finger. But after eight exhibition and ten regular season games, Larry ripped off the tape, announcing that he had "to quit babying himself." The finger would probably need surgery again after the season, yet Larry wasn't about to complain.

Playing in the pros was prompting significant adjustments in Larry's shooting. As a result, Larry was not shooting near the 54 percent average from the field he had maintained in college. First, the ball was different. Larry much preferred the wide-seamed Spaulding ball used in college to the narrow-seamed Wilson ball then used in the pros. Secondly, Larry now had to worry whether anyone was going to block his shot: "The defense is so much better in the pros.

I always have somebody like Bobby Jones to worry about. You can never fake them out. You just have to make your move and shoot it quick. In college I followed my shot a lot. In the pros you can't afford to." But despite his transition problems, Larry was still having a dramatic effect on the Celtics.

The Celtics won 11 of their first 14 games, whereas the year before they had lost 12 of their first 14 games. The difference in the team could mostly be accounted for in terms of Larry's contribution. The Celtics were now looking to pass the ball, emphasizing a selfless style of team basketball, in contrast to the selfish one-on-one style of the year before. Noted Coach Jack Ramsey of the Portland Trailblazers: "He makes the teammates around him play better—that's the sign of a great player."

That the other Celtics were playing better was a reflection of Larry's ability to lead and inspire his teammates by example. "Larry is a tremendous passer. He always looks for the pass first," said Archibald. "He did it from the first day of training camp. As a result, everybody started to move without the ball." Everyone started passing more also. For Larry, the unselfish play was just business as usual: "This is the way we played at Indiana State," said Larry. "One guy will want to make a good pass, then the next guy wants to make one. Pretty soon everybody's doing it."

After the first 19 games, the team's record stood at 15–4, and Larry was averaging 19.1 points, 10.1 rebounds, and 4.5 assists a game. And on November 14, Larry achieved the first triple-double of his professional career with 23 points, 19 rebounds, and 10 assists. The statistics were good, but they hardly reflected the full impact of Larry's effect on the team. The Celtics soon extended their record to 20–6. The season was one-third over, and no one was claiming that the amazing record was a fluke. And by the time Larry came off a 30-point 11-rebound performance against the Pacers, it was obvious that Larry had made the shooting adjustments necessary to increase his offense.

With the coming of December also came the hype of the first of two Celtic-Laker games, featuring the first rematch of Larry and Magic since the NCAA final back in March. CBS and the NBA, in desperate need of higher ratings, were heavily promoting the game: "The Magic Man versus The Bird" and "Can the Magic Man pull a Bird out of his hat?" Larry bristled at the one-on-one comparison.

"Guards don't play forwards," he said. But the TV rating for the first game was 52 percent higher than it had been the previous year, with an 8.5 rating, more than double the 4.0 rating of the next NBA game of the week. The media hype had been responsible for a certain amount of distance between the two players to begin with. Says Magic: "He thought I was Hollywood, egotistical and stuck on myself, things of that nature. I thought he was this country guy who couldn't relate to me and the other guys." Indeed, Larry had served notice about their distinct differences when he referred to Magic's "show-time" approach: "I can't come out here [on the floor] for a game smiling and joking. To me this is serious, and I have to give my complete attention."

Despite their lack of communication, Larry knew that the two of them would continue to command the competitive spotlight long after their first collegiate battle. "Even then I sensed it," says Larry. "I knew that whatever team he played for and whatever team I played for were going to be battling for whatever's there." So Larry had begun to anticipate the first pro matchup with extra zeal. That the game would be a grudge match for Larry was noticeable to Rick Robey. "[Larry would] like a little revenge. You can tell it in his eyes."

The December 28 game at the Forum was being billed as "The Greatest Show on Earth," but in reality, neither player dominated, as the Lakers won 123–105, with Magic outscoring Larry 23 to 16. More interesting was the confrontation between Larry and Magic well after the contest had already been decided. With less than three minutes remaining, Magic drove down the lane and Larry fouled him hard, knocking him to the ground. Magic leaped to his feet, and the two exchanged words. "If he thought I was going to lay down for him he was crazy," said Larry. "He wasn't going to back down, and I wasn't going to back down," said Magic. The two players would have another opportunity to continue their incendiary rivalry just sixteen days later when the Lakers and Celtics battled for the second and last time at the Garden.

With members of the national media like *The New York Times, Newsweek,* and *Time* planning coverage of the game, attention focused on the two-man race for Rookie of the Year honors. Magic was at a disadvantage for two reasons. First, he had joined an already good team and merely made it better. Second, the Lakers were still considered Kareem's team, whereas the Celtics were already considered Larry's team. Moreover, opinions around the league had crystallized almost immediately. Within the first week, Larry had been unofficially certified by NBA coaches as a "player." But the jury was still out on Magic because of his suspect outside shot and questions about his ability to run a half-court offense (a prejudice of most coaches then), since the Lakers ran a fast-break offense almost all the time. An example of the general sentiment around the league was the opinion of former Celtic Coach Tommy Heinsohn: "Magic is the better athlete. He's 6'8", plays guard, and is quicker. But I think, as a basketball player, Bird is better." The statistics of the two players at the time of their second meeting were virtually identical. Although both were averaging over 19 points a game, Magic was averaging 7.5 assists to Larry's 5. Larry, on the other hand, was averaging 10 rebounds to Magic's 5.5.

Despite all the media buildup, both players were hobbled for the second game. Larry had hurt his hand the night before against the Knicks, and Magic had pulled a groin muscle against the Bullets. Thus, Larry attempted only 10 shots all night long, although he ended up with 14 points, 12 rebounds, and 3 blocked shots. Magic scored just 1 point. However, with Larry being held to only 2 second-half points, the Lakers won again 100–98. Despite the Laker win, Magic was troubled with his injury for some time thereafter, while Larry continued to improve the rest of the season. Therefore, the statistical gap between the players widened, and Larry eventually won the Rookie of the Year award by a 63 to 3 vote (the vote was concluded before the playoffs). But like Larry's college player of the year award, the first-year award would be little consolation for losing to Magic's team in both games.

Shortly before the second Laker game, Larry had been named the *New York Post*'s 1979 Athlete of the Year, winning over the likes of Pete Rose, Björn Borg, Terry Bradshaw, Sugar Ray Leonard, and Larry Holmes. It was a stunning honor for an athlete only one month past his twenty-third birthday. But Larry had little time to savor his distinction; after the second Laker game, the Celtics were scheduled to make their annual west-coast road swing—in the midst of Cowens's twenty-seven-game absence due to foot problems. But Larry rose to the occasion, averaging a whopping 28.4 points per game in Cowens's absence. Before the midseason break and the league's annual All-Star game, Larry totaled 36 points in a romp against San Diego; after the break he scored his season high of 45 points along with 13 rebounds against Phoenix.

In the All-Star game, Larry was a substitute for the East and didn't play much, though at one point he made a brilliant, blind behind-the-back pass on the break, which players across the league were still talking about long after the game was over. With the score tied at 126 with 37 seconds remaining, East Coach Billy Cunningham sent Larry into the game and Larry promptly knifed a twenty-two-foot pass to Moses Malone inside for a 2-point lead. But the West tied the score. In overtime, with 2:30 left, Larry first assisted Malone for a 134–132 lead, and then he hit from twenty to push the score to 136–134. Twenty seconds later, Larry provided the winning margin with a gut-check three-pointer. Then in the waning moments he rebounded a missed shot and in one motion redirected the tip to George Gervin to make the score 144–136. "Larry didn't play the most minutes, he didn't score the most points, he didn't get the MVP. He just won the game," said one writer covering the game.

The transition from college to the pros *off* the court had proved more difficult. Larry had managed to establish some ground rules that seemed to be respected by the press covering the pros. He would not discuss anything personal, only basketball. Larry also found that if he stayed in the trainer's room after games he could avoid much of the hassle with the press, since that was one area off-limits to the press. But Larry's distrust of reporters, or of strangers for that matter, resulted in his being perceived as aloof and even, occasionally, nasty by outsiders and the press.

This situation was a source of great frustration to Woolf. "Larry's so different in private than he is in public that it's a shame more isn't known about that side of him. I really love this kid. He's so down-to-earth and so intelligent that I wish more people could know what he's about. But he's shy around strangers, especially reporters." Said Larry: "I know people think I'm a loner, but that's not true. I have a lot of friends. I just enjoy my privacy, my home, my family. What I don't enjoy is the celebrity thing."

Larry especially struggled with his growing celebrity on the road. As a result, he rarely went out in public. The few occasions that Larry did venture forth were enough of a culture shock, as it were. Larry's first trip to New York with the Celtics produced another frustrating experience with New York restaurant prices. "We had a steak dinner," said Rick Robey. "It cost $52 for both of us to eat. 'In French Lick you can eat on that for a week,' Larry said. I told him, 'Larry, we've got to leave a tip.' Larry wasn't too happy. He said we should get the dishes and the tableware." But, for the most part, to go out in public was to ask for all sorts of unwanted attention. Says Robey, "He can't go anywhere. We get harassed sometimes. He gets it all the time." To make matters worse, Larry's tendency toward moodiness made him even more sensitive to the intrusions on his privacy. "Some days," he'd say, "I can handle it; some days I can't. Some days I can relate to people, and some days I don't want to."

Larry's usual response to all the attention was to withdraw as much as he could. He had always tended to sleep a lot, anyway. Plus, he had, likewise, tried to expend as little energy as possible when not playing basketball (or training). So, to find seclusion in the anonymous hotel rooms across the country, while on the road, was only natural. Said Rick Shaw, "A couple of times when I was with the Pacers, I'd go over to the Hyatt and see him, and he'd come out and eat food; he might even walk to a McDonald's or something like that and eat, but that's it. He's in his room the rest of the time. I don't know if he's graduated to room service yet or not, but I think that's pretty extreme."

Whether in seclusion or not, waiting for the game to begin was one of the most difficult aspects of the NBA for Larry to get used to. "I hate the time before games, from 3:00 P.M. until it starts. I just want to play so badly—still do—that I can't stand waiting around," Larry would say later in his career. Larry was also surprised at the toll of life in the NBA. All the traveling and playing, night in and night out, while at the same time often nursing injuries, was much more than Larry had expected. "[The pros compared to college] is a lot more difficult.... You've got to play hurt a lot and be on the move. You're confronted with stuff you've never been confronted with before. It's very tough. I never did think in my wildest dreams that it would be this tough." It was also tough on the court. "I could do more things in high school and college than in the pros, because the players had weaknesses. Once you get to the pros, you've got to slow it down a bit. There are other players out there who can play the game just as well or better."

But Larry was still playing well, regardless of how talented the opposing players were. By the beginning of March, the Celtics were battling the Philadelphia 76ers for the conference lead. And Larry was continuing his torrid midseason pace. The day before the Celtics were to play the Pistons on Georgia's birthday, Larry told Mike he would get 50 points. Larry did fall short, but not by much, scoring 41. Larry's "a lot better now than he was three months ago....I think you have to consider him for the MVP along with Doctor J. and Abdul-Jabbar," said Fitch. Fitch's pitch for the MVP was no coincidence. The *Boston Globe*'s Bob Ryan, one of the NBA beat's most respected writers, had been touting Larry for MVP, as well as Rookie of the Year, for much of the season.

The Celtics finished their season two games ahead of Philadelphia, thus earning the home-court advantage for the playoffs with the best record in the NBA. Their record of 61 wins and 21 losses was a milestone of sorts. Never before had a single player been responsible for so dramatic a turnaround—32 games—in one season. In the history of basketball, Kareem and Walton were the two other obvious examples. Jabbar had sparked a 29-game turnaround when he came to the Milwaukee Bucks in 1969, and Walton had sparked a 12-game turnaround for the Portland Trailblazers in 1974.

Larry possessed an exceptional ability to help his teammates raise the level of their games. Still, that alone could not account for the largest single-season turnaround in NBA history. An explanation for the turnaround would have to start with Larry's uncanny ability to "see" the floor. He could instinctively decide the exact play that needed to be made. "I call him 'Kodak,' because his mind takes an instant picture of the whole court. He sees creative possibilities," said Bill Fitch. "Larry can create off a set play, and in the context of that play he can invent something that's never been done." Not only did his vision and instincts allow Larry to do what few had ever done, but it enhanced the other aspects of his game as well.

And it was the wide array of Larry's talents that impressed other coaches around the league. "He has all the skills you admire in a team player. He passes, sets screens, rebounds, gives the quick outlet pass, works hard at his defense and on improving his game." For Jack Ramsey, Larry "does all the things a player should do." Similarly, Hubie Brown, then of the Atlanta Hawks, also saw an idealized version of the game embodied in Larry: "He's a complete player, a definite all-star. He's a beautiful player to watch. He epitomizes how the game is supposed to be played."

Cowens believed Larry developed a game to fit his particular physical abilities, a game which he did not try to go beyond. "He is a very inventive player. He has good hands and he has confidence in his ability to control the ball. He has good vision and depth perception.... He has some skills coming into the league that a lot of guys never acquire. He knows how to play within his game." And such a clear understanding of what he could and couldn't do provided Larry with the confidence to take over a game when necessary.

Only Kareem and Erving finished ahead of Larry in the MVP voting at the end of the season. Larry averaged 21.3 points, good enough for fourteenth in the league, and 10.4 rebounds, which was tenth in the league. In addition, Larry had the third-highest three-point field-goal percentage, and his 58 three-pointers would stand as a record for rookies over the next eight seasons. Among the NBA's forwards, only Seattle's John Johnson had more assists than Larry, who averaged 4.5 per game. By season's end, Larry had more than justified his magnificent salary, helping to attract $1.3 million in regular-season ticket revenue alone and another $750,000 during the playoffs. It was quite a contrast to the previous season, where the only sellout all year had been opening night against the Cleveland Cavaliers, who won by 14 points. Larry had backed up his early-season prediction about attracting fans and winning. "If I can give to the Celtics what I want to give, the place will be packed every night, and that's what they want. There musta been somethin' wrong here cause they didn't win many games the last few years, but I think that's over."

In all of Celtic history, 1977–1979 was the only two-year period without a playoff appearance. However, the period was, indeed, over when the Celtics opened the postseason against Moses Malone and the Houston Rockets. They had earned a first-round bye* and would host the first two games. And Boston swept the series, winning all four by a margin of at least 17 points. Unfortunately, the next opponent, arch rivals the Philadelphia 76ers, would not be nearly as easy to beat. They started a front line featuring 7'0" Caldwell Jones, 6'11"

---

*A bye allows the team to automatically advance to the second round without having to beat another team in the first round.

Darryl Dawkins, and Erving. The guards were Maurice Cheeks and Lionel Hollins, with defensive specialist Bobby Jones and Steve Mix coming off the bench.

Game 1 at Boston Garden went about as expected in the first half with the Celtics taking a 53–44 lead into intermission. In the third quarter, though, the Sixers took the lead and won 96–93, as the stunned Celtics couldn't catch up despite Larry's 27 points. The second game, also at home, started in desultory fashion as Larry missed his first three shots. Then Larry hit 10 out of his next 13 to take a sizable lead in the first half. Although the Sixers briefly took the lead, after the third quarter the Celtics weren't seriously headed, winning 96–93. The series shifted to Philadelphia for the next two games, and Boston needed to win one of those games to even the series. Meanwhile Sixer Coach Billy Cunningham, unhappy with Larry's ability to exploit Julius Erving on the inside, shifted the seven-foot Jones onto him. The switch was immediately effective, though Boston was able to lead by two at the half. Then the third quarter proved to be the Celtics' undoing again, with the Sixers exploding to take a commanding 12-point lead. Larry and the late-season acquisition, Pete Maravich, led a fourth-quarter charge that just fell short to allow the Sixers a 99–97 win.* Larry had scored 22, but it had been a struggle, with Jones denying his inside game while proving to be tough to shoot over.

With their backs against the wall, the Celtics had to win the fourth game or the series was virtually over. The first half was tight again, but disaster overtook the Celtics in the third quarter again as the Sixers took the lead and held on to it throughout the fourth quarter for a 102–90 victory and a 3–1 lead in games. To win the series, the Celtics were faced with the unenviable task of having to win three straight, a feat which had only been accomplished twice before. Moreover, although Larry led the team in scoring again with 19 points, his performance had been, for the most part, lackluster. He was suffering from the flu and looked especially fatigued. And with a tired Larry Bird and Tiny Archibald left to run the offense, it was the Sixers who looked more like the ultimate team players. Thus, game 5 seemed almost beside the point as the Sixers dominated from start to finish, winning 105–94.

---

*Maravich, the late, great college and NBA star, was at the end of his career and would play only for the rest of the 1979–80 season before retiring the following year.

The Sixers' twin towers, Dawkins and Jones, had dominated the smaller Celtics inside, allowing the team to pull off a major upset. And Larry had looked like he had trouble catching his breath the entire game. He had his worst performance, scoring only 12 points. Larry was bitter that he and the Celtics had not come close to playing up to their potential. "We had the best record in the NBA, and they put us away like nothing. We never played a good game [in the series], not even the one we won."

For Larry, the season's premature conclusion had been as unexpected as many of his other experiences in his first professional season. Yet this year of firsts had been a triumph, if only because Larry had proved that he could adapt. And while the adaptation was sometimes a little rough around the edges off the court, it was brilliant on the court. But if the success of his first year was to have any bearing on the future, the next season a wiser, more experienced Larry Bird would not be going home early.

13 / The First Championship Season: The Boston Celtics, 1980–1981

For Red Auerbach, the team's current success had been especially gratifying in light of the past two seasons, although the ensuing dramatic decline in the playoffs had been all the more frustrating. Nobody, including Auerbach, had expected the kind of regular-season success the team had enjoyed, simply because nobody had expected Larry to be such a dominant pro player. "Larry, I felt, had that potential—yet I didn't realize how quick he was. I had no knowledge of his rebounding abilities. I knew he had a court presence on offense, but I didn't realize he had one on defense, too. And I had no sense of his leadership qualities, or his ability to motivate other people as well as motivating himself. I had no great insight into his character, or his personality, or his willingness to play in pain. I have never had an athlete in my 39 years in the league who liked to play more than Larry does and who would make every effort to play whether he was hurt or not....I call him a pro's pro. Knock him down again, he'll get up again. He won't take any crap from anybody. He far exceeded anything I expected, not only as an athlete but as a person."

Yet even Larry's basketball virtues could not hide the fact that the Celtics had been overmatched in the frontcourt against the Sixers. Auerbach was prepared to make a major move in order to counter Philadelphia's dreaded huge front line (7'0", 6'11", 6'7", compared to the Celtics' 6'8", 6'9", 6'8" front line). Fortunately, the Celtics had the resources to get their big man. Auerbach had managed to salvage two of the three original first-round draft picks he had been marshaling before John Y. Brown's arrival. And the first pick was Detroit's first pick, which also proved to be the first pick of the draft, due to the Piston's woeful season. The second first-rounder obtained from Detroit wasn't bad either; it was the thirteenth choice overall.

Auerbach had the option of using the first pick to draft 7'1" center Joe Barry Carroll of Purdue or of using the picks to engineer a trade for a veteran center. Carroll was projected as the top collegiate available in the draft. But Auerbach was not sure. He liked Kevin McHale, another Big-Ten player from Minnesota, at least as much. McHale had impressed the pro scouts with his postseason appearances and was projected to be a high first-round pick. At the same time, Auerbach had received word that Golden State was not only interested in dealing their 7'1" center, Robert Parish, whom Auerbach liked for his rebounding and shot-blocking ability, but that they were also extremely interested in Carroll.

Warrior general manager, Scotty Stirling, was so covetous of Carroll that he agreed to swap the Warriors' first-round draft choice, the third pick, for the Celtics' first pick (thus being assured of getting Carroll) and agreed to give Parish to the Celtics in exchange for the Celtics' other first-rounder, the thirteenth pick. Auerbach would not only get Parish, but he wouldn't have to give up anything in return, since he would still be able to get McHale with the third pick. So the trade was completed and on the next day the Celtics drafted McHale. It was yet another in a series of brilliant player moves Auerbach had made throughout his career.

Meanwhile, in French Lick, Larry was attempting to fully comprehend the season's-end collapse. He had now been frustrated in his attempts to win a championship both in college and in the pros. The Philadelphia series, in particular, ate at him, specifically the ineffectiveness of his inside play. So, over the summer, he set out to develop an inside game to go along with his outside game.

That summer Larry was willing to do whatever was necessary for him to be able to take the team to the next level. However, one of the biggest stumbling blocks to this resolve was Fitch's relationship with the players. Throughout the first season they had had difficulties with Fitch's dictatorial personality. His manner was especially difficult for the veterans on the club, and Fitch was largely responsible for the premature retirement of Pete Maravich, in the middle of training camp the following October. Unlike other players on the team, Larry responded to Fitch in a positive manner, for he took

Fitch's demands as a challenge to play his best. And Fitch's tendency to overwork his players, whether on the practice floor or in the video room, certainly didn't bother Larry. Indeed, the biggest reason why Fitch and Larry got along, according to K. C. Jones, was that they were "the two hardest workers on the team."

However, the success that the team had been able to achieve in the previous year was a testament not to Fitch's demands but to Larry's ability to assume the coaching role on the floor. Even Fitch had to admit he had little to do with the positive changes: "I'd like to take credit for [the team's sudden ability to pass] but I can't. I didn't go to training camp and preach good passing. You stress ball movement and hitting the open man, but we teach those same things every year.... This is a team game—but on this team, Larry Bird influences how well or poorly we do. He does everything that we ask of him. He inspires other players to sometimes play beyond their ability." And beyond that, the Celtics' offense was designed around Larry. "Bird is the reason the Celtics are so successful. All their plays revolve around him," said Washington Bullet Coach Gene Shue. "He's the best passing forward in the league by far—and maybe one of the best ever."

There was no doubt that Larry, just as he did in college, coached the team on the court as a kind of surrogate or extension of the coach. Or it could be said that sometimes he coached the team in spite of Fitch.

Yet Larry was commonly perceived to be dumb. Part of this may have been attributable to his facial structure, with its "receding chin and slack jaw," as the poet Donald Hall describes it. Also, Larry's southern Indiana argot and ungrammatical speech tended to give a lot of people a mistaken impression. But as Jones remarked, "Don't be misled by his down-home Indiana style,... Larry is one of the most perceptive people I have ever met in my life." And coaches and players alike remarked on Larry's mental powers. "He's so intelligent. He always seems to know where the ball is going," said Billy Cunningham, coach of the Philadelphia 76ers. Said Robert Reid of the Houston Rockets: "He's the smartest player I've played against." As Tom Nissalke explained: "The number one thing Larry's got going for him, besides being a good athlete, is basketball brains. That's something in short supply. The college game is a coach's game. He's got all week to take smart kids, dumb kids, and get them ready for a game. The pro game is a player's game, even though there's a lot of coaching. You have to think so quickly. Bird is like a coach on the floor.''

In short, the evidence was overwhelming that the Celtics were Larry's team. Yet Larry possessed a public modesty that made him resist that idea. "I don't think I'm the leader out there...but I was around a lot of great guys and it made my job a lot easier." But according to Carr: "He is a silent leader. He doesn't get out in front and lead, instead he stays with us,...Larry's a quiet leader—he leads by example. He's not the sort to say, 'C'mon guys, let's go.'"

In his second season, his abilities as a leader would be tested more than Larry or anyone else could have imagined. In the first place, besides a difficult coach and an aging backcourt, there were a number of problems with the team. Archibald was staging a contract hold-out and had missed all of training camp; Maravich retired right at the end of training camp; and Kevin McHale was at an impasse over his Celtics contract. Only an eleventh-hour intervention by owner Manguerian ensured that McHale would play his rookie season in Boston. Then, without warning, Dave Cowens walked onto the team bus and bid everyone farewell. The seven-time all-star and 1972–73 league MVP was retiring.

With Archibald still holding out and the season a week away, the future looked bleak. Cowens's unexpected retirement effectively reinforced the view of some that Parish wasn't ready to take over from Cowens full-time. There were, however, some positive signs. Parish was already impressing a number of observers at training camp by showing an unusual facility for blocking shots with his left hand. Furthermore, McHale was progressing rapidly. And then, seven days before the Celtics' opener against Cleveland, Archibald signed a one-year contract.

In their opener, the Celtics were victorious before a sellout crowd at Boston Garden. But the Celtics lost 3 of their next 5 games as they adjusted to all the abrupt personnel changes of the past month. With a 3–3 record, the Celtics beat the Washington Bullets on the road, but lost M. L. Carr for the next forty-one games because of a broken foot. If that weren't enough, the 76ers were off to one of the best starts in that franchise's history. People were already comparing them to the 1966–67 Philadelphia team, widely regarded as the best in NBA history. The two teams met in the tenth game of the season in Philadelphia, their first encounter since the Sixers' playoff triumph the previous spring. The game went down to the wire, with Philadelphia winning in overtime, 117–113. Erving and Larry dueled like superstars, with Erving pouring in his career-high 45 points and Larry countering with 36 points and 21 rebounds.

The Celtics' troubles continued just two games later when they suffered their first home loss to the Milwaukee Bucks, 102–101, despite Larry's 29 points and 14 rebounds. The team's record stood at a mere 7–5, as the Celtics fell 3½ games behind the Sixers in the divisional race. Moreover, it seemed as though the fans had begun to lose confidence—only two of the first six home games sold out. Characteristically, Larry felt the blame was his. He was upset that in both the Milwaukee game and the Chicago game two nights before, he had not gotten Maxwell involved enough in the offense. "Max isn't scoring enough and it's my fault, because I should be getting the ball to him. I know how to do it, and I haven't been doing it" (The next night Maxwell led all scorers with 25 points). Larry's frustration was an indication that the team's offensive scheme was still tuning up. First, Parish was taking some time to acclimate, both mentally and physically, to Boston's running game, after having played a strict half-court game at Golden State. Plus, the team had to readjust its guard concept with the reacclimation of Archibald and the injury to Carr. And McHale, like all rookies, was still getting a feel for NBA life and his role in the front-line rotation. Larry himself was fighting some nagging injuries as well as adjusting to a new role.

Larry's role in the team's offensive and defensive strategies had changed significantly as he realized that the offensive burden needn't depend on him as much as it had during his first season. In contrast to his rookie season, Larry was playing more of a power forward position, leaving more of the outside shooting to the guards and helping to beef up the team's inside scoring. And by concentrating more on rebounding, Larry was initiating additional fast-break opportunities while running the wings less often. Finally, instead of having one inside passing target, as with Maxwell the previous year, Larry now had both Maxwell and Parish. As Larry became comfortable with his new role, so too did the rest of the players. By the second month the team, in Larry's words, had "jelled." He discussed this transition after the season. "Everything began to come together and we began to understand each other as a team. We learned to look for each other. I found out that I didn't need to be a 30-point scorer. I could score 15 to 25 a night and not hurt the team, particularly since there were other areas where I could help out."

The first evidence of this came in the November 21 game against the Golden State Warriors in the Boston Garden. Boston brought a 5-game winning streak and a 12–5 record into the contest. Golden State surged to a 21-point lead, but the Celtics came rushing back in the fourth period, spurred by a scrambling team defense which utilized the shot-blocking abilities of McHale and Parish, as well as Larry's ability to roam like a football free safety. The Celtics won, 108–106. Larry contributed 27 points. Yet the Celtics dropped 2 of their next 4 games, for a 15–7 record, and found themselves still 6 games out of first place. Unfortunately, the Sixers, the hottest club in the league, had an amazing 22–2 record, which constituted the best start in NBA history. However, the Celtics now began to play really good basketball and won 8 of their next 9 games.

Despite the dramatic win over Golden State at home, the team had sold out only one of its last six games. Still, the attendance had yet to drop below 12,200 as Larry's popularity helped buoy the team until the city became convinced the Celtics were going to be a dominant ball club. No longer would the club find it necessary to peddle free tickets as part of supermarket or breakfast cereal promotions. Boston now had the NBA's top fan attraction, be it home or away. "[Larry] has sold more tickets, as an individual attraction throughout this league, than any player before him," says Auerbach. "He's become the best box-office draw in the history of the NBA." The club was so confident of Larry's popularity that they raised ticket prices. Not only was Larry the white superstar the city had hungered for, but his attitude and style of play reinforced his popularity. "A lot of people who come to our games work hard—six days a week, long hours. What I try to do every time is give the best I can. You can't always score 30 points a game or get 20 rebounds, but you can run for 48 minutes. I like to think that I give the people their money's worth."

Of course, Larry's work ethic was not just to please the fans: "I'd play just as hard if I was playing on a playground somewhere and nobody was watching." The tradition of the Boston Garden provided no extra motivation for a player who was already so self-motivated. "When you go into Boston Garden, you're supposed to look up at all those championship banners, and in New York you're supposed to play harder because of all the tradition [there]. Hey, I played hard in Indiana. I want to make my own tradition." Yet at this stage in his career Larry was not ready to predict that any championships might result. "I'll pass and hustle and play with nicks, scrapes, and scratches. And I'll try to help the other guys on my team. I'm not saying I can make them champions. But maybe I can make it more exciting for the fans."

In the Celtics' next game, on Christmas Day against the Knicks in Madison Square Garden, the team won its ninth-straight game, 117–108. Larry led the way with 28 points, 20 rebounds, and 8 assists, marking the third time in the last six games that he had grabbed 20 rebounds. After the game Larry discussed the 76ers' 32–4 record and 4½-game lead. "We think the Philadelphia 76ers are peaking out. We'll get them." At the time, Larry's remarks seemed brazen in light of how well the Sixers had been playing. The Knicks game was the first of the Celtics' six-game road swing with four games on the west coast. They managed to win the first 4, pushing their winning streak to 12 and their overall record to 30–8. The winning streak had been the product of a remarkable run of defensive efforts that would become the hallmark of the 1980–81 Celtic team. Beginning on December 3, the Celtics held opponents under 90 points fourteen times during the regular season, and the team had lost only 1 of those 14 games.

When the team brought its 12-game winning streak into the Oakland Coliseum, an unusual event occurred: Larry did not score a single point—the only time in his pro career he had failed to score and the first time since junior high. Without Larry's customary 22 points, the Celtics were overwhelmed and Golden State won 121–106. Larry's reaction was similar to his reaction to the playoff debacle of his rookie season. "[Larry] was unusually silent during the trip to Oregon [following the Golden State game], and in that game's opening minutes, we understood why," says Carr. "He took over completely, rushing through the pack to grab loose balls, seemingly to take the ball physically from our guards for shooting opportunities. He swished his first 5 long jumpers, finished with 35, and led us to an important road win." (Larry finished with 33 points in the 120–111 victory.)

The Celtics finished their road trip with a 5–1 record; Philadelphia had not fared as well on theirs, dropping 3 out of 6. Larry's Christmas Day prediction was looking more attainable as the Celtics came back to the Garden only three games out of first place. In fact, a 12-game winning streak resulted, and Philadelphia's lead was reduced to 1 on the eve of only the second matchup between the two teams all season. With a 104–101 win, the Celtics gained first place and accomplished what only a month earlier had looked nearly impossible. If they could go on to win the division, they would secure the all-important home-court advantage for the playoffs. Moreover, the winning team would earn a bye, and the second-place team would face a first-round miniseries and second-round matchup against the Milwaukee Bucks. Winning the division could prove the difference between winning and losing the championship.

With the Philadelphia victory, the Celtics had won 25 of their last 26 games and Larry was finally content with his game. As he explained after the season, "I was playing great basketball for about a month. I reached my potential. For one stretch there, I was averaging about 28 points, 14 or 15 rebounds, and 7 assists. I felt like I had control of every game I played." However, in the Sixers game Larry was literally jolted out of his contentment when Darryl Dawkins's knee collided with Larry's thigh, which turned a deep purple for the next two weeks. "I've been hurt before, but I never had pain through my leg and back like that. It felt like my hip came out through my ear. And Darryl didn't even know he hit me. A while later I see him and he said, 'I'm sorry, Larry. I thought I felt something against my leg that night. I read in the paper the next morning that I hit you.' I never did get it back until the playoffs."

But Larry played the next night in Chicago, purple thigh and all, and refused to sit out the All-Star game the following night, though he was still in terrible pain. He had been denied a starting spot on the All-Star East team because of ballot stuffing by the Atlanta fans on behalf of forward Dan Roundfield. Asked if he was upset, Larry simply said, "It doesn't matter. I know the people in Boston love me. I know the Celtics love me. They signed me. The All-Star team didn't sign me." But Larry wasn't about to miss the game. He had never missed a game in college or the pros because of injury; playing with pain was a great source of pride for him.

In fact, Larry played only 18 minutes in the All-Star game and

could only manage 2 points on 1 for 5 shooting. In the three following regular-season games, Larry averaged only 27 minutes a game
and scored just 38 points on 14 for 37 shooting. Not surprisingly, the
team lost all three games, so the Celtics' possession of first place
lasted all of twenty-four hours.

The Celtics finally broke their three-game loss skein with two wins
in the Garden, and though Larry's thigh was better, it would not be
completely healed until the end of the season. In the meantime, the
Celtics had their west-coast swing and played the Lakers in the Los
Angeles Forum. Magic Johnson had required surgery on his left knee
for torn cartilage and had to miss the first meeting between the two
teams in Boston Garden on January 18. The Celtics won that game,
98–96. Johnson was nearly ready to come back for the second game,
but the doctors decided to hold him out another week. Magic or no
Magic, Larry wanted to pay LA back for their sweep of the season
series the year before.

He paid back that debt, and then some, by playing the most perfect game of his pro career. He hit 15 of 17 shots, including 8 in a
row, from mostly long-range, to total 36 points. He also had 21 rebounds, 6 assists, 5 steals, and 3 blocks. The Celtics won 105–91.
Ironically, two years earlier the Laker General Manager Jerry West,
a noted skeptic, had voiced some doubts about Larry's prospects in
the NBA. This night if he wasn't humbled by Larry's performance,
at least he had to admit its brilliance. "It wasn't the 36 points I liked.
I've seen that before. But Bird was a thought ahead of everyone all
night. You don't ordinarily see basketball played like that."

Two nights later against Utah, Larry proved himself once again,
but this time not in basketball terms. Utah sixth man, Alan Bristow,
and Larry had been verbally sparring with each other for much of
the game. Later, Larry and other Celtics speculated that Bristow's
provocation might have been part of a grand design to tempt Larry
into a fight to get him out of the game. Premeditated or not, that was
what happened. Utah had been leading all the way, though the Celtics
had come back behind Larry's 25 points and 12 rebounds, when
Bristow and Larry got tied up in the backcourt. Bristow ended up on
the floor with Larry standing over him, refusing to move. When
Bristow asked Larry to move one more time and was still refused,
Bristow tackled Larry, knocking him to the floor. Larry bounced back
up and leveled Bristow with a left to the jaw. Both players were

ejected, and Utah went on to win, 104–89. The incident wasn't the first time that a player of far less value to his team had confronted Larry, but Larry wasn't about to be intimidated. K. C. Jones likes to refer to Larry as a "street fighter." And Fitch, for one, harbored no illusions about Larry's "mean" temperament once he stepped on the court. Indeed, that quality had a lot to do with Larry's prowess as a player. "He's one of the meanest sons of a bitch in the league," said Fitch. "He's as tough and as rugged as you could ask. He has no fear threshold. He may be a 'hick from French Lick' but he's street-wise. If you bully Larry Bird, you picked the wrong guy."

The Celtics ended their road trip 3½ games out of first place with just nineteen games left to play. But by winning their next six games, including a 114–107 win against the Sixers in the Garden, the Celtics tied for first. Yet both the Celtics and the Sixers continued to battle down to the wire as they juggled half-game leads back and forth until the final game of the season—at Boston Garden. On March 29, Philadelphia held a 62–19 record; Boston was 61–20. A Boston win would produce a tie and require a tiebreaker, the first of which would be the two teams' head-to-head record which was 3–3. Only a third tiebreaker, representing the teams' records against other divisional opponents, could determine a winner, and Boston had the better record. So if the Celtics won they would be the division winner. As a result, the season and the probable conference championship came down to a single game.

In front of a national TV audience and 18,030 rabid fans (including 2,500 standing-room-only), the Celtics won for the third time in three home games against the Sixers, 98–94. Larry finished with 24 points. It was an appropriately dramatic finish to one of the most competitive divisional title battles in NBA history. Moreover, the battle was between two historic rivals, each outspoken in its dislike for the other. For Larry, the win was a gratifying conclusion to a remarkable regular season. He could now rest his still-aching thigh. Yet the division championship would be meaningless if the Celtics could not convert it into a division championship in the playoffs, like the previous year. So, the team was cautious in its enthusiasm. They could not afford to celebrate yet.

Still, no one had expected the Celtics to capture the division, especially after the first month of play. No one was more surprised with the final turn of events than Larry himself. "If you asked me last fall

if I thought this team would win 62 games, I'd've said 'no way.'"
Besides Larry, a large part of the reason for Boston's success had
been Robert Parish, whose game had finally begun to flourish. Along
with McHale, he gave the Celtics a formidable shot-blocking presence. That shot-blocking ability was probably the biggest factor in
the team's increasingly effective defensive play. Larry had increased
his own shot-blocking ability, improving by 10 over his rookie total
of 53. In fact, Larry improved in every statistical area except scoring, where his average declined one-tenth of one point to 21.2. His
field-goal percentage had gone from 47.4 to 47.8, his free-throw percentage from 83.6 to 86.3, his steals from 143 to 161. Larry's improved
performance was no surprise since it was, to a large extent, a part of
the NBA learning experience.

Larry's game had undergone some specific changes. For one, he
essentially played a different position than he had in his rookie year
when he played more small forward. But with Fitch's greater emphasis on a power-oriented inside game, Larry played more power
forward. "I went up against people more my size and quickness, and
it helped my rebounding and defense. As for defense, I anticipated
better." Larry didn't discern any dramatic differences in his game:
"I don't think I'm much better. What I've tried to do is improve a
little in each area, and it is reflected in my stats." One change that
Fitch noticed was that "he was no longer bashful about asserting himself when the game was on the line. He used to be more conscious of
passing the ball before looking for the shot. Now he knows there are
times when we need him to score. In a tight game, he now feels he
can take over."

Although, according to Martin Manley's Most Valuable Player
rating, Larry was the league's MVP by a wide margin over Julius
Erving, he was runner-up to Erving for the official MVP award in
the voting.

But Larry's contributions to his team went way beyond mere statistical improvement, and they could not be quantified. A Celtic official had this perspective: "Some superstars are arrogant. There
would be a lot of teams in this league who would be better off if the
stars treated their teammates better. Bird treats everyone well—on
and off the court." Although Larry himself and others have always
characterized him as an extremely moody person, Larry always managed to leave his mood at the arena door. "It doesn't matter what

mood I'm in when I get to the arena. I can always get ready to play. In fact, I'd rather be mad when I come in, because then I know I'll be ready to bang and do some work." In addition, his enthusiasm for the game and his level of play motivated his teammates to enjoy the game more. Auerbach explains: "When you play with a guy like Larry, a guy who will get the ball to you when you're open, it makes you try harder. It makes you enjoy the game. No matter what kind of shot Larry puts up, nobody resents the play because they know they would get the ball if they were open. He makes everyone who plays for us happier, and when players remember that he's only been in the league two years and that he's going to be with us for a while, then you see the influence and effect Larry has on the franchise."

As usual, Larry attempted to play down his role. "I'm just a player...I do what I'm supposed to do. I fit in with the team. I try to do what I do best...a bit of everything." As a result, Larry inspired little resentment for all the media attention he received because his teammates understood how he worked for the team. If his teammates knew Larry was going to play despite a lot of pain, they were likely to do the same. "He's one hell of a competitor," says Kevin McHale. "You can tell he is hurting, he's not running as well as he should, he's pulling back. But you say, 'Larry are you all right?' And he says, 'Yeah,' and goes out there and does his job. Those are the kind of guys you go across the river with, guys you go over the mountain with. I've never known another player who is so loyal," says McHale. "If you're Larry's teammate, you're one of the most important people in the world to him."

Larry was also one of the leading comedians on the team. A loose, jocular environment was essential to his happiness and to all those around him. So, he took upon himself the burden of making sure that those around him were having a good time. "This is the same atmosphere I knew in college. Everybody is razzin' somebody." No one was exempt from the razzing either—not even the general managers and coaches. K. C. Jones remembers "one day in a tight game at halftime, I was yakking away at the blackboard and pointing out mistakes on the videotape. It seemed to me the guys were all having mouth and face trouble. Their hands were rubbing around their lips, and chins, and cheeks. I was in the middle giving out the word from on high and started to walk to the other side of the blackboard. I jolted to a stop and almost fell over. My shoelaces were tied together. Mister L. Bird was lying on the floor by my feet. That was the end of that halftime sermon." After playing Auerbach in a game of one-on-one, Larry pointed out to reporters afterward that "[Auerbach] is the only guy who goes one-on-one with an oxygen tank on his back." Larry also worked at making sure that everyone was made to feel as significant as possible. For example, when he realized that eleventh man, Eric Fernsten, didn't have a shoe contract, he quietly went to Woolf and helped get him one.

After receiving a bye for the first round of the playoffs, the Celtics were to take on the Chicago Bulls, who had won 10 straight, and 15 of their last 17 games. However, the Celtics won the first two games handily. Games 3 and 4 were back in Chicago and were expected to provide more of a challenge. But even though Chicago led at the half of game 3, 60–57, Boston rallied to win by six behind Larry's 24 points, 17 rebounds, and 10 assists.

The fourth and final game was a nip-and-tuck battle in front of what Larry called "one of the loudest crowds" of his career. And in this game Larry displayed the fervor that made him such a great competitor. Says Kevin McHale, "We were about to sweep the series, leading in the fourth game, and I came in to substitute for Larry. He had just crashed into a table diving for a loose ball, and when he walked past me he said, 'Kill these guys.' He had the same intensity in his voice at the end of the series as he did at the beginning." A few minutes later, after reentering the game, Larry produced "the best shot of my life." "Fourth game, tied up, their place, time out just before the fourth quarter and they got about 20,000 fans just going nuts. Coach Fitch says, 'Let's do something to quiet this crowd down.' We threw the ball in, messed around with it for awhile, I made a three-pointer...then stole the ball, went back, laid it in....We went up five within 40 seconds. I mean, that crowd just went 'Whoooo!' Stopped. From then on it was over."

The Celtics' rivals for the conference championship, the Sixers, had beaten the Indiana Pacers two straight in the first round and then needed all seven games to narrowly defeat the Milwaukee Bucks. This meeting was the eighth time in the last seventeen years that Boston and Philadelphia had met in the playoffs. And there was no love lost between the two teams. However, in contrast to their last meeting, the Celtics had had playoff experience and were more likely to play up to their potential. But if the first game was any indication, the team was going to need a lot more experience. After a close battle, Philadelphia built a commanding 9-point lead with less than two minutes left and held on to win the game 105–104.

Just as they had the year before, Philadelphia had reversed Boston's home-court advantage, forcing the Celtics to have to win on Philadelphia's home court—something they had failed to do on nine straight occasions during the Bird era. In game 2 at the Garden, Larry wasn't about to have another game slip away; he totaled 34 points, 16 rebounds, and 5 assists to inspire a 118–99 victory. Game 3 in the Spectrum was never in question either as Philadelphia won by 10.

In game 4 the Sixers hung on at home to win 107–105 and to gain a seemingly insurmountable 3 to 1 edge. Like the year before, the Celtics' tentative play had been matched by the Sixers' aggressiveness. Historically, the odds of winning 3 straight were not good. In sixty-seven previous 3-to-1 advantages, the trailing team had been able to come back and win the series only three times.

The historical odds didn't bother Larry. He confided to friends that the Celtics were going to win 3 straight, conveniently ignoring the team's loss of all 11 games they had played in the Spectrum since Larry had been in the league. Similarly, Fitch said, "This club is capable of winning 3 games in a row from the 76ers." But at the beginning of game 5 in Boston Garden the Celtics once again played tentatively and trailed 59–49 at the half. Carr describes the mood at intermission: "We filed quietly into the locker room for our meeting, trailing, time slipping away. Fitch was a great coach that year—he treated us correctly and sensed perceptively what we needed as a team. 'Listen right now,' Fitch hollered to the group, 'I don't mind losing, but I do mind seeing you guys go out and play passively. You're not doing anything out there, and you're forgetting what got you to this level. I'm warning you men. If you go out like this, you'll find it hard to live with yourselves all summer. I don't want to end my season tonight.'"

Through the rest of the second half, the team played more aggressively, and near the end of the third period they were leading. But Andrew Toney, ever the streak shooter, got hot, and the lead changed hands. With 1:51 to go, the Sixers led by six. The Celtics' season once again was coming to a premature end against the Sixers in just five games. However, Maxwell blocked a Toney shot, and Archibald took the ball all the way to the hoop and was fouled as he scored. He then hit the free throw to reduce the margin to 3. Then the Celtics' vaunted fourth-quarter defense suddenly kicked in, forcing a turnover, and Larry drove the baseline with 47 seconds remaining, to bring the team within one at 120–119. Twenty seconds later, the Boston defense forced another turnover with Larry picking up the ball and driving to the basket. He drew three defenders, and so even though he missed, Carr was able to get the rebound, drawing a foul on the follow-up. When he sank both free throws with 20 seconds left, Boston led 110–109.

Philadelphia decided to work for the last shot. With Larry and Maxwell double-teaming Erving, he gave the ball up to a wide-open Bobby Jones, who drove the lane to the basket. Larry and Parish converged, with Parish between Jones and the basket. As a result, Jones threw up an off-balance left-hander which Carr garnered for the rebound, while drawing the foul. The clock showed 1 second left, and the game appeared to be clinched. At the time-out, Fitch instructed Carr to make the first free throw and then miss the second. He reasoned that the ensuing struggle for the rebound would exhaust the clock. Carr did as he was told, only Philadelphia was able to gain possession of the missed second throw and call a time-out before the clock ran out. Larry harassed Jones on his attempt to inbound the ball, and Parish stole the ball, giving the Celtics an astounding comeback victory. In a little over a minute-and-a-half, they had scored the final 8 points to win 111–109. Larry's 32 points and 11 rebounds were both game highs.

Despite their exciting comeback triumph, the Celtics' postgame celebration was marred by some controversy when Auerbach, along with some other former Celtics, excoriated Fitch for his decision to have Carr miss the free throw. Then too, the team could not afford to celebrate in any meaningful way because there were still two games to win, including the next one at the Spectrum.

In an effort to break the Spectrum jinx for game 6, Fitch had each of the players dress at different lockers and warm up at the opposite end of the court from where they ordinarily began each game. It didn't seem to help. Philadelphia completely dominated most of the first half and led, 51–42, at intermission. The Celtics looked doomed. The scoreboard overhead was even informing fans that tickets for the Philadelphia-Houston championship series could be purchased after the game. In the first minutes of the third quarter, the Celtics were having trouble even making the game competitive. The team desperately needed a catalyst to stem the Sixers' traditional third-quarter, game-clinching runs.

That catalyst came when Cedric Maxwell, partially by design, went into the stands after a heckler. From that point on the Celtics were inspired, and over the next eight minutes outscored the Sixers 26 to 14, as Larry scored 11 in the run. In the fourth quarter, with less than a minute remaining and Boston ahead 98–96, Toney stole the ball and went in for the score that would have tied the game. But Kevin McHale swooped in, blocked the shot, and saved the rebound—as well as the game. Maxwell's two free throws provided insurance against the last Philadelphia basket, resulting in what mere minutes before had seemed impossible: a 100–98 win in the Spectrum.

Pandemonium reigned on the tarmac at Logan Airport when the Celtics' charter landed late that evening. Hundreds of fans were waiting to cheer the team that had engineered such an improbable comeback. The impending seventh game had generated greater fan interest and anticipation than any other in Celtic history. Carr describes the mood in the warm-ups before the seventh and final game. "We were skying, on an emotional high coming out of the locker room. During the warm-ups, with about a minute to play before we were to be blown off for the introductions, we started dunking, high school style. At first slowly, Henderson, Maxwell, and Carr. Then in a cascade of dunks Bird, Ford, McHale, and Parish followed slam, slam, slam! The crowd began applauding and screaming." Yet when the game began, the Celtics fell behind once again. And they were still trailing at the end of the first period, and at the end of the half were down, 53–48. But with Larry and Maxwell leading the way, Boston trailed only 75–71 at the end of the third. With 5:23 remaining, Philadelphia took an 89–82 lead.

When Boston answered with a basket and then Larry stole the ball from Erving, the score was 89–86. Larry stole the ball once again and was fouled by Erving. He hit both free throws to tie the game at 89. When Darryl Dawkins threw up a shot that missed there was just over a minute left. Larry rebounded and went the length of the court, pulling up at twelve feet to fire a leaning banker over Erving. The Celtics had their first lead since the first quarter, 91–89, with 1:03 remaining on the clock. On the next possession, Erving again threw the ball away, but Maurice Cheeks stole the ball back and was fouled on his way to the basket with 29 seconds left. However, Cheeks missed his first free throw and the Celtics ran down the 24-second clock until Carr missed. There was a scramble for the rebound, and when Philadelphia gained possession with just 1 second left, they called a time-out. Then Bobby Jones inbounded at half-court against Larry's pressure, which forced him to throw a lob pass for Erving off the top of the backboard. The game and series were over. The Celtics were the divisional champions.

Boston had achieved one of the greatest comebacks in NBA history. The Celtics had come from 6 points behind with less than two minutes in game 5. They had rallied from 17 points down in game 6. And in game 7 they had held the Sixers without a basket for the last 5:23 to come back from a 7-point deficit. Only 1:51 away from winning the series in game 5, the Sixers had collapsed. The closeness of the final result wasn't that surprising, considering how evenly matched the two teams had been. "We played these guys 13 times this season, and the whole season is decided by one point," said Sixer Assistant Chuck Daly. Larry's final shot in game 7 had provided that season-ending margin, and he surprised reporters after the game with his bravado: "There was no place in the world I wanted that ball except in my hands." Indeed, Larry had dominated the series. His season-long battle with MVP Erving had been a mismatch. Despite having several different Sixers guarding him, Larry had averaged 26.7 points, 13.4 rebounds, and 4.6 assists in the series. He pulled down 29 more rebounds and scored 48 more points than anyone else in the series. "Bird is brilliant; what more can I say?" said Sixer Coach Billy Cunningham.

Standing between the Celtics and their fourteenth NBA championship were the Houston Rockets, a team the Celtics had beaten 14 straight. Although their top player, Moses Malone, had been dominant throughout the season (he averaged 27.8 points and 14.8 rebounds), the team had suffered through a 40–42 season. The Rockets had opened the playoffs against the mighty Lakers and were expected to lose the series, as they had the previous year against Boston. Instead, the Rockets won 3–2, benefiting from a series of wretched performances from Magic Johnson, who was not completely healed from his surgery. Johnson's late-season comeback also threw the Lakers' offense out of synch after they had painstakingly changed their game to accommodate his absence. The Rockets then barely survived San Antonio in a seven-game series to earn the right to meet the Kansas City Kings in the conference finals. They bounced the Kings, another team with a 40–42 record, in five games.

Most of the NBA and fan attention had gone to the seven-game series between Philadelphia and Milwaukee and then to that between Boston and Philadelphia. That series was considered to have been for the championship, and the upcoming series with the Rockets to be a mere curiosity. The Boston fans and players even celebrated the Celtics' victory over the Sixers as if it had been the championship itself. Two days later, when the Celtics actually had to play for the championship, they looked as though they had left their championship game back with the Philadelphia series. The problem was less a case of the brilliance of the opponent, as was the case in the series with Philadelphia, and more a case of the lethargy of the Celtics. No one was particularly worried, even though at the half Houston led 57–51. In the closing minutes of the third quarter, Boston gained its first lead only to lose it again; with the fourth quarter just under way, Houston held an 83–76 lead.

The fourth quarter belonged to Larry when, by sheer force of will, he refused to allow the Celtics to succumb. He began with a twenty-two-footer launched from the right side. Robert Reid, who was guarding Larry, ended up watching the ball. Larry knew immediately that he had missed the shot. Anticipating that the ball would carom off the rim along the right baseline, he launched himself toward the ball like a long jumper. He met the ball in midair, but his momentum carried him over the baseline about 12 feet to the right of the basket. Larry instinctively knew that if he put up the ball with his right hand, it would hit the backboard. Thus, in midair, he switched the ball to his left hand and lofted a soft little left-handed shot just before he landed beyond the baseline and out-of-bounds.

The shot was so remarkable that after the game it would become the main subject of conversation in both locker rooms. "Bird sort of flipped it. What can you say on a play like that?" said Reid.

"Only other play I've seen like it was made by Russ [Russell] a long, long time ago," said Auerbach. "Larry Bird is a player of destiny. He's going to go down in the history of this game."

The Rockets scored twice to reduce what had become a Celtic lead to 96–95 with 19 seconds left. But Larry then helped keep a rebound alive, and out of the Rocket hands, by grabbing it on the third tip and putting it in left-handed to save the game and give Boston a 98–95 victory. The Celtics had come away with their fourth come-from-behind win in a row.

Regardless of the extent to which the team made its own breaks, there was no denying that Boston was leading a charmed existence. In the first period of game 2 in the Garden, the Celtics fell behind for the ninth-straight game. Although the team rallied to take a 46–42 lead at the half, Fitch was so angered by the team's complacency that he punched a hole in the backboard at halftime. It did not serve to shake the team out of its doldrums. Houston rallied behind Moses and won 91–90. The Celtics had lost their home-court advantage again. And the Rockets had served notice that they were not to be taken lightly. The loss might have been just what the Celtics needed. "Sometimes a slap in the face wakes you up," said Carr.

In the third game, at Houston, the Celtics finally got out of the box, and took the lead, 12–11, after 7 minutes of play. The game quickly turned into a blowout as Boston emerged victorious, 94–71. Larry's game was about as strange as the one he played in. He scored only 8 points, but contributed 13 rebounds, 10 assists, and 5 steals. And he got into a shoving match with Reid, maybe because Larry was frustrated over his play.

In the fourth game, at Houston, the teams were tied at the intermission. Houston Coach Del Harris determined to use only six players in the game. The Rockets came out aggressively to begin the third period, and by its end led 75–67. With Larry in the midst of a tough shooting slump, Boston could get no closer as Houston tied the series at two with a 91–86 victory.

Larry had 12 rebounds, but surprisingly had been held to 8 points for the second game in a row. Perhaps the large number of minutes he had played during the regular season and playoffs had begun to take their toll. Although in his second season Larry had come into camp in much better shape and better understood the importance of pacing himself, he played 284 more minutes during his second sea-

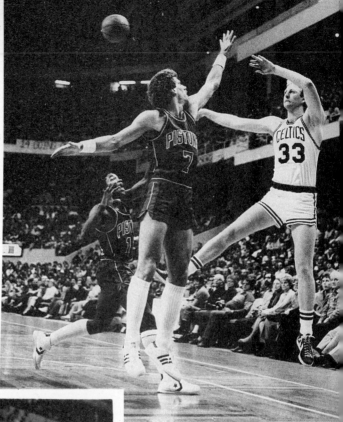

Passing while being double-teamed by Isiah Thomas and Kelly Tripucka of the Detroit Pistons. (Courtesy UPI/Bettmann.)

Passing without looking to Kevin McHale, during the 1986 Championship series. (Courtesy Phil Huber, *Sports Illustrated*.)

October 17, 1983, confrontation with Sixers' Mark Iavaroni. Both players were ejected from the game. (Top left and bottom photos courtesy AP/Wide World; top right courtesy UPI/Bettmann.)

LEFT: Cheap shot by Bill Laimbeer of the Detroit Pistons during 1987 playoffs. (Courtesy UPI/Bettmann.)

BOTTOM: Larry retaliates by hurling the ball at Laimbeer. (Courtesy Rich Clarkson, *Sports Illustrated*.)

Larry takes on three big scorers and one big mouth.

LEFT: Against Bernard King of the New York Knicks, seventh game, 1984, Eastern Conference semifinal. (Courtesy UPI/Bettmann.)

BOTTOM: Against Kareem Abdul-Jabbar of the Los Angeles Lakers, 1984 Championship series. (Courtesy Richard Mackson, *Sports Illustrated.*)

TOP: Against Ralph Sampson of
the Houston Rockets, 1986
Championship series. (Courtesy
UPI/Bettmann.)

RIGHT: Against Dennis Rodman
(at right) of the Detroit Pistons,
1987, Eastern Conference
Championship series. (Courtesy
UPI/Bettmann.)

Larry Bird triumphant after stealing game 5 against the Pistons in the 1987 playoffs. (Courtesy AP/Wide World.)

Analyzing the game during a rare rest in the 1987–88 season. (Courtesy Peter Read Miller, *Sports Illustrated*.)

Passing while falling over Rick Mahorn of the
Washington Bullets, January 24, 1983.   (Courtesy
UPI/Bettmann.)

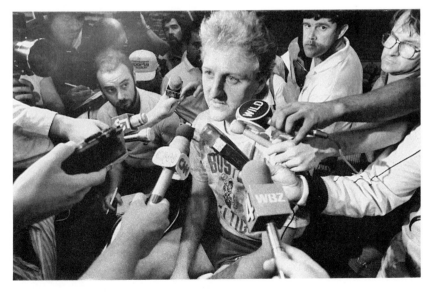

Surrounded by the press as usual, 1987 NBA Championship series.   (Courtesy
AP/Wide World.)

Victory over the Detroit Pistons, 1987 playoffs.   (Courtesy UPI/Bettmann.)

son (an average of 3½ more minutes a game) than his first. Whether Larry wanted to admit it or not, he was tired. Then, too, in this early part of his career, Larry tended to go through cyclical shooting streaks. He had shot significantly better than his season average in the eleven previous playoff games (49.1 percent compared to 47.8 percent)—so he was due for a couple of poor outings.

However, another factor was about to provide the Celtics with a shot in the arm. In the playoffs, players try to avoid controversial statements. Aroused emotions can often spell the difference between two evenly matched teams or allow an overmatched team to upset its opponent. Moses Malone, however, chose not to heed this rationale. After the game in which the Rockets tied the series, Malone launched a tirade against the Celtics: "I could get four guys off the streets of Petersburg, Virginia [his hometown], and beat [the Celtics]. I don't think they're all that good....I don't think they can stop us from doing what we want to do." If the Celtics had been guilty of complacence before, Malone's comment aroused in them an intensity similar to that which they had in the Philadelphia series. "The man threw down a challenge, and this is a team that responds well to challenges," said Maxwell.

Midway through the first quarter of game 5, Houston led 18–15; it was the last they would see of the lead. The game turned into a relentless payback with the Celtics finally winning by a massive 29 points—109–80. Larry's slump continued as he scored 12 points along with 12 rebounds. But it didn't matter; he was leading both teams in rebounding, assists, and steals: 15.8 rebounds, 7.4 assists, 2.6 steals. "Reid has stopped my offense, but I'm pleased with the rest of my game. I'm happy with every part of my game except my shooting."

Even though the Celtics had been only spurred on by Malone's comments, he wasn't through. For, after game 5, he said, "The Celtics are still chumps. I'm speaking from the heart now, and I want everybody to understand. I have respect for those guys, but they just aren't that good. If we play our game, they can't beat us. Tonight we didn't play our game....The Celtics aren't going to drink champagne after game 6, they'll drink Gatorade...to get their strength back." Malone's fresh war of words certainly didn't hurt the Celtics' motivation as the team headed back to the Summit for the sixth game and what would be their ninety-ninth game of the season.

Boston took a 53–47 halftime lead, and Larry was shooting well.

In the third quarter the Celtics mercilessly built their lead to 15 points, 82–67. But with the Houston crowd refusing to give up on their team, one of those abrupt and dramatic shifts in momentum took place. The Rockets managed to close within 3 points, 86–83, with 4:28 left in the game. The crowd was in a frenzy, and the Celtics were back-pedaling, both literally and figuratively. In the final four minutes, Larry took over, hitting a twelve-footer from the baseline to push the lead to 88–83. Then he came down on defense and drew a charge from Tom Henderson to give the Celtics back the ball. He then stuck a foul-line jumper. The score was 90–83, but Houston was not finished. Four-straight free throws brought the margin to 90–87, with 2:20 left. The crowd was on its feet. Larry took the ball out on the left side of the Celtics' end and threw a clutch lob pass to Maxwell for a score off the inbounds play. Calvin Garrett quickly came back to hit a jumper at the other end to make the score 92–89 with less than two minutes left. Larry next came down the court and found himself free in the left corner. He simply took one step back behind the three-point line and calmly sank his first three-point shot (and only the sixth by either team) of the series for a 95–89 lead. The shot not only silenced the crowd, but clinched the game and the championship. The Celtics' 102–91 victory made them the 1980–81 NBA champions.

"That shot was the killer," said Garrett. "I got caught in a tangle under the basket, and Larry got away from me. He made the big shot in a clutch situation. What can you say? He's a great player." Commentator Bill Russell believed the key to the shot was Larry's confidence: "Larry knew it would go in, because he had rehearsed it in his mind hundreds of times before." According to Larry, "The shot was there, so I took it. It's no further out than where I usually shoot from, so I never hesitated." The Celtics, to a man, had been concerned when Houston came back, but confident that Larry would pull them through. "There's nobody in the world I'd rather have taking a big shot for us. He's just one-of-a-kind," said Fitch. Ford commented: "Larry is a money player and when it was on the line he came through."

In the locker room after the game, the CBS cameras rolled, the champagne flowed, and the players mugged for the camera. Larry for once basked in all the media attention as he and Auerbach, who was smoking his trademark victory cigar, were being showered with champagne. And with about as much audacity as it took to attempt a three-pointer with the game on the line, Larry stole the cigar out of Auerbach's mouth. After one deep inhale, he coughed and announced, "We're the champions," and everyone, including Auerbach, broke up. Meanwhile, Auerbach reminded one and all that Larry was "a 6'9" Bob Cousy, a player who will go down in the history of the game as one of the all-time greats." Afterward, settling into a chair near the shower, away from the mob in the middle of the locker room, Larry quietly reflected upon the championship: "From the start of this series, everybody said we had the best team and were supposed to win every game. The pressure was always on us and now, thank God, it's over." The victory certainly helped erase the bitterness of the loss to Michigan State, two seasons before. "This means a little more because you're going against the best players. In college there are limitations on both teams." The championship was even sweeter for Larry because it had been such a team effort. "With the Celtics, the burden is not always on me. And that makes it even better that we won the NBA title. It's just good to be part of a championship team. It's what we worked so hard for all year."

Overall, Larry registered a memorable postseason. He finished the Chicago series with two breathtaking performances, clinching the final game on a three-pointer; then against Philadelphia he had three 30-point games and spearheaded comebacks in the last three games, including the seventh and deciding game; and against Houston he provided back-to-back 21 rebound games, before clinching the championship with a three-pointer. In seventeen playoff games, Larry totaled double-figure rebounds in every game. He averaged 21.9 points, 14.0 rebounds, 6.1 assists, 2.3 steals, and 1 block per game, while shooting 89.5 percent from the foul line in 44.1 minutes playing time per game. Though teammate Maxwell averaged, in contrast, only 16.1 points, 7.4 rebounds, and 2.7 assists, Maxwell was voted playoff MVP. The vote had been influenced by all the media attention focused on Larry's midseries slump against Houston and because Maxwell had averaged 17.7 points to Larry's 15.3 points in the final series. Afterward Fitch argued that Larry got a raw deal on both the season and playoff MVP awards. "Bird should have won both of them," said Fitch.

All of Boston turned out en masse to fete the new NBA champions. The Boston police estimated that 1 million fans lined the parade route to catch a glimpse of the championship motorcade with Larry in the front holding the championship trophy. At City Hall anywhere between 40,000 and 100,000 fans (plus millions tuned in on TV) gathered to hear the traditional serenades of Boston, as well as the bromides about the glorious season. The crowd saved its greatest response for their reluctant hero from the midwest. Bostonians had always desired to claim him as one of their own. However, the gulf between Larry's background and the Boston milieu was, in the final analysis, too great to be bridged. He'd given an indication of where his true identification lay in an interview after the final game on national TV, when he dedicated the championship to French Lick.

In front of that huge Boston throng, Larry simultaneously dampened both the cultural pride and the fan adulation that up until then had marked the occasion. Larry lampooned both autograph seekers and the Boston mayor's office, and also noted that he would rather be in French Lick. Though there was no doubt about the jocular nature of Larry's comments, the response was a mixture of cheers, boos, and nervous tittering. Furthermore, Larry's adolescent side, appealing as it was to his similarly inclined teammates, wasn't as successful with this broader audience. Explaining that "I love to play around," Larry glimpsed a sign in the audience with a scatological reference to Moses Malone and went on to announce to everyone, "I think, after all the hollering and screaming, I look out in the crowd and see one thing that typifies our season. Moses does eat shit!"

Proper Bostonians, urban sophisticates, and editorial writers mindful of the limits of public decorum were outraged. Larry was surprised that anyone was offended, but he apologized anyway. Larry also apologized to Malone who, given his own proclivity for blunt speech, had probably been far less offended than those in Boston. Later, Larry commented, "I've said a lot of things I wished I never had, but, hey, that's me. I'll do a lot more before I get older. There's nothing I can do about it once I've done it. What people think of me could hurt a little if they think bad. I'm sure there are people in this world who hate me, but there are a lot who love me. I'm just me. I try to be honest." Larry was, in large part, able to be philosophical because he was secure enough by now not to be overly concerned with presenting a palatable public face.

Yet Larry still had some ambivalence about the reaction to his Moses Malone comment. A part of him badly desired acceptance, and this was so ever since he had been a shy youngster from a family poor enough and transient enough to be outcast, even in the valley.

But despite having his intense desire for acceptance by his fans, Larry couldn't care less whether the people in Boston liked him. To him, the Bostonians were akin in many ways to the outsiders who had invaded and then abandoned the valley. And like his friends back home in the valley, Larry had a fundamental distrust of people who are incapable of understanding, or unwilling to understand, his admittedly small-town values and experience. To be sure, Boston would never be known as a city of understanding, much less sympathy, for those of "different" social and cultural backgrounds. It was a city defined by boundaries, where the sophisticated eastern establishment with its Ivy League airs uneasily coexisted alongside the city's intensely ethnic provincials. And those boundaries hardly lent themselves toward an understanding of Larry Bird, the man from Indiana, as distinct from Larry Bird, the Boston Celtic basketball star. In response, Larry came to especially value those people and those things nearest to his experience. In other words, for Larry the world consisted of his girlfriend Dinah, his brothers Mike and Mark, his teammates, and a constant stream of friends and family from the valley and Terre Haute. As he had said during the season, while registering his uneasy accommodation of Boston, "Just as long as I can live the simple type of life I want, I'll be all right."

The topic of Larry and his public was a complicated one. No matter how deprecating his remarks about Boston or how surly his demeanor with fans, Larry continued to be the most popular athlete in Boston. People lived through, identified with, and cheered Larry on for what he did on the court. And the public was only too willing to go along with Larry's desire to keep his life separate from his basketball exploits, for they desired perfection in their heroes. They didn't want to be told of Larry's "flaws" any more than they liked to be reminded of their own problems.

However, Larry was more willing to be the subject of fans' identification and fantasies than he was to assume the other burdens attendant to being a public figure. According to Robey, "Larry's pretty happy with his life and his public, so he figures his free time is his own." Said Larry, "If I did half the things people wanted me to, I'd be busy all the time and I'd have no time to play ball." As Larry grew better able to handle the distractions, he also was more successful at being open with the public. Even during his second season, he was doing things that would have been unthinkable in his rookie season. Once, when he was in the Dallas airport, before playing the Dallas Mavericks, he was greeted by a couple, "Don't be too hard on our Mavs." He entered into a ten-minute conversation with them and even seemed to enjoy himself, smiling throughout. He still, however, had a problem with signing autographs. "I'd prefer that somebody shake my hand and have a conversation than ask for an autograph. When people ask to talk to you, they want to know about you. That's the kind of people you give your time to." It was a curious comment from someone who had always resisted attempts from strangers to get to know him better.

Larry was much more willing to autograph for kids than for adults. Still, in his first couple of seasons, he was likely to turn down children as well. On at least one occasion, he was taken to task by his mother for refusing a child in her presence. Most of the time, Larry's position on the responsibility of athletes to their public was close to that of former Celtic great Bill Russell. According to Red Auerbach, "[Bill] insisted: 'All a performer owes is a good performance.' Beyond that he felt nothing was owed, including autographs, appearances, and small talk on the street."

Like Russell, Larry almost never made appearances, even though the league, for one, always asked Larry to appear. "I don't do stuff for them 'cause I don't work for the league. I work for the Celtics." Of course, Larry didn't make appearances on behalf of the Celtics either. The difference was that Auerbach knew enough not to ask Larry in the first place.

While Larry did make an effort to be more accommodating to the press in his second season, he continued to hide out in the trainer's room until the very last minute. "I'd rather do it that way," he said, "instead of answering the same question over and over." Yet as the season wore on, there was a perceptible difference in the way he handled the press. Instead of looking down and mumbling, Larry developed a clear and more assertive delivery. As he spoke, his eyes focused somewhere over the heads of the surrounding newsmen rather than down at the ground. It was plain that he would rather be anywhere else, and his answers to questions were almost always dutiful and perfunctory rather than informative. But by the time of the playoffs, he had become one of the better Celtic interviews. And following the sixth-game victory over Houston, he actually stayed at the victory party until 6:30 the next morning drinking beer and chatting with reporters.

After spending the summer in French Lick luxuriating in the aftermath of his first-ever championship, Larry was eager to begin the quest for another title. Moreover, he was ready to establish himself as the premier player in the world; he wanted to win the MVP. And in fact, Larry was certainly admired by all the experts including coaches like Jerry Sloan of the Bulls and Kevin Loughery of the Nets, and players like Bobby Jones. Said Sloan: "I don't think there's ever been a better player in the league than Larry." Loughery said: "[Larry's] simply the best we [the NBA] have." Said Jones: "He's the best in the game today." For teammate Dave Cowens, Larry's greatness was encompassed in his unique mental capacity for the game. "It's a savvy, or something. Larry's got it. Something mental that other players with more physical talent don't have." And teammate Chris Ford remarked on the breadth of Larry's skills: "Larry never fails to amaze me. He can do so many things well. He may have a bad shooting night, and it won't mean a thing. He can lead us with his passing or his rebounding or his defense. He can do it all. When he does, he's the greatest there is." Larry, too, was confident about his abilities. "At times, I think I'm the best player in the league," Larry said. "Now I figure three out of four nights I'm gonna play better than anybody else in the game." With each season and every success, Larry continued to build upon the confidence that K. C. Jones, three years before, had noted was the greatest he'd ever seen. It would only be a matter of time before that greater confidence and the growth it inspired in Larry's game would culminate in his official recognition as the league's most valuable player.

14 / *Building to Greatness: The Boston Celtics, 1981–1984*

On October 30, 1981, the Celtics opened at home against the Washington Bullets, but first they hung their fourteenth championship banner from the rafters of Boston Garden. Larry was selected by his teammates to address the Garden fans, despite the controversy that had followed the last speech he had given. This time there was no controversy, only satisfaction: "Every time I walk into the Garden, I look up and see the 1981 flag, and it makes me feel good because I know that thing will be hanging there until the building falls," said Larry. "What I want to do now is win another, no matter how long it takes." But not since the Celtics had repeated in the 1968–69 season had a championship team been able to come back and win the crown again. Accordingly, the Celtics were tabbed to finish second in the division, behind Philadelphia.

Still, many believed that it would be a Boston-Philadelphia dogfight for first and that the Celtics had a good shot at getting their second consecutive 60-win season. There are a multitude of reasons why a championship team usually doesn't repeat, but one of the most important is that a team rarely can sustain the same winning balance and chemistry. M. L. Carr recalls a comment Auerbach had made the previous season: "He pointed out at us—the players and coaches laughing and talking, moving with the familiar rhythms of practice like kids on the playground, happy to be just there....Red commented, 'I hope these guys realize what they have....These types of feelings among players don't last long.'" And the Celtics found out fairly quickly that sustaining that chemistry would be more difficult than they had imagined.

In December, the team was unexpectedly presented with what would ordinarily have been a wonderful bonus in the form of still-another brilliant acquisition by Auerbach. Danny Ainge, a third baseman with the Toronto Blue Jays, had become a college basketball star in his senior year at Brigham Young. When Ainge had signed with the Blue Jays in his junior year, he had no reason to believe that he would develop into the basketball player that he became in his senior year. Plus, signing with the Jays allowed him the opportunity to play professional baseball in the summers and at the same time to pursue a degree at BYU without jeopardizing his college basketball eligibility.

If Ainge hadn't been under a long-term contract to the Jays, he would have been a top five pick in the 1981 draft, but, since he was and, in addition, had not shown any interest in playing basketball, it was assumed he was untouchable. But Auerbach, with the encouragement of agent Ron Grinker (Grinker also represented Maxwell), decided to take a chance on such a gifted player in the second round of the 1981 draft. Auerbach figured if Ainge ever determined that he wasn't going to be able to consistently hit a major league curve ball, then he would join the NBA. Ainge had grown dissatisfied with baseball. With Ainge's consent, the Celtics went to court to get Ainge released from his contract. They claimed that Ainge had been given a verbal release by the Jays due to his increasing unhappiness with baseball. After hitting in the .240s in 1980, Ainge's average had slipped to .187 in 1981. After his surprisingly effective senior basketball season, Ainge's thoughts had begun to turn to basketball. The more he struggled at the plate, the more he thought about basketball and the unhappier he became. Though the Jays won the court case, Ainge had announced that he wasn't going to play baseball anymore. The Jays had no choice but to release him.

By December 9, Ainge was in a Celtic uniform. Ainge's appearance should have been welcome insurance for the aged backcourt. But instead, it only aggravated a burgeoning problem: playing time was scarce. Ainge's need for minutes upset an already-precarious balance of playing time. And his appearance was even less welcome because a player cut or trade would be necessary as soon as Carr came off the injured list. Even Larry was upset, saying, "They better not trade M. L." So it was no surprise that Ainge was virtually ignored by the entire team in his first appearance. At the same time he was wildly cheered by the Garden crowd. Those cheers would eventually turn to occasional boos, while his acceptance by his teammates would continue to be problematic. Meanwhile, the Celtics were playing "sluggishly," in Carr's words. The team had developed a habit of blowing big leads. Regardless, they were still in contention for first place with Philadelphia in the division and Milwaukee in the conference race.

One month after Ainge's inaugural appearance, the Celtics hosted the Chicago Bulls. In what Fitch called "the worst basketball in my three years here," the Celtics blew the lead in the second half and eventually lost by 14. With the season one-third over, the team seemed to believe it could turn it on at will. The attitude, as announced by Larry, was "We'll be all right for the playoffs. That's when it counts." Nevertheless, the Chicago loss seemed to shake the team out of its lethargy to some extent. Larry had been held to 9 points in the Chicago game—his first single-digit game of the season. So, if the Chicago loss didn't galvanize the rest of the team, it certainly galvanized Larry. He proceeded to play the greatest basketball of his life for the rest of the month. He had his first 40-point game since his rookie year, against the Pistons in Hartford. He then had two triple-doubles in three nights against New Jersey and Atlanta. A week later, Larry had 39 points against the Knicks in Madison Square Garden, followed by dominant performances in three home games against Indiana, Seattle, and the Knicks again. Fittingly, Larry was named NBA player of the month, and also earned the All-Star game MVP on January 31. Larry continued to maintain his high level of play as the season progressed. Before each home game, during the playing of the national anthem, he would prepare himself by looking at Bobby Orr's retired number, a ritual he continues to this day. And Bostonians were attending games as never before. Even during the most inclement weather against the worst teams, it was near-impossible to get a ticket.

On February 21 the Celtics were near the end of their annual west coast odyssey; they were now about to go over a month without losing. By February 28, the Celtics had a three-game winning streak. Three games later they played in a nationally televised game at the Garden against the Milwaukee Bucks, who had the best record in the NBA. Late in the second period, the Bucks' Harvey Catching swung around and caught Larry with a vicious left elbow to the face.

As Larry lay motionless on the parquet, a pall fell over the Garden. Meanwhile, the game television coverage repeated replays of the blow in slow motion. Larry, tough as ever, got up and left the court under his own power. In the locker room, his face was stitched up as he missed the entire third period, during which the Celtics lost the lead.

At the beginning of the fourth period, a murmur went through the crowd, and then everyone was standing and screaming as Larry emerged through the tunnel to reenter the game. Within a few moments, Larry received the ball on the right side, where he aggressively wheeled to the basket and dunked. The crowd went wild, and the momentum of the game was irrevocably reversed. Larry went on to score 6 more points which made the difference as the Celtics won 106–102. Larry's performance was all the more impressive considering that x-rays showed a fractured cheek bone which would require plastic surgery. (The injury was also reported as a fractured cheek and as a fractured jaw.) Unfortunately, the injury would force Larry out indefinitely.

Without Larry, the team managed to win the five games of their Texas swing to increase their winning streak to nine. Larry, not yet completely recovered, was disconsolate over having to miss any games at all. Thus, when the team next traveled to New Jersey, Larry declared himself ready to play. But Fitch, ever-superstitious, didn't want to interfere with the team's winning chemistry. He asked Larry to come off the bench as the team's sixth man—at least until the winning streak ended. Though Larry had started in every basketball game he had played since his junior year of high school, he acquiesced. Said Fitch, "We've got a lot of 'we' people on this team and from the beginning Larry had been one of the biggest promoters of this concept. He's concerned only about playing basketball and winning." If Fitch's comments were meant to both mollify and cajole Larry into more fully accepting his new role, Auerbach also seemed to be trying to do the same thing. "He's unselfish. He doesn't ask 'What's in it for me?' when you ask him to do something to help promote the club." The common theme throughout both Fitch's and Auerbach's messages was Larry's readiness to submerge his ego for the good of the team. Larry always had been willing to subscribe to the team ego first; however, the team imperatives had never before diverged from the demands of Larry's own ego. Although Larry obviously tried to put a good public face on his coming off the bench, the matter wasn't as simple as it seemed on the surface. For a player of Larry's calibre to be asked to accept a reserve role for an indefinite amount of time was unprecedented. But Larry accepted that role.

It couldn't have been easy, for over the course of Larry's career, no other player has averaged as many minutes per game. And many of the minutes were accumulated when his presence was hardly necessary to win the game, even though those extra minutes tended to have a deleterious effect on Larry at the end of the season. But no other player guarded his minutes like Larry. "I have only one real goal in this league: to play every minute of every single game....Man, if you can't play 45 minutes a night you're not taking care of yourself, not getting enough rest after the game....We're in the prime of our lives. We're paid to play 48 minutes. What's the big deal—unless you're injured?" Why was Larry willing to risk injury and exhaustion at the end of the season simply to preserve his minutes? Part of the answer can be explained by Larry's sheer love of the game: "Basketball is fun for me. I don't consider it work." The other part of the answer can be explained by Larry's enormous ego.

To talk of Larry's ego seems to contradict the picture of Larry as the ultimate team player. The common assumption about Larry as a player without an ego is in large measure due to people like Auerbach, Fitch, and Woolf, who confuse "playing without an ego" with selflessness, since for many people, the term "ego" conjures up images of superstars only concerned with their own statistics. Yet Larry's ego fostered an intense altruism, the genesis of which was the substantial ego-gratification Larry gained from giving the ball up to teammates. "Passing the ball is what I like the best...because if I can get the ball to a guy and he scores and I see the gleam in his eye when he's running back down the court, it's about the greatest feeling in the world." That Larry had been able to incorporate such a level of selflessness into his basketball ego was a rare phenomenon. It has become a point of pride for Larry to eschew his own statistical gain on behalf of other players. If Larry needed one more point at the end of a game to break a record and he saw a teammate in a better position to score, he would give the ball up rather than try for the record. Larry believed most statistics or records had little to do with how well he really played. "If I wanted to break records, I wouldn't be the all-around player that I am. How many championships you've won...how many games you've won...those are the important things. Individual records don't really excite me.... What [John] Papanek said about me in *Sports Illustrated*,...that I was the best all-around player in the game, that's what I like." Larry was at once both selfless and in the possession of the biggest ego in the game. It was that rare balance of such polar opposites that allowed Larry the will to dominate the game and at the same time the ability to involve his teammates to the highest degree.

The Celtics' 9-game winning streak increased to 11 as Larry played sixth man. Then Larry, in his third game off the bench, had one of the greatest games ever recorded by a sixth man, with 31 points and 21 rebounds at Washington. Boston continued winning: With the defeat of Detroit on March 26, by a score of 125–104, the Celtics established a new team record for most consecutive wins with 18. It was also the third-longest winning streak in NBA history. Larry rewrote sixth-man history once more with 35 points and 17 rebounds against the Bulls. The contest marked the eighteenth-straight game in which Larry had come off the bench. Finally, Fitch put Larry back into the starting lineup for the team's final three games.

The great winning streak had propelled the team to a 63–19 record. Only six teams in NBA history had recorded more victories in a season. And the team's victory total was all the more ironic, because both Fitch and Auerbach had predicted in January that the team was heading for a rude awakening because of its poor play in the early part of the season. Yet the Celtics had wrapped up the home-court advantage, a first-round bye, and the privilege of letting Milwaukee and Philadelphia beat up on each other in the conference semifinals again. Many people around the league were already starting to talk of a Celtic dynasty, since the Bird era had shepherded in 60-win seasons in each of Larry's three years.

Larry's season had been tremendous. His improvement between his second and third seasons was much more dramatic than between his first and second. In fact, if Larry had not been injured, he would have had an even better season. He had career highs in points, rebounds, steals, blocked shots, and assists per game. His most dramatic improvement was in field-goal percentage, where he went from 47.8 percent to 50.3 percent.

Moses Malone won the sportswriters' vote for league MVP. But Larry was named first-team all-pro for the third-straight time, honored as the All-Star game MVP, and named to the second team of the All-Defensive squad by the league's coaches.

In the first round of the playoffs, the Celtics eliminated the Washington Bullets in five games, but four of the five games were close. In the other semifinal, Philadelphia came up with a 4–2 series win that was no easier than the Celtics' victory.

Once again the most intense and evenly matched rivalry in basketball was about to be staged. In game 1, the Celtics won in an amazingly lopsided rout, 121–81. Unfortunately, the size of the victory probably did more psychological harm to the Celtics than it did to the Sixers. Boston had a difficult time regaining its intensity in the second game and lost their home-court advantage, 121–113. Back in Philadelphia, the Celtics regained their intensity and looked to have a good chance to regain the home-court advantage when Archibald went down with a separated shoulder in the third quarter. The Celtics seemed to be in a fog without their playmaker, and lost, 99–97. Game 4 was even worse as the team appeared dazed by Archibald's absence, losing 119–94.

Parish finally figured out Philadelphia's defense and played well in the fifth game, after playing terribly in games 2 and 4. At the same time, Boston adjusted its defense to double on the Sixer guard, instead of Erving, when Philadelphia went into their two-man game. As a result, the Celtics won big, 114–85. The Celtic fans taunted the Sixers by chanting, "See you Sunday," implying that Philadelphia would do the implausible: lose at home on Friday to set up a seventh-game showdown at the Garden on Sunday. The certain upshot would be a second straight collapse after a 3–1 lead. But when Philadelphia surged to a lead of 48–42 at the half, the Celtics had to figure out a way to be the first team in the series to win after trailing at halftime. However, the Sixers could manage only four field goals in the last 18 minutes of the game. It was the 1981 collapse all over again as the Celtics forced a seventh game with their 88–75 victory.

The fans at the Garden had been right; they would be seeing the Sixers on Sunday after all. Yet in one of those strange turns of fate, it was the Sixers who came to the Garden with a loose and aggressive attitude. And the Celtics, who expected to find the Sixers as tentative as usual, found themselves on the defensive. This was in spite of the wild scene in the stands involving five fans dressed in hooded sheets printed with "The Ghosts of Celtics Past" on the front, and the names and numbers of Russell, Havlicek, Sam Jones, Tom Sanders, and Don Nelson on their respective backs. When Erving spied the hooded fans, he said, "That's when I got scared. I thought it was the Klan." (Given Boston's prevailing racial situation, it's not unreasonable to assume that the same thought crossed the minds of the fans who wore the garb.)

But at that point Cunningham did a smart thing; he took the team off the floor with three minutes remaining in the warm-up in order to have them gather themselves within the refuge of the locker room. Philadelphia came out loose, and dominated the first half. With Philadelphia leading 64–54 in the third quarter, everyone sensed that Boston was about to make its big move. Larry scored 6 of the next 8 points and assisted on the other score to cut the lead to 64–62. But Ainge made horrendous passes on consecutive trips down the court, and Philadelphia scored twice to break Boston's momentum and give the Sixers a 70–62 lead. Realizing that the Celtics hadn't been able to make a run in the third quarter, the Sixers came out for the final period with renewed confidence. When "the Boston Strangler," Andrew Toney, got hot in the fourth quarter, there was little the Celtics could do. The Sixers won, going away, 120–106. The Boston fans, in a sportsmanlike move of concession, serenaded the Sixers with chants of "Beat L. A." in the waning minutes.

Regardless of the fans' sportsmanship, the Celtics were shocked by the loss. "We thought we could beat them; we should have beaten them. But couldas, wouldas, and shouldas don't count. We had our chance. We had a terrible letdown," said Kevin McHale. However, the final result shouldn't have been so surprising. The two teams' talent levels and records the past two years had been almost identical. If nothing else, the law of averages simply dictated that the Sixers weren't going to collapse and lose 3-straight games both years. And the collapse was even more unlikely with Boston's loss of a key player like Archibald. In fact, the Celtics were lucky to win games 5 and 6. And Larry could do relatively little. For such is the nature of a team sport, that even a superstar can't always will his team to win. But even if Larry had been the ultimate guarantor of the Celtics' fate, they probably still would have lost. Larry was never completely himself after his cheek injury. While he still led the Celtics in rebounding, assists, steals, and minutes during the playoffs, his shooting and scoring had dropped off. He was far from the dominant player he had been, and Parish led the team in scoring. Larry's numbers of 41 minutes, 17.8 points, 12.5 rebounds, 5.5 assists, and 1.9 steals per game were clearly subpar for his standard of play.

The Celtics' failure to repeat was difficult for Larry to accept. He had improved every season, but both his and the team's performances in the playoffs were a letdown. He left for French Lick immediately after, thankful to be returning to Indiana. The lack of privacy in Boston had begun to take its toll. "It's tougher this year than ever to get around without being recognized....Overall, I can deal with it, but I need my summers back home." And summers back home involved the pleasures that he'd always most enjoyed: drinking beer, mowing the lawn, fishing, playing golf, and hanging out with his friends. Though Larry didn't offer his friendship easily, the vast majority of his friends had been his lifelong friends. They asked nothing of him, and he asked nothing of them. And he guarded those friendships with the utmost zeal. "I'll say this much," said another old friend, "you won't find a finer person than Larry. He hasn't changed one little bit. He comes back [to French Lick] in the summer every year and doesn't want anyone to know he's around except his closest friends." Fame and fortune had hardly affected him. He eschewed ostentatious displays of wealth, remaining wedded to the simple pleasures he had always valued. "He wears nicer clothes now. That's about it," said college roommate Bob Heaton. "He's not the type of guy who's going to drive a $35,000 Mercedes." Of course, to say that Larry wore nicer clothes was merely to say that the warm-ups and jeans and tee-shirts he continued to prefer were a little nicer. Approximately 40 warm-up suits and some 600 baseball-style hats were his only sources of sartorial pride.

The often-sullen and resistant persona that big-city sportswriters had come to know was transformed when he returned to the comfort of home and friends. With the help of a few beers, Larry was even likely to be open and voluble in a way that few who knew him from the Celtics had ever seen. But Larry still didn't talk about his father's suicide; and his former marriage and his daughter were not welcome topics of conversation.

Indeed, many of his Celtic teammates knew nothing of these areas of his life. For, as *Boston Globe* writer Bob Ryan had pointed out, "It is quite possible that nobody knows the *real* Larry Bird. He may not even know that person himself." This was not as surprising a statement as might initially be assumed, for Larry's behavior was typical of that of children of alcoholics. Knowing the "real" Larry Bird was as difficult for his family as for everyone else. "Even those of us who know Larry Bird best, including his mother Georgia, often feel like saying, 'Will the real Larry Bird please stand up,'" says Larry's aunt. "Georgia has often said she could pretty much well figure out what her other children were thinking, but Larry could hide his feelings from her completely. She used to say she never knew or understood Larry." Larry had assumed so many defenses, such as his sarcasm, his distancing himself from others, and his suspiciousness, that the true Larry Bird was rarely glimpsed by others—or, for that matter, by Larry himself. "[Larry] thinks people are out to take advantage of him. He is aloof from everyone, including his family, and is suspicious of anyone he doesn't know," one family member says. Another adds, "I sometimes wonder if Larry loves anyone." Larry's behavior was not unusual for adult children of alcoholics. He obeyed the three dominant internal commands as outlined by Claudia Black (one of the pioneers in the understanding of those children): "Don't talk, don't trust, don't feel."

As the summer before his fourth professional season neared an end, the revived Larry began to yearn for the new season and its prospect of redemption. The failure to repeat had gnawed at him: "I definitely want to get [the title] back. I don't play in this league to come in second. If I did, I'd go out and get a job somewhere else. ...I don't step out there for pleasure or to entertain. I love basketball but I've always been taught to win. If I do well and the team doesn't, it isn't enough." Though many believed the Celtics possessed the talent to repeat, Auerbach had not been idle over the summer.

When the retired Dave Cowens professed a desire to return to the game, Auerbach shrewdly engineered a trade so that the front-line heavy Celtics could receive much needed assistance in the back-court.* The Milwaukee Bucks, much in need of frontcourt help, reluctantly gave up their point guard, Quinn Buckner, who was on the verge of attaining all-star status, for the rights to Cowens. As a consequence, there was a confidence and an excitement among the players as they headed into training camp. Buckner's acquisition re-inforced early predictions that made the Celtics a favorite to win the NBA crown.

The Celtics came out of training camp with very solid personnel from one through eleven on their roster. Only unproven rookie Darren Tillis, euphemistically referred to as "a project," looked to be insig-nificant. With that kind of depth the team was expected to wear down the opposition. Along with Larry, Maxwell, and Parish in the front-court, Ainge was penciled in to start with Archibald in the backcourt. Plus, Henderson and Buckner were scheduled to receive a lot of min-utes, in addition to McHale, the league's best sixth man, and Robey and Carr. Yet the Sixers themselves had made a sensational move over the summer by signing free-agent league MVP Moses Malone. At last, after losing to the Lakers for the championship in June, it seemed as though the Sixers themselves might finally be able to win the NBA crown. As a result, the rivalry between Boston and Phila-delphia was likely to be more intense than ever. They were sched-uled to meet in the season's fifth game, at Philadelphia.

Both teams won their first four games, and predictably their first battle was a war. Philadelphia won it by four. With the season a quar-ter over, the Celtics' record stood at 18–4, with Larry off to the great-est start of his career. He was averaging 40 minutes and 25.5 points per game, along with almost 12 rebounds and over 5.5 assists. Most significant was Larry's torrid shooting. His field-goal percentage was over 54 percent.

Yet both the Sixers and the defending champion Lakers were keeping pace; they each had 18–4 records too. In January, Auerbach made another ingenious player move, hoping to strengthen the team for the stretch run against the still-hot Sixers. For Darren Tillis, a first-round draft choice, and some cash, the Celtics received former all-pro Scott Wedman from the Cleveland Cavaliers. On paper the

---

*Though Cowens had retired two years earlier, the Celtics still retained his player rights and therefore enjoyed the luxury of being able to trade him.

trade looked great, but in reality the trade exacerbated an existing Celtic problem: There was no possible way to provide the kind of minutes each player deserved. "Scott is an excellent player, but most of us couldn't help but think, 'That's great that we got him. But where the heck can you play him,'" said a Celtics player.

A week after the Wedman trade, Larry suffered a severe ankle sprain against Cleveland, but continued to play on it without complaint. And on February 23, Larry had another virtuoso performance at the L. A. Forum, with 32 points, 17 rebounds, 9 assists, and 4 steals. The victory gave the Celtics a sweep of their season series against the defending-champion Lakers. Three days later, at Phoenix, the Celtics found themselves trailing 101–100 with 1 second remaining. They immediately called a time-out. Before each team huddled, Phoenix rookie David Thirdkill (later a Celtic) taunted Larry that the Suns would stop him on the game's last play. Larry remembers, "I told him what was going to happen, that I was going to hit [the winning shot]." On the inbounds play, Larry received the ball behind the three-point line with his back to the basket. In one motion, he turned and fired, without taking time to size up the rim. The ball homed in on the basket and the buzzer went off while it was still in midair. A split second later, the ball swished through the twine to give the Celtics an improbable 1-point victory. The Phoenix fans and team sat stunned as Larry sought out Thirdkill and then pointed at him and laughed. The shot was the first time in his career Larry had thrown in a shot at the buzzer to boost his team to the win. It would, however, not be the last.

On March 30, Larry set a new Celtic regular-season scoring record for a single game with 53 points against the Pacers in Boston. But three embarrassing losses to the Pacers, Bulls, and San Diego Clippers indicated problems and foreshadowed more difficulties to come. The team had been unable to keep pace with the torrid Sixers. Though the Celtics had won 37 of their first 47 games, they trailed by 5 games. "You began to wonder whether it was an impossibility to beat out Philly," said Henderson. "We'd win four or five straight and still be in the exact same position in the standings, no closer to our goal.... Once it became clear that we weren't going to catch them, I think subconsciously we suffered a letdown." Certainly something went wrong, because the Celtics managed to win only 19 of their last 35 ball games to finish with a 56–26 record. It was the first time the Celtics had failed to reach the 60-win level since Larry had turned pro.

There were a multitude of reasons for the Celtics' decline during the last two-fifths of the season. The level of motivation was certainly one. But there were other factors at work, namely problems surrounding Bill Fitch. Self-centered concerns had begun to replace the Celtics' usual team-oriented values. "Last year we didn't help out enough," said Larry the following season. "You can't have five individuals out there. You need people working together. In this league it's the only way you win." As the season wore on, more and more, the public line became "Wait until the playoffs."

K. C. Jones was then an assistant coach, or at least was supposed to be, except that Fitch, in his dictatorial way, wouldn't allow him to take on any of the duties of an assistant coach. Fitch had never been good at delegating authority. And his tendency to browbeat and discipline players worked when he first came to the Celtics. But, as the team grew older, the effectiveness of Fitch's style began to wear thin. Jones describes the mood of the team: "The time when we were champions, driven by pride and acceptance of roles, was gone.... We were woefully inconsistent.... Larry seemed genuinely hurt and puzzled. [Parish] withdrew, disgusted. [Maxwell] played inconsistently. ...Meanwhile, we faltered." The team opened the playoffs with a much-tougher-than-expected win against the Atlanta Hawks, and veteran Celtic watchers had plenty of reason to be worried about the upcoming semifinal matchup against the well-rested Milwaukee Bucks.

According to M. L. Carr, "The climax of the year came after game 1 of the infamous playoff sweep by the Bucks over the Celtics. I'll never forget it; the Bucks won that game, 116–95, but the score didn't report the event accurately. It was a 30-point defeat—at least it felt that way. When we walked into the locker room afterward I was thinking—'Gee, those cats really killed us tonight.' There was no fire! No anger, just a resigned acceptance of defeat. That wasn't the Boston Celtics." Three games later, a vast number of fans at the soldout Mecca were hoisting brooms signifying sweep, as the Bucks humiliated the Celtics in their worst playoff showing in history. There was no doubt that the Celtic breakdown was total. While many of the players—and fans—were apt to blame Fitch for much of the team's troubles, Larry was one of the few Celtics to have a good relationship with Fitch. Larry had grown up with enough verbal (not to mention physical) abuse in his own family. Any troubles in the Celtic family caused by the petulant but, at least, reliable and consistent Fitch, were mild by comparison. When the season was over, Larry was Fitch's only defender. "He's the best coach I've ever had. No one could have gotten us better prepared. What [the Bucks' sweep] amounted to is that we [the players] weren't ready."

Larry conveniently ignored the fact that it is also the coach's responsibility to get the players ready. He seemed to have a better sense of that in his response to Fitch's resignation immediately following the season. "I think Bill wondered if he could get the guys to play the way they did for him before." As coach, Fitch had been unable to counter Milwaukee's free-lance offense which utilized extensive clearouts and either one- or two-man isolations for both Marques Johnson and Sidney Moncrief. But had that been his only failing, there would not have been the hue and cry that followed the series. Fitch's dictatorial and demeaning methods were cited by almost everyone as the major reason for the team's downfall. Essentially, the team quit on Fitch in the playoffs. Fitch's treatment of the team, as depicted in the memoirs of both K. C. Jones and M. L. Carr, was indefensibly dehumanizing. Larry was probably attempting to put a good public face on what was an intolerable situation, especially since he had never been one to make excuses. So he was understandably loath to say anything that might be construed as shirking his responsibility for the Celtics' performance.

The magnitude of the Celtics' discontent wasn't confined to a few players. Virtually everyone on the team was unhappy. While Larry was the only player who didn't blame Fitch, Larry was not immune to the ennui that had set in after countless hours of excessive Fitchean video replays and browbeatings. But Larry wasn't about to turn on the hard-working coach who had helped him so much, no matter how difficult Fitch had become.

Yet Larry's general unhappiness and the uneven quality of his performance in the playoffs were partly the result of how much his game was dependent upon team harmony (he also suffered from the flu during the series). When the team began to pull in separate directions, Larry was less able to play well, and this, in turn, affected the team's performance. But it really wasn't until the playoffs that

Larry began to appreciate what a deleterious effect Fitch's regime had upon the other players. The severity of the 1982–83 coaching problem would be brought into sharper relief with the upswing in player morale the following season. The sea change to come would be almost exclusively at the behest of new coach K. C. Jones.

The date was May 2, 1983, and the scene was the Celtic locker room following their sweep at the hands of the Milwaukee Bucks. The atmosphere was morose. Some players, like Archibald, sulked. Archibald knew that the game was quite possibly his last as a Celtic. Others, like McHale, talked about money. McHale had been unable to resolve contract negotiations and was anxiously awaiting his impending free agency.* Larry sat by himself and said, "This just makes me want to work harder than ever. I'm going to punish myself all summer so this doesn't happen again next year." It was a common assumption in the press that Larry had always punished himself in the summer. But, as has been discussed, Larry had previously used his summers to unwind and rest up after a long and arduous season.

However, in 1983, Larry had a whole new set of motivations. First, he had never been on a team that had been embarrassed to such a great degree. "You're only successful personally if your team is successful. There are a lot of guys in this league who have great stats on losing teams. To me, that's not what the NBA is about." Larry also believed that he needed to get in better condition. "I had suffered more injuries than I ever had—a broken finger, sickness in the second game of the Milwaukee series, and I felt more run down than I ever had before." Larry also "wanted to improve [his] game and win a championship."

Maybe the biggest motivation of all was the reaction of people everywhere, whether in French Lick, Boston, or of all places, Israel.† "A day didn't go by without somebody asking me what the hell hap-

---

*In March, the NBA players and owners agreed to a salary cap for all teams, which limited the flexibility of the various teams in obtaining free agents.

†If there was one example that demonstrated Larry's growth over the past six years, it was his willingness to go to Israel, not to mention his enjoyment of the trip. His ostensible reason for being there was to do instructional clinics for Converse. But in Israel the NBA is the most popular spectator sport and Israeli television presents CBS's NBA games live. As a consequence, Larry was trailed everywhere by kids and adults.

pened to the Celtics.'' Larry's response was to dedicate his summer to preparing for the new season. ''This was more of a work [summer] for me. Some friends and me built a basketball court at my house. It got a lot of use once it was finished. I also did quite a bit of running, maybe three or four miles a day. And I spent a good deal of time just going over our season, trying to figure out what had to be done this season.''

''My house,'' where Larry built the basketball court, was actually the house that he more often described as belonging to Georgia. He had built the house on Joe's parents' property in West Baden, which he had bought for back taxes. Larry sometimes referred to the house as ''my house'' because, as relatives explain, it was intended eventually to become Larry's home. Nevertheless, Larry's intent for the time being was to have Georgia and his younger brothers, Jeff and Eddie, live there. Larry built an apartment off the family room for his use. Publicly, and even privately, Larry talked about the house as if it were Georgia's, but he treated it as his own. Within the typical Larry Bird mythology, the home was a symbol of Larry's devotion to his roots and to his mother. What was more ambiguous was Larry's relationship with Georgia and his attitude toward money. Both of those issues crystallized with regard to the house.

When Larry had signed his first pro contract he announced that he was ''thinking about the family and about giving my mother the kind of security I've always wanted for her.'' Yet, for a variety of reasons, that security didn't arrive quickly. And when it did, it was only at the insistent urging of financial advisor and friend Max Gibson. In Larry's defense, part of the initial problem was rooted in his desire to be prudent. He had heard horror stories about free-spending rookies who squandered all their contract money. On top of that particular apprehension, Larry was unable to fully appreciate the extent of his wealth. His early experience of poverty had distorted his perceptions. The family's economic straits had dictated that fifty or sixty dollars a week was good pay. When Larry later earned $100 a week working for the city, that was considered real wealth. The contract was worth almost two-hundred times what Larry had formerly thought real wealth was. Whether he was making fifty thousand or a million (his salary plus endorsements) was irrelevant. Both figures seemed not only vast, but totally unreal. One of Larry's relatives explains: "He didn't see the money [it went directly to his financial advisors, who had Larry turn over his bills to them], and didn't feel it. It wasn't in his pocket; he didn't believe it." The money might as well have been play money for all the assurance it provided Larry in the beginning. To make matters worse, as soon as Larry signed his contract, everybody in the family assumed that Larry would give them a helping hand. However, Larry construed these appeals for help as an expectation of not only immediate but continuing support—i.e., that some family members would quit their jobs and live off him, an idea which was antithetical to Larry's intense work ethic. According to Eddie, Larry "tries to push us, he gives the family things, but he wanted my brother [Jeff] and me to work this summer [1987] to learn to make a living, and not just lay around."

Jeff is more independent and refused the college-car *quid pro quo* that Eddie accepted. He likes to do everything at his own pace, which, according to one Bird family member, is "slow." In high school, Jeff was the one who told Coach Holland he'd rather play second string on the basketball team so there would be less pressure. Yet, last year, at the age of 23, Jeff entered Indiana State, thanks to Larry, no strings attached.

Larry also wanted to be cautious about giving money to relatives because he feared that if something were to happen to his pro career, then everyone relying on him would go under. This dread was not so unusual, given the valley's unfortunate history of dependence upon the fickle rich. Thus, Larry's financial assistance to family members mostly involved loans that were to be paid off through honest, hard work. Larry co-signed loans for Mark's liquor business. And Larry helped Mark obtain his Trans Am, but did not give it to him. Larry did bail Mike out of bankruptcy (although one relative adds that Mark had to convince Larry that it would look terrible if Larry Bird's brother had to declare bankruptcy). Similarly, Larry loaned Mike money when his twins had medical complications at birth. Mike subsequently came out to Boston to help Larry adjust to his new environment and to work in order to pay off the debt. (It's said that Mike is the one person in the family who has the ability to make Larry feel guilty about not helping the family enough.) And after a few years, Larry began to better understand his wealth and became slightly less wary about spending his money, but the subject had become very much an issue the year following his contract signing. Georgia had spoken publicly about her desire to have a new home. "Just once I'd like to have one without scratches in the wall or a warped door," she said. But Larry was hesitant. "I've been wanting to get a home for my mother, but I wanted to wait until I was sure I was financially stable. I know a lot of guys go off the first year they come into money and buy everything in sight. Then they find out they didn't have as much money as they thought they did." There was a house on the market for $55,000 that Georgia had fallen in love with. By the time Larry heard about the house, the price had increased to $80,000. His response was, "Mom, forget it. We ain't gonna pay more just because I'm a ball player."

Another reason Larry didn't buy the house was that he had begun to think about building on Joe's parents' property out on Abbeydale Road, on between ten and fifteen acres of land. He would be able to build a house far more cheaply than an existing house would cost. There was yet another consideration: Larry's concern about appearances in the valley. He didn't want to do something that might be construed as ostentatious. Some of his old friends had been intimidated about coming around because Larry had signed a lucrative contract. Larry worried that people might think the Bird family was putting on airs. Larry eventually realized that "that thinking was ridiculous. My Mom deserves that house, and so do my younger brothers. I grew up in a house where seven kids shared two bedrooms. Why should she have to wait longer?"

As far as Larry's concern for his mother's needs, according to a number of relatives, the public face masked a less palatable reality. "If it wasn't for Max [Gibson], his mother would still be living on Washington Street [in the home she had lived in since 1972] and still working despite her poor health," said a relative. Georgia had hip problems and blood clots in her legs, which were, no doubt, partially the result of the strenuous work she had done all her life. Moreover, the idea that it was Georgia's house was, to some extent, a fiction served up for the sake of the press. "Georgia doesn't feel that it is her house," says a relative. "She's just living in [Larry's] house and keeping it up and cooking for him when he's there in the summer. ...This is the first time Georgia has had anything, but she is totally dependent on Larry." And now Larry has added on to the house, in anticipation of his eventually living there when his career is over. In response, Georgia is pushing Larry to look for another home, one that would truly be hers alone.

Furthermore, relatives readily admit that were it not for Gibson, Larry would make his mother pay for the house's upkeep. His original plan had been to put a trailer on the property and rent it so that Georgia would have that income to pay for food and utilities. But Max insisted that Georgia send her utility, telephone, and grocery bills to him and not to worry. Nonetheless, family members report that on numerous occasions Larry berated his mother to the point of tears over grocery, electricity, and phone bills that he considered excessive. At the same time, the media mentions in glowing terms how Larry may be a millionaire, but he's still enough of a regular guy to be concerned with something as mundane as an electricity bill. No wonder Georgia, at her most frustrated, will hyperbolically protest that she wished she still lived on Washington Street. That isn't to say that Georgia isn't reasonably content with her present life or that she'd really rather live in her old home. But the house as a symbol of Larry's generosity and devotion to his mother was yet another of the myths perpetuated by a credulous press ever-willing to sanctify Larry, no matter how difficult he was, as the perfect all-American hero. Larry happily bought into the media's gullibility; it meant another layer of obfuscation to protect the imperfect reality of his privacy. "I'm basically an honest person....I don't lie to people, but that doesn't mean I tell 'em the whole story or everything that's on my mind....I read stories people write about me, and they're generally the same. One day I figured out why. It's because I give them the same old stuff." And each new layer of myth was one more small victory over the still-despised press. The "dumb hick" had outsmarted the "sophisticated" press yet again. But the mythology so heavily contributed to by Larry and his friends was also often inspired by a desire for a little entertainment, something that Larry and his friends could wink about. The wealthy outsiders could abandon the valley and then later look at it as a cultural backwater and oddity. But people in the valley could revel in their own form of cultural pride and chauvinism. After all, they knew something the rest of the world didn't; they knew the unvarnished Larry Bird. That isn't to say they weren't susceptible to the same tendency to idolize him.

Besides, the more perfect the image of Larry Bird, the better it reflected on the community that had nurtured him.

By August, Manguerian, who had tried to sell the club since the middle of May, had finally found a reputable group of buyers. Gulf and Western executive Donald Gaston and former Nets Chairman Alan Cohen would be the active partners. They, along with Paul Dupee, bought the club for $15 million. The other news in August was that Larry had been determined by a computer to be the best player in the NBA. The sponsor of this inaugural analysis was the Seagram's liquor company, which presented Larry with $10,000 and a case of whiskey. "All I got to say is thank God for computers because every time the press votes for MVP, I come in second," Larry said in accepting the award. Larry had just finished as runner-up to Moses Malone in the league MVP race for the second year in a row.

The Seagram's award was presented just before negotiations were to begin on Larry's new contract. His original five-year $3.25 million contract was set to expire at the end of the upcoming 1983–84 season. Larry had revised his intention of playing only five seasons and retiring. However, he refused to negotiate the contract during the season. He wanted to focus on playing. If he wasn't signed by the opening of training camp on September 29, he would not discuss the contract until after the season, when he would become a free agent.

It behooved the Celtics to sign Larry sooner rather than later. Larry's announced desire was "to be paid with the class of the league." And since Moses Malone had been paid approximately $2.25 million (counting incentives) the year before, reporters expected another titanic struggle between Auerbach and Woolf. But discussions between Woolf and Auerbach began without the acrimony that had characterized negotiations for the first contract. "[Reporters] wanted to know what my strategy would be; here's what I told them," said Auerbach. "'Normally, when you negotiate with an agent you look to a player's faults,...but with Larry there are no buts....I wish I was his agent. There's simply no case to be made against that kid.'" And true to his word, Auerbach didn't give Woolf a hard time, for once. "I never had to sell Red on the worth and value of Larry Bird," said Woolf. "I felt he should be the highest-paid player in the game.

Every Hall-of-Famer and former coach will tell you he's the best all-around player ever. Red didn't need much coaxing."

Of course Auerbach didn't forsake his reputation as a tenacious bargainer. Larry explains: "I looked at what the other top players were gettin', and I asked Red what he thought—and in an hour we had a contract. If I was demanding to be highest-paid, with Red, I'd still be in there arguing." If this sounds as though Larry handled much of the final negotiations himself, that is because he did. The shy youngster from the little town had come a long way. Larry signed a contract for what was initially reported to be $15.2 million over seven years, although that estimate was later lowered to $12.6 million. In either case, the contract gave him the highest yearly contract (without incentives) and third-highest total contract in the league.

Though Moses Malone was still making approximately $300,000 more per year, Auerbach had always maintained a principle of not negotiating incentives or perks into Celtic contracts. Without the incentives, Malone's contract was slightly less lucrative. Moses made $14.47 million for seven years, and Magic made $25 million as part of a twenty-four-year package.

The new contract provided even more motivation for Larry, yet he refused to set any personal goals. Any goal independent of winning the championship he considered irrelevant. Plus, Larry was realistic enough not to expect perfection every time he walked on the court. Consistency was the key. "You play your game and worry about nothing else....I don't want to play perfect, I just want to make sure I never play bad. I expect a lot from myself—but not anything close to perfection."

The most turbulent summer in Celtic history had begun with the resignation of Fitch and his replacement by Jones. Then Auerbach had prevented the New York Knicks from signing McHale to a free-agent offer sheet by tendering offer sheets to three Knick free agents. Since the Knicks had to match the offers or risk losing the three players to the Celtics, they had to go over the salary cap and didn't have enough money to sign McHale. Auerbach then signed McHale to a four-year contract for $4 million. But Archibald and Charles Bradley were, respectively, waived and cut. Robey was traded to Phoenix along with two second-round draft choices for Dennis Johnson, plus first- and third-round picks. Draft choices Greg Kite and Carlos Clark were added to the roster, giving the team at least two players who wouldn't complain about playing time. D. J., who had been all-defensive first team for five straight years, was obtained in part because of the need to stop players like Toney and Moncrief in the playoffs. Also, getting D. J. would allow Henderson to move to the other guard spot and Ainge to the bench.

The difference between the coaching styles of Fitch and Jones was drastic. Fitch had always been the consummate strategist, a real X and O man; yet he eventually alienated almost everyone he coached. Jones was the consummate player's coach; he was less interested in the details of the game than in harmony on the team. "I think everyone is more at ease," said Maxwell. "We have older players on this team. We know what to do without being chastised or scolded." Even Larry, who had at one point imposed a moratorium on discussing Fitch or the past season, said, "Coach Fitch was very demanding. Night in and night out, he wanted you to do something at times you felt was impossible." Fitch refused to delegate and ran the team as if he were the only one who could ever be right (with the exception of Larry). Jones allowed the players great freedom and had faith that they would generally make the right decisions. He was as democratic in his leadership as Fitch was totalitarian. If K. C.'s style was to prove helpful to the team, it could be critical toward winning the first game against the world champion Sixers: The outcome of the psychological warfare between the two teams could make the difference at the end of the season.

The rivalry between the Philadelphia 76ers and the Boston Celtics was already the most intense in professional sport. And the fact that the Sixers had won the 1983 world championship only made the rivalry more intense. The Celtics were scheduled to meet the Sixers in the Garden to open the exhibition season. Auerbach's address to the team before the game proved to be a harbinger of the game, if not the entire season. "Last year we let [Philadelphia] intimidate us with all that physical crap. I don't intend to wait until the regular season to find out what we're made of. I want you guys to make a stand tonight." It didn't take the Celtics long to do so; only 2:23 into the game, Maxwell was tackled by Malone under the basket after Malone had missed a shot. Maxwell then threw the ball at Malone. Within the next minute Maxwell and Mark Iavaroni almost came to blows. Twenty-eight seconds later Larry got into the act as he and Iavaroni began pushing each other, and then each grabbed the other's jersey.

Larry then smashed Iavaroni in the mouth. When Larry and Iavaroni began trading blows, both benches cleared. Then Larry and Malone had words and had to be restrained, and Larry went after Iavaroni again. Next Larry and Sixer Coach Billy Cunningham almost went at it. When the referees called double technicals, Auerbach charged out onto the court to join the fray. Cunningham, incredulous at Auerbach's coming out of the stands, ripped his own sportcoat almost in half. In the meantime Malone and Auerbach were exchanging words. "Hit me you big bleep," Auerbach taunted Malone, as he took off his glasses. "Go ahead. I'm not big, hit me, you bleepin' son of a bitch." Afterward, Auerbach commented, "What's the worst thing that coulda happened? If the son of a bitch had hit me, I'd own him. Unless, of course, he killed me." Auerbach was fined $2,500, and Larry was fined the most of all the players on both teams at $2,000, "because he participated in an altercation and renewed the fight after it had been broken up." Afterward, Sixer owner Harold Katz angrily implied that Larry's willingness to fight was a recent development. "How are you supposed to play Bird now? I think Bird's temperament has gotten to the point where if he doesn't like the way you are playing him, he'll belt you."

In a way the altercation at the Garden had been a first effort by the Celtics at overcoming the humiliation of the previous season. Then, too, Auerbach had believed that Cunningham was trying to intimidate the Celtics to get the all-important psychological edge. Said Auerbach: "The season hadn't started yet. I didn't want Billy and his team thinking they could come in and control my building."

Indeed, the team had effectively served notice to the Sixers and the rest of the league that they had recovered and were ready to do whatever was necessary to win the title. Larry had predicted as much before training camp; "Talentwise, I just don't think we lack what it takes to reach our goal. . . . If the attitude is right, there's no reason why we can't go all the way." By the end of the preseason, Larry had seen what he was looking for. "Everybody had their minds on only one thing, playing basketball. . . . There were a lot of reasons why I was optimistic. . . . Everything so far has been 'we.' You don't see guys staring at stat sheets after a game. The score is enough to tell them the whole story."

After all that, the Celtics lost their season opener to the Pistons in the Silverdome. Yet they went on to win their next 9 games, which proved to be the longest winning streak in the league all season. They matched that win streak twice. Then Boston lost four straight, including two at home. The team had yet to fully adjust to K. C.'s coaching style. But Larry was able to adjust even when the team could not. Larry's fourth triple-double in the first three weeks of the season came at the Garden against the Sixers, yet the Sixers were able to win for the second time in two games. Despite the losses against the Sixers, the Celtics improved their record to 24–8 and passed the Sixers to go into first place on New Year's Eve.

By the end of January, the Celtics had boosted their record to an impressive 35 wins against only 9 losses; they led the slumping Sixers by 6½ games. Marring what was becoming a truly impressive season were two blowout losses. One was at Houston, where Bill Fitch had resurrected himself, and the other was on national TV at Milwaukee. They quickly avenged the Houston defeat by winning 114–101 in Boston. Larry was playing the greatest basketball of his career and not coincidentally, the Celtics were playing the best of his career, too. "This is the best I've seen [the Celtics] play in six years," said New York Assistant Coach Rick Pitino. "Emotionally they have more going for them this year, and Bird has taken it upon himself to challenge everybody to get the most out of their abilities."

With the end of the season nearing, the Celtics clinched the best record in the league for the fourth time in Larry's five seasons. And they readied themselves for the playoffs by running off another 9-game winning streak.

Yet there were some major question marks as the Celtics prepared to enter their first-round miniseries against the Washington Bullets. Could this team win against the good teams like the Sixers or the Lakers? They had suffered a second humiliating national TV loss at home against the Sixers and ended up with a 2–4 record against their main adversary, not to mention losing both their games against the Lakers.

Despite the team's question marks, Larry had performed at the highest level of his career and was the leading candidate for the league's MVP trophy. He had career-high averages in scoring, rebounding, assists, and steals. And he was named to the NBA All-Defensive second team for the third-straight year.

*   *   *

The team with the best record in the league no longer received a first-round bye, and so the Celtics opened the playoffs with a 3–1 victory over the Washington Bullets. Meanwhile, in New Jersey, the Nets had shocked the defending-champion Sixers in their miniseries and insured, once again, that a repeat champion would not reign in the NBA. In Detroit, the Knicks won in overtime of the final game in a wild series that earned them the right to meet the Celtics. In that series, Bernard King, the league's leading scorer and Larry's main competition for the MVP, had averaged an astounding 42 points a game against the Pistons.

In game 1, the Celtics blew out the Knicks, who were still dragging from the aftereffects of their series against Detroit, which had concluded only 36 hours earlier. Larry came out firing in the second game and had 37 points along with 4 steals to lead the Celtics to another easy victory. It looked as though the Celtics would clinch the series easily. But the Knicks surprised the Celtics with two close wins at Madison Square Garden. Fortunately, for Boston, two of the next three games would be played in the Boston Garden. Game 5 was another Celtic home blowout as Boston won 121–99, with King having a subpar game. However, King came back to score 44 points back in New York to lead the Knicks to a 2-point win. The series had come down to a seventh game—to be played in Boston.

The series had also evolved into an informal precursor to the MVP vote (though the vote did not reflect postseason play). In Boston, Celtic fans chanted "MVP" every time Larry went to the foul line, and in New York, Knick fans did the same for King. In addition, the series had been physically brutal, with ten technicals, three ejections, and one full-scale brawl punctuating the competition. It was in that context that, on Mother's Day, Larry came out firing. Scoring the first basket of the game, he struck for 15 points in the first quarter, and the Celtics were on their way, 36–26. When the first half ended, Larry had 28 points, three more than King would score all game. The coup de grace was Larry's three-pointer, ending the third quarter, and giving Boston a 21-point lead. With the fans screaming "MVP" the entire game, Larry had played his finest playoff game ever. He had surpassed his regular season performance with a brilliant series in which he outplayed King in every facet of the game.

He averaged nearly 40 minutes per game with an average of 30.4 points, 10.6 rebounds, and 7.1 assists. He also shot an astounding 58.5 percent from the field and 90 percent from the line.

One of the most satisfying aspects of the win against the Knicks was that it enabled the Celtics to seek revenge against the Milwaukee Bucks, who had won the other conference semifinal against the New Jersey Nets. The memory of jubilant Milwaukee fans waving brooms while the Celtics went down to their fourth-straight defeat was etched into the collective Celtic consciousness. Although Milwaukee had plenty of rest time after dispatching the Nets in six games, Boston overwhelmed the Bucks just two days after beating the Knicks. Two nights later, they routed the Bucks again, then proceeded to beat Milwaukee at Milwaukee, 109–100. Milwaukee came back to win game 4, but Boston clinched the series in game 5, 115–108. Larry redeemed himself for his performance the year before by dominating again with a per-game average of 27.5 points, 10 rebounds, and 6 assists, in addition to shooting 50 percent from the field and 90 percent from the line.

After a two-year hiatus, the Celtics had made their way back to the finals. After the frustrations of the previous year, it was an impressive achievement. Most exciting of all, the Celtics were slated to meet the Lakers for the championship. Larry versus Magic; they had only met seven times since they had gone head to head in college. Now they could meet as much as seven times in two weeks, with a championship hanging in the balance. The matchup of Larry and Magic at times threatened to overshadow the series itself. The public was fascinated by the prospect of the two playing each other. Each had exerted so much influence upon the game that they transcended position. They were both "once in a lifetime" players. "Me and Larry's just different from everybody else," said Magic. When Larry and Magic entered the league, the NBA was in the second year of a four-year contract with CBS that paid $16 million per year. USA Network paid the league $400,000. In contrast, today CBS pays $44.75 million a year, and WTBS will pay $27 million for the 1989–90 season. This 450 percent increase in TV revenue, plus a 26 percent increase in league attendance since Larry's second season, and more than a 100 percent increase in the league's gross revenue are thought by many to be largely a result of Larry's and Magic's impact. Says Russ Granick, executive vice president for the league, "There's no question that Bird and Magic together, with the rivalry they brought us, was an important factor. It's hard to quantify it." As in college, the Bird-Magic rivalry garnered the highest TV ratings ever for an NBA game.

While acknowledging that they did similar things, Larry emphasized that he and Magic had accomplished their basketball tasks differently. Larry, as usual, bent over backward to praise Magic while belittling his own contributions: "With me it's usually scoring, but with him it's always his passing. He's got his hands on the ball more than I do, so he has more control of the situation. You really can't compare us. He's more flashy and can make more things happen than me, make them happen quicker. I think of him as one of the three top players in the game today, maybe the best. He's a perfect player." Similarly, Magic sought to compliment Larry: "[Larry's] definitely the best player at this time. But it's no personal battle— me against him. We never let it be personal, trying to outdo each other. Because that's going to be hard to do. He's the best, so you've got to bring your best. The boy is bad." Magic's contention that Larry was the better player was true—at least at that point in their careers: The Lakers still built their game around Kareem; the Celtics built theirs around Larry—who was having his best year as a pro. Jerry West, general manager of the Lakers, seemed to give the nod to Larry also: "Bird whets your appetite for the game. He's such a great passer and he doesn't make mistakes. Magic handles the ball more, and he makes more mistakes because he has it more....The one that best approaches the kind of game I would recommend a young player model himself after is Bird. He's a genius on the floor."

Despite all the comparisons, it was impossible to really compare the two players because they didn't play the same position, they didn't take each other on defense, and they didn't have the same responsibilities. "As much as people want to talk about who's the best, you'd get a better idea who plays the greater game [only] if they matched up against each other," said West. Larry, as might have been expected, played down all the public furor: "Comparisons don't mean nothing to me." But West, for one, saw through Larry's protective guise. "If somebody were to tell you that they weren't aware [of the comparison], they'd be lying. It's like the opening of a great play. Everybody's waiting to see it.''

After winning the Western Conference championship on a Friday night, the Lakers were forced to fly immediately to Boston and play the well-rested Celtics Sunday afternoon. Nonetheless, within six minutes, the Lakers led 20–6 by double teaming the Celtics' big people, thus forcing the guards to shoot from the perimeter again. Another problem was that K. C. had decided to put Gerald Henderson on Magic, since Magic was guarding Henderson. His reasoning was that by letting the Lakers dictate the matchups, the Celtics would have an easier time finding their defensive assignments, when making the transition from offense to defense. In that way he hoped to help slow down the Laker fast break. However, if anything, the move helped encourage the fast break by removing the one possible major irritant to the inception of the Laker break: D. J. Yet K. C. stubbornly refused to concede any error until midway through the third game, when the Celtics were on the verge of being down 3–0 in the series. Only a miraculous steal by Henderson of a lazy inbounds pass by James Worthy in the waning seconds of game 2 had allowed Boston to avoid a near-impossible deficit.

But the fact that the Celtics managed to steal game 2 merely seemed to indicate that the Lakers would win the series by 4–1 instead of 4–0. The Lakers were so thoroughly dominating that after their 137–104 victory in game 3 (despite Larry's 30 points), most pundits felt the series was a foregone conclusion. However, those experts underestimated the ability of Larry to rally his teammates; after the embarrassing game 3 loss, he went public with his complaints: "We played like sissies," Larry told the press. "I know the heart and soul of this team, and today the heart wasn't there, that's for sure. I can't believe a team like this would let LA come out and push us around like they did. Today I didn't feel we played hard. We got beat bad and it's very embarrassing.''

Larry took his own advice in the first half of game 4 and sent Michael Cooper flying into the stands with a forceful rear-end blockout even though Cooper was already out-of-bounds. McHale subsequently clotheslined Kurt Rambis on a breakaway when the Lakers were leading by six in the third quarter. Moments later, Larry and Kareem almost came to blows after Kareem elbowed Larry in the head. The tide was turning, though the Lakers had led throughout, and with 16 seconds remaining, Larry tied the game to force it into overtime. In the extra period, Larry hit a sixteen-foot turnaround jumper over Magic to clinch the game. The Celtics had tied the series at two games apiece.

In game 5, the Garden, a building both antiquated and without air conditioning, would prove to be the major factor. Throughout the game the temperature on the court was an incredible 97 degrees. The heat was so oppressive that the Lakers were forced to take oxygen and cool down with huge fans when they returned to the bench for time-outs and substitutions. If there was one man who was capable of willing himself to transcend the adverse conditions, it was Larry. In a magnificent performance, once again, Larry hit 15 of 20 shots on the way to totaling 34 points, along with 17 rebounds, as he played more minutes and for longer periods than any other player. In the final outcome, Larry's play inspired the Celtic game to a new level. "This is probably the best game we ever played," said D. J. And Pat Riley had to admit that "the man who made the difference was Bird. He was just awesome. He made everything work."

In game 6, back in the Forum, the Celtics had an opportunity to clinch the championship. Once again, Larry lifted his game to help motivate his teammates. However, this time Larry didn't get the ball enough to affect the outcome. As a result, despite 28 points, 17 rebounds, 8 assists, and 3 blocked shots, Larry was powerless to stop the Lakers from winning 119–108. The 1984 season had come down to a seventh game between the Lakers and the Celtics.

Most observers felt while the Lakers had played well enough the first four games to sweep the series, they had proved mentally fragile. If the Celtics could maintain enough pressure, it was likely that the Lakers would break down. And yet another mental aspect might come into play again also. For, in the history of Celtic-Laker playoff matchups, the Celtics had won all six, including two that were decided in the seventh game.

With the confidence of such a mental advantage, as well as the home-court advantage, the Celtics entered the game and proceeded to chalk up a whopping 52–33 rebound edge, including an even more amazing 20–9 advantage on the offensive boards. With Larry scoring 20 points and adding 12 rebounds, Boston built a lead of fourteen with 8 minutes remaining. LA could get no closer than three as Magic had a shot blocked by Parish and was stripped by D. J. in the waning minutes. It was over. The Celtics had beaten the Lakers in a championship series for the seventh time in seven meetings. It was their fifteenth world championship.

Larry was the unanimous choice as the MVP in the playoffs, and winner of the first series matchup between Magic and himself. Though Magic totaled a series record 95 assists, Larry led both teams in scoring, rebounds, and steals. He averaged 27.4 points, 14 rebounds, over 3.5 assists, and 2 steals in 43.5 minutes a game. Larry also won the MVP vote for the regular season (King was second, Magic third). By winning both the regular season and playoff MVP, Larry became only the fourth player in NBA history to achieve such a distinction (Willis Reed in 1970, Jabbar in 1971, and Moses in 1983 were the previous winners). Larry was also only the third noncenter in the last ten years (along with Erving and Robertson) to win the award. While Larry had coveted the award ever since his entrance into the league, he would just as soon have passed up the pomp and circumstance of the ceremony, and as discussed, had to be dissuaded from mowing his yard in West Baden to attend. Of course, he wasn't about to get dressed up, so he became the first MVP winner in NBA history to accept the trophy wearing an open-collared bowling shirt.

Through constant striving and hard work, Larry had reached, in K. C. Jones's words, "the pinnacle." But now that he was at the top, he wasn't about to let up. And Larry would continue to build on his past successes in an effort to take his game to an even higher level. Off the court, as always, his success would be more limited on the eve of a season that at all levels could be best termed a turning point in the amazing life of the young superstar.

15 / *Turning Point: The Boston Celtics, 1984–1986*

The 1984–1985 season proved to be a watershed year for Larry both in the development of his game and in his growth as a person. For the first time in his pro career, Larry thought of his primary role with the Celtics in terms of being a scorer. So, he spent the summer before the 1984–85 season working harder than usual and polishing his basketball skills, especially his shooting, on the new court at his home.

Auerbach believes that one of the most important keys to Larry's success is his level of self-motivation. "I honestly don't know when he'll stop improving," says Auerbach. "Here's the difference between Larry and a lot of other guys with talent. The average guy worked hard to get into the league. But once he got to the top, he figured he'd made it. The work stopped—or lessened a lot. Now Larry, he didn't reach the All-Star level and give himself a rest. He'll spend an hour after practice working on a little move that might or might not work." Even though Larry knows he'll never reach perfection, he's not content to accept his game as unimprovable. "The important thing is he's never satisfied."

Except for Henderson, who was traded to Seattle for a 1986 first-round draft pick (that draft pick proved to be Lenny Bias), the Celtics went into the 1984–85 season with their championship roster virtually intact. And Larry started the season where he left off: on fire. By November 9, Boston had won its first four games and was to face Philadelphia in the Garden. Larry had been magnificent in all four games.

Against Philadelphia, Larry simply destroyed his favorite matchup other than Magic: Erving—getting 42 points in contrast to Erving's 6. When Erving started hammering Larry without penalty, Larry retaliated and got called for it. That was the final straw; Larry started taunting Erving, and then shoved him. Erving shoved back, and soon it was an all-out brawl. The Celtics went on to win 130–119, and Larry and Erving were fined $7,500 each—the second largest individual fines ever handed out by the NBA. The incident was surprising not only because the two superstars did commercials together but because Erving was known as a player of great decorum.

Although Erving eventually apologized for the incident, he said, "I still feel Larry was the instigator....He felt he could do whatever he felt like doing in his arena." Larry refused to apologize. "The fight was just something that flared up in the heat of the battle. The Philly-Boston series brings those emotions to the surface. It didn't mean I hated Julius. The press made a bigger deal of it than it was. Growing up, I had fights with my brothers on the court all the time, ...but they were still my brothers—I loved 'em."

But Larry's response to any competitive situation was also very much a reflection of his overriding will to win. "The guy would kill to win at a game of jacks," said Fitch. And rival coaches had similar comments. "He will cut your heart out to win," said former Philadelphia Coach Matt Goukas. "He's a killer. He'll do anything to win," said George Karl, when he coached at Cleveland. "It's the competition," said Larry, trying to explain the fight. "The NBA is like that every night....Nothing personal, but that's the nature of the business." Even more so, it was the nature of the man.

Larry's competitive attitude was so fierce that he regarded opposing teams as "The Enemy." After an exhibition game between the Sixers and the Celtics in Knoxville later that season, members from both teams were drinking at a bar. Said Al Domenico, the veteran trainer for the Sixers, "Bird walked in and took one look around at us and turned his back—we were the enemy." As Mo McHone, Cleveland's one-time assistant coach, once commented: "You have to realize that Larry Bird isn't a nice guy."

Larry readily admits that "nice" is something foreign to his perspective. Once, when K. C. was commenting on how nice a particular player was, Larry answered, "Hey, I could be a nice guy too. I just don't have time. There are games to be won."

Larry was not only *not* a nice guy, he was often vicious: he would do anything to get a ball or to psyche out an opponent. For example, in the 1985 playoff game when Isiah Thomas and he were both going for the ball, Larry gouged Isiah's eye to get it. Many witnesses and Isiah were furious. But Larry merely shrugged. He was playing to win. If that meant occasionally hurting another player, that was too bad.

"I've represented over 2,000 athletes," says Bob Woolf. "The man has a toughness like no athlete I've ever known." Others took a less enlightened view of Larry's behavior, calling him a dirty player—a charge Bill Fitch has reacted to angrily. "That's just pure bull. Just watch the beating he takes night after night, . . . but he toughs it out and doesn't complain. Sure, he . . . doesn't back down from anyone. That's all part of the reason why he's one guy who can beat you." Although he equivocated more than Fitch, Erving himself was not ready to level the dirty-player charge. "I don't think Larry goes out of his way to play dirty," said Erving. "But I think he'll do anything he has to do to get the upper hand." This relentless will to win was in evidence early on in Larry's life and extends beyond just basketball. Jim Jones says: "He just hates to lose at anything. If we're fishing, he has to weigh everything. . . . If you beat him, he made you stay at it; he refused to believe he was going to lose."

Following the Philadelphia game, the Celtics lost in Washington, and then won 10 straight for a 15–1 record. Philadelphia, however, was also playing well and challenging for first place. But Larry was having the kind of season that even a few years before, he could have only dreamed about. On December 9, with the season only five-weeks old, Larry had his third 40-plus effort with 48 points in a 128–127 Celtic win at the Garden. As in the first four games of the season, Larry continued to dominate the end of close ball games. On January 27, against Portland in the Garden, Larry took a pass deep in the left corner with Boston trailing 127–126 and 1 second remaining. With two Portland defenders in his jersey, he launched a twenty-two-foot shot that arched over the corner of the backboard from behind as he fell out-of-bounds. K. C. recalls, "Everyone was quiet in the arena. You could see the ball spinning in the air." When the ball fell through the net giving Boston a 128–127 victory, the crowd went crazy. Two nights later, against the Pistons in the Garden, Larry got the ball in the left frontcourt about fifteen feet from the basket with the Celtics trailing 130–129 and only a few seconds left. He banked in a one-handed runner just before the buzzer sounded, for a 131–130 victory. At no time in recent memory has an NBA player brought his team from behind to victory at the buzzer in consecutive games. Moreover, there weren't many players willing to take the kind of shots that Larry took—let alone make them. Larry made the shots for two reasons: practice and concentration. Studies have shown that children of alcoholics often perform better under stress or in moments of crisis than those who grew up in homes without the influence of alcoholism. Children of alcoholics have had so much more practice dealing with stress and crisis. Similarly, the more pressure there is in a game, the better Larry performs. "I guess my concentration gets better when [the game] gets close." But that concentration goes hand in hand with Larry's extensive practice; it's not just a matter of being able to deal with crisis. "Some days I've shot as many as 2,000 times. That's why I like to take the last shot in a game even when we're down by a point." The security which derives from that practice helps produce a sense of total calm when Larry is in a position to win a ball game with a last shot. "I know I do things down the stretch in games without even thinking about it. I'll go back and see a game on film and say, 'Damn, that was a big shot I made; I can't believe I took it.' Then I think back to what I'm feeling at that point in the game and I remember that I felt calm, more calm than at any other time in the game. That's the way it is every time."

While Boston was relying on Larry to pull games out in the last second, K. C. was relying almost exclusively on six players. The team eventually picked up free-agent Ray Williams, hoping he would be better-suited for the guard rotation than Quinn Buckner. Then on February 17, Maxwell blew out his knee, and Boston fell to LA at the Forum. On February 18, against Utah, Kevin McHale moved into the starting lineup to stay. On March 3, Larry persistently passed to McHale in an effort to help him break Larry's Celtic single-game scoring record of 53. When McHale tired near the end, Larry chided him that he should've gone for 60, because McHale's record of 56 points was still vulnerable. It took Larry only nine days to break McHale's record. On March 12, against the Atlanta Hawks in New Orleans, he tossed in 60 points. What was remarkable about his performance was that Larry scored his points in two short intervals. "He burned 32 points—over half—in two little stretches over maybe 14 minutes," said D. J. "I mean, it was *frightening*. Everything he touched, he threw in like a guided missile, from no matter where. First, we were laughing, then we were in shock."

In March, the Celtics finally shook the Sixers with a 10-game streak that pushed their lead to 6 games. Their record stood at an astonishing 59–14 with nine games still to go. They had played the best regular-season basketball since the Bird era had begun. And much of the reason for the team's success was Larry's play, fueled by his confidence at an all-time high. However, during the previous seven games, Larry had been bothered by a nagging elbow injury, which was variously described as bursitis or a problem with floating bone chips. The elbow hurt every time Larry shot. Surgery was contemplated, and, at the same time, the Celtics began to rest their starters and, hence, lost 5 of their last 9 games.

While it had been both Larry's and the Celtics' finest season, Larry's chronic late-season elbow problem and the team's fade in the final nine games produced some worry. The fact that Larry averaged the most minutes per game of his career probably had something to do with his elbow injury. That and the cumulative impact of six seasons of diving to the floor and into the stands for basketballs. "I remember when I was a rookie," said Larry. "The veterans would say, 'If you don't slow down, you'll pay for it.' I didn't understand then, but I do now. These [injuries] crop up more often and hang around longer. But I can't change the way I play. I might not feel 100 percent, but when they toss the ball up I'm going to go hard. The day I start coasting, I'll know it's time to get out." Further hampering him were back problems and the sense that the Celtics had lost much of the momentum they had gained during the season.

The Celtics' opponents in the first round of the playoffs were the Cleveland Cavaliers, a team the Celtics were expected to beat easily. Yet they barely won the first two games in the Garden, 126–123 and 108–106. Larry was the difference in both games, playing brilliantly, despite experiencing considerable pain. In game 3, the pain was bad enough that the coaches decided to hold Larry out. Without Larry, Cleveland won 105–98. At the end of the game, the Cleveland Coliseum crowd chanted, "We want Bird," to which Larry replied in the paper the next day, "They want me? I'm gonna throw both barrels at 'em tomorrow night. They want me, they're gonna get me."

The Cleveland fans were outraged by these and other comments ridiculing their intelligence and came out to jeer their new favorite villain. It was just the kind of challenge Larry was hoping for. And he even upped the ante by walking up to Phil Hubbard, who would be playing defense against him, two hours before the game and saying, "I'm coming at you all night long." With the Cleveland fans taunting, "Larry," every time he touched the ball, Larry collected 34 points, 14 rebounds, and 7 assists, helping the Celtics to hold off the Cavs by only a basket.

The incident with Hubbard and the Cleveland fans was just another in a series of increasingly provocative public comments by Larry that dated back to Larry's publicly berating his teammates in the finals against LA the year before. K. C., for one, welcomed Larry's bluntness. "I don't mind when Larry says something about the team, because he's saying it for a reason. The sissies comment—he included himself in that. He said we had to wake up and he was right." Erving attributed Larry's increased vocalism and cockiness to "the Boston influence. He's up there with M. L. Carr and Cedric Maxwell—guys who talk a lot of junk. Personally, I don't think Larry needs that. He's too good for that." Larry's response to Erving seemed like an evasion: "I play hard all the time. I guess people interpret that different ways. If I'm still diving for loose balls with a 15-point lead, maybe they think I'm showing up the other team. I'm just playing the only way I know how. Talking? I don't talk anymore than anybody else. People said I ran up the court saying, '42 to 6' to Julius before we had our scuffle. That's not true. I have too much respect for Julius to do something like that."

But a year later, Larry gave another explanation for the change in his on-court behavior—one closer to Erving's: "I guess I try to carry myself in a certain way on the court. It's funny because nobody else in my family is like that. It's not that I don't have respect for my opponents. When you lose that, you've got nothing. But tradition is important here: You've got to act like a Celtic." The master of intimidation and cockiness was the combative patriarch of the Celtic family, Auerbach. He had been known to do almost anything to win, including setting off fire alarms at the opposing team's hotel to disrupt the team's sleep before a game. He was also known to have fiddled with the thermostat in the opposing team's locker room, producing severe heat and then sometimes severe cold, before and during a game. That intense desire to win had rubbed off, creating the winningest franchise in sports history. The Celtics knew they were "bad" and wouldn't mind telling everyone about it. "But though we were called cocky, dirty, and many other things, when the season was over, everyone called us champions," said M. L.

Two factors in Larry's personality account for his increasing public statements. First, Larry makes a point of telling the unvarnished and, often, too-blunt truth. Rick Robey says: "He doesn't try to pull anything over on anybody. If he's mad, he will tell you." Second, Larry was consumed with the game: "All I know is I only play one way—all out." And Larry had become more extroverted through the years. Jim Jones talks about how in college Larry silently went about achieving on the court and gradually became less and less silent. "If you needed a basket, he got it done. That was it. But he got more vocal every year. Now he's an extrovert."

Since Boston's upcoming series with the Detroit Pistons was likely to be more difficult than that with Cleveland, the status of Larry's elbow became a prime concern. Yet the injury took a back seat to the Celtics' 31-point victory in the first game. However, the elbow again received attention after Larry's 42 points inspired Boston to a 7-point win in the second game. Larry had gotten rid of his protective elbow pad at halftime. (He had always been suspicious of players who have to don all sorts of protective padding: In his view, a truly tough player took the court unadorned.) He then was decked by a Bill Laimbeer elbow, which cut his chin. The result was that in games 3 and 4, Larry appeared to be suffering, and the Pistons went on to two straight wins. Larry obviously felt a lot more comfortable in the Garden, where he answered in the next game with 43 points. After Isiah Thomas led a Piston run in the fourth quarter, Larry went up to him and asked, "Are you through?" Thomas answered back, "No." Larry had other ideas: "Well, you're through now, because it's my turn." Larry then took over, leading Boston to a 130–123 win. In game 6, at the Pontiac Silverdome, Larry again played poorly, but his teammates picked up the slack to help Boston win, going away.

In the conference finals, the Celtics resumed their rivalry with the Philadelphia 76ers with only 48 hours to prepare after their dispatch of Detroit. But the team's struggle against the Cavs and the Pistons had helped prepare the Celtics mentally. Following another opening-game blowout victory in Boston, the Celtics won the next two games by decisive margins and were up 3–0. They lost the fourth game in Philadelphia and prepared to go back to Boston hoping to clinch the series in the fifth game. Philadelphia fans hoped the series would come back to Philadelphia for a sixth game. Charles Barkley reported that "some guy in the stands told Bird, 'See you next Friday [for game 6 in Philly].' And Bird said, 'You have a better chance of seeing God.'" The Sixers might not have appreciated Larry's cockiness, but Larry couldn't have been more correct. The Sixers had the ball at midcourt, trailing 102–100, with less than 10 seconds left. As Andrew Toney brought the ball upcourt, Cunningham screamed to get his attention. As Toney paused to focus on Cunningham, Larry stole the ball with 4 seconds left to ensure that there would be no game 6.

Larry's scoring during the playoffs was a study in contrasts. Against Detroit he had averaged an outstanding 28.2 points, 10.25 rebounds, and 6.3 assists in only 40 minutes per game. Despite his high scoring average, Larry's shooting dropped precipitously to 45 percent. Against Philadelphia, Larry's shooting dropped even more, along with his scoring and rebounding. Still, in the first two games he'd averaged 26 points and 8.5 rebounds. It was in the last three games, when Larry showed up with a bandaged right index finger, that Larry's numbers really began to decline—he managed just 16 points and a mere 6.3 rebounds.

No one could remember Larry injuring the finger during the series, and rumors started to spread that there had been a mysterious altercation involving Larry between games 2 and 3. Supposedly, the altercation began in a Boston bar and spread to the parking lot, where Larry knocked someone out. Both Larry and the Celtics claimed the finger was hurt during the series, though they gave no specifics.

The Celtics entered the finals against the Los Angeles Lakers with a considerable handicap. Their star player was physically subpar, hampered by a bad elbow, a bad back, and now an injured index finger on his shooting hand. During the season, the Celtics had looked like a sure bet to break the repeat-championship jinx. Suddenly they looked quite vulnerable. Moreover, the Lakers were hungry to redeem themselves after falling apart the year before. But if game 1 of the 1985 series was any indication, they had a long way to go. In a bizarre and dominating performance, the Celtics trounced the Lakers by an almost-incomprehensible 148–114 margin.

But the laughter proved to be a psychological albatross, as the Celtics failed to rise to the occasion for game 2 and lost 109–102, relinquishing the home-court advantage. Larry, whose nose was bloodied by a Jabbar elbow, was the only Celtic to play well, but his shooting was still off. In game 3, it was the Lakers' turn to blow the Celtics out, as LA won 136–111. "What we should do is meet them out in the parking lot and have a fight and get it out of our system," said Larry in frustration after the game. It was an ironic suggestion considering that Larry was suspected of suffering from the aftereffects of just such an altercation.

Larry's frustration showed little sign of abating in game 4 when, with less than 10 minutes left, the Lakers owned a 92–85 lead. The Forum fans, eager to clinch the title at home in game 5, began chanting, "We're not going back [to Boston]." But over the next three minutes Larry scored 8 straight points to regain the lead. The Lakers fought back, and with 12 seconds remaining, the Celtics had the ball with the score tied at 105. Everyone knew the Celtics' final shot was going to be taken by Larry. So, when he was double-teamed, leaving D. J. wide open, Larry delivered the ball to him. D. J. hit the twenty-footer just ahead of the buzzer to give the Celtics the win and tie the series at two games apiece.

Game 5 was a lackluster losing performance for the Celtics. The Celtics could console themselves that they had the final two games at home and that the Lakers had never beaten them in the playoffs in seven tries. But the bigger jinx seemed to be that no NBA champion had repeated in 16 years. And once game 6 began, the only mystery concerned the Celtics' inability to shoot. Despite a number of open shots, Larry could only hit on 12 of 29, which paled in the face of the even-worse shooting of the Celtic guards. The Lakers won the game and the world championship.

Larry had slumped to just 45 percent from the field. Before his finger injury, he had averaged 30 points and 10 rebounds a game; after, his averages declined to 22 points and 8 rebounds. Although Larry fulfilled his burning desire to win another MVP, it was a bittersweet triumph: "Your goal is to win a championship, and if you don't win it, you're a failure." Later, Larry would add, "To tell the truth, I wish they'd take it back and give it to someone else. It didn't feel right. It should have gone to a championship player."

*   *   *

The mystery of Larry's injured right index finger ballooned into a major media event over the summer, especially in Boston. The story broke in the *Boston Herald* and was then reluctantly picked up by the *Boston Globe*. Apparently, on a Thursday evening, May 16, one of the off-days between the second and third games of the Boston-Philly series, Larry, Quinn Buckner, and a friend, Nick Harris, went to Larry's favorite bar, Chelsea's. There Larry and Mike Harlow, a bartender from another bar (Little Rascals), became embroiled in such a heated argument that Larry knocked Harlow out and in the process damaged his already permanently altered index finger. As the story began to emerge, there were at least two different versions. One, sympathetic to Larry, was essentially the story known among the *Boston Globe* writers and at least some witnesses in the bar. In this version, Larry's friend Harris was beaten severely by Harlow when he attempted to make advances to Harlow's girlfriend. Larry, ever the dutiful friend, did what "poor boys from hardscrabble towns in Indiana do as an article of faith": He knocked Harlow out in an alley adjacent to the bar. Harlow threatened to sue because of the jaw injury he suffered as a result of Larry's punch. An out-of-court settlement (of $21,000, according to one source, and between $15,000 and $20,000, according to another) was reached by the fall of 1985. (By the way, Harris was indeed admitted to Massachusetts General Hospital that evening.)

The *Boston Herald* later reported that Harris, a 39-year-old used-car dealer, had previous convictions for selling drugs, fixing odometers, and "fraudulent bookkeeping." Further, the *Boston Herald* reported that the Massachusetts State Police had been asked by the Celtics to run a background check on Harris—a story which the Celtics denied but the Massachusetts State Police confirmed. The paper also reported that the Celtics had earlier asked Larry to sever his friendship with Harris, but that he refused. Both Larry and the Celtics denied this. Larry did say later that he eventually broke off the friendship on his own initiative. At the time, most of Larry's relatives apparently knew nothing of the incident. Georgia initially thought the injury was sustained in the series.

The story that Larry went for Harlow after Harris tried to hit on Harlow's girlfriend is at some odds with an AP version of what happened and inside information from the *Boston Herald*. According to the AP story, a woman with Harlow claimed that Larry assaulted them. "It's just so contrary and uncharacteristic of Larry Bird," said

Bob Woolf in the story. "In a case like this, I think everyone certainly has to reserve any judgment until all the facts are out." But the facts never did get out. Woolf's other comment, "[This] year I've seen him do some things that made me wonder," along with "It's just so contrary and uncharacteristic of Larry Bird," should be noted. Sources at the *Boston Herald,* as well as some of Larry's friends, report that Bob Woolf himself was literally begging Larry's closest friends to help persuade Larry not to hang around with Harris. Sources at the *Boston Herald* report that the unidentified woman who filed charges along with Harlow was Harlow's girlfriend and that Larry had made advances toward her. However, this version of the story doesn't explain why Harris was beaten so badly.

Incidents such as the Chelsea fight are virtually endemic to the culture of southern Indiana, where young men are expected to spend the night out drinking, brawling, and chasing girls. Larry had hardly been immune to his cultural influences. Indeed, in Indiana, there are countless such stories, episodes, and incidents reported about Larry, often secondhand and most likely considerably embellished, that never became public. As Woolf had pointed out after the Chelsea incident, "If this happened in Indiana, it would have been nothing because this is what happens in Indiana." But when that kind of behavior occurred in Boston and began to impinge upon Larry's life in the public arena, then it was clear that changes would have to be made. Yet, Larry's stubbornness didn't allow the repercussions of the Chelsea incident to sink in right away. And his habits remained pretty much unchanged. However, during the 1985–86 season, Larry began to reassess his lifestyle and also began to curtail his drinking. In fact, by the spring of the 1985–86 season, Larry entered into a pact with the other Celtic starters, plus Jerry Sichting and Bill Walton, to stop drinking for the last month of the season and the duration of the playoffs. It was a vow made to demonstrate the team's determination to dethrone the Lakers. The pledge ultimately led to two-and-a-half months of abstinence. While Larry liked his beer, that attraction paled in comparison to his desire for another championship.

Larry consulted a number of specialists at the end of the regular season and immediately following the playoffs in June, and was advised to hold off surgery on his elbow. What was recommended instead was conservative treatment: no shooting until the middle of July. Not long after the first day that he was allowed to shoot again, Larry went down to the court in front of the homestead with his two younger brothers. According to his brother Jeff, "Larry, Eddie, and me were on the court, and Larry picked up this old, deflated basketball and threw it from one end of the court to the other. And it went right in the basket. Then he picked it up and did it again. When it went in the second time, Larry was jumping around like he won the world title. You know, I think that's the most amazing thing I ever saw Larry do." However, toward the end of the season and especially over the summer, there had been talk in Boston papers that Larry's career was threatened because of the elbow problem. Larry was furious. "That's just totally absurd." But then, late in the summer, Larry aggravated a back injury suffered at the end of the previous season. Again, the papers' response proved upsetting: "Everyone started saying that my career was over. You're the best player they've seen until you come down with an injury, and then 'Bird is getting too old.'"

No matter how much the stories about Larry's injuries angered him, they hardly had the impact that the reporting of the Chelsea's incident had, and the incident itself had affected his playoff performance (some said the Celtics' ability to repeat). In September, when Larry came back from Indiana, it was with a wide range of emotions: anger at the reporters who pursued the Chelsea's story; chagrin that his image had been tarnished; reticence, because he felt his privacy had been violated; plus, perhaps, embarrassment and regret for what, after all, had been an immature mistake. But in his anger at the press, Larry canceled his subscriptions to both Boston papers. He also imposed a semiboycott of the press for the entire upcoming regular season. In other words, Larry essentially talked to the press at away games only. Ironically, over the prior couple of seasons, Larry had painstakingly built up an excellent relationship with the press. By 1985, there were no complaints from media people who regularly covered the Celtics. Local writers reported that Larry was as giving and as helpful as possible.

Later in the 1985–86 season, Larry finally admitted that it was the Chelsea's incident that he was most sensitive about. By then, his anger at the press had dissipated somewhat. During the playoffs, Larry lifted all restrictions on his communications with the press. "I haven't been very good with the press this year....If I knew they wanted something that was really going to help their stories I wouldn't snub 'em so bad. How much more can I say? I've been here six years and talked to the same guys night after night. The press has treated me fair, except probably that one incident...mostly I communicated less at home because I was conserving my energy as much as possible....I really don't care what's written if it's the truth. In college I did, but now I don't.''

Larry's current sensitivity to the press had to do with his concern with his image. "The Legend Grows" and "The Legend Continues" were some titles of journalistic outpourings on Larry. *New York Post* basketball writer Peter Vecsey took to calling Larry "Larry Legend" after he wrote an article entitled "Larry the Legend." And *Sports Illustrated* ran a story in March 1986 with the title, "The Living Legend," gracing the front cover.

Larry had learned to feed into this idolatrous and mythologizing press. Says a relative, "Larry tends to believe what the newspapers say about his being the greatest player of all time." But Larry was also mindful of the pitfalls of being placed in such a position. "First they put you on a limb, way up there, now they're trying to knock you down. I've been in this league seven years and I've exceeded everything anybody ever felt I'd do, because I can't jump and I'm not a quick runner, but I made up for it. I play five hours a day in the summer, work on my game all the time."

Perhaps the most revealing aspect of this comment is that Larry is guilty of some of the same hyperbole of which he accuses the press. Except for the summer after the Celtics were swept by Milwaukee, Larry never came close to always putting in "five hours a day." And friends report, with bemused smiles, that he didn't play five hours a day that summer either. But in consciously buying into the press's image of himself, Larry played down his natural talents and painted a picture of a man who only works and never plays. Of course, there has never been any doubt that Larry works as hard as anyone during the season. Larry *is* slower and less of a leaper than many other players, yet his physical skills are simply overwhelming. Hundreds of players with similar work habits haven't come anywhere near making the NBA, let alone making a claim for being the greatest player of all time.

Larry likes to depict himself as resistant to press attention. But the truth is that Larry loves the attention—but only on his terms.

"Larry's not camera-shy; he's one of the biggest hams I've ever met. He enjoys being in the limelight. But it's important that he have control about what's said....He's suspicious of most people and thinks most people are out to take advantage of him," says a relative. In college Larry didn't have that control. But in the pros, Larry was in control, and the press, which painted him as a hero, was happily compliant.

As training camp for the 1985–86 season got under way, the Celtics were, once again, a different team. M. L. Carr retired; Quinn Buckner was released. Auerbach came up with another player coup, acquiring 6'1" Jerry Sichting—like Larry, a small-town Hoosier pure shooter—as a free agent. A starter with the Pacers, Sichting hailed from Martinsville, home of John Wooden.

However, Auerbach's key personnel moves of the summer were a trade of Cedric Maxwell, and a 1986 first-round draft pick and some cash in exchange for Bill Walton. Maxwell had been a valued member of two championship teams. But he had always felt resentment because he wanted to be the man the team built the offense around. And he finally had asked to be traded.

Walton had stated that he was willing to play only for the Lakers or for the Celtics. But he had been turned down by the Lakers not long before because a physical examination revealed stress fractures in both of his feet. But Celtic doctors assured management that Walton had played with the fractures in the past and would be able to continue to do so. Walton once had the makings of the greatest center of his time. And over parts of three seasons, especially when he led the Portland Trailblazers to the 1977 NBA championship, he seemed to be on his way to fulfilling that promise. Yet, 174 games over three seasons does not a career make; so people had always looked at Bill Walton in terms of what could have been. He was, pure and simple, the victim of fragile feet. What was more remarkable was that he was still playing at all. He had officially retired five years before, and had had reconstructive surgery on his left foot in the hopes of being able to walk normally again. The surgery was so successful that he revived his career after a two-year absence. With the Celtics, he was projected to play not over 20 minutes per game.

While the rest of the team was shaping up, Larry was not. His physical condition was way below par. His back was in such horrible shape that he could barely bend from the waist, never mind touch his toes. In fact, there was serious concern that Larry would never play effectively again. Regardless, in the opener, Larry proved that at 60 percent efficiency, he was still pretty good. But Walton played abominably, and the Celtics blew a huge lead and fell to the lowly New Jersey Nets. Larry continued to struggle, but Walton improved and McHale was playing brilliantly.

When Larry managed to score 47 points against the Pistons, bad back and all, it was clear that the Celtics were still the premier team in the east. Although that ranking was on precarious ground after their televised Christmas Day disaster when they managed to blow a 58–32 third-quarter lead to the Knicks. In an ugly and embarrassing display, the Celtics shot only 34 percent in letting the lightly regarded Knicks win in two overtimes. It was their fourth-straight road loss. The biggest problem was that Larry was shooting only 44 percent, and the season was already one-third over. However, the Knick game proved to be a turning point. After that humiliation the team won 17 of their next 18 games. Besides the will to make amends and improve their play, the Celtics began to play great basketball because they had the old Larry Bird back. An orthopedic physical therapist, Dan Dyrek, had begun treating Larry, and by the end of December he was better. This enabled him to begin a regimen to get in shape. Conditioning was critical in order for Larry to play at his usual intensity for the 38 or 40 minutes he generally averaged.

As Bill Walton began to feel comfortable with the Celtic system, he became a source of pleasure rather than frustration for the Garden throng. On January 22, the Celtics got sweet revenge in their first regular-season meeting against the Lakers, as Larry compiled 21 points, 12 rebounds, and 7 assists. The crucial difference, though, was Walton. He had 7 blocked shots and earned four standing ovations in sixteen minutes to help Boston win easily, 110–95.

For the first time, the All-Star game was to feature a three-point shooting competition. Naturally, Larry was one of the favorites. But the rules were so elaborate that there was no sense that the best three-point shooter would necessarily win. Each contestant had 60 seconds to shoot 25 times from the three-point range. There were five racks of five balls each positioned at the far corners of the baseline, at the top of the three-point circle and in between on both sides. The fifth ball on each rack was worth 2 points, allowing for 30 possible points. The competition among the eight competitors would be divided into three rounds, with the top-four scorers emerging out of the first round, and the top two emerging out of the second round for the final round.

In a practice in which he attempted to simulate the conditions, Larry had not done particularly well. That and Craig Hodges' 25 points in the first round were enough to give Larry pause. Moreover, Ainge and Scott Wedman tried to psyche Larry out. "They said I didn't have a chance to win," said Larry. But as McHale explained, "When I found out Birdie could make ten grand by shooting basketballs in one afternoon, I knew it was all over." Indeed, Larry seldom, if ever, lost a bet concerning his own talents. One of the first things Larry did was to psyche out the competition. He began in the locker room. Larry found a seat, put his bag down, looked around the room, and said, "We know whose name is on the first-place check. Which one of you gets second?" The other players sat in disbelief and apparently proceeded to get nervous. "Leon Wood might be the best three-point shooter in the league, but I kept telling him what a slump he's been in....I went up to Craig [Hodges] and told him I thought he had a good chance for second."

Continuing his "psyche-out," Larry didn't deign to take off his warm-ups during the competition, and then just eased into the second round on the basis of a shootoff which broke a tie with Dale Ellis. Larry scored 15 points; Hodges scored 25. In the second round, Larry got better, while everyone else got tired. Larry scored 18, and Hodges scored 19. He and Hodges were paired in the finals. A coin toss that Larry won allowed him to select Hodges to shoot first. Just before Hodges went out, Larry reminded him, "Now I know who's going to come in second....That money's got my name on it." Hodges had tired; the competition had taken a toll on his legs, his concentration, and his stamina. Like the rest of the contestants, who averaged 6'3½", he had relied on his legs to provide much of the strength he needed to shoot threes as jump shots. Larry was so much bigger and stronger that he had the luxury of shooting without his feet having to leave the ground. As the other players' legs went, so did their shots. So, it was no great surprise when the exhausted Hodges finished his round with just 11 points. Larry went out and missed his first shot, then hit the next eleven in a row. Larry ended the competition with a two-pointer as he deliberately banked the last red, white, and blue ball in for 22 points on 18 of 25 shots. With his arms raised, Larry left the court jubilantly shouting, "I'm the three-point king! I'm the three-point king!" He was especially happy because it had been a new challenge. When he arrived in the press room a few minutes later, he was hardly done luxuriating in his victory. "Anybody can dunk, but not everybody can shoot three-pointers." And once the weekend was over, with 5'7" Spud Webb winning the dunk competition and 6'1" Isiah Thomas winning the All-Star game MVP, Larry noted, "This was the week of the brilliant and the short people. I was brilliant. The rest of the people were short."

Following the All-Star break, the Celtics traditionally went west-ward immediately. And traditionally, the west-coast swing was something that Larry thrived on. Not only was the defense less intense, but the tempo was a little quicker; the game less physical; and credit for assists was more liberal. Against the Portland Trailblazers, Larry hit a runner around the foul line in traffic with 6 seconds left to tie the game. In the overtime, at the buzzer, Larry fired in a fourteen-footer with Jerome Kersey in his face and several Trailblazers sur-rounding him. It was a near-perfect way to finish a masterpiece of a game. Besides Larry's two game-saving shots, he managed 47 points, 14 rebounds, and 11 assists. Even more impressive was Larry's use of his left hand. He hit on 10 of 11 left-handed shots. Among the more impressive makes were a left-handed dunk, and his last three lefties of the game: a ten-foot jumper off the glass, a ten-foot hook, and an eight-foot double-pump one-hander while being fouled. Larry's ambidexterity had always been an important component of his game, but in the past year he had been using his left hand more and more. Larry eats and writes lefty and signs autographs with either hand. Predominantly a right-handed player, he was still named the 1987 Na-tional Association of Lefthanders' Male Athlete of the Year.

By February 20, the Celtics had won 21 of their last 25 and were 42–11 for the season. They had beaten the Lakers at the Forum with-out McHale and surprisingly won 16 of the 19 games while he was out with injuries. But it was also the time of year when Larry's value extended to the practice floor. On March 6, the day before a game against the Knicks, K. C. dared anyone on the team to take a half-court shot. If the shot was good, there would be no practice. Every-one looked at Larry; so he calmly walked to the ten-second line and swished a set shot. Practice was over before it had begun. "The legend continues," said the magazine *Celtic Pride*.

The Celtics' success paralleled Larry's brilliance. Over the last 29 games of the season, the Celtics were nothing short of phenomenal. And when the smoke cleared, the Celtics had compiled the greatest record in the team's history. They had won 67 games and lost only 15. Even more amazing was the fact that the record was achieved in the face of injuries to the team's two best players. In fact, so domineering were the Celtics that Martin Manley, using his statistical analysis, rated the team as the fourth most dominant team in NBA history and the most dominant team in the last fourteen years.

At the same time, Larry cemented his grip on a third straight MVP. In one nine-game stretch, Larry hit on an almost incomprehensible 25 out of 34 three-pointers for 73.5 percent. Over the final 50 games, he averaged 27 points, 10 rebounds, and 7 assists and shot over 52 percent. Thus, despite his poor health during the first 32 games, Larry was still only the second player in the history of the NBA to finish in the top ten in five categories.

The Celtics blew out the Bulls twice to win their first-round playoff series, 3–0. Meanwhile, the Atlanta Hawks, after barely beating the Pistons in a rugged seven-game battle, were slated to face the Celtics next. The Hawks were a young, confident, upstart team. The Celtics shook their confidence by dominating the first two games in the Garden. It was on to Atlanta for game 3, where the Hawks were much tougher. But after trailing all the way in a close game, the Celtics methodically turned the intensity level up another notch and overtook Atlanta about midway through the fourth quarter. They led the rest of the way to take an all-but-insurmountable 3–0 lead into the fourth game. There they played a little loosely, and stumbled, sending the players back to Boston in an angry mood; for they had wanted to get the series out of the way.

In game 5 the Celtics led 78–61 with 5:17 left. Then for the rest of the quarter, Boston outscored Atlanta, 24–0, to end with a 102–61 lead. "It was just the finest exhibition of basketball I've ever seen," said Atlanta's Doc Rivers. "They would have beat the Lakers by 40, too. They would have beaten anybody by 40 points. It was awesome."

The Celtics were to play the Milwaukee Bucks once again for the conference championship. The Bucks had beaten the Sixers at the buzzer of the seventh game of their playoff series. Despite their fatigue and the fact that Boston had beaten them 5 out of 5 during the season, Milwaukee had hopes. Those hopes were not to be realized, as Boston won the first game by 32 points. Larry hinted that the Celtics were aiming at a sweep when after the game he mentioned the 1983 debacle against the Bucks. "There was no way we should have allowed something like that to happen. No way." And taking Larry's cue, the team came out and decisively beat the Bucks again in game 2. "I usually feel good when Larry says we're going to win," said McHale, "because we usually do." The Celtics won the third game and, in the fourth, Larry backed up his boast of sweep by outscoring the entire Buck team in the fourth quarter 17–16 to break open a close game. "The Celtics don't come to split. They come to sweep," Larry said afterward.

The champion Los Angeles Lakers' hopes of repeating, along with the Celtics' hopes of revenge, were dashed when the upstart Houston Rockets handily whipped the Lakers 4–1 to win the West. And it remained to be seen if the Celtics' intensity was going to be affected by either that outcome or by the delay in starting the series. The first game of the finals was pushed back to a Monday because CBS didn't want to go head-to-head with the Indianapolis 500. Larry wasn't pleased: "Heck, I'm bigger than the Indianapolis 500—even in Indiana." But the Celtics didn't seem to be affected much in game 1, which they won easily. They also won game 2 in a 22-point blowout.

The disappointed Rockets went back to Houston aiming to show Boston that they were just as dominant on their court as Boston was in the Garden. In game 3 with just 3:41 remaining, the Boston juggernaut had a 102–94 lead. But this time everything went wrong, and inexplicably Boston lost. "We haven't given one away like this since Christmas," said Parish. "We were too slow in developing our plays," said Larry. The unavoidable conclusion was that the Celtics didn't seem so invincible anymore. And game 4 certainly gave no indication of any Celtics dominance. With just 3 minutes left, the score was tied at 101.

However, Bill Walton hauled down a rebound and outletted to Larry on the right wing. At 2:25, Larry pulled up abruptly and launched a three-pointer. At the time it seemed an odd moment for that shot. However, Rocket Coach Bill Fitch understood but could

only watch helplessly from the sidelines: "I could see it happening.
...I hollered to somebody on the weak side to get over there." It
proved to be the winning shot, though Walton added an insurance
bucket to give the team a 106–103 victory.

Game 5 was an opportunity for the Celtics to clinch the coveted
championship. But no matter what they did, the game had a surreal
edge to it. With Houston leading by one at the 9:40 mark of the second period, Ralph Sampson threw an elbow at Jerry Sichting. But
Sichting, like Bird, was from southern Indiana. And, like his more
well-known teammate, he was not one to ignore a challenge. "I'll
get you for that," said the 6'1" Sichting to the 7'4" Sampson. This
precipitated Sampson's punches and then a full-fledged melee. Said
Larry, "I can't believe [Sampson] picked a fight with Sichting. Heck,
my girlfriend could beat him up." In reality, Larry and the rest of
the Celtics were furious after having inexplicably fallen apart following Sampson's ejection. Larry promised the next game would be different. "I think Ralph will have a hard time in Boston. He better
wear his hard hat."

The following day, K. C. merely showed the team the film of game
5. With no outlet, the Celtics' frustration was pent up until Saturday,
when there was a practice scheduled. But K. C. called it off in the
middle. "The intensity level was just incredible....I had to call it off
before they killed each other....I was just going to go five baskets
and a half-court scrimmage, but these guys went at each other like
Muhammad Ali and the gorilla. I have never seen anything like that."
When game time finally came around on Sunday, "The usual cutup
stuff in the locker room wasn't there," said Sichting. "Kevin and
Larry are usually the cutups, but they were mum." "Nobody had to
say anything to us before the game," said Larry. "We knew what
we had to do." Not surprisingly, Larry's performance epitomized
the locker room atmosphere. "I got more psyched up in this series
than in any I've played." Of course, after all that, it was inevitable
that Larry and the team would open the game with a vengeance.
"Then they just went out and were as aggressive as any team I've
ever seen," said K. C. "The only team that's played as aggressive
as we did in the first quarter is the Chicago Bears." At halftime the
lead grew to 17, at 55–38, and the Celtics never let up. At the third
quarter the score was 82–61. Psychologically, the game was over. The
Celtics had won another championship. The final score read 114–97.

Larry's stat line said enough: 29 points, 11 rebounds, 12 assists, and 3 steals (all in the first half).

Yet the statistics only told part of the story. Larry's psychological importance had been so much greater. Larry had set the tone for the Celtics, emotionally, defensively, and offensively. Said K. C., "Houston didn't know what hit them." To be sure, at least one of the Rockets was a true believer. "He's the best," said Houston's Jim Peterson. "I never saw anyone demoralize a team [single-handedly] the way Larry did. That's why he's the MVP of the NBA. I saw him take on five guys by himself. At times, he doesn't need teammates." "That guy makes them all better, never mind on the floor, but in the locker room," said then-Knicks Coach Hubie Brown. "There is nobody like him in the league. He's the last of the cops.... Larry Bird is a legitimate, bona fide cop. He don't give a bleep about nobody. He's in their face all the time at practice. You see him in the games, he goes right in their face. That's why I say [the Celtics will] never go down until the guy starts to fall apart physically."

If there was one key to the season, besides Larry's remarkable play, it was the addition of Bill Walton. "If he stays healthy we have a great shot at winning more championships," said Larry. Walton, for his part, credited Larry. "Larry was exhausted out there, but he was in constant motion, moving, moving, moving.... One of my main reasons for coming here was the opportunity to play with Larry Bird." The championship was all the more gratifying for Larry, because he had overcome such injury problems in the last season and a half. Larry had averaged 24 points and almost 10 rebounds and 10 assists per game in the series and was thus rewarded with his second play-off MVP.

Three other postseason awards put Larry's athletic achievement in perspective: In January Larry was named the 1986 Associated Press Athlete of the Year by an overwhelming margin. He was the first basketball player ever to win the award in its 65-year history. Larry was also named the Sporting News Man of the Year—again, the first basketball player so honored. Finally, Larry became the first non-center in the history of professional basketball to be named MVP three-straight years. Only centers Bill Russell and Wilt Chamberlin had previously accomplished such a feat.

*   *   *

After a year of tremendous growth on and off the court, Larry began to feel that he had finally achieved real success and contentment. Dinah's decision to stay in Indiana much of one season along with the Chelsea's incident had spurred change in Larry's attitude off the court. And his third consecutive MVP complimented his more mature attitude. At 29, Larry had begun to achieve some perspective on his life and the world. "Oh, there's no question I feel happy in life," he said to one interviewer. "I feel successful in everything I've done. I tried to be the best basketball player in the world, and I've succeeded. I tried to make a good living for myself, and I did. A lot of people are miserable in their jobs; I make a good living doing what I do best, and love best, and I don't take for granted what I do like a lot of people do. It's a bunch of bull if somebody says they go around every day just happy-go-lucky. Everybody has their ups and downs. I have my downs. Not every day is a great day for me—I don't always feel like a million bucks. But I'll tell you what—I'm getting to the point where I say, 'Hell, I've succeeded in this life.'"

16 / The Legend: The Boston Celtics, 1986–1987

After the Celtics won their third NBA title of the decade, basketball experts believed that they were the one team that could repeat for the first time in eighteen years. Not only had they arguably been the most dominant team of the modern era, but Auerbach had parlayed the Gerald Henderson trade into the number-two pick in the talent-laden 1986 draft. On June 17, the Celtics made a brilliant selection, choosing the best athlete in the draft, Len Bias from Maryland. Bias elicited comparisons to Michael Jordan, only he was bigger and stronger. The Celtics knew first-hand how talented he was; they had invited him to their rookie free-agent camp the previous summer, where Bias had stunned everyone, including Auerbach, with his prodigious talent. The thought of Bias coming off the bench along with Walton, the winner of the NBA's Sixth Man Award, was enough to inspire discussion of another Celtic Dynasty. Many believed that with the Bias pick the Celtics had laid the groundwork for a championship reign lasting the rest of the decade. Larry was so elated by the pick that he announced he would attend the rookie camp in August just to play with Bias a month before the veterans reported.

But the fate of returning champions has not been kind in the modern NBA era. Two days after the draft the 22-year-old Bias died of "cardiorespiratory arrest brought on by cocaine intoxication," while celebrating his selection by the Celtics in his dorm room. "It's the cruelest thing I've ever heard," said Larry. His sentiments mirrored those of people across the country as details became known. Auerbach's words would have an eerie prescience in the coming weeks: "It's so hard to repeat unless you've made some trades down the road to get a good pick as we did last year—until this unforeseen and unfortunate happening. I think if we had Bias this year we would have been a favorite to repeat. We're going to miss him an awful lot. As it is now, so much will depend on injuries.''

Bias's death was likely to cause repercussions for the Celtic franchise through the rest of the decade, if not beyond. ''[The Celtics] have been dealt a pretty tragic hand,'' said Laker Coach Pat Riley. ''That was devastating to them...when you lose that type of opportunity, it's going to devastate the growth of your franchise. They've lost a whole year.'' Yet as tragic as Bias's death was, there was no telling what his impact upon the team would have been in view of his drug problem. ''You know what I think of guys using cocaine,'' said Larry. ''I believe that if you do it, you pay the consequences. A guy like him could have destroyed the team. I'm not glad he's gone, but I'd hate to see him come into this situation on cocaine.'' Larry's view about drugs was as hard-line as his view about the necessity of hard work. ''I'd be willing to go to any extent, even if it means undergoing drug testing, in order to help rid ourselves [the NBA] of this problem,'' said Larry. ''I don't understand how kids can do drugs when they see how it can bleep us [athletes] up, how it can bleep up their lives.''

Despite the Bias tragedy, it was a good summer for Larry. Said Larry, ''You can wake up ticked off in the morning, and all you have to do is think about winning the championship and your whole day is made.'' When he received the MVP trophy, Larry had announced that he was going to take a two-week break and then ''really work hard this summer.'' As usual, the press relayed this information, singing praises for Larry's inexhaustible and never-ending quest for improvement. At the end of the summer, when a close friend was asked if Larry had been working hard on his game, he laughed. ''Maybe he plays an hour here and there, but mostly, Larry ain't doing nothing but playing a lot of golf and sleeping a lot.'' Larry ran early in the morning most of the time. He then returned home to take a nap until eleven or so, when he ate lunch.

Larry did, however, manage to play on the same team as Magic in an All-Star game before a sellout crowd in Los Angeles on August 10. Delighting the crowd with some great passing, Magic and Larry worked well together. The Celtics, upset that Larry might risk injury in a nonsanctioned game, had forbidden him from playing. Larry called the Celtics' front office and two days later the Celtics announced they would let Larry play after all. (They refused to let him play in the same event the next summer.) The game, a benefit for the United Negro College Fund, also included a black-tie dinner which Larry declined to attend. "Some people aren't tuxedo kind of guys," explained Magic.

Fierce arguments about whether Magic or Larry was the better player had followed the two since their entrance into the league. But after winning three-straight MVP titles, even Johnson supporters had begun to admit that Larry had raised the level of his game a notch above all players, including Johnson. In fact, the number of voices arguing that Larry was the greatest player had multiplied in those three years, reaching a crescendo with the 1986 season. John Wooden, Don Nelson, Red Auerbach, Matt Goukas, Billy Cunningham, Bob Cousy, George Irvine, Dick Vitale, and Frank Layden were just some of the coaches who had gone on record to declare Larry the greatest player of all time. There was a definite reason for the abundance of coaches who appreciated Larry's skills. "I don't know if there's ever been a player with his knowledge of the game," said Doug Collins. "You can't appreciate him until you coach. When you're playing against him, the game goes too fast. Watching him on film, he is a clinic on the way to play basketball." Similarly, it took repeated tape viewings for George Karl to finally see the game like Larry. "He sees the game on the floor the way I do after four viewings. That's scary."

In addition to being named Man of the Year by the AP and *Sporting News,* both the *New York Post* and the *Boston Herald* named Larry 1986 Athlete of the Year. *Consensus, Basketball Digest, Basketball Weekly,* and Miller-Lite all named him MVP for the year. Larry began to receive awards outside of basketball, too. When he was notified that he had been selected by *Esquire* as one of the Young Leaders of America, his reply was, "Yeah, sure. Me and Cindy Lauper." Larry was getting a little tired of all the awards. He'd never liked receiving them to begin with. On top of that, there seemed to be a feature on him everywhere he went. Asked if there was anything that wasn't known about his life, he answered, "The public knows about as much about me as I do, there are no skeletons in my closet."

All in all, Larry seemed pretty much over the Chelsea episode. So, with the season ready to begin, Larry resumed the open posture with the press that he had begun in the playoffs. "I have no problems with the press now....I look out there during these interview sessions and I see a lot of faces I recognize....90 percent have treated me fair.''

Boston opened its season on October 31, against Washington, by raising its sixteenth championship banner. But the ominous foreboding that began with Bias's death in the off-season continued into the preseason. Walton broke a finger and then suffered an unusual ankle injury which put him on the injured reserve list. Scott Wedman was also on the injured list; Ainge had suffered a back injury and began the year on injured reserve as well. But Larry carried over his brilliant play from the previous season and led the team to its first four victories.

Given how important Larry's role had become in the face of the team's injuries, his own health became crucial. Larry discussed his health as he approached his thirtieth birthday. "I'm healthier than I have been in almost two years. The elbow and back pains are gone. Playing a lot of minutes has never been a problem for me. I've always wanted to play around 40 minutes a game. The more I play, the better I feel and the better my game gets." The team increased its record to 9–1 as Ainge prepared to return from the injured list.

But Sichting began having problems with an intestinal disorder, and wound up battling the virus throughout the 1987 season. Then, the rosy comments that Larry had made about the state of his health proved to be short-lived when he had to sit out a number of practices with an injured ankle (he refused to miss the next two games).

It was, indeed, shaping up to be a bizarre season as the Celtics pushed their record to 10–4. In the next game, at Hartford, Connecticut (technically considered a home game), the Celtics' remarkable 48-game home winning streak was broken. In the loss against Washington, Larry experienced an Achilles tendon problem and missed the next three games, two of which the team lost. Larry's frustration reached its height on his thirtieth birthday when he ripped off his walking cast and got rid of his crutch, saying, "The injury's history. I want to play tomorrow." Larry then came off the bench and scored 35 points on 15 of 21 shots in 30 minutes against New Jersey. Two days later the team suffered its first Garden loss in 42 games to the Lakers. It was not a good omen for the rest of the season.

The Celtics were saddled with more bad news when a second bone scan on Walton's injured right ankle and foot revealed abnormalities in the navicular bone in the foot. An arthroscopy was performed, and Walton was to be sidelined until the middle of February. The team's misfortunes seemed to escalate as if Walton's plight had damaged the Celtics' psyche. Larry missed three more games because of a bad back. At the All-Star break, Boston owned a 35–12 record, a record barely on target for another 60-win campaign. Nevertheless, considering the extent of the Celtics' injuries, it had been a more than satisfactory first half.

For the second year of the Long Distance Shootout (the three-point shooting contest), Larry threatened to pull out unless the prize was equal to that for the Slam-Dunk Competition. The shooting competition had offered only $10,000, and the dunk competition $12,500 the year before. When the league agreed to $12,500 for the shootout, the prize became known as the "Larry Bird Fund."

For Larry, perhaps the biggest factor in the competition was the money. Larry's frugality was legendary. Teammate M. L. Carr once said that "The most incredible thing he ever saw Larry Bird do was pick up a check once." Friends and relatives laugh and nod vigorously when told of the anecdote. They all say it fits Larry perfectly. When the comment was mentioned in an interview, Larry smiled knowingly and agreed, "Ain't no question." For the multimillionaire who still lived as if he were only making $20,000 a year, the painful memories of abject poverty were still strong. Larry doesn't bet on athletic events, horse races, or anything speculative. But betting on himself was hardly "speculative." In fact, it is the surest investment there is. "I don't bet. Unless I'm out shooting three-pointers against somebody. I'd do that. I'd go up to $50,000. Against anyone." One reason Larry could be so confident was because of the hard work that provided the foundation beneath his skills. He was comfortable taking the last shot because he had taken that shot in practice hundreds of times before. It is easy to forget that Larry was not always a great free-throw shooter: "I was only 60 percent in high school, so I practiced an hour before school every day. In college I was 75 percent. Now, because I've continued to work on it, I'm over 90 percent. I'm convinced anyone can be good at it if they're willing to pay the price."

That kind of work merely fueled the legendary Bird confidence. So, in the locker room before the Long Distance Shootout, according to Ainge, "Someone came in and said, 'They want the winner to come to center court after it's over,' and Larry said, 'How long do they want me to stay out there?'" Yet once the competition began, Larry again started slowly, tying for the last spot in the semifinals with Hodges and Ellis. The other competitor, Detlef Schrempf, then scored high enough in the second round to go on to the final round. So did Larry. Upon winning the coin flip, Larry decided to go first to put pressure on Schrempf, who was only in his second year in the league. As Larry's clock began, someone in the stands yelled, "You're going to choke." Larry said later, that was when "I knew I'd run that rack." So he hit his first 8 shots, quieting the crowd and psyching out Schrempf, to win for the second time in as many years, 16–14.

At the halfway mark of the season, Larry was averaging 26.3 points, 9.0 rebounds, and 7.25 assists, while shooting 51 percent. On the west coast, Magic had done as he promised and raised his own game a level. There was talk that Magic might break Larry's hold on the MVP. Larry, for one, said he believed Magic deserved it, and, anyway, he was too busy worrying about the Celtics and their season to worry about the MVP. Meanwhile, Larry had already missed six games due to injury, and Auerbach suggested that Larry might be able to lift his game and increase his resistance to injury by losing some weight. Larry was 238 pounds, which was more than he usually weighed at that stage of the season.

On March 11, Walton came back. But four games later, his health had now become a day-to-day issue. Larry was raising his game for the stretch run. Over the next 6 games, Larry scored over 40 three times and led the team to 5 victories, finally ending a 5-game losing streak on the road, the longest of the Bird era. Larry had also begun to lose weight. His diet was strange but, initially, effective: it consisted of popcorn, salad, and 7-Up. At the same time, the Celtic starters again swore off alcohol for the last portion of the season and the playoffs.

By the middle of April, Walton made another attempt to practice. Yet his very presence had a terrible effect on the team's morale. Every time he made some progress, the team would brighten up. But when he couldn't play, they would be demoralized. Only the inspired play of Larry and of Kevin McHale, who was having the greatest year of his career, gave the Celtics any real hope. In the meantime, the Celtics' problems on the road were bad beyond belief. They had lost 9 of their last 10 road games. Even Larry's continued great play couldn't help. And on April 10, the Celtics were assured of their first season without 60 wins since 1983, when they were beaten at New Jersey.

Larry's last twenty-seven games had been stunning in terms of his personal dominance. He had lost 17 pounds on his diet and that, along with relative good health, seemed to have a strong effect upon his play. Yet even Larry couldn't prevent 8 road losses in those 27 games. Larry had gotten stronger as the year went on, but he had gotten stronger during the regular season in 1985, too. The question remained whether he would be stronger by the end of the playoffs.

In the first round of the playoffs, the Celtics quickly dispatched the Bulls in three games. In the conference semifinal against the Bucks, the Celtics discovered that McHale had aggravated a still-healing stress fracture in his right foot. Walton came up lame once again. This latest setback effectively rendered him useless for the duration of the playoffs. In the meantime, the Celtics won the first two games.

Game 3 proved to be a thrilling battle as the stage moved to the Mecca. There were 29 lead changes and 12 ties as the Bucks forged ahead, 114–108, with 1:16 left. But the Celtics scored the last 6 points of the game to send the game into overtime. But the Bucks dominated the extra period and the final score read: Bucks 126, Celtics 121. Game 4 brought McHale's return to the starting lineup and yet another dramatically close affair in a double overtime. With Larry and McHale both playing 56 minutes, the home-court advantage and the fatigue factor both seemed to favor the Bucks. Yet the Celtics clinched the game, 138–137, in the final seconds. And Larry produced his second 40-point performance with 42 points, 7 rebounds, and 8 assists. The win provided some breathing room for the Celtics, leaving them with an almost-insurmountable 3–1 series lead.

In game 5 Boston took a 102–97 lead into the fourth quarter, but Sidney Moncrief played a brilliant game, scoring his career playoff high. When Parish went down with an ankle sprain, the Bucks won, 129–124.

Game 6 went back to the Mecca, and CBS Commentator Billy Cunningham noted that Larry looked very tired. Larry had averaged 47.66 minutes per game against the Bucks. This was on top of the league-leading average of minutes he had put in during the season. Larry reacted defensively when asked about his high number of minutes. "Hey, in the regular season, you play two or three nights in a row. In the playoffs, you play 40 minutes and then one or two days off. You can't get tired unless you stay out all night." Well, Larry wasn't staying out all night, but he wasn't playing 40 minutes, either.

After the Celtics' loss in game 6, which forced the Celtics to go back to Boston for the deciding game, Larry still denied he was tired. But Larry came out for game 7 determined to play all 48 minutes, if need be, and to play as intensely as he knew how.

Having won 2 in a row, Milwaukee had all the momentum, and they took it to the Celtics for the full extent of game 7. With just 5:52 remaining, Milwaukee led 108–100. Not only had Milwaukee dominated most of the game, but Parish, who had missed game 6, was limping; McHale was limping; and Ainge was in the locker room with a knee injury. Yet somehow, Boston came back, and Larry keyed the comeback by scoring 10 of the last 19 points to finish with 31 points, 10 rebounds, and 8 assists for a 119–113 victory. The Celtics' comeback against such great odds was a fitting conclusion to a series that would rank as one of the best in NBA history.

During the regular season, Celtic players had missed an extraordinary 206 games due to injury. But the Celtics were actually much more banged up going into the series against the Pistons than they had been all season. Moreover, the Pistons were coming off an impressive 4–1 playoff victory against Atlanta in the second round, and entered the series believing they could win. Still, the Celtics were able to win the first two games at home. Heading into game 3 at the Silverdome, Larry confronted the Celtics' greatest worry: "We're strong [at home]. But we're not a very good road team." That the Pistons won game 3 by 18 and game 4 by 26, was evidence that the Celtics' only chance to win the series was to win all four games at home.

Game 5 will go down as one of the most memorable playoff games in Celtic history. Boston had won 34 of its last 35 games in the Garden, and the Pistons had lost 16 straight on the parquet floor. The Pistons, coming off two lopsided victories in Pontiac, were young and healthy. Boston, with three of its five starters dealing with assorted leg and foot injuries, had no bench to speak of. Yet there was enough bad blood between the two teams to revivify the "old guys." Before the series, Larry had encapsulated the team's feeling toward one Piston in particular, Bill Laimbeer: "We don't like him too good." Accordingly, Larry had gone after Laimbeer following a gratuitous Laimbeer undercut which slammed Larry to the floor in game 3. Because Larry received a number of death threats after the Laimbeer fight, his bodyguard, Indiana State Trooper T. H. Hill, was brought along to Detroit. Still, Larry was unable to shoot before the games, as was his normal routine, because of the threats. With the Pistons back in Boston for game 5, the Garden fans were angry at Laimbeer. If the jeers of the Garden faithful weren't enough, then Parish's three punches to Laimbeer's face got the message across.

Not surprisingly, the Celtics came out with intensity and built a 12-point lead in the second quarter. But by the fourth quarter, with just 6:40 remaining, Detroit had a 93–88 lead. However, the next four minutes produced a 12–6 run for the Celtics and they took a 100–99 lead. When Larry hit a fallaway from the corner to make the score 104–101, there was just over a minute remaining. A Laimbeer basket, then a score by Isiah on a turnaround, gave the Pistons a 107–106 edge. A win would allow them to go back to Detroit and get the certain home-court win that would propel them into the championship round. After a time-out, Boston, of course, got the ball to Larry for the final shot. Larry drove along the baseline and softly put the ball up. But Dennis Rodman knocked the ball away. It hit Jerry Sichting before going out-of-bounds to give Detroit the ball and the lead with only 5 seconds. That was the game—or should have been. The Pistons simply needed to call a time-out and set up a last play to run out the remaining seconds. Indeed, Coach Chuck Daly was screaming from the other end for a time-out. Instead, Isiah thought he could best run down the clock by inbounding the ball before Boston could prepare defensively. The Pistons were already celebrating. Rodman and Mahorn were dancing down the court, thus leaving only center Bill Laimbeer down in the backcourt near Isiah. Joe Dumars was around midcourt. Meanwhile, Larry's momentum had left him sliding on the seat of his pants along the baseline beyond the basket.

Larry picked himself up and prepared to guard Dumars. Dumars had made his way to the foul line, and Larry's movement toward him induced Isiah to inbound to Laimbeer, who was open 10 feet away from Larry and 7 feet from the sideline. But "Larry was going to the ball before Isiah even threw it," said Sichting. Plus, Laimbeer didn't see Larry and thus failed to go out and meet the ball. Isiah didn't see Larry either.

Once Isiah's pass was in midair it "seemed to hang there forever," according to Larry. Larry darted in front of Laimbeer and tapped the ball away toward the baseline. He then managed to keep his balance, grab the ball, stay inbounds, and begin moving toward the basket—all in one motion. Then as Larry's body weight shifted toward the basket he continued to count down to himself, calculating that there was still time to take a better shot. It was then that he spotted Dennis Johnson, or actually "his jersey," cutting toward the basket from along the left side of the lane. Larry whipped the ball left-handed to D. J., allowing just enough of a lead so that D. J. wouldn't have to break stride. In remarkable synchronization, D. J. caught the ball at full speed, and ducked under Dumars to make a difficult right-handed lay-up from the left side as he went past the baseline. The ball rolled lightly around the rim before falling through with still a second to spare.

The magnitude of the feat wasn't lost on the other participants. "We had the game won," said Isiah. "I didn't see him." Daley thought the same thing, "I thought we had it." Auerbach called it a "miracle finish and a miracle victory." When Assistant Coach Chris Ford was asked how it happened, he replied, "Easy, because he's Larry Bird." The press immediately saw the event as one of epic proportions. "Adding yet another story to his legend, Bird...," said the *Hartford Courant*. *The New York Times* called it "another chapter in the great moments of pro basketball." The headlines on the front page of the *Boston Herald* read, simply, "Steal of the Century."

For game 6 the Celtics were without Parish, who was suspended for punching Laimbeer, and K. C., who would be attending the funeral of his mother. McHale had the flu. All this was enough of a handicap for a team that had lost its two previous games in Pontiac by a total of 44 points. Larry did an impressive job keeping the team alive until the fourth quarter, scoring 35 points on 14 for 20 shooting, but Detroit won 113–105. So, it was on to Boston for one more momentous seventh game. McHale was feeling better; Parish was off his suspension; K. C. was back in the coaching box; and Larry wasn't about to let his team lose, even if it meant playing every minute. Still, the Pistons came out undeterred in the Garden's 88-degree heat, and through the first three-and-a-half quarters, there were ten lead changes. But then at the end of the third period, the Pistons' Adrian Dantley and Vinnie Johnson, two vital offensive performers, collided while diving for a ball and knocked each other out. In the last six-and-a-half minutes, the game could not have been any closer as the tension built, and the crowd's intensity soared. When Larry hit a fourteen-foot running jump shot off the glass, left-handed no less, the Celtics went up 99–97. Dumars's follow-up tied the game at 99. Yet it was the next offensive sequence that, in many minds, was the turning point. Ainge missed an open jumper, but the Celtics controlled the rebound. And over the next 65 seconds, Boston controlled five offensive rebounds and took six different shots before Ainge was able to connect on a three-pointer to give them a 112–109 lead. "That was the biggest sequence in the game," Larry said later. "Danny's shot was the play of the game." The Celtics won 116–110. Detroit had lost its eighteenth straight in the Garden, and Boston had won 36 of its last 37 games on the parquet.

It had been an immensely satisfying victory. Boston won with its two big people Parish and McHale, playing at about 75 percent. "The way we had guys playing hurt and in pain makes this one special," said Larry. "But you have to have that, everybody hurting and playing hard if you want to get to the championships." Plus, the game had been satisfying to Larry on a personal level. Despite his large number of minutes and nutritional deprivation, he had maintained a stunning level of play through the series.

In the opposing locker room, a massively disappointed Isiah launched into a tirade against just about everyone. He included his teammates, especially Laimbeer, and his opponents, especially Ainge and Larry. In the midst of his remarks he was asked if he thought Boston had a chance of repeating. "No, none at all," came the angry reply. Chris Ford would later retort, "Yeah, but we're gonna get the chance to try. And he's not." It was that realization which weighed heavily on Isiah, a man of fierce pride and ego. As much as

Larry, Isiah hated to lose. Unlike Larry, who kept the intensity inside, Isiah tended to lash out when he lost. It had happened numerous times in his career, but after this seventh game his ire was at its worst. He subjected reporters to his venom for a good half hour before rookie Dennis Rodman made his comments about Larry's skin color—that Larry was "overrated" and that his three MVP awards had come, by virtue of his being white—and Isiah rushed to agree, adding, "I think Larry Bird is a very, very good basketball player, an exceptional talent, but I have to agree with Rodman. If he were black, he'd be just another good guy." In the next week, a tremendous public furor developed over Isiah's comments. Isiah went on national TV, with Larry's assistance, to make the questionable claim that the comment had been a joke. Larry had gone out of his way to appear at a news conference called by the NBA to defuse the controversy and defend Isiah, whom he considered a friend. "Isiah apologized to me, but he didn't have to. I knew right off the bat those remarks didn't come from the heart; they came from his mouth. And what he said didn't bother me, anyway. If it didn't bother me, and after I explained it to my family it didn't bother them, [then] it shouldn't bother anybody else, either. If Isiah calls me on the phone and tells me he didn't mean those things the way it sounded, I believe him. I don't think Isiah's stupid. He knows I'm a bad player. The only thing I've got to say is that Isiah should know better than to listen to Rodman. You never agree with a rookie."

"Larry saved my career," Isiah says today. Yet Georgia claims that Frank Deford's *Sports Illustrated* article was incorrect in describing the phone call Isiah made to Larry after the incident. The article says that Larry hadn't taken Isiah's remarks seriously and that he had handed the phone to Georgia because she was the one who was upset. On the contrary, Georgia says Isiah called Larry and her separately. After Georgia accepted Isiah's apology, he replied, "My mother [Mary Thomas] can quit crying now." Georgia explained, "Isiah, it's you today, tomorrow it'll be somebody else."

As the Celtics went into the finals against the Lakers, no one gave the team much chance of repeating. McHale had a fracture of the navicular bone in the right foot, as well as a sprained right ankle. Celtic team physician, Dr. Thomas Silva, had determined that McHale could do no more damage to the foot than he already had, and McHale decided to continue playing. Parish was still hobbling, but his ankle was greatly improved. Boston was injured; they were weary; and they had lost 14 of their last 18 games on the road. The Lakers, on the other hand, were fresh; they were healthy; and they had been the best team in the league during the season. Fans held out hope that Larry and company could pull off another miracle, but in a seven-game series, the odds against the Celtics were overwhelming. However, game 1 still surprised everyone as the Lakers ran all over the Celtics (who acted as though they were suffering from jet lag), and won 126–113.

Game 2 was more lopsided than the first. Boston started out hot, but a 75–56 Laker halftime lead culminated in a 141–122 blowout. The Celtics' only remaining hope was to win the next three games in Boston and then somehow manage to win one of the remaining two games in the Forum. However, many experts were predicting a Laker sweep. Boston went home and dug in for game 3. They were tough enough, despite their handicaps, to avert a sweep. And yet, the Lakers led early in the second quarter before Boston came back. In the fourth quarter, Boston went on to win 109–103. Still, it had been telling that the signs in the Garden before game 3 had boasted only that the Celtics would not be swept, not that the Celtics would win the championship.

In game 4 the Celtics held a 16-point lead at 79–63 midway through the third period. When the Lakers came storming back, Boston struck right back and took a seemingly insurmountable 101–93 lead with only 2 minutes left. But the Lakers made one of the great comebacks in recent championship series history and regained the lead with 34 seconds left. Larry surprised no one by sinking a clutch three-pointer from the left corner to give Boston the lead back at 106–104. But Magic launched a perfect one-handed jump hook from 18 feet to put LA in the lead with 1 second left. A desperation, off-balance twenty-five-footer from Larry barely missed to ensure that Boston would have to win three straight to win the series.

The series was all but a foregone conclusion, yet the Celtics' pride was on the line in game 5 on their home court. "Would we roll over and quit?" said Larry after the game. "This team has worked too hard all season for us to do that now." Boston went out to a 63–48 lead at the half and were never headed after that en route to a 123–108 win. Down 3–2, the Celtics needed to win both the remaining games on a court where they hadn't been able to stay even close for more than a quarter-and-a-half. The team, as they had been all year, was game; they played near-perfect basketball in the first half to go into the locker room with a 56–51 advantage. Nonetheless, LA was just too strong, and they stormed to a 81–68 lead. The cumulative weight of too many minutes, too many injuries, and too many comebacks seemed to overwhelm the Celtics. LA ran away with the title, 106–93.

Even if Boston had been able to win game 4, it was hard to believe that they could have beaten the Laker machine on its home floor. Regardless, the defeat was difficult. But the pain was mitigated by the triumph of a season spent overcoming injuries that should have denied them any chance of making the finals. For Larry, it had been a frustrating final series. When Cunningham had noticed that Larry looked tired in the Milwaukee series, Larry still had sixteen more playoff games to go. And for twelve of them, Larry had hung in and played masterfully. In game 6 of the final series, however, he looked pale, wrung out, exhausted. Too many minutes had finally taken their toll. But such an ordeal also had its positive side. In the loser's locker room following game 6, Larry tersely announced he was going to lift weights over the summer for the first time and come back as a better player than ever.

The summer following Larry's eighth pro season would be different from previous summers. He spent his time shuttling between Terre Haute and West Baden tending to new business ventures and domestic matters. For the first time, Larry became an active partner in local businesses bearing his name. His associates were Lu Meis and Max Gibson, two of the Terre Haute businessmen who had befriended Larry in college and then managed his investments when he became a Celtic. As a result of the extreme care they exercised in investing his money, Larry's financial position was more secure than that of most athletes. Bob Woolf boasted: "You hear these athletes say they are financially set for life, but I guarantee you he is more financially set than ninety percent of them." Furthermore, Meis and Gibson have earned Larry's trust. "I've known them for a lotta years," Larry says. "I don't know about business, but both these guys, just look at what they do. Just look at them; how successful they've been throughout their lives. You've got to put your trust in them. I feel comfortable with these types of businesses, I feel comfortable with the business decisions that are made with them.''

One of Larry's new ventures was a hotel, called Larry Bird's Boston Connection. Initiated in association with Gibson, the hotel is part of an effort to enable Larry to give something back to the community, and at the same time, to profit from a creative investment. The hotel is a Bird fanatic's paradise—truly the unofficial museum for Larry's accumulated basketball achievements.

While the hotel is a shrine of sorts, it is no narcissistic exercise in megalomania. To avoid the hotel's entire focus being only on his exploits, Larry established the Wabash Valley Hall of Fame, also to be housed at the hotel. Inductions of the area's finest athletes are to be made annually. However, Larry has since relinquished control over most of the details to Gibson. He has neither the time nor the desire to manage them. ''I can honestly say that I'm not a businessman. I'm a basketball player. That's my job. Everything I've done, I've done with friends.'' Gibson, an intense fan as well as one of Larry's closest confidants, has been taking memorabilia off Larry's hands for years, because Larry has so little inclination to hold onto that type of thing. ''I don't like trophies. I don't like getting them. I enjoy receiving the awards, but not the trophies. If other people enjoy them, that's fine,'' says Larry. Despite that, Larry is pleased with the hotel. ''Max [Gibson] assured me it would be in order. I think it's fabulous the way it turned out. . . . As far as the beauty and what it does for Terre Haute, I think it's great.''

In addition to a swimming pool with a free-throw lane painted at the bottom, the hotel features a gift shop with every Larry Bird–inspired item imaginable: sweaters, caps, tee-shirts, replica jerseys, posters, etc. The hotel has four floors, each with its own motif. The first is the Boston Celtic floor, featuring the Larry Bird Suite, the Coaches' Suite, and the Red Auerbach Room. The second is the Indiana State floor. All rooms have extra-long mattresses, remote-controlled TV, and bath accessories all featuring an illustration of Larry poised to shoot a free throw. What's more there's a shower curtain with the same illustration greatly inflated in size. The gift shop sells them for $19.95.

The hotel also boasts three restaurants. The Bird's Nest Lounge offers drinks, as well as full food service, including Onion Hoops, NBA Nacho Chips, French Lick Fries, and sandwiches called the Three Pointer and Springs Valley Special. An exhibit of ninety-four photographs depicts other area athletes. There are also continuous-running videos of many of Larry's performances, music videos, and live music every night. The MVP Club, on the other hand, requires a $500 annual donation and functions as a power restaurant in the manner of many big-city establishments. Burnished leather is every-where, and most striking, Larry's three MVP trophies are displayed in the front of the room. A *Holiday* magazine four-star chef does the cooking.

However, the primary attraction is the Boston Garden Restaurant, offering "the kind of down-home Hoosier cooking that is al-most as famous as basketball." The menu explains that "Larry Bird himself chose the things he likes best to eat" such as "Melt-in-your-mouth tender Swiss Steak by the platter-full, with bowls of real honest-to-goodness mashed potatoes and gravy, vegetable of the day, dressing, and noodles, salad, rolls, and coffee or tea." One featured item is Georgia Bird's "famous" sticky buns.

More spectacular are the furnishings in the Boston Garden Restaurant, starting with a glass-enclosed free-throw area with a parquet floor and a regulation NBA glass backboard—so the kids can shoot hoops while waiting for a table or burn off the excess after too many sticky buns. On the walls are some 194 laminated or framed items—magazine covers, book covers, advertisements, photographs—of Larry. Plus, Larry's uniforms from ISU, the World University Games, the Celtics, etc. Plus, at least twenty-five trophies and game balls, in-cluding Player of the Year, Rookie of the Year, and Most Valuable Player trophies from college and the pros. And, as in the real Gar-den, there are sixteen championship banners waving overhead.

Though he had no idea that Max Gibson and his friends had mar-shaled so much memorabilia, Larry takes it in stride. When asked how it felt to be in a restaurant with so much of himself on the walls, Larry replied, "I'd rather go in there and look at myself than look at Max [Gibson]."

Similarly, Larry has begun to get used to the fact that his name and fame are being put to the test of selling cars and trucks to Hoosiers from all over the state. People are bypassing their local car agencies and sometimes driving as much as 200 miles just to have a

Larry Bird Ford-Lincoln-Mercury sticker attached to the vehicle of their choice. The dealership is the latest investment project spearheaded by the other half of Larry's financial team, Lu Meis. The agency opened last fall in Martinsville, Indiana, where legendary Coach John Wooden and former Celtic teammate Jerry Sichting grew up along with the son of Sichting's high school coach, Sam Alford (Alford's son Steve was a star player at Indiana University). The 20,000-foot dealership boasts a showroom with an oak parquet floor like the one in Boston Garden, with a bright-green border. And hanging above, the sixteen championship banners. Customers are encouraged to use the baskets at either end while pondering a deal. Free-throw shooting (with Larry Bird Spaulding Signature series balls) has been known to determine more than a few final sticker prices when price discussions bog down. Like the hotel, the showroom also has the essential Larry Bird gift shop.

The summer's domestic matters involved charges that Larry threatened to beat up his estranged brother-in-law, Ben Campbell, from whom his sister Linda was getting divorced. Campbell charged in court that when he called Linda at Larry's home in West Baden to determine when he could visit the couple's two children, Linda told him if he attempted to see them, she would "see to it that her five brothers...beat [Campbell] to death." Campbell also claimed that in three subsequent phone calls, both Mark and Larry threatened him. The next month, Campbell dropped his charges, saying "It was a family matter, and they would work it out themselves."

Campbell had begun dating Linda when she was 16 (Larry was a high school sophomore at the time). After their marriage, the couple moved to Vincennes so Campbell could attend college there. However, after two kids and moves to Chicago and Decatur, Illinois, it had become apparent that Campbell had a drinking problem. Things eventually culminated in a bad incident in which Linda ended up in the hospital for four days.

Linda filed for divorce and then dropped the suit several times— just as her mother had done with Joe. As did her mother, Linda needed a restraining order against her husband once the divorce proceedings were under way. Georgia says that just as she had felt sorry for Joe, Linda always felt sorry for Ben. Linda finally left Campbell when his pledge to attend A.A. went for naught, and she moved into the mobile home Larry promised to buy her if she left

Campbell. Larry's indignation with Ben also stemmed from Linda's sneaking Ben onto Larry's property after their separation. Larry had put the mobile home on his property in West Baden so Linda's kids could also be close to their grandmother. When visitation rights were granted to Campbell, Larry forbade Campbell from coming onto his property. Instead, Campbell and Linda met at Ben's mother's place in Paoli where he again attacked Linda. It was just a short time later, when Campbell tried to set up a visit, that the threats allegedly occurred.

At the same time, Larry was finally coming to the point of making a more difficult, but much happier, decision than the ones involving Linda. After almost eleven years he decided to ask for Dinah Mattingly's hand in marriage. His proposal was supposedly, "You can wear this if you want to," as he handed her the ring. Georgia says he proposed at home instead of in the car, as Frank Deford reported in *Sports Illustrated*.

Dinah has a business degree from Indiana State. She went to high school in Terre Haute, where her father was the head of the local F.B.I. office. Her family now lives in Indianapolis, where her father works part-time with the Indianapolis Colts helping them with security. When the couple first moved to Boston, Larry insisted that she work even though he had just signed a $3.2-million contract. Larry believed that Dinah should at least be able to pay for her own clothes and nonessential items, so she worked as a Kelly Girl for approximately two years. Everyone who has come into contact with Dinah describes her as "a saint." To a person, people point out that she helped keep Larry's life in order. Jim Jones, like everyone who knows Larry well, explains that Dinah is absolutely indispensable to Larry's life today: "Larry couldn't function without her." They also point out how difficult it is to live with Larry and how extraordinary Dinah has been in weathering the last decade at his side. Indeed, there have been separations. "One year they spent a lot of time apart," says a friend. "She visited her parents for a couple of months at a time." And Larry has supposedly asked her to leave a few times. But everyone says that their relationship is much better now. In a recent *Sports Illustrated* article he says, "Dinah was with me through [everything]. I don't know how many times that poor girl stood under the basket and passed the ball back to me. Over and over standing there, throwing it back to me so I could shoot. And then all the time takin' care of my injuries.... 'Course we've gotten a lot of beer drinkin' in together, too," explains Larry.

The significance of Larry's engagement to Dinah is that it allows him to get over one of the most traumatic events of his life: his first marriage. Unfortunately, Larry's unhappy memories of his marriage have led him to resist his ex-wife's attempts to get him to see their child.

Larry's intense resentment toward Janet has prevented him from seeing his daughter, Corrie, according to Janet and some of Larry's friends. Even Janet acknowledges that the issue isn't whether or not Larry wants to see Corrie. "I imagine Larry right now would love to see Corrie. I imagine he's hurting because he doesn't get to see her. But it's pride." He has seen Corrie once in the last five years, even though he spends much of the summer in West Vigo County, where she lives. While Janet has been bitter in the aftermath of the divorce, she would like nothing better than to have Corrie see her father. And she has communicated that fact numerous times through other parties. Yet Larry, privately and publicly, believes that Corrie does not want to see him and that Janet does not want her to. Larry told Frank Deford that he is not allowed to have much time with Corrie. He recently told a family member, "Corrie doesn't want to see me, but I hope when she gets older she can sift through all this crap and want to see me." Larry also suspects that Janet plants terrible ideas about him into Corrie's head, though Janet says she has "never done that." However, from all indications, the lack of time spent with Corrie, regardless of Janet, is Larry's decision and no one else's.* "Ed [Jukes] thinks that the reason that Larry doesn't see Corrie right now [is] he doesn't know how to act towards her," says Janet. "[Corrie] was kind of scared of him before, when she was 5, and [Larry] doesn't know what to say to her, and he doesn't want her to be afraid of him, and he's not around kids. But I don't know who's supposed to crack the ice. I sure have tried."

By the end of 1987 Larry admitted that his worldview had changed. "From time to time, I've changed my philosophy of life. I've seen people; I've been all over the world. It's been an education."

---

*Janet says that Dinah was supportive and very helpful when Larry did see Corrie.

If there was ever a time for Larry to take stock and possibly temper some of his more youthful behavior, that summer was it. Larry had "slowed down," in Jim Jones's words, over the last two years, largely as a result of the Chelsea's incident. And he became particularly devoted to a more domestic lifestyle after Georgia suffered an angina attack over the summer. Larry now takes Dinah with him when he goes out with the boys in the summer. In fact, for the majority of the summer Larry and Dinah retired around nine in the evening.

And there were other motivations. The end of his career loomed ahead, even if not as close as the Boston press imagined. It was time for Larry to fully recognize his responsibilities beyond the basketball court and beyond the end of his career. "[Larry] has slowed down quite a bit," says a friend today—which is to say that Larry is hardly a choirboy these days but that his drinking has moderated. Larry also, in turn, began taking a greater interest in financial matters. Previously his money had been more of an abstraction to him, but with the help of financial advisors, Lu Meis and Max Gibson, Larry started to take more of an interest in his investments. Today, he reads each monthly financial report and understands where and how his money is invested.

With more financial security and a growing awareness of the world beyond French Lick, Larry entertained a desire to become more well-rounded. He further tested some of his still-evolving assumptions with a new friend. Back in the summer of 1984, Larry really got to know Magic Johnson for the first time. They filmed a commercial together in French Lick, where they spent a considerable amount of time talking the game and the world. Larry found that he and Magic were quite similar. And while Magic had a taste for the "best cars and clothes," Larry came to understand that didn't necessarily mean a compromise of values or integrity, much less the level of one's game. Earlier in his career, he had said, "I don't buy things just to buy. Some players have to have the best cars and clothes. I think when people start changing the way they live, their game starts changing." Of course, Magic's game was beyond reproach, and Larry gained an appreciation that Magic's values remained inviolable regardless of their trappings.

Back in 1986, Larry received a once-taboo Mercedes Benz as a gift from the Celtics (for winning the MVP three times), and he now actually drives it much of the time. Larry also bought Dinah a BMW to assuage her anger over his seeing other people, says Georgia. Only a few years earlier, Larry had pronounced about foreign cars—Mercedes and all that: "They're nice cars, but I can't see putting $50,000 or $60,000 into a car when our house was worth only $10,000." Other changes have been manifested: Dinah has influenced his willingness to wear a sports coat and tie at more formal functions. Open-collar shirts are no longer the rule, although he still refuses to wear a tux. New Year's Eve in San Francisco found Larry at Boz Scags' (Springsteen, eat your heart out) chichi and very expensive new club located south of Market. Larry even admits to liking once-hated Boston now. But big cities don't compare to home. An addition to his house in West Baden has been built in anticipation of the time when Larry lives there year-round or close to year-round. Initially Larry was worried that Dinah would be unhappy in the valley, and as a result they looked at homes in Indianapolis. But over the last few summers, Dinah has made some good friends in the valley and is now quite comfortable there. That has no doubt had some influence on Larry's decision to become engaged and to add to his home in West Baden. Larry has prepared for his retirement there with Dinah by building tennis courts and a pool as well. And even if strength is desire, Larry began lifting weights last summer for the first time.

But as Larry prepares to make his way from basketball to business, he must cope with the knowledge that his gifts are most attuned to the former. Larry Bird without the game that has nurtured him? It seems almost impossible.

Of course not only is the game inextricably linked to Larry's concept of self, it is his very lifeblood. The feeling Larry experiences when he plays he describes as "unbelievable. I wish I could drink it. I mean I've never done drugs—yeah, some beers, and with them you get a little tipsy and think you can do anything. But [when you play ball], it's more like being scared, except you're not. You somehow get real cool and in control at the same time." That initial shot of adrenaline is not that far removed from the fear that used to consume him before games when he was younger. But today the fear has given way to a sense of calm grounded in the confidence that has developed over years of practice. It is that control that Larry had always sought as a kid when he played by himself. Thus, to a large extent the pleasure Larry derives from the cycle of practice and games is more than just the intrinsic joy of the game. It is more the fulfillment of a lifelong quest that began when he was an insecure youngster who feared failing. "He really doesn't believe he's that good. So he practices and then believes he can take over the world," says one of Larry's coaches. For Larry it is the ultimate cycle—practicing to satisfy the residue of youthful insecurity which in turn helps create the confidence and the refinement of skill necessary for success. "That's why I spend all them hours before the game taking those extra shots. Because making them later is one of the greatest feelings you can have." But a pure love of the game is not Larry's only compulsion. There are other challenges on the horizon; that is, Larry still has some championships left to win, and he faces the challenge of not only defying expectation but defying age, as well. "One thing I know is that you won't see Larry in his fifteenth season getting 20 minutes," says Kevin McHale. "And you shouldn't. I don't want him to be the Everly Brothers, just hanging around after their prime. Larry Bird is like Elvis. He's got to get out while he's the King." Even if McHale is right, Larry could still play five more years and get out before he is in his fifteenth season.

And in this, his ninth season, at the age of 31, Larry is having his greatest statistical year ever. Is it possible that he's going to just keep getting better with age? Bear in mind that the role his summer conditioning and weight lifting has played is critical. There's no reason why Larry can't maintain or even improve his physical condition. So the question of when he will retire is still up in the air. Larry himself leaves the door open. Two years ago he addressed the issue when he had four years left on his contract. "I feel that I could play six more years at this level. But it'll probably be four. Red said that after that period of time, ten, eleven years, you tend to lose it. And I don't know if I want to leave with a lot of pain. Of course, what I should tell Red is that I'm different than a lot of people he's coached."

Epilogue: 1988

With the 1987–88 season half over, Larry earned his third-straight three-point title during the All-Star weekend's Long-Distance Shoot-out. Larry needed to make 8 of his last 10 shots including his last three in order to beat Seattle's Dale Ellis. But while the last shot still hung in the air, Larry's index finger was raised. He didn't need to see the shot swish through the net to know that he had continued his reign as the league's most effective outside marksman. Larry's hot shooting extended beyond the All-Star game as he seemed to defy father time by playing perhaps the most dominant basketball of his career. Coming off the team's west-coast swing, Larry scored at least 39 points in six games of a nine-game stretch, including a three-pointer with 4 seconds left to beat Dallas and 16 points in the last 9 minutes to nip Portland. And all this was despite a broken nose and a fractured eye socket during the latter part of the streak. Moreover, the Celtics would likely have lost all six of those games without Larry's heroics. But instead of gloating after such an amazing stretch, Larry was plainly worried. "I don't think I can keep scoring 40 every time and have us win the championship." Indeed, it was necessary for Larry to score at the most productive clip of his career to enable the Celtics to gain the best record (and home-court advantage in the playoffs) in the conference. Yet the team still failed to reach the 60-win plateau for the second straight year.

Larry's dominance also reflected the fragility of the once-great Celtics. Never before had the Celtics been so vulnerable that they needed to rely on one player to score such a significant portion of their points. And considering that almost all the points would have to emerge from a half-court offense made the burden on Larry all the more dismaying.

The final third of the regular season offered signs that the Celtics' dominance over the Eastern Conference for five of the last seven years might finally be coming to an end. Inconsistent play was highlighted by two home losses: the first against the dreadful New Jersey Nets and the other involving the inexplicable loss of a 22-point fourth-quarter lead over the Philadelphia 76ers. In each of the losses Larry played poorly and fatigue seemed to play a large role. With almost no bench strength, if Larry didn't offensively dominate, the Celtics were in trouble.

Nevertheless, Larry had been so dominant following the All-Star break that the lack of depth and inconsistent play weren't as urgently addressed as they otherwise might have been. As weak and ignored as the Celtic bench was in the 1986–87 season, the bench was even worse in 1988. And this was despite the late-season acquisition of former Portland Trailblazer All-Star Jim Paxson for Jerry Sichting, who was just coming off knee surgery. Though many pundits predicted that Paxson's arrival would push the Celtics over the top in their quest for a seventeenth world championship, Larry was skeptical on the eve of the playoffs. His skepticism proved prophetic. "Our problem is the bench. Paxson is a good addition, but we don't have the luxury of other teams, being able to bring in a lot of guys who can help every night.... So the starters play a lot of minutes. People ask if we get tired. Hell, yes, you get tired.... But improve our depth, and who knows how long we can play?"

That Larry averaged 29.9 points per game did, however, reflect to a large degree the first extensive off-court physical fitness regime of his career. "I [maintained the regime] so I could be the best basketball player I can be.... After last season I was really fatigued. When the season was over I was glad. I had never felt that way before. I also thought the weights would strengthen my back and elbow which I'd had problems with. I wanted to come back strong, and felt that if I lost weight, and did some work with free weights, that I'd be stronger at the end of the season than I was last year." Larry not only averaged the most points of his career but had career highs in field-goal and free-throw percentage while making more three-pointers than ever before. He also had the two longest strings of consecutive free throws in his career with 53 and 59 (the fourth longest in NBA history). And though the NBA writers voted Michael Jordan MVP both in a midyear poll at the All-Star game and in a vote following the regular season (Larry was runner-up), the sixty writers still elected Larry as the best player in the league when they were polled at the All-Star game. A week earlier, Red Auerbach had surprised everyone by announcing for the first time that he felt Larry was the best basketball player he had ever seen. Previously, Auerbach had refused to choose between Larry and Bill Russell as the greatest in the history of the game.

Though Larry was stronger than he had been the previous years, his goal of being stronger at the end of the season was not to be. In the final third of the season, Larry maintained his level of play. And with no fast break and the resulting easy baskets, cold shooting by Larry or any of the other Celtics spelled doom for their half-court offense. As any shooter knows, when fatigue sets in, the shot is always the first to go. So, Larry and the Celtics valiantly struggled through the final 25 games of the season and the first-two rounds of the playoffs, just able to compensate for the occasional poor shooting efforts. To make matters even worse, Paxson fell victim to back problems in the postseason and was ineffective. Thus, forced to use essentially five players in the playoffs, the Celtics squared off against three teams each of which used a nine-player rotation. Eventually, the Celtics and Larry wore down.

Against the Knicks in the first round of the playoffs, the Celtics managed to beat their younger and less experienced opponents in three out of four games. Larry was disappointed in his shooting effort, but in the playoffs it was always more difficult to shoot a percentage equal to regular-season highs for a variety of factors. A slower and more physical game resulted from the difference in the way officials called the playoffs compared to the regular season. Teams also tended to play with greater defensive intensity and had the luxury of preparing for only one team over the course of a week or more with as many as seven games. In the second round against the Atlanta Hawks, it was more of the same. But Larry single-handedly outscored the Hawks 24 to 23 in the first quarter of the first game, setting a Celtic record while helping to determine the victory. Yet Larry's final playoff heroics for the 1987–88 season would not be displayed for another five games, not until the seventh and deciding game against the Hawks at Boston Garden. What was seen was one of the finest playoff games in the history of the NBA, with the Celtics winning 118–116. The fourth quarter, in particular, was brilliant. "That's the greatest quarter I ever saw in 42 years in the NBA," said Red Auerbach. The quarter was remarkable because Atlanta scored on 17 of its 22 possessions, shot 66.7 percent from the field, outrebounded the Celtics, committed only two turnovers, and still managed to lose even though they were tied early in the quarter. Both turnovers, a steal and a blocked shot, were forced by Larry, not to mention that he hit 10 of 11 shots from the field in one of the most dominant fourth quarters ever played in the playoffs. "I never saw a fourth quarter like his in all my years in basketball," said Detroit Piston Coach Chuck Daly. Afterward, Larry explained some of the reasons for his great success in the game. "One of the keys is 'feetwork.' That started to come to me in the fourth quarter. I was coming off the picks and I was in rhythm, and I was getting squared off and in good balance. A lot of times you think you're well-balanced and you're not....I had the touch today."

But the touch which so suddenly materialized in the fourth quarter against the Hawks just as suddenly deserted Larry against the Pistons. After the Atlanta series, Larry was shooting 51 percent from the field. But against Detroit, he slumped to 35 percent. Not surprisingly, the explanation for the sudden desertion was much the same as the explanation for the sudden arrival of the "touch." Against Detroit, Larry had consistent difficulty coming off the picks in rhythm and in balance, and squared up to the basket. "I'd have to say [the Piston defense] is giving me a lot of trouble....Part of it is that I was getting the ball a little late coming off the pick, and that gave the guy time to get up on me. I'm used to coming off the pick and getting the rhythm and shooting." That the series with Detroit was unusually physical further prevented Larry from finding his rhythm. "One of Larry Bird's problems is that he's getting pushed on shots. I don't think he knows what it's like now to shoot without a push. No wonder he's had trouble getting his rhythm," said Boston Assistant Coach Chris Ford. "[The officials] are definitely not protecting the shooters. I've seen Larry get hit several times on the shooting arm," said Danny Ainge who had his own shooting woes, hitting only 31 percent for the series. Robert Parrish suffered similar shooting problems with his percentage against the Pistons falling 16.7 percent from his regular-season percentage (Larry's percentage dropped 17.6 percent and Ainge's fell 17.7 percent).

There were other factors involved in Larry's shooting slump. Larry had never shot well in the Pontiac Silverdome, a notoriously bad venue for shooters because of its lighting and backdrop. In the first seven games of his career, Larry shot less than 38 percent and going into the series was still under 47 percent from the field in Pontiac. In addition, the Celtics' poor shooting resulted in, or was caused by, the team's poor ball movement. "You like to invite the double team on one side of the floor and kick it back and around real quick. But the problem was that we had guys standing around," explained Larry. Nonetheless, Larry attributed most of the blame for the team's shooting woes to himself. "I let my team down in the shooting aspect (he led the team in rebounding, steals, and blocked shots, and he committed the fewest turnovers among the starters). We shoot 53 percent all year, and then all of a sudden we're in the low 40s. (43 percent)....My shots don't go in, and it carries over to everybody else....I played my worst series ever.''

But like any shooter, going through a slump was an occupational hazard. During his entire career in the playoffs, Larry has shot under 40 percent for stretches of two and three games every year except for 1984 and 1986. "It's happened before; it's going to happen again. It's just every time I shoot I think it's gonna go in....I've shot the basketball maybe a million times this year, and if it don't go down, it don't go down. There's no use me worrying about my shooting....It's been awful good to me over the years.'' Moreover, Larry tried to shoot through his slump, but naturally started to hesitate and lost confidence in his shot, which only made things worse. "My confidence [against Detroit] is not as good as it was in the fourth quarter against Atlanta....I'm starting to hesitate a little bit....I was starting to think 'pass' before my shot, and that's what really bothered me.''

Yet similar to his slump in the final three games against the Lakers in 1987, it was fatigue that probably played the biggest role in his poor shooting. And not only did the Pistons play unusually physical defense, but they rotated three fresh defenders on Larry during the game. In contrast to Detroit's starters, who played only 67 percent of the team's minutes, Boston's starters were forced to play an amazing 84 percent of the time in the series. Considering the age of the starters and how many minutes they all had to play in the regular season, it's no wonder that Larry and the rest of the team ran out of gas. "Our bench wasn't as good as we'd like. You can't play five guys for 48 minutes,'' said Larry. Indeed, Larry averaged nearly 45 minutes a game in the 1988 playoffs, exceeding the remarkable 44-minutes-per-game average the year before.

In Larry's case, the fatigue was so palpable that there were rumors throughout the Atlanta and Detroit series that he was suffering from mononucleosis, or at least that he had been tested. It is curious that the national wire services and all the individual newspapers covering the series except for the two Boston daily papers reported rumors of the illness. Larry was so exhausted during the series that he deviated from the normal routine he follows when mired in a slump. Instead of taking more shooting practice, Larry did less and less as the series wore on. Normally Larry takes about 300 shots two hours before each game. But against the Pistons he took only about a hundred, often shooting for no more than ten minutes. Obviously the series had exacted a mental toll, too. "Mentally and physically, we were wore down a little bit," Larry explained. As for himself, when he was asked after the series if he was a little tired, Larry corrected the questioner: "No, I'm a lot tired."

For many, the Celtic loss was a death knell for the future success of the team. But the doomsday prophecies seem to be premature. Long-time Celtic Assistant Jimmy Rodgers has been named head coach for the 1988–89 season. Rodgers has developed a reputation as a coach who would support the idea of younger players getting a lot of minutes. So players like Reggie Lewis and Brad Lohaus can expect to get significantly greater playing time next year. Analogies between these two players and the Pistons' Dennis Rodman and John Salley are not that far-fetched. In addition, a 7'2" Yugoslavian player is expected to be on the 1988–89 roster. But maybe the most underrated change for the Celtics next season will be the presence of Bill Walton. The standard assumption is that his career is over. It should be remembered however, that eight years ago he had his left foot surgically rebuilt. He then sat out two years, but has not had a single problem with that foot since. A year ago, he went through the same procedure for his right foot, and he will be fully healthy by the beginning of the new season. With a new coach dedicated to developing the younger players on the bench and the addition of Walton, the team is destined to improve even if the starters are a year older. And with Lohaus and Lewis in the lineup, Rodgers has announced that he's going to attempt to get back to the traditional Celtics' style of fast-breaking, which should relieve some of the offensive burden from Larry's shoulders.

Yet the likelihood of a strong Celtic team in the 1988–89 season is best guaranteed by Larry himself. The coming season will in all probability bring an even better conditioned and more motivated Larry Bird. With the expectation of more rest and an even more rigorous physical conditioning routine in the offing, Larry may be on the verge of his most satisfying effort yet. Besides, he's never gone more than two years without an NBA championship. Cynics who are predicting the demise of the Celtics and an over-the-hill Larry Bird are providing just the kind of challenge he thrives on. Larry Bird in decline? Don't bet on it. K. C. Jones says it best: "I learned long ago never to be surprised at being surprised by anything Larry Bird does."

Larry's Stats as a Boston Celtic

BOSTON CELTICS—REGULAR SEASON

YEAR	G	MIN	AVG	FG	FGA	PCT	FT	FTA	PCT	TPM	TPA	PCT	REB	AVG	A	AVG	ST	BL	PRO	PTS	AVG
79–80	82	2955	36.0	693	1463	.474	301	360	.836	58	143	.406	852	10.4	370	4.5	143	53	25.3	1745	21.3
80–81	82	3239	39.5	719	1503	.478	283	328	.863	20	74	.270	895	10.9	451	5.5	161	63	26.7	1741	21.2
81–82	77	2923	38.0	711	1414	.503	328	380	.863	11	52	.212	837	10.9	447	5.8	143	66	29.2	1761	22.9
82–83	79	2982	37.7	747	1481	.504	351	418	.840	22	77	.286	870	11.0	458	5.8	148	71	30.0	1867	23.6
83–84	79	3028	38.3	758	1542	.492	374	421	.888	18	73	.247	796	10.1	520	6.6	144	69	30.0	1908	24.2
84–85	80	3161	39.5	918	1760	.522	403	457	.882	56	131	.427	842	10.5	531	6.6	129	98	34.4	2295	28.7
85–86	82	3113	38.0	796	1606	.496	441	492	.896	82	194	.423	805	9.8	557	6.8	166	51	31.3	2115	25.8
86–87	74	3005	40.6	786	1497	.525	414	452	.910	90	225	.400	682	9.2	566	6.6	135	70	34.3	2076	28.1
87–88	76	2965	39.0	681	1672	.527	415	453	.916	98	237	.414	703	9.3	467	6.1	125	57	34.0	2275	29.9
Total	711	27371	38.5	7009	13938	.503	3310	3761	.879	455	1106	.411	7282	10.2	4367	6.1	294	598	30.6	17783	25.0

PLAYOFFS

YEAR	G	MIN	AVG	FG	FGA	PCT	FT	FTA	PCT	TPM	TPA	PCT	REB	AVG	A	AVG	ST	BL	PTS	AVG
79–80	9	372	41.3	83	177	.469	22	25	.880	4	15	.267	101	11.2	42	4.7	14	8	192	21.3
80–81	17	750	44.1	147	313	.470	76	85	.894	3	8	.375	238	14.0	103	6.0	39	17	373	21.9
81–82	12	490	40.8	88	206	.427	37	45	.822	1	6	.167	150	12.5	67	5.6	23	17	214	17.8
82–83	6	240	40.0	49	116	.422	24	29	.828	1	4	.250	75	12.5	41	6.8	13	3	123	20.5
83–84	23	961	41.8	229	437	.524	167	190	.879	7	17	.412	252	11.0	136	6.0	54	27	632	27.5
84–85	20	815	40.8	196	425	.461	121	136	.890	7	25	.280	182	9.1	115	5.8	34	19	520	26.0
85–86	18	770	42.8	171	331	.517	101	109	.927	23	56	.411	168	9.3	148	8.2	17	11	466	25.9
86–87	23	1015	44.1	216	454	.476	176	193	.912	14	41	.341	231	10.0	165	7.2	27	19	622	27.0
87–88	17	763	44.9	152	338	.450	101	113	.894	12	32	.375	150	8.8	115	6.8	36	14	417	24.5
Total	145	6176	42.6	1331	2797	.476	825	925	.892	72	204	.353	1544	10.6	932	6.4	277	135	3559	24.5

ALL-STAR GAME

YEAR	G	MIN	AVG	FG	FGA	PCT	FT	FTA	PCT	TPM	TPA	PCT	REB	AVG	A	AVG	ST	BL	PTS	AVG
1980	1	23	23.0	3	6	.500	0	0	.000	1	2	.500	6	6.0	7	7.0	1	0	7	7.0
1981	1	18	18.0	1	5	.200	0	0	.000	0	0	.000	4	4.0	3	3.0	1	0	2	2.0
1982	1	28	28.0	7	12	.583	5	8	.625	0	0	.000	12	12.0	5	5.0	1	1	19	19.0
1983	1	29	29.0	7	14	.500	0	0	.000	0	1	.000	13	13.0	7	7.0	2	0	14	14.0
1984	1	33	33.0	6	18	.333	4	4	1.00	0	0	1.00	7	7.0	3	3.0	2	0	16	16.0
1985	1	31	31.0	8	16	.500	5	6	.833	0	0	.833	8	8.0	2	2.0	2	1	21	21.0
1986	1	35	35.0	8	18	.444	5	6	.833	2	4	.500	8	8.0	5	5.0	0	0	23	23.0
1987	1	35	35.0	7	18	.389	4	4	1.00	0	3	.000	6	6.0	5	5.0	7	0	18	18.0
1988	1	32	32.0	2	8	.250	2	2	1.00	0	1	.000	7	7.0	1	1.0	2	1	6	6.0
Total	9	264	29.3	49	115	.426	25	30	.833	3	12	.250	71	7.9	38	4.2	20	3	126	14.0

G = game; MIN = minutes; AVG = average; FG = field goals; FGA = field goals attempted; PCT = percentage; FT = free throws; FTA = free throws attempted; TPM = three pointers; TPA = three pointers attempted; REB = rebounds; A = assists; ST = steals; BL = blocks; PRO = productivity rating; PTS = points.

SOURCES

Writing a book on Larry Bird can be a frustrating experience because access to Larry, his family, and his friends is limited if not impossible. This explains why Larry is possibly the best-known athlete in the world to have never had a full-scale biography written about him. Yet persistence and naïveté worked well for me, and eventually friends of Larry and even family members who had never before spoken about his life cooperated in my research for this book. Because this is not an "authorized" biography, all quotes attributed to Larry, Mark, and Mike Bird, as well as Lizzie Kerns, were derived from secondary sources.

There is, of course, a plethora of information on Larry from secondary sources. I have tried to cull the best of that information in order to augment the material I have gleaned from those people who have been a part of Larry's life. Following is a chapter-by-chapter overview of my principal sources. I have also provided a brief and subjective description of the books and major articles which were used.

Chapter 1 / A Gift

Basketball's Magnificent Bird: The Larry Bird Story by Frederick Lynn Corn (New York: Random House Sports Library paperback, 1982) is one of the five best overall sources of information about Larry. Written primarily for adolescents, the book has excellent photographs, and it enjoyed the cooperation of Lizzie Kerns and of coaches Butch Emmons, Jim Jones, and Gary Holland. There are some historical inaccuracies, however, and the book concludes in 1981.

Chairmen of the Boards: Erving, Bird, Malone and Johnson by Bill Gutman (New York: Grosset & Dunlap Tempo paperback, 1980) is another relatively good source of information, though it only includes Larry's first pro season.

From Valley Hick to Boston Celtic by L. Virginia Smith (self-published, 1982) caused a furor in the Bird family when it was released after Larry's first pro season. Larry still has difficulty reconciling himself to Smith (Georgia's sister), who has always been one of Larry's biggest fans. The unhappiness over the book stemmed mostly from Smith's candid portrayal of Joe Bird. There are some inaccuracies, and the book concludes in 1980.

Hoosier Hysteria! by Bob Williams (South Bend, Indiana: Icarus Press, 1982) is an excellent introduction to Indiana basketball, although it tends to be slightly tedious if the reader is not already familiar with the subject. Williams's chapter on Larry, which was written after Larry's second pro year, is excellent.

Rebound (Boston: Quinlan Press, 1986) by K. C. Jones is a fairly typical as-told-to sports book. Of note is K. C.'s guarded but still revealing discussion of his difficult relations with Bill Fitch.

I have also referred to and quoted from various articles: *Sports Illustrated* November 9, 1981, and March 3, 1986; the *New Yorker,* March 24, 1986; *Inside Sports,* May 1986; *Time,* March 18, 1985; *The New York Times,* the *San Francisco Examiner,* and the *Boston Globe.*

Celtic Pride, a monthly magazine devoted to the Celtics, as well as information from the Indiana Department of Agriculture and the Sports Information Department at Vanderbilt was helpful.

Chapter 2 / Hoosier Hysteria

Hoosiers: The Fabulous Basketball Life of Indiana (New York: Random House Vintage Books paperback, 1986) by Phillip Hoose is the best book ever written on Indiana high school basketball. Hoose not only writes well, but his vignettes and anecdotes are fascinating. His chapter on Larry is probably the best short piece ever written about him. Hoose benefited from the cooperation of Mark Bird, Beezer Carnes, and Jack Carnes.

Hoosier Hysteria (self-published, sixth edition, 1985) by Herb Schwonmeyer is an excellent reference book for Indiana high school basketball, which includes box scores from the four teams in the state finals for every year of the tournament.

My Indiana (Englewood Cliffs, New Jersey: Prentice-Hall, 1964) by Herb Liebowitz is a bit dated, but it remains a revealing and intelligent portrait of the culture of the state. It also provides an excellent perspective on the significance of basketball within that culture.

Indiana High School Record Book which is put out annually by Gene Milner and the Indiana Basketball Coaches Association is a cornucopia of statistics past and present. The *Underclass Report* provides statistics for the leading seventh- and eighth-grade teams across the state in addition to covering the up-and-coming players in the ninth through eleventh grades.

"Back Home in Indiana," Bruce Newman for *Sports Illustrated,* February 18, 1985, remains one of the best articles ever written on the phenomenon of Indiana high school basketball.

Chapter 3 / The Valley

Georgia Bird, Jim and Dorothy Ballard, Jim Jones, Gary Holland, Doug Gromer, John Carnes, Jim Tolbert, Audra Qualkinbush, Patsy Nelson as well as other Bird family members provided information that was used in this chapter. Also, articles from *Outdoor Indiana,* February 1986; *The New York Times,* the *Detroit Free Press,* and the *Boston Globe* were useful.

Chapter 4 / Joe and Georgia; Larry's Childhood

Children of Alcoholism: A Survivor's Manual (New York: Harper & Row Perennial Library paperback, 1985) by Judith Seixas and Geraldine Youcha is one of the best books written on children of alcoholism. Other books that were helpful included *Children of Alcoholics* (New York: Simon & Schuster Fireside paperback, 1983) by Robert J. Ackerman; and *It Will Never Happen to Me* (Denver: M.A.C., 1981) by Claudia Black. *Foul! Connie Hawkins* (New York: Warner Books paperback, 1972) by David Woolf is probably the best basketball biography ever written. *Basketball's Magnificent Bird: The Larry Bird Story* by Frederick Lynn Corn; *Chairmen of the Boards: Erving, Bird, Malone and Johnson* by Bill Gutman; *From Valley Hick to Boston Celtic* by L.

Virginia Smith; *Hoosiers: The Fabulous Basketball Life of Indiana* by Phillip Hoose.

"A Player for the Ages" by Frank Deford in *Sports Illustrated,* March 21, 1988, is the most comprehensive article ever written about Larry. Deford's full access to Larry allowed for a rare glimpse of some of Larry's feelings about his father and first marriage. *Sports Illustrated,* November 9, 1981; and articles from the *Boston Globe* were used. In addition, information from Georgia Bird, Jim Jones, Gary Holland, Doug Gromer, John Carnes, Jim Tolbert, Audra Qualkinbush, Lorraine Campbell and Jim Ballard, as well as other Bird family members was helpful.

Chapter 5 / Springs Valley High, 1971–1974

Hoosiers: The Fabulous Basketball Life of Indiana by Phillip Hoose; *Basketball's Magnificent Bird: The Larry Bird Story* by Frederick Lynn Corn; *Chairmen of the Boards: Erving, Bird, Malone and Johnson* by Bill Gutman; *From Valley Hick to Boston Celtic* by L. Virginia Smith; *Hoosier Hysteria!* by Bob Williams; *Sports Illustrated,* March 21, 1988 and Georgia Bird, Don Bates, Jim Jones, Gary Holland, Doug Gromer, John Carnes, Jim Tolbert, Audra Qualkinbush, Patsy Nelson, and Jan Hargrave as well as other Bird family members provided information.

Chapter 6 / 24 Days with Bobby Knight and the Indiana Hoosiers, 1974

Jim Wisman, Stan Evans, Georgia Bird, Jim Jones, Gary Holland, Doug Gromer, Patsy Nelson, and Jan Hargrave, as well as other Bird family members provided information.

Chapter 7 / Joe's Death, 1975

Basketball's Magnificent Bird: The Larry Bird Story by Frederick Lynn Corn; *Chairmen of the Boards: Erving, Bird, Malone and Johnson* by Bill Gutman; *From Valley Hick to Boston Celtic* by L. Virginia Smith; Stan Evans, Georgia Bird, Jim Jones, Gary Holland, Jan Hargrave, as well as other Bird family members provided information.

Chapter 8 / Bursting onto the Scene: Indiana State, 1975–1977

Basketball's Magnificent Bird: The Larry Bird Story by Frederick Lynn Corn; *Chairmen of the Boards: Erving, Bird, Malone and Johnson* by Bill Gutman; *From Valley Hick to Boston Celtic* by L. Virginia Smith;

Hoosier Hysteria! by Bob Williams; the 1975–1976 and 1976–1977 ISU Press Guides; the *Indiana Statesman,* the *Chicago Tribune,* the *Chicago Daily News,* the *Indianapolis News,* the *Indianapolis Star;* Rick Shaw, Tom Reck, Don Edmond, Tom James, Stan Evans, Georgia Bird, Jim Jones, Gary Holland, and Jan Hargrave, as well as other Bird family members provided information.

Chapter 9 / "A Phenomenon": Indiana State, 1977–1978

Basketball's Magnificent Bird: The Larry Bird Story by Frederick Lynn Corn; *Chairmen of the Boards: Erving, Bird, Malone and Johnson* by Bill Gutman; *From Valley Hick to Boston Celtic* by L. Virginia Smith; *Hoosier Hysteria!* by Bob Williams.

Sports Illustrated, November 28, 1977, and February 9, 1978; the 1977–1978 ISU Press Guides; the *Indiana Statesman,* the *Chicago Tribune,* the *Chicago Daily News,* the *Indianapolis News,* the *Indianapolis Star;* Bob Heaton, Craig McKee, Rick Shaw, Tom Reck, Don Edmond, Tom James, Stan Evans, Georgia Bird, Jim Jones, and Jan Hargrave, as well as other Bird family members and friends provided information.

Chapter 10 / The Final Four: Indiana State, 1978–1979

On and Off the Court (New York: Macmillan, 1985) by Red Auerbach is another as-told-to autobiography. While there is little that is surprising, there are quite a few of Auerbach's pithy observations which make the book worthwhile to read. *Rebound* by K. C. Jones; *Basketball's Magnificent Bird: The Larry Bird Story* by Frederick Lynn Corn; *Chairmen of the Boards: Erving, Bird, Malone and Johnson* by Bill Gutman; *From Valley Hick to Boston Celtic* by L. Virginia Smith; *Hoosier Hysteria!* by Bob Williams; *Sports Illustrated,* February 9, 1978, and February 5, 1979; the 1978–1979 ISU Press Guides; the *Indiana Statesman,* the *Chicago Tribune,* the *Chicago Daily News,* the *Indianapolis News,* the *Indianapolis Star;* Bob Heaton, Craig McKee, Rick Shaw, Tom Reck, Don Edmond, Tom James, Stan Evans, Georgia Bird, Jim Jones, and Jan Hargrave, as well as other Bird family members and friends provided information.

Chapter 11 / The Committee, the Contract, and a New World, 1979

On and Off the Court by Red Auerbach; *Basketball's Magnificent Bird: The Larry Bird Story* by Frederick Lynn Corn; *Chairmen of the Boards: Erving, Bird, Malone and Johnson* by Bill Gutman; *From Valley Hick* to *Boston Celtic* by L. Virginia Smith; *Hoosier Hysteria!* by Bob Williams; *Sports Illustrated,* November 9, 1981; the *Indianapolis News,* the *Indianapolis Star,* the *Spectator,* the *Boston Globe,* the *Boston Herald;* Georgia Bird, Jim Jones, and Jan Hargrave, as well as other friends and Bird family members provided information.

Chapter 12 / Rookie of the Year: The Boston Celtics, 1979–1980

Breaks of the Game (New York: Alfred Knopf, 1981) by David Halberstam is the definitive work on the NBA and most likely will be for years to come. This is indispensable reading for those interested in the NBA.

Don't Be Denied: My Story (Boston: Quinlan Press, 1987) by M. L. Carr is quite similar to K. C. Jones's memoir. Again, what is probably most notable is Carr's discussion of his relations with Fitch.

Martin Manley's Basketball Heaven 1987–1988 (Topeka: Facts, 1987) by Martin Manley is the only full-scale work that has attempted to analyze past and present NBA players from a statistical perspective. Similar to what Bill James has done for baseball, Manley's book succeeds admirably. I have yet to see another statistical method as logical as Manley's Productivity Rating in measuring players' effectiveness over the course of a game and season.

On and Off the Court by Red Auerbach; *Basketball's Magnificent Bird: The Larry Bird Story* by Frederick Lynn Corn; *Chairmen of the Boards: Erving, Bird, Malone and Johnson* by Bill Gutman; *From Valley Hick to Boston Celtic* by L. Virginia Smith; *Hoosier Hysteria!* by Bob Williams; *Sports Illustrated,* November 9, 1981; *Inside Sports,* October 1979; the *Spectator,* the *Boston Globe,* the *Boston Herald;* Jim Ballard, Lu Meis, Ed Jukes, Georgia Bird, Jim Jones, Jim Wisman, and Jan Hargrave, as well as other Bird family members and friends provided information.

Chapter 13 / The First Championship Season: The Boston Celtics, 1980–1981

Don't Be Denied: My Story by M. L. Carr; *Martin Manley's Basketball Heaven 1987–1988* by Martin Manley; *On and Off the Court* by Red Auerbach; *Basketball's Magnificent Bird: The Larry Bird Story* by Frederick Lynn Corn; the *Boston Celtics' Official Yearbook* 1979–1980 and 1980–1981; *Sports Illustrated,* November 9, 1981; *Inside Sports,* October 1979; *Celtic Pride, The New York Times,* the *Boston Globe,* the *Boston Herald;* Georgia Bird, Jim Jones, as well as other Bird family members provided information.

Chapter 14 / Building to Greatness: The Boston Celtics, 1981–1984

Rebound by K. C. Jones; *Don't Be Denied: My Story* by M. L. Carr; *Martin Manley's Basketball Heaven 1987–1988* by Martin Manley; *On and Off the Court* by Red Auerbach; the *Boston Celtics' Official Yearbook* 1981–1982, 1982–1983, and 1983–1984; *Sports Illustrated,* November 9, 1981; *Inside Sports,* October 1979; *Sports Illustrated,* March 3, 1986; *The New Yorker,* March 18, 1985; *Celtic Pride, The New York Times,* the *Boston Globe,* the *Boston Herald;* Georgia Bird, Jim Jones, as well as other Bird family members provided information.

Chapter 15 / Turning Point: The Boston Celtics, 1984–1986

Rebound by K. C. Jones; *Don't Be Denied: My Story* by M. L. Carr; *Martin Manley's Basketball Heaven 1987–1988* by Martin Manley; *On and Off the Court* by Red Auerbach; the *Boston Celtics' Official Yearbook* 1984–1985, 1985–1986, and 1986–1987; *Sport,* May 1986 and March 1987; *Sports Illustrated,* March 3, 1986; *The New Yorker,* March 24, 1986; *Inside Sports,* May 1986; *Time,* March 18, 1985; *Celtic Pride, The New York Times,* the *Boston Globe,* the *Boston Herald,* Georgia Bird, Jim Jones, Tom Clark, Jim Ryun, as well as other Bird family members and friends provided information.

Chapter 16 / The Legend: The Boston Celtics, 1986–1987

Rebound by K. C. Jones; *Don't Be Denied: My Story* by M. L. Carr; *Martin Manley's Basketball Heaven 1987–1988* by Martin Manley; *On and Off the Court* by Red Auerbach; the *Boston Celtics' Official Yearbook* 1984–1985, 1985–1986, and 1986–1987; *Sport,* May 1986 and March 1987; *Sports Illustrated,* March 3, 1986; *The New Yorker,* March 24, 1986; *Inside Sports,* May 1986; *Time,* March 18, 1985; *Celtic Pride, The New York Times,* the *Boston Globe,* the *Boston Herald,* the *Terre Haute Tribune Star;* Georgia Bird, Jim Jones, as well as other Bird family members and friends provided information.

ACKNOWLEDGMENTS

First and foremost I'd like to thank my parents for their unconditional support. It's hard to imagine what would have happened without the shrewd advice and calming influence of my agent, Eric Kraus. My editor, Elisabeth Jakab, never failed to maintain her enthusiasm for and belief in the project. Deborah Palacio was there when it all began; she'll never know how much her friendship meant to me. Bo Manning has been a believer for years. Matt Love and Tom Larson were the great validators. Sy Jacobs put the wheels in motion. Cynthia Copeland was extraordinary as a research assistant. Kelly Mladick and Caroline Mulder were dedicated transcriptionists and supporters. Catalina Salas was a late but critical contributor. Meg Slavin lent late but soothing support. Tim Colenback fed my "basketball Jones." Dr. Richard Gracer and Dr. Teresa Pantaleo helped my back and my head. Debi Applebaum, Katie Cavanaugh, Wayne Pate, Matt Hoffmann, Jeff and Jodi Olin, Marissa Smith, Debbie and John Bernlohr, Steven Stiller, and Joan Levine all played roles. Hal Jacobi helped to keep me afloat. Mary Farrell, Susan Jacobs, Gail Peteryell, Nick Monti, Margery Luhrs, and Charles Casale indulged my eccentricities. And thanks to all the role players that time and space prevent me from mentioning.

Lu Meis, Jim Ballard, Georgia Bird, Stan Evans, Jan Hargrave, Doug Gromer, Rick Shaw, Jim Jones, Tom Clark, Don Edmond, Craig McKee, Jim Wisman, Gary Holland, Audra Qualkinbush, Doc Welty, Bob Heaton, Patsy Nelson, Jim Tolbert, John Carnes, Tom Reck, Don Bates, Jim Ryun, Ed Jukes, Alex Wolf, Bruce Newman, the ISU Sports Information Department, L. Virginia Smith's book, and all the friends and relatives who wish to remain anonymous but who made this book live—to all, thanks. Of course, I'm responsible for all errors.